SHADOW ELITE

SHADOW ELITE

HOW THE WORLD'S NEW

POWER BROKERS UNDERMINE

DEMOCRACY, GOVERNMENT,

AND THE FREE MARKET

JANINE R. WEDEL

BASIC BOOKS

A Member of the Basic Books Group
New York

Books published by Basic Books are available at special discounts for bulk purchases in the United
States by corporations, institutions, and other organizations. For more information, please contact the
Special Markets Department at the Perseus Books Group, 2300 Chestnut Street, Suite 200, Philadel-
phia, PA 19103, or call (800) 810-4145, ext. 5000, or e-mail special.markets@perseusbooks.com.

Designed by Jeff Williams

Library of Congress Cataloging-in-Publication Data
Wedel, Janine R., 1957–
   Shadow elite : how the world's new power brokers undermine democracy, government, and the
free market / Janine R. Wedel.
      p. cm.
   Includes bibliographical references and index.
   ISBN 978-0-465-09106-5 (alk. paper)
   1. Corruption. 2. Political corruption. 3. Power (Social sciences) 4. Elite (Social sciences)
5. Privatization. 6. Government accountability. I. Title.
JF1525.C66W43 2009
320.9—dc22
                                                                                    2009038735

10 9 8 7 6 5 4 3 2 1

To my parents,
Arnold and Dolores Wedel

CONTENTS

PREFACE

In my work as a social anthropologist, people often tell me unusual stories. For instance, in Poland recently, a scholar and former speaker of the parliament described to me an interaction in police headquarters a few years ago. As one of several esteemed members of a task force advising the national police on how to transform itself into an institution compatible with democracy, he met with the chief of police and the other advisers. During a break in the meeting, he thought he smelled more than the usual cigarette smoke. When he ribbed his fellow advisers, they acknowledged that they, indeed, had been smoking marijuana during the break.

While my friend told this lighthearted story to amuse me, sensing I would appreciate its absurdity, it is actually telling. It is the kind of tale that one hears in a society with a long experience of upending official rules—a society that persisted, despite occupying armies, imposed regimes, and the attendant scarcities, repressions, and hardships. High-ranking Polish government advisers ignoring prohibitions against smoking marijuana may be inconsequential, but in fact this tale illustrates a willingness, even delight, in flouting rules. Rules were made to be broken, goes the old saying, but rules are also what we live by. Yet rules, I have discovered, are being flouted on a wide scale. Nowadays, even in the democratic-model-for-the-world United States, people are systematically upending rules and authority, not in search of either personal enjoyment or basic necessities, but to wield high-level power and influence.

I have come to this bold conclusion after spending the better part of three decades observing people as they employ teamwork, flexibility, and ingenuity to work around the rules, and studying the conditions that encourage them to do so. I did this first in Eastern Europe under communism and as countries in the region moved away from it. Then I charted the activities of archetypal players who flouted rules and authority to wield influence, this time on a global stage, and investigated the conditions that encourage them to do so in the wider world and especially in the United States.

I have written this book to explain the new breed of transnational players who, far from something as trivial as smoking marijuana, toy with official rules and not only get away with it, but often make decisions about policies that affect us all—in areas ranging from the economy and foreign affairs to government and society—while fashioning new rules of the game to benefit themselves.

In a twisted sort of way, examining eastern Europe up close—through its transformations away from communism over the last quarter century—has been excellent preparation for making sense of what is happening in the United States today. In communist Poland, the necessity of getting around the system bred absurdities, ranging from the employee who "lifts" a desk from a state-owned factory to sell for cash and then complains when a fellow worker "steals" it from him, to the employee at Communist Party headquarters who doubles as an underground publisher, printing his leaflets at headquarters. While the totalitarian nature of the state necessitated such strategies, America today seems increasingly to offer up absurdities of its own.

I have written this book to offer readers a lens through which to view what I identify in this book as a new system of power and influence, and to explain the players and networks that drive it in a rapidly transforming American and global environment. As an anthropologist, I'm trained to go behind the scenes, beyond what people say they are doing, and beyond government and bureaucratic organizational charts. But all of us must do so now because that is the only way to see that how the world is organized has changed, amid such developments as the breakdown of bureaucratic and professional authority and new information technologies. The new players and networks of power and influence do not restrict themselves to activities in any one arena. Rather, through their activities, they connect state with private, bureaucracy with market, political with economic, macro with micro, and global with national, all the while making public decisions—decisions backed by the power of the state. As influencers perform overlapping roles and networks of policy deciders snake through official and private organizations, creating a loop that is closed to democratic processes, we have to focus on them—their roles, activities, and sponsors—and how they maneuver these levels if we want to get to the bottom of power and influence.

That is why, as I realized over the course of this project, the frameworks and terms that we've long used to understand power and influence are no longer sufficient to explain what is happening. While it became clear early on that terms like "lobbyist" or "interest group" don't suffice, naming this new breed of players and networks proved to be a challenge. Here I am grateful to two scholars in particular. "Flexian" grew out of a conversation with Lloyd "Jeff" Dumas, "flex net" from a conversation with Susan Wright. I am indebted to both. As well, terms like "conflict of interest" and "corruption" also proved inadequate to explore how agenda-wielding players actively structure, indeed create, their roles and involvements to serve their own agendas—at the expense of the government agencies, shareholders, or publics on whose behalf they supposedly work. These players not only flout authority, they institutionalize their subversion of it. Thus, I have also written this book so that people can see the trade-offs they inadvertently make as they tolerate, even approve of, this state of affairs and suffer from loss of democratic input, control, and accountability.

In my quest to explore how societies work—in contrast to how they are supposed to work—I have found common ground with people from many walks of life and professions, scholars from a variety of disciplines (not only anthropologists), journalists, government researchers, and investigators. Several sociologists were especially astute observers of the movers and shakers who positioned themselves at the nexus of state and private power amid the ruins of communism (sometimes in conjunction with global operators who descended on the region like carpetbaggers). These players, of course, were operating in an environment where new rules were being invented—and sometimes even inventing them themselves. In Poland I am grateful to the scholars who offered insights and opportunities for discussion, in particular

Antoni Kamiński, Joanna Kurczewska, and Jacek Kurczewski. Alina Hussein of NIK, Poland's equivalent of the U.S. Government Accountability Office, helped provide important trend-line data, in particular about appropriation of the state budget to private, unaccountable organizations through the 1990s and into this decade. Grzegorz Makowski and Barbara Pomorska pulled together supplemental materials on these trends, as well as on the Rywingate scandal that publicly illuminated under-the-table, yet pervasive means of influence. I thank them all.

I am also grateful to the many experts and informants (far too many to name) who assisted me in recognizing drivers of transformation beyond Poland as I traveled to other parts of central Europe, Russia, and Ukraine after the fall of the Berlin Wall and into this century. I tracked a new generation of operators who seemed to have internalized the worst of the Wild East (even when they had never set foot there), such as financial wizards playing on the latest innovations. For providing opportunities to further explore and discuss these players and phenomena, I am indebted to British sociologist Paul Stubbs. Based in Croatia, he invited me to workshops he organized there in 2006 and 2007 that brought together dynamic local and international scholars and practitioners to explore changing systems of governing, power, and influence. These trips were learning opportunities of the best sort, and enabled me to give lectures and get feedback from those steeped in law, economics, and other fields.

The networks of interlocking players I charted at the nexus of state and private in eastern Europe, as well as those operating in and around global grey zones, are what led me to explore the networks and modus operandi of certain players in the United States. When, in the early part of this decade, prominent neoconservatives were regularly in the news, I began to look into the social networks and overlapping connections in government, ideological initiatives, foundations, think tanks, business, and family ties of a small set of neoconservatives who have been working together for as long as thirty years to put their ideology into action. I was struck by the similarity of the modus operandi of this "Neocon core"—a dozen or so interconnected players with Richard Perle as their linchpin—with many influential groups that had shaped government, politics, business, and society in transitional eastern Europe. In both contexts, players straddled official and private organizations, were remarkably successful in achieving their group goals even at the expense of the institutions they supposedly served, and skillfully skirted liabilities resulting from their activities.

I studied the activities of the Neocon core first by delving into the wealth of material published on them and then by interviewing people associated with them (including "defectors" from the group); frequenting meetings, lectures, and gatherings in which they participate; and, eventually, interviewing some of the key players themselves. In this exploration, I thank Steve Clemons for his excellent blog (thewashingtonnote.com) and steadfast support, as well as members of the "Garden Club." I am especially indebted to Jim Lobe, a journalist who has long tracked and written about neoconservatives, read multiple drafts of my chapter on the subject, and loaned me a boxful of books and resources. Eli Lake may not agree with the conclusions I have come to, but I greatly appreciate his perspectives and willingness to engage in conversation. Although studying the Neocon core helped me to identify influencers and their workings in their American habitat, the book draws on examples from across the political spectrum.

Observing the achievements of players and networks led me, in turn, to explore the contexts in which they operate. Seeing firsthand the machinations at the nexus of state and private in eastern Europe, as state-owned resources were being privatized, led me to wonder what "privatization" in the United States is about, especially given America's history of contracting out government services, and, increasingly, functions. Reams of GAO reports, inspectors general findings, and other government documents, as well as scholarly treatises, provided the background needed to grasp the import and extent of the changes under way. Countless hours were spent talking with experts, investigators, and participants in contracting out (in sectors ranging from military and homeland security to energy and education) and other aspects of U.S. governing, including the drain of brains, information, and authority away from government. For guidance on these issues, I am especially indebted to Richard Loeb and Richard Miller, as well as to Scott Amey of the Project On Government Oversight.

My subject is replete with theoretical issues. I am very fortunate to have had the generous help of Ted Lowi and Bob Jervis, both of whom read parts of the manuscript multiple times and provided detailed and supportive critiques. I am eternally grateful to both of them. I also thank Simon Reich, who illuminated crucial perspectives on American government and reviewed my work, and James Galbraith, who highlighted important economics perspectives.

I am grateful to Teresa Hartnett for stimulating my conceptualization of the project early on, and Stacy Lathrop, who did the same in the latter stages. Both reviewed and edited drafts and provided incisive suggestions. Other readers, including Ethan Burger, John Clarke, Des Dinan, Jeff Dumas, Carol Greenhouse, Jeanne Guillemin, Jessica Heineman-Pieper, Antoni Kamiński, Don Kash, Ted Kinnaman, Leonid Kosals, Wendy Larner, Charles Lewis, Michael Lind, Barry Lynn, William Odom, Steven Rosefielde, Dorothy Rosenberg, Louise Shelley, Irena Sumi, Susan Tolchin, Ty West, and Anne Williamson provided valuable feedback on the manuscript. Adam Pomorski, as usual, offered keen guidance throughout the project.

I am also indebted to a number of scholars for offering fora that enabled me to get feedback on papers I delivered, including: James Galbraith, for an American Economics Association panel on "The Abuse of Power" (2005) and a Communitarian Summit session on "Working Toward a Criminology of Economics" (2004); Carol Greenhouse and participants in 2005 workshops at Princeton University on "Ethnographies at the Limits of Neoliberalism"; participants in my panels at the 2006 Civil G-8 Conference in Moscow; Hugh Gusterson and Catherine Besteman (organizers) and Jeanne Guillemin (commentator) at a 2006 MIT workshop; Susan Wright and Cris Shore for the 2006 panel on "Policy Worlds" at the European Association for Social Anthropology meeting in Bristol, UK; Winifred Tate and participants in the 2007 workshop at Brown University on "Ethnographies of Foreign Policy"; Don Kalb and others at the Central European University in Budapest who organized my 2007 talks there; Jon Abbink, Sandra Evers, and Tijo Salverda for the Anthropology of Elites conference at Vrije Universiteit, Amsterdam, in 2007; Monique Nuijten of Wageningen University, the Netherlands, in 2008; and the organizers of sessions where I delivered papers on topics relating to this book at annual meetings of the American Anthropological Association, the American Political Science Association, and the American Economics Association.

For research assistance, I am grateful to Kanishka Balasuriya, Maya Ellis Brown, Joseph Sany, and especially to Emily Gallagher, Ben Katcher, Jeff

Meyer, Faith Smith, Mandy Smithberger, and Sarah Willyard. I thank Karen Coats, Nan Dunne, and Caroline Taylor for editorial comments.

I am especially indebted to independent editor Sarah Flynn, who worked with me tirelessly to shape the book. Her unflagging commitment to the project, her enthusiasm for finding the best way to express my ideas, and her effectiveness as both sounding board and wordsmith have seen me through every draft of the manuscript, from its beginnings as a proposal. I am also grateful to Sarah for introducing me to my agent, Michael Carlisle. Michael "got" the book right away, and I am grateful to him not only for his confidence in me but also for his insights into the nature of the topic. Insights were also provided by Bill Frucht, who acquired the book for Basic Books, and Tim Sullivan, who saw it through to publication and provided keen suggestions that helped focus parts of the manuscript. I thank Irina Kuzes, a graphic artist, for her original creations, steadfast commitment to the project, and willingness to make changes as it developed.

The New America Foundation has generously provided me a research home and numerous resources that aided this project. For that and for research assistance and collegiality with a dynamic group of policy writers, analysts, and scholars, I am deeply indebted. My permanent base, the School of Public Policy at George Mason University, and my dean, Kingsley Haynes, have been extraordinarily supportive and generous, and for that I am grateful. I also thank the Ford Foundation, which funded some of my research related to the project.

Finally, I thank friends who both put me up (when on the road) and put up with the project, in particular Antonina Dachów, Ted Kinnaman, Aśka Mikoszewka, Terry Redding, and the Occasional University of Lewes. As always, I am especially and profoundly indebted to Adam and Basia Pomorscy for their generous and abiding help.

Many people provided input about the phenomenon that today's shadow elite represents, the conditions that give rise to the new players and networks, and the implications of both for democracy, government, and society. But while this project might not have come to fruition without the generous assistance of so many, I alone am responsible for the final product.

JANINE R. WEDEL
Washington, D.C.
July 2009

CHAPTER ONE

Confidence Men
and Their Flex Lives

WE LIVE IN A WORLD OF FLEXIBILITY. WE HAVE FLEX TIME, FLEX workers, flex spending, flex enrollment, flex cars, flex technology, flex perks, mind flex—even flex identities. "Flex" has become an integral part not only of how we live, but of how power and influence are wielded. While influencers flex their roles and representations, organizations, institutions, and states, too, must be flexible in ways they haven't been before. The mover and shaker who serves at one and the same time as business consultant, think-tanker, TV pundit, and government adviser glides in and around the organizations that enlist his services. It is not just his time that is divided. His loyalties, too, are often flexible. Even the short-term consultant doing one project at a time cannot afford to owe too much allegiance to the company or government agency. Such individuals are *in* these organizations (some of the time anyway), but they are seldom *of* them.[1]

Being in, but not of, an organization enables these players to pursue a "coincidence of interests," that is, to interweave and perform overlapping roles that serve their own goals or those of their associates. Because these "nonstate" actors working for companies, quasi-governmental organizations, and nongovernmental organizations (NGOs) frequently do work that officials once did, they have privileged access to *official* information—information that they can deploy to their own ends. And they have more opportunities to use this information for purposes that are neither in the public interest nor easily detected, all the while controlling the message to keep their game going.[2]

Take, for instance, Barry R. McCaffrey, retired four-star army general, military analyst for the media, defense industry consultant, president of his own consulting firm, part-time professor, and expert, whose advice on the conduct of the post-9/11 U.S. wars was sought by the George W. Bush administration and Congress. Crucial to McCaffrey's success in these roles was the special access afforded him by the Pentagon and associates still in the military. This included special trips to war zones arranged specifically for him, according to a November 2008 exposé in the *New York Times*. McCaffrey gleaned information from these trips that proved useful in other roles—and not only his part-time professorship at the U.S. Military Academy, which the Pentagon claimed is the umbrella under which his outsider's perspective was sought.

At a time when the administration was trying to convince the American people of the efficacy of U.S. intervention in Iraq, the general appeared frequently as a commentator on the television news—nearly a thousand times on NBC and its affiliates. He was variously introduced as a Gulf War hero, a professor, and a decorated veteran, but not as an unofficial spokesperson for the Pentagon and its positions. He also was oft-quoted in the *New York Times*, the *Wall Street Journal*, and other leading newspapers. Further, in June 2007, according to the *Times*, he signed a consulting contract with one of many defense companies he had relationships with, which sought his services to win a lucrative government contract. Four days later, McCaffrey did the firm's bidding by personally recommending to General David Petraeus, the commanding general in Iraq, that the company supply Iraq with armored vehicles, never mentioning his relationship to it. Nor did he reveal these ties when he appeared on CNBC that same week, during which he praised Petraeus, nor to Congress, where he not only lobbied to have the company supply Iraq with armored vehicles but directly criticized the company's competitor.[3]

Using information and access to link institutions and to leverage influence is what General McCaffrey and other such players were expected to do by an administration seeking public support, media in need of high ratings, industry pursuing profits, and academia in search of superstars. But because only the individual player bridges all these institutions and venues—by, for in-

stance, enlisting access and information available in one to open doors or enhance cachet in another—only he can connect all the dots. Such a game involves a complex, although subtle, system of incentives that must reinforce its
players' influential positions and access to knowledge and power. And the
players must uphold their end of the bargain. When McCaffrey criticized the
conduct of the war on the *Today* show, Secretary of Defense Donald Rumsfeld quickly cut off his invitations to Pentagon special briefings. Tellingly, Mc-
Caffrey went back on the air, reiterated the Pentagon's line, and regained entry
into those briefings.[4]

McCaffrey owes some of his access to a Pentagon public relations campaign that enrolled retired, high-status military personnel as "message force
multipliers" in the media, according to an earlier piece in the *Times*. McCaffrey was among the most high-profile members of the campaign, during
which, from 2002 to 2008, the Pentagon provided the seventy-five analysts
access to military campaigns and initiatives through private briefings, talking points, and escorted tours. Following the exposé and congressional calls
for an investigation, government auditors looked into whether the Pentagon
effort "constituted an illegal campaign of propaganda directed at the American public," as the *Times* put it. The Pentagon's inspector general found that
Pentagon funds were *not* used inappropriately and that the retired military
officers didn't profit unfairly from the arrangement. President Obama's Pentagon later rescinded the inspector general's report, but no new one was issued. Even when they are not whitewashed, such government audits are not
designed to capture the reality of today's influencers and the environment in
which they operate—a reality that poses potentially much greater harm to a
democratic society than a mere drain on taxpayer dollars. While millions of
viewers, Congress, and General Petraeus were led to believe that McCaffrey
was offering his expert, unbiased opinions, McCaffrey's interlocking roles created incentives for him (and others of his profile) to be a less-than-impartial
expert. The *Times* understatedly remarked, "It can be difficult for policy makers and the public to fully understand their interests."[5]

Meanwhile, the official and private organizations in and out of which such
movers and shakers glide either just go along to get along or are ill equipped
to know what these actors are up to in the various venues in which they operate. In McCaffrey's case, no institution, from the Pentagon to the defense

contractor to NBC, had an incentive to be anything but complicit. Operators like the general have surpassed their hosts, speeding past the reach of effective monitoring by states, boards of directors, and shareholders, not to mention voters. And while the players sometimes cause raised eyebrows, they are highly effective in achieving their goals—and often benefit from wide acceptance. Much more than the influence peddlers of the past, these players forge a new system of power and influence—one that profoundly shapes governing and society.

This new breed of players is the product of an unprecedented confluence of four transformational developments that arose in the late twentieth and early twenty-first centuries: the redesign of governing, spawned by the rising tide of government outsourcing and deregulation under a "neoliberal" regime, and the rise of executive power; the end of the Cold War—of relations dominated by two competing alliances—which intensified the first development and created new, sparsely governed, arenas; the advent of evermore complex technologies, especially information and communication technologies; and the embrace of "truthiness," which allows people to play with how they present themselves to the world, regardless of fact or track record. While it may be jarring to mention such seemingly disparate developments in the same breath—and to name "truthiness" as one of them—the changes unleashed by these developments interact as never before.

The proliferation of roles, and the ability of players to construct coincidences of interest by those who perform them, are the natural outcome of these developments. So, for example, increased authority delegated to private players (facilitated by privatization, the close of the Cold War, and new, complex technologies) has enabled them to become guardians of information once resting in the hands of state and international authorities. While supposedly working on behalf of those authorities, such players (working, say, as consultants for states or as special envoys or intermediaries between them) can guard information and use it for their own purposes, all the while eluding monitoring designed for the past order of states and international bodies. And they get away with it. Appearances of the moment have become all-important in today's truthiness society, as comic Jon Stewart expressed in his quip: "You cannot, in today's world, judge a book by its contents."[6] Today's premier influencers deftly elude such judgment. Pursuing their coincidences of interest, they weave new institutional forms of power and influence, in which official and private power and influence are interdependent and even reinforce each other.

The phenomenon I explore in *Shadow Elite* is no less than a *systemic* change. A new system has been ushered in—one that undermines the principles that have long defined modern states, free markets, and democracy itself.

Naming the Animal

I call the new breed of influencers "flexians." When such operators work together in longstanding groups, thus multiplying their influence, they are flex nets. Flexians and flex nets operate at one extreme of a continuum in crafting their coincidences of interests.

Performing overlapping roles can be—and often is—not only benign, but can serve the interests of all the organizations involved, as well as the public's. Yet in an international arena that "multiplies the possibilities for double strategies of smugglers . . . and brokers . . . there are many potential uncertainties and mistranslations surrounding individual positions," as two political-legal scholars point out. Take, for instance, the individual who acts "as a political scientist in one context . . . and a lawyer in another; a spokesperson for nationalistic values in one context, a booster of the international rule of law in another." This peripatetic political scientist/lawyer is not necessarily engaged in a "double strategy." But his activities on behalf of one organization can be at odds with those on behalf of another—even to the point of undermining the goals of either, or both. Flexians take these coincidences of interest to the nth degree. When an individual serves in interdependent roles, and is in the public eye promoting policy prescriptions, *and* when fundamental questions lack straight answers—Who is he? Who funds him? For whom does he work? Where, ultimately, does his allegiance lie?— we have likely encountered a flexian.[7]

To get a sense of flex activity as we could watch it becoming acceptable, let's take a look at Gerhard Schroeder, the Social Democratic chancellor of Germany from 1998 till 2005. While he did not flog a cause as do true flexians, he exhibited certain flex features and *almost* crossed the boundary into flexian-hood. In September 2005, before losing his bid for reelection,

Schroeder signed a pact on behalf of his government with Gazprom, the Russian energy giant that commands a quarter of the world's natural gas reserves and represents a murky mix of state and private power. The agreement was to construct a Baltic Sea pipeline to run directly from Russia to Germany and supply gas to Germany and other western European nations. That December, after the election, he accepted a position as the head of Gazprom's shareholders' committee, a post roughly equivalent to board chairman. As the *Washington Post* editorialized, through his actions, Schroeder "catapulted himself into a different league."[8]

Germany paid a political price for the deal. Some Western Europeans warned that the pipeline would saddle Europe with greater dependency on Russian gas. And with the Russian navy ordered to protect the pipeline, critics foresaw new potential for espionage. Moreover, the two countries' central European, Baltic, and Ukrainian neighbors, bypassed by the pipeline's sea route, were outraged at being relegated to nonpartner status. In Poland, the deal unleashed sentiment recalling the Hitler-Stalin pact that had carved up the nation like a side of beef.[9]

Other peculiarities characterized the deal. The pipeline consortium's chief executive is Mathias Warnig, an ex-Stasi captain. As an East German spy, Warnig had worked with Vladimir Putin in the 1980s when the Russian president was overseeing the KGB bureau in Dresden. (The chair, or once deputy chair, of Gazprom's board of directors from 2000 to 2005 was Dmitry Medvedev, a Putin associate from St. Petersburg who became first deputy prime minister in 2005 and took over as president in 2008.) And according to Russian sources, while the German public learned of the pipeline deal in fall 2005, certain elites in Moscow had heard of it a full half year earlier.[10]

In this episode, crudely put, one sovereign state bought the chancellor of another state, one that is not only sovereign but the third largest industrialized nation in the world. Schroeder's arrangement with Gazprom evokes the unregulated deal making of a disintegrating command economy, such as those of 1990s transitional eastern Europe, and the circumvention of the free market by a public officer. During the Cold War, obviously, the deal would have been impossible. The Soviet Union did not have private companies, even ones thoroughly entangled with state power as it does today, to make private pacts with foreign leaders. The idea that the chief representative of a key ally of the United States would strike a deal with its rival that could potentially undermine its own national interest seems unthinkable; and the idea that word of such a deal would be spoken of in Moscow long before Berlin, equally unthinkable. Yet the end of the Cold War has shaken up not only relations among states but also their relations to markets, while creating new opportunities and incentives for the merging of official and private interests and power. Gazprom stands as a monument to what a Russian sociologist has called the "privatization of the state by the state"—a practice that apparently is becoming more acceptable.[11]

The Gazprom-Schroeder covenant challenged previous convention among Western democracies. Even though many people found Schroeder's behavior unacceptable, even scandalous, social pressure or cultural restraint did not deter him. More than four years after he accepted the position with Gazprom, he remained board chairman. If neither public opinion nor available mechanisms of states or international systems can hold Schroeder accountable, then who or what can? What he was able to get away with demonstrates an emerging standard of acceptability in which flexians and almost-flexians operate.[12]

Schroeder's deal with Gazprom does not seem so very different from some of the dealings exposed by the American financial crisis, which have evoked a public outcry about the collusion of high finance and government. Goldman Sachs, the vast investment bank with a wide reach of subsidiaries, investors, and friends—among them Henry Paulson, the former Sachs CEO and secretary of the Treasury who presided over the bailout of the company as the financial crisis came to a head in the fall of 2008—has been called "government Sachs."[13]

The new breed of players, who operate at the nexus of official and private power, cannot only co-opt public policy agendas, crafting policy with their own purposes in mind. They test the time-honored principles of *both* the canons of accountability of the modern state and the codes of competition of the free market. In so doing, they reorganize relations between bureaucracy and business to their advantage, and challenge the walls erected to separate them. As these walls erode, players are better able to use official power and resources without public oversight.

Flexians craft overlapping roles for themselves—coincidences of interest—to promote public policies (and sometimes their personal finances as well). These players, who generally work on more fronts and are more elastic in their dealings than similar operators in the past, both make the new system work and demonstrate how it does so. Consider, for example, Bruce P. Jackson, unofficial envoy, lobbyist, business professional, NGO founder and officer, and Republican Party activist. An operative with longtime ties to prominent neoconservatives Richard Perle and Paul Wolfowitz, as well as to Dick Cheney, Jackson served both in the Department of Defense and as a U.S. Army military intelligence officer from 1979 through the 1980s. After leaving government, he entered the private sector as a strategist for Lockheed Martin, today the largest federal contractor.[14]

In 1996, while Jackson was employed by Lockheed as vice president for strategy and planning, he and other neoconservatives founded the U.S. Committee to Expand NATO (later renamed the U.S. Committee on NATO) to push for the entry of former Eastern Bloc nations into what had been a Cold War defense group. Members of the board included Perle and Wolfowitz. (Jackson was also a project director of the Project for the New American Century, whose signatories included Wolfowitz and Cheney.) Jackson served as president of the committee while still working for Lockheed, where, in 1997, he was made responsible for securing fresh international markets for the company after the end of the Cold War. NATO enlargement, of course, would supply that in spades. In 1996 and 2000 he served on and chaired, respectively, Republican Party platform subcommittees responsible for national security and foreign policy. According to journalist John Judis, the efforts of Jackson and the committee proved important to winning Senate approval for expanding NATO to include Poland, Hungary, and the Czech Republic.[15]

With that success in hand, Jackson and his fellows worked to further enlarge NATO and set up a spinoff organization with the same principal officers in the same offices as the U.S. Committee to Expand NATO. In congressional testimony, Jackson credits himself with creating the "Big Bang" concept of NATO expansion that the would-be (second-step) NATO allies largely later adopted. This endeavor meshed nicely with another goal halfway around the world: to overthrow Saddam Hussein via American power. That effort was exemplified by Jackson's creation in 2002 of another neoconservative-powered lobbying group, the Committee for the Liberation of Iraq, which he chaired. During that same year, in which he cut his formal ties to Lockheed, Jackson burnished his profile as a de facto representative for the George W. Bush administration in eastern Europe. Jackson was characterized by the U.S. ambassador to NATO as "an indispensable part of our efforts in reaching out to these [former Soviet bloc] governments" and by Georgia's president as "an official with clout." (The government of Romania also signed Jackson up to facilitate its entry into NATO, according to *Le Monde* and Romanian newspapers, though Jackson denies this.) Jackson's standing as a Bush administration envoy in the eyes of American and eastern European officialdom was indispensable to his efforts to convince the NATO hopefuls to do the administration's bidding—that is, to back the U.S.-crafted invasion of Iraq. Toward that end, Jackson helped draft a declaration supporting the invasion that was signed by the foreign ministers of ten nations then up for NATO membership—later called the Vilnius Ten. This declaration was politically significant, for it came at a time when the administration was eager to show that its "Coalition of the Willing" had substance.[16]

Players like Jackson, ostensibly a private citizen, yet working stealthily for U.S. executive branch masters, peddling and helping to craft policy, are accountable only to their patrons. Such players are not confined by government diplomacy or lobbying rules, yet they routinely perform those functions in a way few diplomats or lobbyists would have the portfolio to do. The whole package that constituted Bruce Jackson—from the exact source(s) of his marching orders, to the source(s) of his funds, to the promises he supposedly made on behalf of the United States to foreign governments, to the fallout from those promises—is saturated with ambiguity.

Jackson's type of brokering has become much more necessary in the post–Cold War world, with its expanded fragmentation of power and frequent relinquishing of information by states to all manner of private players. But such an enterprise is also much more fraught with potential ambiguity, making spies and even double agents look like the simplest of animals. The ability of brokers like Jackson to flex their overlapping roles is made easier when dealing across national, legal, and cultural contexts and in societies in political

and legal flux. The reorganizing world has stimulated opportunities for flexians, without establishing balances to check these players' activities. Obtaining reliable information about a player's roles, sources of funds, and actual
track record may be difficult, and viable monitoring systems are usually lacking. Flexians can thus continue unchecked to convert their environment into
one that is friendly to them.

Now let's turn to a flexian who has championed, mastered, and made acceptable what he calls the "evolving door": Steven Kelman. He is a living example of how the new system has changed the profile of many of today's most
successful influencers, moving them beyond the revolving door of the past. In
the grand tradition of academics trooping to Washington to put their theo-
ries into practice, Kelman was invited by President Bill Clinton in 1993 to
come from Harvard's Kennedy School of Government to assume the top contracting job in the federal government, heading the Office of Federal Procurement Policy (OFPP), part of the Office of Management and Budget.[17]

Kelman would perform a lead role in the Clinton administration's efforts
at reinventing government. Known for his belief that the rules designed to
prevent collusion between government contractors and public officials in-
hibited more efficient and innovative contracting practices, he set out to reform that system by deregulating the awarding of contracts. While Kelman's
reforms did streamline the process, they also encouraged privatization of
heretofore officially available information and processes (as detailed in Chapter 4), advanced the partnership idea, and spurred more opportunities for
nontransparent deal making between government and contractor officials.[18]

Soon after his departure from government in 1997, Kelman became a
member of a Department of Defense (DOD) task force charged with identifying "DOD Policies and Practices that Weaken Health, Competitiveness of
U.S. Defense Industry." One of the stated concerns prompting the formation
of this body, according to a DOD press release, was the "beating" that the defense industry was taking on Wall Street at the time. While the task force presented Kelman's credentials as affiliated with Harvard and as a former OFPP
administrator, he simultaneously served on the board of directors of, and held
an equity interest in a company with nearly billion-dollar per year average
sales, almost all in government contracts.[19]

Kelman also put his punditry skills to work. He began writing a column for a trade publication, *Federal Computer Week*, distributed to nearly 100,000 readers, mostly government personnel involved in IT, contracting, or program management. In his column he has endorsed contractor-friendly policies for more than a decade. To his readers, Kelman is just a former OFPP administrator and Harvard professor promoting "good government"; his industry connections and consulting projects are rarely revealed. And this points to another feature of flexian performance: the tendency to hide behind one's most appealing role. In the world of media and punditry, flexians want to appear objective and devoid of self-interest. There they generally identify themselves to the unsuspecting public in their most honorable, least partisan role, thus concealing or downplaying other agendas. This is strategic: A high-prestige imprimatur like Harvard's enables Kelman and flexians like him to promote views for which they might not get a hearing if they had to fall back on their less neutral roles, such as those of company or industry consultant.[20]

A *Washington Post* news report's use of Kelman's "expert" commentary is one of many such cases. The *Post* article concerned a controversial government financing scheme championed by the Bush II administration, known as Share in Savings contracting. The *Post* quoted Kelman as a Harvard professor and former Clinton procurement policy chief who supported the technique. But he was at the time a registered lobbyist for a government contractor that was one of the largest beneficiaries of such contracting. While the *Post* issued a correction after the matter came to public light, most presentations by flexians are made with impunity and go unnoticed.[21] In an equally revealing incident, Kelman, in a *Post* op-ed, decried inspectors general reports that "generally advocate more checks and controls." Earlier an IG had recommended that a government contractor, in which Kelman held an equity interest and served on the board of directors of, be debarred from receiving federal contracts. "Small wonder he has it in for IGs," commented the Project On Government Oversight, a public interest organization.[22]

◊ ◊ ◊

ALL THESE PLAYERS, operating in and around diverse organizations and geographical areas, and of diverse ideological persuasions, surge beyond standard roles and responsibilities, as well as beyond standard rules and practices of Western states and international organizations. In the process, their operations swirl in and above the institutions for which they supposedly work—state, corporate, international, or other.

These players also have in common that their activities may sound like a simple litany of questionable ethics. They elicit shock from some: "Wow, did you see what he arranged/did/got away with/accomplished?" Observers are hard pressed to find comparable cases within their own institutional memories. But, just as often, the response is tolerance—and sometimes downright admiration for the flexians' sheer nerve.

Another common response to the actions of flexians is to label them "conflict of interest" or "corruption." Yet while parties to corrupt activities typically engage in them for profit, the same cannot be said of flexians, who seek influence and to promote their views at least as much as money. And "coincidences of interest" crafted by the players to skirt the letter of the law are often difficult, if not impossible, to pin down as conflicts of interest. When those coincidences span the globe, limited organizational reach and the limited jurisdictions of legal systems can only further empower the players, who seek to derail any mechanisms of accountability that might apply. Flexians are additionally hard to challenge because, while some of their activities are open and appear eminently respectable, others are murky or hidden, often just below the surface.

Thus, while it may be virtually impossible to determine whether flex activity today is statistically on the rise, it does appear to be widely tolerated. Tongues may click in public expression of disapproval but, in the end, passive acceptance and the entrenching system encourage recurrence. The very people who engage in these activities continue to command public respect and influence, sometimes even garnering more. Moreover, national and international governments and organizations are often attracted to, and reward, flexians because they get things done.

Journalists and public interest watchdogs have excavated and published details of activities by all these players, but to little consequence. All of them continue to operate unbridled by institutional constraint or adverse public opinion; their careers—and their likely bank balances—soar ever higher. And the public interest falls by the wayside. But merely exposing certain activities is not enough; framing them is essential.

Evolution of the Species

My longtime focus on central and eastern Europe, studying communism as it really worked and then came undone, was excellent preparation for charting this new phenomenon. For it was there that I observed the sophisticated practices of dealing under the table, reading between the lines, shifting self-presentations, and social networking for survival. These were not only art forms in a society (Poland) where the "authorities" were far removed from the will of the people; they also helped nudge formal bureaucracy and economy away from communism. And when that system unraveled and informal maneuvering was given free rein, self-enfranchising individuals and networks acquired information, resources, and influence heretofore in the hands of communist authorities. These players maneuvered the power vacuums created by crumbling command systems (made obvious by the 1989 fall of the Berlin Wall and the 1991 breakup of the Soviet Union), sometimes joining forces with outside operators as they rushed into the same vacuums.

In late-1980s/early-1990s Poland, as it was sprinting away from communism, a revealing practice attracted my attention. Many officials I was interviewing gave me multiple business cards bearing different job titles. It's hard to count how many times I was given one, two, three, or even more cards by the same official.

This happened first in Poland, then in Hungary, Czechoslovakia, and later in Russia and Ukraine after the Soviet Union fell apart. A deputy minister of privatization, a housing and environmental official, and a key presidential adviser each gave me multiple business cards. In all these countries my interlocutors had established new roles, in fact several roles at once, each to be trotted out as the occasion arose. Typically they knew little about me. As a Western scholar with entrée in the region, they clearly reasoned, I must have potentially useful contacts among Western foundations, businessmen, or aid agencies.

When interviews with officials were winding down or turning more personal, they would hand me their official government card, followed in quick succession by other hot-off-the-press business cards—also theirs. Then they would fill me in on their activities: It seemed that, in addition to their government job, they also headed a consulting firm, a "foundation," or an NGO (often one they or their wife had founded). Sometimes these entities even did business with the government offices these officials supervised.

Those exhibiting flexian features first revealed themselves to me as I observed both native and foreign operators during the so-called transition to democracy, as they facilitated and profited from the changes under way. The edgy players who adapted to the new environment with the most agility and creativity, who tried out novel ways of operating and got away with them, and sometimes were the most ethically challenged, were most rewarded with influence. In the study of foreign aid I undertook in the 1990s, these traits were exhibited in abundance. I saw how the overlapping roles, networks, and sponsors of the actors involved in the aid process were crucial to understanding how certain high-priority aid efforts played out.

Probably nowhere else could flex activity become as integral a part of changes under way and also mingle with global transactions than in the post-Soviet empire. There, legacies of a militarized economy and secret police combined with collapsed command systems, law subordinated to politics, and informal networking, not to mention Western-promoted radical privatization schemes, to accrue spoils to a connected few. There, as well, entire realms of financial practice were created and money laundering reached new heights. Some players who cut their teeth there have taken their skills beyond the region, plying their trade in a global environment where huge sums of money, off the books and largely unmonitored and unregulated by any institution, flow freely and lavishly.

The people I came to call flexians would soon appear on the world stage. Some of them operated across borders in the manner of global elites, international high fliers who ally more comfortably with their fellow global elites than with their own countrymen. In addition to the cross-pollination of practices—and not necessarily "best" ones—among such elites, parallel processes also developed as flexians, transmuting and changing their colors as necessary, carried the tradition of "the fix and the deal" to new levels. Like masterful dancers who push beyond accepted steps and recognized routines, flexians perform on the edge, trying out and inventing new patterns. These players live symbiotically within the system, quietly evading and stretching its rules as they help mediate its transformation. The new system they help fashion blurs the boundaries between the state and private sectors, bureaucratic and market practices, and legal and illegal standing. Ironically perhaps, the formerly communist world and the maneuverings that flowed from its transition away from communism proved an ideal training ground for examining governing, power, and influence in the United States at the dawn of the twenty-first century. There the new era of blurred boundaries is marked by privatization and contracting out, and a resulting fusion (and confusion) of state and private power.

Beyond Old Boys

Flex nets (like flexians) arose to fill a niche that is new. Just as flexians cannot be reduced to mere lobbyists, neither can flex nets be reduced to interest groups, lobbies, old-boy networks, and other such groupings in American society, government, and business. Flex nets are far more complex. Like interest groups and lobbies, flex nets serve a long-established function in the modern state—negotiating between official and private. But while flex nets incorporate *aspects* of these and other such groupings, they also differ from them in crucial ways—and those ways are precisely what make flex nets less visible and less accountable.

Four key features define both flexians as individuals and those influencers who work together as a flex net. Flexians functioning on their own exhibit the modus operandi embodied in all four features discussed below, as does a flex net as a whole. Because members of a flex net benefit from the actions of the collective, pooling resources and dividing labor, not all members of a flex net must exhibit these features individually.

One, *personalizing bureaucracy.* Flexians operate through personalized relations within and across official structures, and act primarily based on loyalty to people, not organizations, to realize their goals. They *use* the formal organizations with which they are affiliated—governmental, corporate, national, or international—but their chief allegiance is to themselves and their networks. Flexians work bureaucracy to their advantage, preferring to operate by means anathema to official, legal, and procedural objectivity—the hallmark of the modern state that harks back to the classic model elucidated by Max Weber, the influential German sociologist.

Members of a flex net, with their loyalty to people over organizations, form an exclusive informal network that serves as *an intricate spine*—the corresponding (first) feature of flex nets. Flex nets draw their membership from a limited circle of players who interact with each other in multiple roles over time, both inside and outside government, to achieve mutual goals. While their roles and environments change, the group provides continuity. For instance, as detailed in Chapter 6, members of what I call the Neocon core, an informal group of a dozen or so members and a successful flex net, have worked with each other in various incarnations for some thirty years to realize their goals for American foreign policy via the assertion of military power. Whereas interest groups promote a political cause or defend the agendas of a particular group, and lobbies offer politicians support and resources in exchange for preference in policies, flex nets are not formal or permanent entities. Their existence is unannounced, and they do not seek to incorporate themselves as such. Moreover, members of flex nets are united by shared activities and interpersonal histories. "Interest groups" and "lobbies" do not convey the ambiguous state-private networks of flex nets, which coordinate power and influence from multiple vantage points—often far removed from public input, knowledge, or potential sanction.[23]

Two, *privatizing information while branding conviction.* Flexians believe— in any event, convincingly assert—that they have complete understanding of the cause that propels them into action. They have a theory. And theory that serves as an organizing catalyst is crucial in times of rapid and intense social change, as Vladimir Lenin famously pointed out. More than the opportunists who have benefited from blurred boundaries and disorder throughout history, flexians operate in today's environment of *perpetual* change. They play on loopholes produced by the four transformational developments. Among them is the vacuum of information left at the end of the Cold War as states could no longer lay exclusive claim to official information. Being frequent gatekeepers of inside access and "knowledge" enables flexians to brand information and control its applications. They are highly skilled at using the media to sell solutions to economic, political, and social ills, sometimes along with their own role in those solutions, so they are also able to convince others of their unique understanding in an uncertain world, one that often takes them on faith. Thus, to keep going on and on (to borrow Celine Dion's phrase), flex-ians offer easy-to-grasp stories and parables to a public yearning for simple ex-planations.[24]

When such influencers work together in a flex net, they exhibit *shared conviction and action*—the corresponding second feature of flex nets. Flex nets, like military elites and religious cults, induce obligation and loyalty through shared ideals and ordeals. Their goals as a unit are ideological and po-litical, as well as to varying degrees financial and societal as a unit or a subset thereof. Members of a flex net act as a continuous, self-propelling unit to achieve objectives that are grounded in their common worldview, and to brand that view for the public. For instance, a cornerstone of the Neocon core's success over several decades has been the skill of its members at chal-lenging official U.S. intelligence, creating alternative versions, and branding them as official and definitive for politicians, government, and the media.[25]

As self-sustaining teams with their own agendas, flex nets cut through bu-reaucracy, connect entities, and streamline decision making. This efficiency can make them attractive to an administration and the public, as was the Neo-con core to the Bush II administration, especially in the president's first term. The sense of mission, perseverance, and ready strategy for advancing its goals that can make it an asset to an administration also means it can become a li-ability if the policies turn out to be unpopular, as did the Neocons'. And while members of a flex net serve "at the pleasure of the president," as does anyone else, they go on and on trying to achieve their goals. They differ from the "Wise Men" of the past such as the influential advisers who refashioned American foreign policy at the end of World War II and John F. Kennedy's "Best and Brightest" who executed the Vietnam War in the 1960s. These men were mainly instruments of the presidents whose policies they pursued.

Three, *juggling roles and representations.* Flexians perform interacting or ambiguous roles to maximize their influence and amass resources. Their repertoire of roles, each with something to offer, affords them more flexibil-ity to wield influence in and across organizations than they would have if they were confined to one role. The juggling of flexians cannot be equated with the "revolving door," in which people move serially between government and the private sector. The revolving door acquired its meaning in an age when the lobbyist and the power holder were the brick and mortar of the influence game. Their roles were defined and confined. The new breed of players is more elastic in its engagement. In the United States, for example, where players in policy and governing are just as or more likely to be *outside* formal (federal) government (in, say, consulting firms, think tanks, NGOs, and quasi-government organizations) than in it, players can occupy more roles than in the past and more easily structure their overlap to create a coincidence of interests. The ambiguity inherent in the interconnectedness of flexians' roles that can be kept separate, merged, or played off against each other at will yields not only flexibility but deniability. Ambiguity is not a mere byproduct; it is a defense. It enables flexians to play different sets of constraints off each other, skirting accountability in one venue by claiming they were operating in another. They need not necessarily break the rules; they merely shift around them. In this way, flexians defy scrutiny and public accountability while advancing their own agendas.

The corollary to flexians' juggling roles and representations is that members of a flex net form *a resource pool*—the corresponding third feature of flex nets. The influence of a flex net derives in part from its members' effort to amass and coordinate both material and interpersonal resources. As members parlay their roles and standing into influence opportunities by placing themselves in positions and venues relevant to their goals, the network as a whole can wield far more influence than an individual on his own. The Neocon core, for instance, is an example of how a ready-made network of players with its own private agendas can straddle a state-private seesaw to: prescribe and help coordinate government policies of monumental import and impact; sell them to government officials, legislators, the media, and the public; help implement them; and continue this strategy, both to justify what they have done and to influence policies that follow from the course taken. While highly effective, such a group is elusive and more difficult to hold to account than lobbyists, interest groups, and the like.[26]

Four, *relaxing rules* **at the interstices of official and private institutions.** As flexians inhabit and shift among overlapping roles, they relax rules. They achieve their goals in part by finessing, circumventing, or rewriting *both* bureaucracy's rules of accountability and businesses' codes of competition, thus helping to create many of the choices and structural positions available to them. In (re)organizing relations among official and private institutions, flexians fundamentally change the qualities of each, fashion a new fusion, and give birth to an altogether new beast.

Collectively, members of a flex net help create *a hybrid habitat*—their corresponding fourth feature. A flex net's strength lies in its coordinated ability to reorganize governing processes and bureaucracies to suit the group's purposes. Members of these groups both use and supplant government, as well as establish might-be-official, might-be-unofficial practices to bypass it altogether. Poised to work closely with executive authorities, flex nets eschew legislative and judicial branches of government that may interfere with their activities. The Neocon core did all of these things to help take the United States to war in Iraq. As flex nets infuse governing with their supple, personalized, private-official networks, they transmogrify their environment, whether temporarily or more lastingly. While these groups might call to mind old notions such as conflict of interest, they illustrate why such labels no longer suffice. As a Washington observer sympathetic to the neoconservatives' aims told me, "There is no conflict of interest, because they define the interest."

◊ ◊ ◊

THE RISE OF FLEXIANS and flex nets (and almost flexians and flex nets) illustrates the evolution of the American system of governing. In the old days, when an individual handed someone his business card, there was less doubt about who he represented and what activities he was engaged in. On a collective level, networks within government and political elites that undermine democracy are, of course, nothing new. One study of American political power from the Civil War to the New Deal, for instance, depicts the web of ties among government officials and the threat that those connections pose to the notion of democratic government. Most famously, a half century ago, in his treatise *The Power Elite*, sociologist C. Wright Mills described the interlocking group of government officials, military leaders, and corporate executives at the pinnacle of the nation's establishment, who, he argued, effectively "controlled" major political and social decision making. The rise of flex activity augurs for an even less democratic era. Rather than climbing

Mills's pyramid of the political, military, and business establishment, members of flex nets wield influence by forging coincidences of interest among an array of roles across organizations, whose boundaries and purposes often blend. Emergent forms of governing, power, and influence thus play out not in formal organizations or among stable elites, but in social networks that operate within and among organizations at the nexus of official and private power. The players in this system are less stable, less visible, and more global in reach than their forebears. Flex nets are a paradox: more amorphous and less transparent than conventional lobbies and interest groups, yet more coherent and less accountable, as one political scientist has observed. While many activities of flexians, and certainly their views, are public, the full array of their machinations is almost always difficult to detect. And the mechanisms of democratic input and control that could check them are just as difficult to discern.[27]

The new breed of players—today's shadow elite—are as elusive as they are ubiquitous. Agilely evading questions about who funds them, who they work for, or where their loyalties lie, individual flexians as well as those in flex nets benefit from the dust cloud of ambiguity and deniability they leave behind. They are not inherently unethical, in fact they sometimes do good and much-needed works, but they are subject to no greater oversight than their own consciences and the social pressure of their own networks. Their potential "corruption" is so interrelated that mechanisms that might curb their activities have yet to be invented. While charges of corruption may not stick, their activities are potentially more pernicious. They dilute effective monitoring, criticism, and consideration of alternative policies and, wherever they operate, have the potential to reshape governing. The inevitable result is that states, international organizations, companies, and NGOs face a new responsibility of grave proportions: investigating the track records, agendas, sponsors, and allegiances of the movers and shakers who work with them.

Over the past dozen or so years, my attempt to understand and explain the world of players who exhibit flexian behavior has led me to seek out others whose experiences and perspectives can shed light on this phenomenon. One of my many interlocutors has been the irrepressible Jack Blum. A lawyer and longtime observer of U.S. government agencies, he is an expert on money laundering as well as an investigator into Iran-Contra and other lesser-known affairs. In trying to capture the essence of the new breed, he told me one day: "If you're in the academic world, or you're a legal-type focused investigator, you want everything to fit into neat boxes, and none of this stuff fits into neat boxes. It's these multiple roles that these people have. None of these people are neat."[28]

CHAPTER TWO

When Privatization Meets Truthiness

THE NEW SYSTEM USHERED IN BY THE INTERACTION OF THE FOUR transformational developments of the late-twentieth and early-twenty-first centuries has brought new ways of being in the world. A broad array of "non-state" actors—from associates of companies, quasi-government organizations, and nongovernmental organizations to flexians and flex nets—puts these new ways to use every day. Flexibility is undeniably one of them. As a high-powered program director at a high-powered think tank expressed it: "I tend to operate in a 'just in time' mode, sort of like Toyota, because I realize that busy, important people tend not to plan ahead much. They tend to pivot this way and that in a high-flex mode given constantly changing priorities." A look at two individuals who possess the skills needed to maneuver the new environment, without rising to the level of being flexians, tells us much about the wide range of actors who both make and mirror it. Their rich stories, multifaceted lives, and international networks illuminate the texture of this environment.[1]

Ešref-Kenan Rašidagić, thirty-five years old when I met him in 2006, is not a flexian, but illustrates the qualities possessed by the many operators who nimbly manage the new environment. After serving in the Bosnian army in the early 1990s, he made his way to Malaysia, one of the few countries then accepting Bosnians without a visa. There, he earned a degree in political science from the International Islamic University [of] Malaysia. Then, through the Internet, he found out about the American University of Beirut, applied, and earned a master's degree in Middle Eastern studies.

When relative peace returned to his homeland, so did Rašidagić. Settling in Sarajevo, he married and supported himself as a freelance translator of English for various international organizations. He sought opportunities to insert himself into activities that mattered. In 2001, Rašidagić met Paul Stubbs, a British sociologist based in Croatia. Rašidagić was on a short-term assignment as a translator for a project to reform the nation's social sector; Stubbs had been hired to evaluate the project, sponsored by the Independent Bureau for Humanitarian Issues, a local offshoot of an international NGO funded by the Finnish government. Rašidagić impressed Stubbs, who saw his suitability for the post of project manager, a position he has held ever since. As Rašidagić became more established, he performed overlapping combinations of contract work for organizations ranging from UNICEF to the Danish Ministry of Foreign Affairs to locally registered NGOs. At the same time, he contributed input to his country's Poverty Reduction Strategy Paper (sponsored by the International Monetary Fund and the World Bank), which later was adopted as the Development Strategy of Bosnia-Herzegovina. He accepted a full-time university position and did all these jobs simultaneously. Today he works full time for both an NGO and the University of Sarajevo, where he teaches international relations and comparative political systems.[2]

Rašidagić has few counterparts among his countrymen. He exemplifies a genus of engaged citizens who assert themselves through consulting by maneuvering through a welter of international, state, and nongovernmental organizations. Consulting is a means—in some settings, virtually the only means—of positive engagement in helping to build one's nation or civic project.

Consultants like Rašidagić, of course, can play an exponentially greater role in and across fledgling states and unsettled arenas than they could elsewhere. But many of the qualities that today are sought and rewarded in such a context also appear to be sought and rewarded more widely.

A look at the experience of a young American consultant operating in the United States and internationally, who also exhibits flex qualities but does not rise to the level of flexian-hood, is equally telling. In 2000, college graduate Greg Callman, a twenty-nine-year-old when I met him in 2005, found his way to Amsterdam, where he landed a job as a research assistant for an American professor at the University of Amsterdam. In that post, he tracked worldwide "civil society" responses to the World Trade Organization on the Internet and developed a system called an "issue tracker." Callman also began supporting research for the professor's wife's employer, the Open Society Institute (OSI) in Budapest. The OSI is part of the network of organizations founded in the aftermath of the Cold War by the Hungarian-American philanthropist and financier George Soros to encourage democracy, civil society, and human rights. Callman also worked for an eight-person Dutch media company after meeting one of its principals, who spoke at Callman's university. At the same time, he started his own sole proprietorship, through which he hired himself out to employers, and learned to write a business plan and manage a company. While doing all this, Callman earned a master's degree in social and political science from the University of Amsterdam.[3]

The career paths traveled by Rašidagić and Callman are quite different from that of a perennial consultant, say, for one of the "Big Four" (not long ago "Big Eight") accounting firms. For these two (and others like them), "becoming" is a continual life process in which developmental stages are replaced by fluidity as they pursue an uneven mix of business and NGO start-ups and contract work, educational pursuit, and activism. Their paths reflect a much larger pattern: the fact that, more and more, people (not only the younger generation) are building their lives and careers across multiple sectors, institutions, and countries. As Paul Stubbs has noted, our multilayered, rapidly changing world rewards adaptability. Those who are flexible tend to be young and unburdened by either wide knowledge or wisdom, while those with valuable expertise are often older but may be inflexible. "The real challenge is to get both," he said.[4]

Ana Devic, a Yugoslavian-born lecturer and consultant who teaches in the Department of Sociology and Anthropology at the University of Glasgow, is a rare individual who possesses both expertise and flexibility. Lamenting the lower value that consultancy places on knowledge, as opposed to flexibility, she noted: "Every morning [in consulting] we are [starting] from scratch." Her quip insightfully characterizes not only the adaptability required in consultancy, but also the ahistorical, context-free nature of the endeavor, which coexists comfortably with temporary affiliation.[5]

Rather than the West leading the rest, this time states and arenas on the move seem to have something to say to more established or staid environments. While the former show us the qualities encouraged by the new system at their starkest, parallel (and sometimes connected) processes are also very much at work in the latter.

Take, for instance, the United States, where the adaptability required in a consulting life goes hand in hand with declining job security. The U.S. Department of Labor reported that the youngest of the baby boomers (those born between 1957 and 1964) held "large numbers of short-duration jobs even as they approached middle age." Younger workers were likely to change jobs even more frequently. The Department's study, which captured employment duration realities in the 1990s and into 2007, found that, among jobs begun by workers when they were thirty-three to thirty-seven years old, nearly a half ended in less than one year, and more than four-fifths ended in less than five years. Changes in the labor market—fewer good jobs that are harder to obtain and provide less security if you do get one, making more necessary shifts in employment—underpin these trends, which are only intensified by the economic meltdown. When institutions are no longer loyal to their employees, the smart thing is not to be loyal to an institution that may not be loyal to you.[6]

With consulting as a new way, among others, of being in the world, new qualities are prized: Self-managed, self-driving self-starters are in, while company men are out; elasticity is lauded, rigidity is not; "proactivity" is prized, passivity is passé; networks and "networking" are au courant, bureaucracy is scorned. New formations—self-starting organizations and groups, make-it-up-as-you-go-along structures and career paths—are encouraged, along with flexible identities. In short, improvisation and shifting affiliation are rewarded; loyalty to institutions is not. Although in some cases networks replace bureaucracy, mostly they just penetrate, subvert, or otherwise reorganize it. Today's star influencers have little use for the clear-cut arrangements of the past. They merrily innovate as they go along.[7]

These qualities and ways of being have flourished amid the four transformational developments: the redesign of governing; the end of the Cold War; the advent of evermore complex technologies; and the embrace of truthiness. ("Globalization," or the increased flow of goods, services, and capital across nations, is intertwined with all four developments, although this is not a subject of elaboration here.) These developments, or restructuring forces, caused by both design and default, have converged in an interactive spiral to rearrange authority on a global scale and spawn new institutional forms of governing and of power and influence in which official and private are melded, or power is simply privatized. Each development has been accompanied by a narrative—sometimes quite grand, like "the end of history"—that shapes public understanding of the world. Some of the results of these developments have worked to make responsibility more difficult to pin down, and, in time, rendered the public more reliant on the accounts and ethics of the players themselves. Meanwhile, the narratives not only mask the results, but also make it more difficult to see their consequences for democracy.

Redesigning Governing

There are good reasons for the first transformational development, the *redesign of governing*. When (as in Rašidagić's case) government barely exists, people and organizations improvise to get things done—in short, they (re)invent it. On the other hand, when unbending bureaucracies prove exasperating, there are calls in a democratic society for flexibility to make them more user friendly. David Osborne and Ted Gaebler, authors of the influential *Reinventing Government: How the Entrepreneurial Spirit Is Transforming the Public Sector*, published in 1992, criticized governments for their "sluggish, centralized bureaucracies, their preoccupations with rules and regulations, and their hierarchical chains of command." These ideas resonated; *Reinventing Government* became a best seller, even though its dry case studies largely treat state and local governments. The authors gave new voice to a prevalent critique of government that had been expressed before in various incarnations and that would hasten the redesign of governing.[8]

The vision of a streamlined state burst onto the public stage in the United States and the United Kingdom in the early 1980s, with Ronald Reagan and his ideological soul mate, Margaret Thatcher, leading the rhetorical charge.[9] Streamlining the state is part of a grab bag of ideas and policies often referred to as "neoliberalism," a term I employ sparingly because it can describe considerably different policies, not to mention differing local adaptations to them.

While classical liberal philosophy (harking back to the Enlightenment) sought to safeguard individual rights from state power, protect private property, and enshrine laissez-faire economics, neoliberal policies of the past several decades emphasize modest-size government, minimal restrictions on business, and open markets. Thus Reagan campaigned against "big government" and presided over an age of deregulation, relaxing constraints on industry, while Thatcher pressed to privatize the economy by selling government-owned enterprises.[10] The redesign of governing had its origins in these policy reforms (especially those dealing with government itself), as well as in expanded executive power, which often was necessary to implement neoliberal reform. With their roots in the Anglo-Saxon world, neoliberal ideas and policies would travel the globe in varying constellations.[11]

Efforts to limit the size of government, replete with attempts to make government more like business and to enlist private actors in its work, implicitly challenged the model of bureaucracy elucidated by Max Weber in the early twentieth century—one with clear distinctions between the state and private sectors and regulated through professional administration, that is, formal, impersonal structures rather than personalistic ones. Neoliberal policies, first implemented in Anglo-Saxon contexts that comported more to Weber's model (with all models, of course, encountering challenges when they butt up against reality), were hardly friendly to it. In fact, Americans' observation of East Asia, especially Japan, in which the division between state and private never existed in the Weberian sense, may even have contributed to the appeal of neoliberal ideas at a time when America was perceived to be on the decline and falling behind in the competition with Japan. Whatever the impetus, neoliberalism helped occasion a breakdown of the distinction between state and private, bureaucracy and market.[12]

A brief sketch of the trajectory of neoliberal reform sheds light on this breakdown—as the wellspring of today's redesign of governing—and its results. The "Reagan revolution" sanctified the practice of contracting out government services, ostensibly to control costs while letting governing entities concentrate on their central mission. (The United States was already a pioneer in contracting, with the Manhattan Project of World War II and Project RAND, established in 1946, among the templates.) As well, enlisting nongovernmental actors and forging collaborative relations with private entities (as in public-private partnerships) would make government more responsive and efficient. Again, the United States, with its history of private bodies building railroads, universities, and civic institutions, took the lead.[13]

Business was the model for government. In 1976, Ronald Reagan, while running for president, foresaw the ideal state as one in which "modern business practices could make government more efficient, economical, and responsive." The "new public management," which gained currency in the 1980s, sought to apply business principles such as competition and an emphasis on outcomes to government. Heading up President Bill Clinton's "reinventing government" initiative in the 1990s, Vice President Al Gore echoed the point: "We need to adopt the very best management techniques from the private sector to create governments that are fully prepared for the Information Age." An example is his promised civil service reform, "based on an insight that is common in private industry: you pay for performance." (Of course, that maxim has not been applied equally. Many CEOs are not paid for performance but paid *whatever* their "performance.") The injection of business principles into government was reflected in the language: Recipients of state services become "customers" and citizens "shareholders," while hierarchy gives way to "participation" and "teamwork," and rule-driven to "mission-driven" government.[14]

However reasonable these reforms may sound, the fact is that making government more like business constituted a full-frontal challenge (without necessarily declaring it), to the qualities of government and business, in which government operated for the public good and was accountable to the public, and business, ostensibly based on competition, made money. Imbuing government with the character of business could not help but unsettle the accountability frameworks that depended on the clear demarcations that had evolved within many modern democratic states. Graham Scott, the soft-spoken treasury secretary of New Zealand who implemented sweeping "performance-based management" reforms there beginning in the 1980s and an astute student of government reform, is emphatic on this point. "The complexity and networks [brought about by the management reforms] create the demands for old-fashioned accountability. . . . More than ever, we must be vigilant," he told me.[15]

Whatever the benefits of these reforms, they introduced issues of accountability—that of the state to its citizenry. The problem is not only the complexity injected into governing via the increase in entities and actors involved—and not subject to the same rules as government employees—but the necessity to "perform" for the public that has accompanied neoliberalism. Mission-driven government that emphasizes outcomes, particularly government that is outsourced (thus literally, removed from the source), demands, above all, *showing* that the mission has been accomplished. Like teaching to the test, simple story lines, "metrics," and pseudo-quantitative indicators must be contrived to convince an audience far from the context in which the mission is being carried out. Demonstrating how the mission is progressing thus evolves into a performance for those holding the purse strings, one all about the *appearance* of doing a good job, as John Clarke, a cultural analyst of bureaucracy, has observed. *Appearing* to accomplish the mission is rewarded, sometimes at the expense of actually accomplishing it, not to mention that the "mission" may not lend itself to a set of discrete tasks or simple metrics. Anyone who has labored in the international development and "project" world, where work has long been outsourced to private providers, is familiar with the formulaic "success stories" touted in donors' reports and the show-and-tells of testimony before congressional committees. That very term, now used to justify a variety of government programs, captures the need to perform for the public.[16]

The spin inherent in success stories, however, pales in comparison with long-standing narratives—narratives that work to mask ground-level realities of neoliberal reform. In the United States, for instance, the practice of railing against "big government" in fact leads to the creation of still bigger government—and of a less accountable sort (as detailed in Chapter 4). That is because, while federal government was officially being contained in size— as measured in terms of civil servants and others employed directly by government—"shadow government" was getting ever bigger. The 1976 book *The Shadow Government,* published five years before Reagan took office, details the vast off-the-books government workforce already entrenched. Since then, the shadow government has done nothing but grow. Its ranks include all manner of consultants, companies, and NGOs, not to mention entire bastions of outsourcing—neighborhoods whose high-rises house an army of contractors and "Beltway Bandits." Largely out of sight except to Washington-area dwellers, contractors and the companies they work for do not appear in government phone books. They are not dragged before congressional committees for hostile questioning. They function with less visibility and scrutiny than government employees would face. Most important, they are not counted as government employees, and so the fiction of limited government can be upheld, while the reality is that of an expanding sprawl of entities that are the government in practice.[17]

Alongside the narrative of limited government is the idea that government remains in control and accountable even when transferring its functions and legitimacy to the private sector. Officially, only government officials carry out "inherently governmental" functions—the government's term for work that only federal employees should do; they also monitor the contracting process and ensure the quality of work performed by contractors. Yet investigations of on-the-ground operations indicate otherwise. For instance, in a twenty-five-year contract awarded in 2002 to a joint venture of two mega defense companies, Lockheed Martin and Northrop Grumman, to upgrade the United States Coast Guard, key decisions were made by contractors rather than civil servants. On some crucial issues, Coast Guard officials had "limited influence over contractor decisions," according to the inspector general at the Department of Homeland Security. Commenting on this state of affairs to the *Wall Street Journal* (in a front-page article titled "Is U.S. Government 'Outsourcing Its Brain'?"), the inspector general remarked, "Our ignorance [that of the government] is their gain." Just who is minding the government store? While it was subsequently announced that the Coast Guard would gradually begin to assume a leading role (with the two companies continuing their involvement), it will take an estimated three years for this branch of the U.S. Armed Forces to refederalize the operation's intellectual capability and to reassert control.[18] In such an arrangement and many others like it, new forms of governing are created. Yet the façade of a government in control and accountable prevails.

Neutrality is another narrative that accompanies neoliberal-inspired changes nearly everywhere they are implemented. Deregulation and the privatization of state-owned enterprises and services, which became standard international development fare in the 1980s, are presented as technical projects, designed to achieve greater efficiency. The public face of these policies—the legions of fly-in, fly-out economists, accountants, and planners—reinforce that narrative. Clad in the personality and language of efficiency, neoliberal principles, spun off in various forms, have circled the globe, with the international financial institutions as frequent sponsors and sometimes local economists trained in elite American schools playing leading roles, such as ministers of the economy. Yet where neoliberal policies took hold outside the Anglo-Saxon world—and they did not always do so—the charade of neutrality is often unmasked. Privatization and deregulation are, at their core, ideological, value-laden endeavors that stimulated reorganizing, and often came on the heels of unpopular macroeconomic restructuring at the behest of the international financial institutions. Whatever their economic rationale and results, and however democracy-challenged the countries into which the policies were introduced already were, these policies did not tend to mesh well with the encouragement of checks and balances, state-private demarcation, or democratic participation. Moreover, implementing privatization and deregulation often required an expanding executive—backed up, of course, by the power of the relevant international financial institutions—that crowded out checks and balances offered by legislatures and courts. Thus, privatization and deregulation restructured governing and power, forging flex-friendly environments, and were hardly neutral.[19]

Further challenging these three neoliberal narratives is another staple of the neoliberal policy sweep—the establishment of nongovernmental bodies that carry out government functions. Such bodies have the potential to create the ultimate flex-friendly environment. Initiated by international development agencies, these hybrid entities—variously called "quasi-government organizations," "para-governmental organizations," "parastatals," and state-created "NGOs" (all with somewhat different meanings)—might recall the quasi-nongovernmental organizations of the United States and the UK (sometimes called "quangos") that are outside the civil service but funded by the state. But there are differences. Supposedly set up to bypass bureaucratized government, these bodies are sometimes endowed with more authority than the relevant government agencies and enable private players to create and carry out government functions. Whatever efficiency might come from such arrangements, they inspire flex activity because the players who empower them can avail themselves of the best of both worlds—the authority and ability to allocate resources of the state, combined with the profits of the private sector—while weaseling out of both accountability to the state and private-sector competition. Such arrangements put the lie to the neoliberal narratives and lend themselves to governing via fusions of state and private power or simply to its privatization.[20]

The collapse of communism on the heels of this wide deployment of neoliberal ideas suddenly presented a vast new expanse for the employment of neoliberal narratives and policies in the 1990s. Not surprisingly, many a privatization adviser sent by an international development institution or Big Six accounting firm hailed from the United States or the United Kingdom and pushed many of the same reforms as elsewhere, this time into overbureaucratized, inflexible command systems that had lost their command. Rather than helping construct effective state apparatuses, the state was often berated and bureaucracy bypassed by creating quasi-government entities to go around government while doing its work. As the movement advanced with little resistance, privatization exploded around the globe; by 1998, its rate was practically doubling every year. There was power in positive thinking. As two political analysts assessed it, "if economic policy could lay claim to popularity, at least among the world's elites, it would certainly be privatization." This "privatization revolution" encouraged the melding of state and private power. Here again, while the narratives of neoliberalism were at work, including that of neutrality, institutions and policymaking processes were established that distanced citizens from the democratic input and the checks and balances for which they had been clamoring.[21]

Whatever their merits, neoliberal policies could not help but facilitate the blurring of state and private relationships and authority. They could not help but make local environments friendlier to flex activity: When walls separating functions and ensuring balance of power are weak, those functions and power balances are able to be concentrated—enabling intensified influence. This does not mean, of course, that government bureaucracy has been put out of commission. Rather, forces are afoot to reinvent it, to make it more informal, improvised, and more dependent on personalistic networks. Bureaucracy has, as a result, become "multilayered and more diffuse," as one analyst put it. Of course, all this eases the fusion of state and private power and provides a hospitable habitat for all manner of nonstate actors, with flexians and flex nets most in tune with it.[22]

Delivering New World Orders

The *end of the Cold War*—the second transformational development—both intensified and expanded the changes earlier set in motion by the redesign of governing and by globalization. With the dissolution of bipolar authority, George H. W. Bush proclaimed a "new world order." Obstacles, it seemed, had vanished. *The End of History*, touting the triumph of market democracy, told a compelling story and became a popular book—and mantra. Everywhere, it appeared, democracy, civil society, and free markets were on the march.[23]

But the narratives of the era masked new forms of power in the making as private operators, be they transnational networks promoting policies and practices, international financial acrobats, or traffickers in drugs, humans, or nuclear materials, seemingly cooperated or colluded with officials and some-times even stood in for the state. This point was aptly made by an illustrator who lampooned the "new world order" in a 1990s cartoon depicting an arms trader enlisting rogue suppliers to fill "new world orders." The new order in-deed presented myriad opportunities for another kind of "order." That is be-cause the fragmentation of authority brought about by the end of the Cold War opened up new, sparsely governed arenas ranging from borders con-trolled by smugglers and corrupt officials; to the economic reforms of states directed by self-appointed transnational actors, regional policies determined by cross-national industry associations, or human rights or environmental politics set by advocacy networks; to commerce regulated by money laun-derers and financial sectors organized by wizards of finance. The new and re-configured arenas offered profitable targets for all manner of players who could not have enjoyed the same, relatively unfettered license or influence during the Cold War.[24]

The unfettered financial arena is huge and growing. Money laundering, for instance, increased at least tenfold between 1990 and 2005, to an esti-mated $1 to $1.5 trillion, while legitimate global trade merely doubled during the same period, according to economist Moisés Naím. Moreover, as Naím explains: "The Moroccan human trafficker who doubles as a real-estate mogul in Spain, or the Russian arms smuggler who owns a bank in Cyprus—blurs the line that traditionally differentiates legal and illegal business activities." Such players, through their criminal activities, help mesh official and private power as they develop close relations with politicians and bureaucrats wherever they operate. Naím contends that, "in many instances, the relationships are so close that government officials replace the national interest with that of the criminal enterprise." Much of this unmonitored and untaxed activity not only eludes the controls of states and international organizations, but "is taboo in business and government circles," as another expert on the subject observes.[25]

While many more actors have been able to perform roles that matter since the close of the Cold War, means of transparency and accountability have not kept up. Whether doing good works, as many are, or operating on the "dark side" of civil society, the players in these arenas are generally not accountable through traditional means, as corporations supposedly are to shareholders (though not necessarily to anyone else) or democracies to voters. That is, they can powerfully influence the lives of people with little transparency and little established means to recognize this influence and hence hold it in check.[26]

With the end of the Cold War, as with the redesign of governing, organizations and publics have become more reliant on players' performances because lines of authority are often unclear or nonexistent. The rearranging of authority has rendered the track records of many players less visible and made it more difficult, in the absence of clear authorities, to recognize who represents whom and who is doing what. A key reason is because players themselves, not established authorities, are now often the ones with access to information. They can closely guard it while performing for the public, divulging only what is in the players' interest for the public to believe. This has made it easier for today's influencers to create the illusion of expertise at the expense of the real thing, to play roles off against each other, or simply to cover up for themselves. It has made it easier for these players to represent themselves as acting on behalf of the public while in fact acting on behalf of themselves. Thus many an arms trader and transnational organized crime figure has made compelling self-presentations that convinced publics of their civic-mindedness. Many a financial guru endowed with boundless legitimacy has done exactly the same.

In all this, the potential for the privatization of power, the melding of state and private power, and the players to replace the national interest with their own interests is enormous.

Adding Technology to the Mix

The third transformational development—the *advent of evermore complex technologies*—has added a new dimension, one unique in human history, to the redesign of governing and reconfiguration of authority engendered by the end of the Cold War. That is because complex technologies bring along with them new forms of organizing and means of interacting with the world. They lend themselves to new forms of power and influence that are neither bureaucratic nor centralized in traditional ways, nor are they generally responsive to traditional means of accountability. Take complex information technologies, for instance. The grand narrative of such technologies is that they are democratizing, egalitarian, and transparency promoting. And while there is truth to this, and certainly also illusion (I and millions of others receive regular e-mails from "Barack Obama" and "Joe Biden," as if we are personally in touch with the president and vice president), these technologies also usher in new forms of governing that can lie far beyond transparency. For instance, advances in technology, while allowing the public unprecedented access to information, have also given government the tools to hide secrets and impede transparency, as several analysts have documented.[27]

Complex information technologies invite not only governments to skirt transparency. Ever multiplying challenges to transparency and accountability are created by private players whose activities the complex technologies of today make possible when they join with the deregulatory fervor of the first transformational development. Take, for instance, the complex new financial instruments that have ballooned in size and scope. The U.S. government, in the name of financial innovation, has allowed parallel, but unregulated or "dark" (over-the-counter) commodity derivatives markets to operate alongside regulated markets. Dark markets are exempted from transparency and regulation through loopholes codified in the Commodity Futures Modernization Act of 2000. The provision of "legal uncertainty," for instance, disables discretion on the part of regulators and exempts certain derivatives and other exotic financial instruments from government oversight. Exploiting such loopholes and the inherent lack of transparency in dark markets, speculators trading in energy, metals, and agricultural products have driven up the price of food and energy for billions of people around the world. The Bank for International Settlements (which tracks transactions in the so-called G-10 countries plus Switzerland) estimates that the notional value of these over-the-counter commodity derivatives grew from $5.4 trillion to $13.2 trillion between December 2005 and June 2008.[28]

Despite the magnitude and impact of these derivatives markets, the Commodity Futures Trading Commission, the U.S.-based (non)regulator of these trades, not only collects no data on the size of these U.S.-based transactions. In July 2008, President Bush threatened to veto legislation that would provide such authority. The Obama administration is seeking to regulate many, but not all, over-the-counter derivatives; the G-8 finance ministers have called for regulation of over-the-counter commodity derivatives to stem excessive speculation in oil. Effective reregulation, however, is far from certain; the political power of the financial services industry will likely force compromises.[29]

The lack of transparency, the complexity of the transactions, and the dearth of government supervision in these vast dark markets empower investment banks and their lobbyists to define the terms of the debate, threaten capital flight and job loss if the instruments are regulated, and thereby acquire disproportionate power to craft the rules. The constant invention of such unregulated financial instruments encourages megawealthy innovators to play on the margins, shape the rules to their advantage, add layers of insulation that help them avoid notice, and ultimately undermine the foundations of the economy. An anthropologist of finance has found that offshore finance, while appearing to be more regulated than ever before, is in fact "regulated" by the representatives of the financial services commissions of the countries that allow it and by the trust and estate practitioners who design offshore "financial architectures" for their clients. As he assesses, "the effect of these people saying 'let us make the rules' has fed in really nicely to neoliberal ideology of letting the subjects most involved in stuff be responsible for the actions." Financial instruments few understand are invented daily. But unless legislators understand them, they can't regulate them. And, because few grasp what the players are up to, appearances are what mostly matter.[30]

These shenanigans are par for the course in an environment where the only dependable constant is change. As Don Kash, a scholar in the field of technological innovation, expresses it:

The most distinctive thing about our time is that technological innovation has become routine and it occurs in nearly every physical activity and in an increasing number of biological activities. . . . You get
up every morning and there is capability to do things that did not exist
the morning before. . . . Change has become the norm—the routine
experience that we have. Many years ago a fellow wrote a book called
Future Shock. What was the thesis of *Future Shock*? What is culture
shock? First time I ever heard about culture shock, a friend of mine
had an occasion to go to the Middle East, and he was invited to a cel-
ebration in the middle of the desert in a huge tent, and they ate all this
good food sitting on rugs and so on and apparently had a good time,
and when the meal was over, people started belching. His first reaction was "good god, how crude," and then he realized that this was an
indication of how good the food was. And so he belched, and said it
really turned out to be a delightful thing to do because sometimes you
need to get rid of gas, and here you had a culture that made releasing
gas also a compliment of the food. Now culture shock is what happens when you go into another culture and you don't know what the
rules are. What's future shock? . . . Future shock is when you get up
and open the door to a technology that changes the rules of the game
and you close the door, but it is distinct from culture shock because
you can never go home. You can never go back to the place where you
know the rules.[31]

That place was more predictable and safer. But an ability to handle not
knowing the rules with agility—to be responsive—is a quality that is today
required for effectiveness.

Amid such unpredictability, network systems, collectively organized and
sustained, have become an integral part of our society. These modes of organizing have emerged in part because they are better adapted to creating
and using complex technologies. Almost every technology is produced by an
international network—a network that is "self-organizing" and "def[ies] hierarchical and centralized management," as Kash contends.

New modes of network-based organizing have penetrated the most conservative of bureaucracies and helped launch challenges to established au-

thorities. Even the U.S. Army is not exempt. A report by a major government contractor discussed the conundrum facing the U.S. military and many other organizations: how to deal with the next generation of workers who are tech savvy, open-minded, multitasking, and perhaps unprepared for command and control environments? The report was initiated because senior military officers were concerned by the use of new Web practices by young soldiers and officers in the ranks—practices that run counter to the formal doctrine and informal culture and norms of the military. These soldiers are now subject to modes of influence from a variety of sources, including online social media. New information technologies, networks, and practices often don't recognize traditional boundaries and can undermine traditional sources of authority such as government and science. Meanwhile, people are more receptive to new forms of (nonhierarchical, noncentralized, and nonaccountable) governing. In turn, these forms of governing abet organizing outside traditional, centralized bureaucracy and accountability, even as they often rely on official power and resources. [32]

What could be wrong with these new ways of organizing, with their obvious potential, if not for good (recall Rašidagić and Callman), then certainly to be benign? In decision making that is scattered through networks and organizations or centralized it's-not-clear where, it is harder to locate just "who" is responsible for an action or decision. The downside to such self-organizing systems is that they "have changed the meaning of individual accountability," as Kash and a coauthor put it. Assigning responsibility for errors or shortcomings, let alone future consequences for entire populations and the Earth, is like trying to catch a fly by its leg.[33]

THE REDESIGN OF GOVERNING, the end of the Cold War, and the advent of evermore complex technologies have profoundly shaped not only the profile of the influencers who play in the state, but also its very nature. In the years following the end of the Cold War, some prominent political analysts posited challenges to the sovereignty of the state: a "retreat of the state" (Susan Strange), a "power shift" away from states that are "sharing powers . . . with businesses, with international organizations, and with a multitude of citizens groups" (Jessica Mathews), the shift from the "unitary" to the "disaggregated"

state (Anna-Marie Slaughter), and the "increasing inability [of states] to regulate economic and cultural exchanges" and the concomitant "decentered and
deterritorializing apparatus of rule" (Michael Hardt and Antonio Negri). Of
course, some states asserting their national interests are much more exempt
than others from such diminution of sovereignty—"gigantic powers like
China, India and Brazil emerging on the global scene as nation-state projects
that seem to have their own logic," as another political analyst put it. To whatever extent a particular state is retreating, sharing power, or failing to regulate arenas of activity, the point is that the state—whatever its involvement—is
a crucial partner in new institutional formations that meld official and private power.[34]

For instance, today's economic crises are leading to new institutional fusions of power as firms "too big to fail" are partially nationalized, unprecedented power is concentrated in "Government Sachs," and cross-national
links with melded state-private executive authorities are built. The new institutional arrangements rely heavily on monopolies of information and executive power. All this has created even more opportunities for the
"regulators" and the "regulated" to be one and the same, and for the privatiz-
ers of power to do their thing and then to perform their way out of public responsibility. "Our political economy is run by a compact elite able to fuse the
power of our public government with the power of private corporate governments in ways that enable them not merely to offload their risk onto us
but also to determine with almost complete freedom who wins, who loses,
and who pays," assesses Barry C. Lynn, an analyst of America's political economy. Meanwhile, the means by which citizens could know what is going on—
much less have some input into it—are ever-elusive.[35]

Slouching Toward Truthiness

The fourth transformational development—the *embrace of truthiness*—builds
on the first two, and paradoxically also has been enabled by the technologies
and networks of the "information" era that are part of the third development.
The grand narrative here is that these technologies keep us better informed
than in the past. That is sometimes the case. Yet powerful cultural and economic forces also work to do the opposite. Performing is an essential ingre-

dient in today's public sphere, often at the expense of objectivity, expertise, and accurate information. Neoliberalism's encouragement of performance helped spur the emphasis on self-presentation that is today crucial to anyone building a career.[36] Society today cultivates this fertile ground by fostering an environment in which players can easily get away with stage-managing their self-presentations, portraying themselves in ways that baldly contradict their previous presentations and realities. Comedian Stephen Colbert captured this when he coined the satirical term "truthiness" to distinguish fact-challenged accounts gussied up as truth from evidence-based accounts. Listed as Merriam-Webster's Word of the Year 2006, "truthiness (noun)" was defined as follows:

> 1: "truth that comes from the gut, not books" (Stephen Colbert, Comedy Central's *The Colbert Report,* October 2005)

> 2: "the quality of preferring concepts or facts one wishes to be true, rather than concepts or facts known to be true" (American Dialect Society, January 2006).[37]

Frank Rich, the *New York Times* columnist and cultural-political analyst, has traced the origins of truthiness to the mid-1990s "when you simultaneously had the rise of the cable-news networks, the rise of the Internet, the rise of networks covering finance and Court TV—this whole apparatus that's in place now." Sociologist Manuel Castells similarly suggests that it is this "new media," entwined with the "new [technology and information-driven] economy," that creates today's political arena, not the sovereign states of yesterday. And as politics blends with entertainment, which is all about performance, political coverage itself gets reduced to performance.[38]

The performance element is made obvious by the appearances of famous people, who no longer necessarily appear as themselves; they instead *play* themselves. That is why what is real can mesh so acceptably with what is not and why people appearing as themselves and imposters are mixed in the same frame. The period leading up to the presidential election of 2008 is rife with examples. For instance, in a *Saturday Night Live* skit of November 3, 2007, Senator Barack Obama appeared as himself while the roles of other politicians were played by *SNL* cast members. In the skit, Hillary Clinton (played by Amy Poehler) hosts a Halloween party in which she invites all the Democratic candidates to her home. Someone walks in wearing an Obama mask—it turns out to be Obama himself. Then Hillary (fake) and Obama (real) have an exchange about being genuine and having nothing to hide from the American people.[39]

Today, it is the *idea of reality* that is often being performed and sought by the media, leaving the reality much more elusive. Tellingly, the performances of vice-presidential candidate Sarah Palin are nearly indistinguishable from the parodies of her by *SNL* cast member Tina Fey. The media toy with reality even further. On *Saturday Night Live* (October 18, 2008), Palin imitated Tina Fey imitating Palin. Here the reality of Palin is mixed with entertainment using Palin. The *idea* of reality is being performed, but the reality of reality is more difficult to track and often undermined. The focus is on performance and empty rhetoric, not evidence. The "substance" lies in Fey's imitation of Palin—not in anything Palin has to say.

Society's embrace of truthiness is another way in which Western culture has moved away from many of the distinctions it once made. Not only are state and private, bureaucratic and market boundaries blurring, but distinctions between politics and entertainment, work and play, truth and fiction, often are also amorphous. Take the hard line between truth and fiction that is nowadays blurred. Satirical fake news programs, such as Jon Stewart's *The Daily Show*, would be considered fiction by traditional journalism but, much like court jesters of medieval times, they regularly connect the dots and express insights more incisive than the network news. At the same time, market-driven "news" programs, often broadcast by networks owned by multinational corporations, frequently cover more entertainment and features than they do hard news. CBSNews.com's Dick Meyer concludes that "We're so jaded by the continuous supply of intentional lies and deceptions by politicians, celebrities, 'the media' and marketers that we need a word to replace truth, which is obsolete and naïve. . . . Truthiness does [the trick]."[40]

The ideological conflict of yesterday has been superseded by politics disconnected from authority and centered more and more in truthiness. As one philosopher notes, truthiness is associated with a society in which the authority of objective knowledge in general, and science in particular, is subject to question. In America, at least, this authority is under attack from both the academic left and, more recently, the political and religious right, such as with efforts to ban the teaching of evolution.[41] The collapsing of truth and fiction, which reflects this loss of authority, affords people a new kind of legitimacy: They can make up their own standards of evidence while living in ever-diverging universes of facts.

Developments in technology and media support this trend. Distributing news no longer requires starting a newspaper or television program. Anyone with access to a computer can create his own space to "report" or comment on daily events for an Internet audience of who-knows-how-many. Consumers, for their part, can create their own "reality" cocoon: Almost as simply as walking down the street with one's own headset listening to one's own music, everyone can discern their own "truth" and find the supporting "facts" and news outlet to back them up.

Today's mainstream journalism has evolved in its acceptance and adoption of truthiness. The attack on authority has permeated the institution. Expertise or qualifications as a journalist are no longer essential. Even Karl Rove can become one. Rove, George W. Bush's former deputy chief of staff, mimicked George Stephanopolous's move eleven years earlier from the Clinton White House to ABC News. The *New York Times* opined that Rove's new role in the media "marks another step in the evolution of mainstream journalism, where opinion, straight news reporting and unmistakable spin increasingly mingle, especially on television." Here, not only is reality performed, but, via juggling of roles and representations, actors can play one role off of others and few will notice or care, as we saw with the retired military officers cum television pundits discussed in Chapter 1.[42]

Lest we think this phenomenon is confined to the United States, we can simply look at Poland. There, politicians have dismissed well-grounded allegations by the press by dubbing them "media facts" or "press facts." Embedded in those notions is the idea that reality is being performed. Nor is the press immune from the flow of virtual reality. A highly regarded reporter for one of Poland's most prominent media outlets was told by one of his editors: "A master journalist doesn't merely report the facts, he creates them."[43]

Top players of the truthiness game, including flexians and flex nets, use media and its evolving technologies and culture with great proficiency. Unlike the specialists of earlier generations, with technical charts and graphs to build their case, today's premier players are adept at selling their version of reality. They are all about appearances—the appearance of the moment, that is. For in a truth-is-what-you-make-it-based, rather than fact-based, world, empirical facts are trumped by the "reality" of the moment.[44]

Flexians are expert at detecting what the public will find convincing. As jugglers of roles and representations, they are skilled at manipulating appearances—at showing up in different guises to achieve their ends, and flexing whichever of their roles gives them the most credibility at the moment. The truthiness society puts up with this legerdemain in part because of people's demand to be "informed" with up-to-the-minute "news," and the media's constant need to fill the news slot and feed the public's insatiable appetite. The diminishment of authority makes it harder for the public to assess the claims of today's influencers.

The flexians, who thrust themselves to the fore, corner access and information previously in the hands of states and official bodies, or operate in new unregulated arenas. They use this access and information to wield their own influence and can spin it however they like because they are the ones "in the know." They have more leeway than their almost-counterparts in recent history to self-regulate their activities and to circulate "talking points" that justify them. And in comparison with their communist almost-counterparts, they have an advantage: While the citizens of communist societies are inundated by propaganda, they school themselves in skepticism, reading between the lines and discerning the motives of players. The same cannot be said of a truthiness society. As Jon Stewart put it in reference to Vice President Dick Cheney's numerous erroneous statements, "His clout is questioned, and, yet, his clout goes on." These changes in society may well prove to be just as important for democracy as those brought about by privatization or complex technologies.

Frank Rich explains the danger inherent in truthiness. "It's harmless if the stories are trivial, like if people want to believe that [the reality TV show] 'Survivor' really is about life-and-death survival. Where it becomes a problem is when it deals with stuff that affects people's welfare, or the welfare of the country. It does damage to sell a country on a war based not just on faulty intelligence but the kind of hyping that went on with the rest of it." In this vein, a *New York Times* reporter recounted a conversation he had with a senior adviser to President Bush. The adviser accused the journalist of being "'in what we call the reality-based community,' which he defined as people who 'believe that solutions emerge from . . . judicious study of discernible reality.'" But "'That's not the way the world really works anymore,' he continued. 'We're an empire now, and when we act, we create our own reality.'"[45]

Clearly, truthiness enables today's influencers—at the pinnacle, flexians—to exercise power and influence with new consequences. Flexians thrive on ambiguous identities, appearances, loyalties, and borders of practically all kinds. They thrive in an environment of improvised reality, in which the façade counts for a great deal and fiction can practically *become* reality if enough people believe it; in which appearances, self-presentations, and professed motivation are accepted pretty much at face value; in which a "company man" loyal to an institution is in vogue only if the man owns his own company; in which reinvention of self is common, even admired, and where track records often do not track.

If the citizens of a state cannot or are not willing to recognize these new players and their modus operandi, they cannot call for them to be accountable through democratic means. Ironically, perhaps, citizens in postcommunizing states, embracing nothing more secure than the promise of market democracy yet accustomed to reading between the lines, were the first to spot the new breed of players as they emerged in their own countries as well as on the world scene.

CHAPTER THREE

Flex Power in the Wild East

I MIGHT NEVER HAVE COME UP WITH THE NOTION OF FLEXIANS IF I hadn't met the woman I came to call Mama. Mama headed the family I lived with in Warsaw beginning in early 1982. Mama was by no means a flexian herself, but through her dexterous self-presentations and shrewd ability to get the best out of her interlocutors—from sales clerks to the secret police—she gave me the first inklings of flex activity.

As a doctoral student in anthropology at the University of California at Berkeley, I was lucky to win a Fulbright fellowship to study Polish society at a time when the Solidarity movement was making headlines around the world. Wojciech Jaruzelski, the stiff general in dark glasses, had declared martial law six weeks before I arrived, and the nation was suffering under bleak conditions. Communist authorities had crushed the independent labor union Solidarity, which had attracted the support of more than one-fourth of the nation's population, and now it had been outlawed. The government imprisoned Lech Walesa and the movement's other leaders, imposed curfews, and cut phone lines. The country was marked by travel restrictions, roadblocks, virtually closed borders, and, above all, an atmosphere of tension and austerity. Public life seemed bleak and frozen, its vitality squeezed out of existence. Yet over the coming years I would observe in Poland a complex, ingenious society quite different from the communist police state portrayed in Western media. It was a society whose members were adept at managing public self-presentation, and whose lifeblood—just beneath the surface—was vital information about anything ranging from where to obtain scarce meat to what bureaucrat might be approached to "arrange" a permit. Such information was circulated only among friends and trusted colleagues and was not publicly available.

At twenty-three, I was no stranger to Poland, having first visited the country in 1977. Through circuitous connections I found lodging with Mama—a warm and generous retiree in her midfifties and a veritable force of nature—and her daughter Ela, an attractive, vivacious physician in her late twenties. Mama and Ela echoed the advice of others, to keep my eyes and ears open and my mouth shut.

Although food seemed plentiful, little of it could actually be found on store shelves. In Poland's centrally planned systems, political authorities made decisions about production and distribution, and demand always outpaced supply. János Kornai, a Hungarian-born Harvard-based economist, calls this an "economy of shortage."[1] How did people manage, I wondered. Some, it was clear, even did relatively well.

Mama is probably the most resourceful person I have ever encountered. Soon after I arrived, I began to watch her shopping in the market across the street. The market was a complex of stalls lodged in a cavernous one-hundred-year-old warehouselike building that had somehow remained standing after the Nazis destroyed the city. Heading each day (except Sundays) for the market at dawn, she often passed to the head of the many different lines for life's essentials. Mama got this special treatment because of her frequent under-the-table deals with the "gals" behind the counters, whom she always sized up and flattered. Succumbing to her charms, the clerks filled her in on when, say, a delivery of meat or (coarse brown) toilet paper or mineral water might arrive and brought out such scarce items for her when they had.

Mama was what Poles call a Siberian survivor. The Soviets had deported her and her once well-to-do family from the Polish city of Vilnius to a Siberian camp when she was a young teenager. Upon her repatriation in August 1946, Mama began to work in various official institutions of the Polish People's Republic, married another young volunteer tied to allied Communist institutions, and settled in Szczecin on Poland's new western border. After the untimely death of her husband, a Party apparatchik, she and Ela moved to Warsaw. While I was studying at Warsaw University, Ela, the fashionable young physician, was pursuing a specialization in dermatology.[2]

Through Mama and Ela, I was drawn into a lively, high-stakes drama, where everything seemed possible, though nothing certain. The state and its rules threw up constant obstacles. Everyday life was about wheedling bureaucrats to creatively elude them—and sometimes even enjoying the interplay and scheming necessary to affect the outcome.

One morning around five, there was a knock on the apartment door. "Stay in your room," Mama whispered, as I emerged from my small sleeping quarters. Four policemen, the only one in uniform a major, had come to search the apartment. Ela was the target of their suspicions. As I would learn later that day—after they had completed a "routine" and, by the standards of the time, "mild" search of the entire apartment—that same morning, Ela's estranged husband had been arrested for underground activities.

Although this was certainly an unsettling experience, I was not surprised that Mama did not leave the outcome to fate. By this time, I understood that her facility with navigating the challenges of martial law had been honed from the time she was transported to Siberia. Now she played her Communist Party comrades with her characteristic pizzazz. When the major turned away to scrutinize the books on her shelf, Mama quickly concealed underground literature. Speaking a shared Party-tinged vernacular, she skillfully quizzed him and soon established their mutual association with certain people and venues, including the Polish-Soviet Friendship Society.

Meanwhile, the flirtatious Ela worked the three cops searching her room. When it came time to inspect my room (as far as we knew, I wasn't a suspect, even though I was an American), Ela came to my door, with her arm around one of the plainclothesmen, exposing part of her shapely leg by gathering her bathrobe, and announced, "Janeczko, you have the advantage. The best-looking one of all will search your room."

During the course of their search, the policemen gave the two women advice on how to protect themselves. The phone would be tapped, they said, and they should stay clear of suspect individuals. When the four left at midmorning, Ela and Mama, waving heartily, appeared to be saying good-bye to old friends.

As soon as the door was shut, the two women collapsed, indignant and exhausted. For the first time, Mama sent *me* across the street on the daily detail for milk, eggs, bread, and meat—but only after I had promised not to tell a soul, not anyone, about what had just transpired.

I wondered how these women fared as well as they did in affairs of this sort. Both could have been detained on the spot and imprisoned indefinitely. (The incident was laced with irony. The major was interrogating a fellow communist operative. The operative was subtly defending her son-in-law, although he was out of favor with both Mama and her daughter.) Other, less quick-witted people might have reacted with outrage that could have produced undesirable outcomes. Some Poles might even have seen the two women's behavior as "compromised." But Ela and Mama were ingenious and highly adept survivors. Their skillful handling of the policemen typified the only recourse people have when they do not have any recourse.

Mama and Ela's reaction to the police state's intrusion into their home stemmed from a long and treacherous history. Poles, after all, had endured repeated travails—concentration camps, deportations to Siberia, shifting borders, martial law, material scarcities—skirting the system for mere survival. War, revolutions, and hardships were a part not only of the fabric of the nation, which had been smashed by so many occupiers, but of immediate experience.

With good reason, people did not trust or depend on the official world that crept into every corner of society, be it the economy, politics, or culture. Over the years, a sharp divide had developed between "state" and "society." As Václav Havel, the dissident turned president of the Czech Republic, put it, Eastern Europeans learned to "live within a lie."[3] Poles complained under their breath but maintained appearances in public. People could express their opinions only among their most trusted intimates, within their own information universe. Continually presenting different faces, they learned how to say one thing and do another—and to stay sane while living with fundamental ambiguity. They not only tolerated the contradictions of their society, but also stage-managed them creatively.

The qualities and strategies that Mama and Ela employed during the apartment search offer a glimpse into how people cope with rigid structures and repressive regimes. They also gave those who lived in communist states a head start in the reconfiguring world order as communism was drawing down in the late 1980s and early 1990s. Watching how people deal with two extreme environments—first the rigidities of an authoritarian system, and, later, the laxity of one come undone—would help me to recognize other, less obvious contexts for flexian activity and to explore the conditions under which it arises. So, ironically, insight into the communist world of Mama and Ela and so many others is what led me to explore the freewheeling world of today's flexians and flex nets. One of the major themes that has emerged is how so much information necessary for public decisions today rests in private hands. Private guardians of official information can spin stories and erect façades for an unwitting government and public. Like Mama, they stage-manage effectively, but for much more than survival. Moreover, flexians have taken on multiple roles, playing their various parts in a theater arranged for their sponsors and the public. This state of affairs has implications for transforming societies far and wide—even in the United States.

Dirty Togetherness

I witnessed firsthand how people organized themselves for survival, and charted the networks that they used within and outside the bureaucracy and economy to get things done. An environment of scarcity and distrust of the communist state encouraged "dirty togetherness," a Polish sociologist's reference to cliquishness and core relationships of trust—typically family, friends, and trusted associates who help each other out through under-the-table transactions. Being "dirtily" together implies mutual complicity in such dealings. To be on one's own under such conditions was about as far from a recipe for success as one could get. You were only as successful as your support network.[4]

The rigid system that the communist state constructed had to be bypassed so that people could live in even minimal comfort. The key to state power was its monopolistic control and expansive bureaucracy that supervised the allocation of resources. It was a conflated system, one in which economic decisions were made in the political realm, and state and private power were merged in cliques of ruling communist elites.

The conventional image of a communist "command economy" conjures up a centrally planned, managed, and hierarchical state noted for its rigidity and undergirded by a proliferation of laws and regulations: a total state. But control was never quite as total as this popular caricature would have it. In reality, state control inadvertently encouraged the development of systems of informal relationships and practices that penetrated and stood apart from the state, even as it surrounded and existed within those informal relationships.[5]

For instance, demand for consumer goods and services always outpaced supply, resulting in shortage economies. Citizens were forced to finagle to get a lot of what they wanted, leading to an elaborate system of informal distribution of goods and services that paralleled and often overshadowed the official economy. For the Soviet Union, economist Gregory Grossman called this a "second economy" but more familiarly it's known as the "gray" or "underground" economy. While these terms imply two wholly separate economies or systems—the official and the unofficial—they were two sides of the same coin, acknowledged and unacknowledged aspects of a single system in which institutions and networks met far more extensively than official ideologies conceded. In the Soviet Union, this informal system was known as *blat,* "the use of personal networks for obtaining goods and services in short supply and for circumventing formal procedures."[6]

To eke out a more livable existence, nearly everyone engaged in under-the-table deals that Westerners might consider corrupt. Because this activity was risky, trust was indispensable, and personalizing bureaucracy essential. People personalized the little bits of the state that they had to interact with, forming relationships with officials, bureaucrats, and clerks. That meant either building relationships with them through an etiquette of exchange or mobilizing trusted contacts through informal social networks of family, friends, neighbors, and work colleagues.[7]

The most important asset was word-of-mouth information, which could not be gleaned without trusted sources who could point to who, how, and where. Mama, with her uncanny ability to suss out what people could offer, to probe and retain information, and to bring forth favors from the secretary or clerk to the priest or Party director, was not only a veritable information bank. She was a dealer in privatized information—the quintessential "blatmeister."[8]

The quality of people's lives often largely depended on knowing which person—rather than which institution or organization—could help secure routine goods and services. The *who* became far more important than what one needed help with. Among my friends in Poland, a typical list of errands consisted of names of people matched up with tasks. To repair heating, contact Pan (Mr.) Jan; for gasoline, Pan Piotr; for a driver's license, Pan Grzegorz; for prompt medical attention, Pani (Mrs.) Jadwiga; or to reserve a place in a kindergarten or university, Pani Antonina.[9]

Skirting the system—even when one was part of it—became a way of life with its own language, impulses of discretion, and habits of secrecy. If I said I had a matter to *załatwić* (arrange)—which could mean anything from making a telephone call or scheduling a babysitter to buying booze or gasoline on the black market—even the closest of friends would not ask for an explanation. As one of an entire arsenal of everyday usages, words like *załatwić* built ambiguity into often shady or illegal yet routine activities and enabled people to work out their daily existence while keeping up appearances. However necessary for survival, such activities often evoked in their protagonists both pride and shame—pride in having ingeniously gamed the system, shame in having lowered oneself to do so. Everyone had matters to arrange, all the time. Nearly everyone was complicit. Nearly everyone was dirty—together.[10]

Dirty togetherness made almost everyone vulnerable and potentially guilty in the eyes of those in power. Laws were ambiguous, making them easier to apply arbitrarily when called for by political circumstances. This became the ruling irony of the Communist state: Under the rigid hand of state rule seethed a roiling mixture of commonly understood, officially denied complicity that actually made society run. As a popular saying in People's Poland went: "Give me the person, and I'll find the law [that he broke]."[11]

In a system where extra-legal factors often determined the outcome of judicial decisions, legality diverged markedly from morality. Take, for example, attitudes toward state property, which belonged to both everyone and no one. The common workers' practice of setting aside goods belonging to the factory, which was owned by the state, to take home for their side jobs was regarded as merely lifting and morally acceptable. On the other hand, if a worker took goods that already had been set aside for personal use by a fellow worker, this was stealing. It was the difference between loyalty to one's fellows and to the state.[12]

While people exhibited stunning disregard for official institutions, these same institutions depended on the informal practices created by those people to function. The networks and practices typically ascribed to the informal realm also penetrated the workings of the official, formal one, from the economy and bureaucracy to legal, judicial, and political structures, and to communist parties themselves. State-owned enterprises are but one example. As the economist Joseph Berliner wrote in his classic 1957 study of factory operations and management methods in the Soviet Union, "Only by engaging in irregular practices can the manager run a successful enterprise." False reporting (*pripiski*)—used to maintain manageable production targets or to obtain rewards for plan overfulfillment—was the norm, as were "pushers" (*tolkachi*), whose job it was to smooth relations with officials and suppliers and bend the unbendable system of bureaucratic allocation. Such informal practices subverted the system of planning—and rewrote the rules of the game.[13]

Of course, at the system's highest reaches, formal and informal were often fused, as were state and private, bureaucratic and market. The system was tailor-made for the privatization of power: Communist operatives exercised the prevailing influence in state bodies of all kinds, sometimes supplanting their formal prerogatives. In Polish parlance, *układy* are the relational "arrangements" of operatives who can exercise or activate power, especially that of the state—if only to supplant it. These operatives are not only "dirtily" together to achieve a shared agenda, the formidable power alliances they sometimes create play out on the national stage. Within the Communist power apparatus, charges of criminality or corruption by one group against a rival one could render the rival a discredited nonplayer. Likewise, in the Soviet Union, "clans"—closed informal groups "bound by shadow relations [and] hidden norms" and operating in a harsh environment—ran the military industrial complex and other crucial resource enterprises of the state, as economic sociologist Leonid Kosals has documented.[14] Provincial bosses brandished personalized power, and patronage networks virtually ran various regions of the Soviet Union. Thus, while the Soviet state "was a virtual labyrinth of bureaucratic structures, . . . it was a far cry from a rational-legal bureaucratic state," as a political analyst of these networks has written.[15]

Such informal systems of relationships and practices from the communist era—the under-the-radar dealings, dirty togetherness with a trusted few, playing on the margins of legality, and parallel ethical constructs that, through collective activities, moved the system away from its communist intentions—would spring resiliently into action.[16] The upended societies of the "Wild East" were perfect environments for flexian precursors, whether they were savvy insiders, or outsiders testing their fortunes in a world now open to speculation. They would serve as a harbinger of things to come in the region—and beyond.

Flex Net Precursors

Togetherness, whether dirty or not, would prove to be a powerful engine of transformation, even in Poland, one of the best candidates in the region for adapting democracy and free markets after 1989. Poland's "social circles," informal political-economic support groups whose members had cemented their bonds in the face of adversity, would prove pivotal to an understanding of how the nation moved away from communism.

When, after several years' absence, I returned to still-Communist Poland in the spring of 1988, I was surprised to find a heightened flurry of activity emanating from these informal groups and networks, aided by the new reality of glasnost wafting from the Soviet Union. Poles from all sides were turning their political energies into economic efforts, mostly still subterranean, and mingling them with apparently civic activities. Months *before* the revolutions of the autumn of 1989, I saw that entrepreneurship and private organizing were becoming tickets to influence in public life, and that leaders from the Communist government and Solidarity alike were jumping on the entrepreneurship and organizing bandwagons.[17]

Solidarity intelligentsia circles had spawned a new economic elite. Activists who had honed their business skills in clandestine publishing houses in the early 1980s and had languished in jail for their deeds now launched limited liability companies to trade in computers, electronic equipment, and information. Some even ran into acquaintances from home in the streets of Singapore, where they were acquiring computers for sale back in the Polish informal economy. One day I invited such an entrepreneur, a doctoral sociology student in his late twenties, to lunch, intending to pay for it—in the tradition of the supposedly "rich American." I remembered that, after being released from martial-law internment a half-decade earlier, he had returned to live with his parents in their tiny apartment. But now, as he picked up the bill, he confided that he had made $80,000 the previous month and hence could splurge.

Both Solidarity- and Party-affiliated circles were forming clubs and lobbies and financing them through entrepreneurial activities. I began following the voluntary associations that were cropping up everywhere, even in areas for which the state claimed exclusive responsibility, including housing, schools, and the environment. These were not headed merely by public-spirited people with good intentions and time on their hands, as they might be in the West. These organizations—no matter what their ostensible purpose—were, by their very existence, political; their leaders were, by their very leadership, political actors. The *very act* of forming an organization outside of state sponsorship was a political act and a risky one, despite the Polish Communist authorities' toleration of these activities as never before—albeit inconsistently.

Because these novel initiatives sported their own independent financial bases, they were doubly threatening to the communist system. The initiatives intertwined civic and money-making activities, which were partly open, partly subterranean. Again, *who* was involved was more important than *what* the involvement was. A similar constellation of people, usually elites, often took part in multiple initiatives. The same loose circle of people typically created and empowered several efforts.

A case in point is the Economic Association, a flex net precursor. Formally an organization to support private enterprise, it was a seminal initiative of a Warsaw-based intelligentsia circle whose members also revolutionized what was possible by founding environmental organizations and private schools. Prime movers in this circle would later become prime figures in running the country. One such player was Aleksander Paszyński, who initiated the association. Years earlier he had been deputy editor of the influential official weekly *Polityka* (from which he resigned in protest after the declaration of martial law). He exhibited some of the prerequisite qualities of flexians: He was a risk taker and innovator, and, in founding the association, he tested adverse waters by experimenting with whether the communist authorities would allow budding organizations like his to gain legal status (circa 1988) by allowing it to be registered with the state. Paszyński's efforts dramatized the mixed signals of an authoritarian regime losing its grip. After the Economic Association's application for state registration had been pending for some time, the Communist government—in an unprecedented move that revealed both the relaxing of the system and its own desperation—offered Paszyński a cabinet-level position, which he declined. Upon his return from a brief trip to West Germany, Polish authorities strip-searched him at the border, which seemed to indicate they wanted to put him in his place. But then, several days later, the government registered his association with some fanfare, and Paszyński appeared on the state-run news.[18]

The explosion of initiatives such as the Economic Association had gone too far to be easily stopped. The Communist authorities were forced to agree to unprecedented negotiations with representatives of Solidarity. Out of this so-called Round Table came an astonishing deal: the first semifree elections in the Eastern Bloc. Solidarity's subsequent landslide victory in June 1989 was the precursor to the revolutions that capsized the communist regimes of the region that autumn.

The Communists' fall from power left a governing vacuum that would be filled by preexisting social infrastructure: circles like those of Aleksander Paszyński. Indeed, when the first postcommunist government came into office, Paszyński became minister of housing, with the Economic Association his informal political base. A handful of elite circles would serve as key pillars in the nation's governance.

During this period of the early 1990s, sociologists Antoni Kamiński and Joanna Kurczewska observed the appearance of "institutional nomads" (from either Solidarity or Communist milieus), key players in Poland's developing postcommunist system. Players in an institutional nomadic group move in and out of multiple positions and efforts at the top of political, governmental, business, and nongovernmental arenas, as well as Polish branches of international businesses, banks, and foundations. They do so to secure the resources and power necessary to further their group's goals, whatever they might be. Like the flexians I would later identify, these nomads cannot be pegged simply as officials, consultants, businessmen, activists in NGOs, or academics. Their loyalty is not to the affiliations they juggle, but to their groups. Their roles, official and unofficial, are, above all, a means to an end.[19]

Members' loyalties are cemented not only by the access to resources and opportunities that their pooled efforts reap, but also by the awareness that they are all involved in dirty togetherness—and can blackmail one another.

Thus they "willy-nilly must stay loyal and collaborate." Loyalty to one's network—and not to institutions—would emerge as a major theme of the coming era's brightest players.[20]

The Rise of Flex Nets

Such networks of operators would be far from irrelevant as the region supposedly "transitioned" to free market and democratic rule with the demise of communist regimes. While the mantra of "markets" dominated public discussions and media accounts, other logics were at work, in which business agents (*biznesmeni*) danced together to a nonmarket drummer, gaining exclusive access to information and hoarding it for their own purposes—the antithesis of a free market. Likewise, while the ideology of "privatization" reigned supreme, the view from the ground revealed the rearranging of state assets into privatized or might-be-state, might-be-private entities, often with powerful players—themselves mergers of state and private power—at the helm. Networks would help organize all these processes and thereby the emergent systems.[21]

In fact, amid legal, administrative, political, and economic flux, more "network capital" was at play than under communism. That is because, when the command structure of a centrally planned state that had owned virtually all the property, companies, and wealth breaks down and no authoritarian stand-in is put in its place, the existing network-based mode of governing and business moves in to replace it, drawing on the networks and groups that had permeated the old official structures.[22]

As communist states' control over resources crumbled (and even before they embarked on formal privatization schemes), communist managers and other privileged players acquired companies and other resources at fire-sale prices for the benefit of their groups. In this loosest of environments—some scholars have even talked about the absence of a state in Russia in the early 1990s—well-connected individuals could, and did, control resources and wield influence.[23]

In the near free-for-all that was the "Wild East," great incentives moved people to work quickly: Opportunities were often fleeting, opening up for weeks or months, only to close as someone else cornered them, laws or other circumstances changed, or better opportunities came along. The ambitions and activities of the players were frequently unfettered by rules and regulations because such restraints did not exist, were not known, were unenforced, competed with one another, or were simply ignored. Even people committed to a public interest and democracy were forced to embrace, or at least to tolerate, extralegal means just to be successful and sometimes even to survive. Exactly what was legal was often not clear, nor did it matter. Because the line between legitimate and illegitimate was blurred—and because legal and illegal often did not equate with moral and immoral—the practices of those who thrived eventually defined the new rules. The people who were most savvy, energetic, well positioned, and quick on their feet were the most successful at gaining access to resources.

Inside information and resources presented themselves wherever reform appeared—as did networks hungry to take advantage of them. Economic restructuring and the privatization of state-owned industry and agriculture (often introduced with the guiding hand of international financial institutions and Western donors) offered much action, especially in states radically divesting themselves, while systems of health care, social security, and so on also were candidates for overhaul. Because some reforms provided prospects for acquiring resources, even plunder, some fostered the entrenchment of informal groups and networks linked to organized crime. "Reform" would become a permanent fixture: not just a steady mantra, but to this day a process without end in many countries of the region.[24]

Close observers of the transition have struggled with what to call these networks. They weren't quite "interest groups" or "lobbies" or defied characterization as state or private, bureaucracy or market, even legal or illegal. One attempt was the "institutional nomads" of Poland mentioned earlier. In Hungary sociologists found that "restructuring networks" with inside information drove privatization and resulted in property forms neither private nor collective but "recombinant." In Romania "unruly coalitions" controlled many resources—defined by the anthropologist who identified them as loose clusters of largely former Communist Party elites "neither institutionalized nor otherwise formally recognized," and less visible and legitimate than political parties.[25]

Further east, clans mobilized to exert control over arenas valuable enough to deem worth their while, positioning their members in and around the state to best promote a group's political, financial, and other strategic agendas. In the Russia of the early 1990s, the most important clans were those involved in the gas, oil, and extraction industries, which provided returns from exports and were directly linked to top officials, Kosals observes. And, as we shall see in Chapter 5, the Chubais Clan monopolized foreign aid and economic reform, and helped set the country's economic and political order for years to come. [26]

Clans have played an equally significant role in another geopolitically strategic part of the former Soviet Union, Ukraine, where they are regionally based, monopolize many national resources and industries, and underpin much political power. Power is contested among several clans, and alternates among them. The Donetsk Clan, an informal association of business and criminal elite from the southeastern Donetsk region, appeared marginalized by the Orange Revolution, a progression of protests and political actions that took place in late 2004 and early 2005. That revolution brought to power opposition leader Viktor Yushchenko, who many think was poisoned by Russian agents, although that has never been proven. Yushchenko defeated Viktor Yanukovich, the clan's candidate and the incumbent prime minister. But the Donetsk Clan made a fast and triumphant comeback when its political party won a majority in the March 2006 parliamentary elections. The clan also played a key role in the subsequent derailing of the government by successfully working to splinter it. In August 2006, President Yushchenko, who had previously trounced Yanukovich, was forced to confirm his rival as prime minister instead of Orange Revolution coleader and political ally Yuliya Tymoshenko, who had been serving as prime minister in Yushchenko's government. The Donetsk Clan now effectively controlled both branches of government. Following the September 2007 parliamentary election, however, the Tymoshenko-Yushchenko alliance returned to power and continued shakily.[27]

Even in Poland, institutional nomads are alive and well, despite Poland having joined NATO in 1999 and the European Union in 2004, boasting one of the strongest economies in Europe and little evidence of criminal mafia infiltration in the political establishment (as there is, say, in Russia and Ukraine). Kurczewska, cocreator of the theory of institutional nomads, has pointed out that these groups continued to evolve with Poland's admission into the EU.

The sphere of nomadic activity widened to encompass positions and opportunities in Europe available to officials and citizens of EU countries; and, because subnational regions are important in the EU resource and power structure, regional nomads have arisen to establish their influence at the regional level. In short, institutional nomads, clans, and the like have shaped the dynamic environment around them while also reshaping themselves.[28]

Flexing Forward—to the Past

Nomads and clans convey a kind of tribal sense. That's no accident. As uninstitutionalized, unregistered, and unannounced sets of people, they are the antithesis of actors in the Weberian state. They are elusive and difficult to track. Yet their very involvement defines where the action is and who is fashioning crucial political and economic directions.

Operating at the official-private nexus, institutional nomadic groups and clans have a lot to teach us about the potential operations of today's flexians and flex nets. Agilely adapting to their surroundings, these groups and clans have come a long way from their own precursor, the *blat* practitioners of an earlier era. Today they not only personalize bureaucracy through one-time transactions for survival; they *organize* the interrelations between state and private, bureaucracy and market, to, say, allocate state resources for their own benefit, which, of course, flexians and flex nets do as well.

My observation of institutional nomadic groups and clans has helped me theorize about flexians and flex nets and the environments in which they arise. Nomadic groups and clans exhibit most of the features of flexians and flex nets. Like flex nets, nomadic groups and clans operate at the interstices of official and private power—with inside information closely held—and help organize the relationship between them. All these groups position their members at the state-private nexus, ply their skills at skirting government rules of accountability and business codes of competition, and mediate between and blur official and private interests. All are selective about the arenas in which they intervene: They tend to hang out where they can control or exert influence over coveted resources or parts of the state bureaucracy and economy. And while they all *privatize information* and engage in *shared action*—the second feature of flexians and flex nets—they are *not* all propelled by conviction, which this second feature also encompasses. In this respect, flexians and flex nets famously distinguish themselves from their nomadic and clan brethren.

Members of nomadic groups and clans *personalize bureaucracy* (the first feature of flexians), using other members and allies to skirt or skate through it, and form *an intricate spine* (the corresponding feature of flex nets). They anchor themselves primarily in the group rather than in the office or organizations with which they are officially associated; their bread is buttered mostly with the group. Flex nets, too, exhibit all these features.

Members of nomadic groups and clans exhibit the third feature of flexian behavior in spades: *juggling roles and representations.* Like members of flex nets, they interact with one another in multiple roles over time, both inside and outside official structures: in government, business, and NGOs, both domestic and foreign, as relevant to achieving their goals. They form *a resource pool* to bolster their influence. Their power derives partly from their coordination of efforts and roles within the group. Members of clans "can be dispersed," writes sociologist of elites Olga Kryshtanovskaya, but they "have their men everywhere." This also describes flex nets.[29]

All the while, members of clans and institutional nomadic groups work to expand executive power at the expense of checks and balances, which helps them further concentrate information, resources, and decision making in economic, political, and legal domains in just a few hands. The more interdependent these domains, the greater the potential influence of the groups. In Russia, for instance, "Property rights are very conditional . . . to this day. . . . Private business exists only by the grace of the state," Kryshtanovskaya remarked in 2007. The result is, as another analyst reported: "It is still impossible to make one's money yield a profit without negotiations at some point with state agents. Financiers, industry managers, journalists and scholars agree that one's career depends on one's ability to weave political networks." As under Communism, law in Russia is sometimes powerfully used to disadvantage or discredit political opponents. During the 1990s regime of President Boris Yeltsin, accusations of corruption were frequently leveled to force the resignation of heads of investigatory offices. Yeltsin's successor, Vladimir Putin, went a step further. Two well-known cases are the detention of media magnate Vladimir Gusinsky on charges of embezzlement in June 2000, a month after Putin assumed office, and the imprisonment of Mikhail Khodorkovsky several years later, along with the breakup of his massive business empire. This simple message was conveyed, one journalist observed: "If you are loyal, steal as much as you like. If you aren't then watch it!"[30]

Concentrating power in legal, political, and economic domains and gaining the means to control the state-private nexus not only guarantees nomadic groups and clans influence, it offers them the opportunity to organize all these realms. These groups often succeed admirably, just like the flexians who *relax rules* at the interstices of official and private institutions (the fourth feature of flexians) and the flex nets who secure *a hybrid habitat* (the corresponding feature of flex nets) and reorganize both official and private structures to realize their goals. The influence of all these groups is more multipronged and monopolizing than that of interest groups or lobbies. The result is that, while the state can be shaken, as happened in the East, power is remarkably stable. It resides somewhere in the neverland between state and private.

The Neverland of Rywingate

Who operates in this neverland, embodying the merging of state and private? One elusive, yet real, group of institutional nomads that was especially visible in the late 1990s is known as Ordynacka, a long-standing informal Polish association whose members came together during their student days under the umbrella of a communist club. Ordynacka members are connected with each other in multiple ways through business, political, and other activities.[31] It's worth looking more closely at how they operated, to give a flavor of how flex nets have later functioned.

In 2002 Ordynacka developed a formal, overlapping incarnation by registering with the government as an NGO called the "Student Movement Ordynacka Association." Unusual for Polish NGOs, the association's statute outlines a stated political purpose. It specifies that its members can hold public positions; actively participate in the creation of state politics; and expect material, financial, and personal support from other members of the association while using its name and logo. Very little information is publicly available about the group or its activities.

What we do know is that Ordynacka counted among its ranks professionals placed in the most important political and economic structures, including banks, political parties, and the media. The popular Aleksander Kwaśniewski, who served as president of Poland from 1995 to 2005, is among them. An up-and-coming minister of sport in Poland's last communist government, Kwaśniewski joined the SLD (Democratic Left Alliance), the main successor party that emerged from the ruins of the Communist Party following Poland's systemic changes of 1989. In 1991 Kwaśniewski presciently told me that "the next few years belong to Solidarity, but then we [the postcommunists] will be back."[32]

"We" did come back with a vengeance. Ordynacka helped ensure the influence of postcommunist-connected players in the economy, not to mention in politics and the media. Robert Kwiatkowski, president of Polish Television, a public broadcaster that dominates the market more than any other European public broadcaster, was among them. So was Włodzimierz Czarzasty, secretary of the National Radio and Television Council, a politicized body set up in 1992 to regulate Polish Television and other airwaves.[33]

While it is difficult to define what Ordynacka is—it can't be reduced to a political party, NGO, social club, business, or lobbying organization—it is clear that it has wielded power and influence. A glimpse of this was hinted at during the course of a scandal that Poles have dubbed "Rywingate." Prominent members of Ordynacka were part of a "group of power holders," one of the two key parties in a saga that, for several years beginning in 2002, riveted the nation.[34]

Rywingate's chief protagonist is Lew Rywin, the famous film producer whose credits include *Schindler's List* and *The Pianist*. Rywin is well known to have ties to Ordynacka and the "group of power holders," which included the prime minister, Leszek Miller, also head of the SLD and a former Communist Party apparatchik. At the center of the second group was Adam Michnik, a well-known historian and European intellectual, and legendary member of the Opposition during the communist period. He had been a key participant in the Round Table discussions. Michnik was then (and remains) editor in chief of *Gazeta Wyborcza*, at the time the largest circulation Polish daily newspaper. The paper is owned by Agora, a powerful private company, some of whose leaders had been engaged in illegal and risk-laden underground publishing enterprises during the last decade and a half of communism.

The essence of Rywingate was an attempt to privatize the legislative process governing the ownership of the Polish media. In 2002, the government proposed a draft amendment to the Act on Radio and Television, which had been signed into law ten years earlier; the amendment would have prohibited national newspapers from getting a license for national broadcasting. At stake for the parties involved was whether Agora would be allowed to expand its newspaper empire to launch a nationwide television station. One reason for the amendment was to synchronize the law with EU regulations in preparation for Poland's 2004 entry into the Union. While the matter was under discussion, a series of curious events unfolded, including unauthorized manipulation of the actual text of the amendment. Suffice it to say that, by the time *l'affaire* Rywingate was finally put to public rest circa 2004, a parliamentary commission had spent months interrogating witnesses in hearings televised live and gavel-to-gavel on two national networks, and Lew Rywin had been sent to prison. National dirty laundry had been aired, sending shock waves throughout society, as much or more than Watergate did in the United States some thirty years earlier.[35]

The affair was publicly exposed in December 2002, when it was revealed that, during the previous July, Rywin reportedly floated the suggestion to Wanda Rapaczynski, chairwoman of Agora, that it would be possible to influence the drafting of amendments to serve Agora's interests. Rapaczynski informed Michnik about the conversation. One week later, Michnik invited Rywin to his office—why he did this is still a matter of speculation—and secretly tape-recorded their conversation. (The tapes were later judged to be authentic.) During the meeting, Rywin told Michnik that he had been sent by a "group of power holders," and hinted (without stating explicitly) that Prime Minister Miller was backing the group's effort to offer wording in the legislation that would enable Agora to become an instant conglomerate. In exchange, Agora would pay $17.5 million to the SLD and support Rywin's candidacy for the chairmanship of the new television station that would emerge from the deal. More informal meetings with various participants followed.

Things got only murkier. When Agora (allegedly) did not immediately jump at the (allegedly) attempted deal, the actual text of the amendment mysteriously underwent 180-degree alterations, once several times in one day—sometimes allowing, sometimes making it impossible for Agora to embark on a nation-wide television enterprise. The amendment was changed by midlevel func-tionaries, one of whom worked for Czarzasty's Radio and Television Council, another for the Ministry of Culture, whose former boss—former deputy min-ister of culture and reputedly a member of the group of power holders—was now chief of staff of Prime Minister Miller's cabinet. While none of these people were legally authorized to put their hands on the legislation, they apparently tampered with its actual wording—after the document had been signed off on by the executive branch and was ready for parliamentary ratification, and no one had the legal right to change it. The tampering was discovered during a routine check by a conscientious bureaucrat in the government office that re-views final documents before sending them to parliament.

The parliamentary commission that was formed to get to the bottom of what happened questioned dozens of people, conducted four "confrontations" (during which people whose previous statements did not jibe with one an-other were interrogated in each other's presence), and drew up several thou-sand interrogation protocols. Among those questioned were Miller and several of his cabinet ministers; Kwiatkowski, Czarzasty, and people working for them; the marshal of Poland's Senate; and numerous journalists and lawyers. So were the unfortunate underlings who had physically changed the wording of the Act. One viewer described their reactions as she watched them being questioned:

> Suddenly, you are being placed under the eyes of the cameras, with the whole country watching you while you are answering questions during an investigation about corruption and bribery. And all you probably did was to delete two single words from the draft of the Legal Act (or add them at some stage, because these two words kept on appearing and disappearing, as if by magic). You either deleted or added them because you were told to do so. And now the commission is asking you about who gave you the instructions to do this, but there were no instructions!

Don't they know that if your superior tells you to do just this (delete or add two words), that is what you do? You don't ask for any written instructions. It's none of your business why they want these words out at this particular hour, and back again at some other time of the day. They know something that you don't need to know, and they know it from someone who "holds power" or is close to those who "hold power"— whoever that might be. But it's not you. And now you are sitting here, having to answer questions. If you give the wrong answer (which has absolutely nothing to do with whether it is true or not), you might lose your job and might not be able to find another job. You might ruin your whole career.

These witnesses were frightened, terrified. Not frightened because someone might kill them. Frightened because somewhere out there (maybe even among the [parliamentary] commission members themselves), are people connected to this "group that holds power" who had initiated a process during which people like Łopacki and Galinska [two midlevel employees who made technical changes to the legislation] had to just make a simple move, a single simple move, that was just that [i.e., simple] to those "who hold power"—but that could completely ruin the lives of Łopacki and Galinska.[36]

Contrast this with our viewer's assessment of the comportment of members of the group of power holders before the same commission:

All their performances have one striking thing in common. All of these witnesses behaved during the hearings as if they did not regard the commission as having any authority over them, and even demonstrated their deep contempt for the commission. They treated the fact that they had to show up for hearings as an extremely irritating and annoying process they are being forced to go through.

Particularly telling, our viewer reports, was the attitude of Janina Sokołowska, head of the legal department of Czarzasty's National Radio and Television Council, and connected to the group that holds power:

Janina Sokołowska's behaviour during the confrontation gave a very clear impression that it is not the commission's business to keep on pestering her about these things . . . Sokołowska non-verbally seemed to communicate the message that: "It's none of your business, this whole thing is a farce, and after it's over we will all return to the normal way in which things are done."

As millions of television viewers witnessed this unprecedented spectacle unfold, Rywingate unmasked the institutionalized nature of informal power relationships (*układy*) and—as never before—brought the issue into the national conversation. For the first time, what everyone knew to be true but could not be publicly stated was placed before everyone's eyes. While Rywingate provoked public discussion of "corruption," the case was not primarily about corruption in the same sense as, say, bribery. It was about the privatization of power: Had Rywin et al. succeeded, they would have effectively privatized the legislative branch with regard to a key issue of media control and conglomerates. Yet, characteristically, no inquiries got to the bottom of the affair, not the parliamentary hearings, not the investigations by the Warsaw prosecutor, not those of Michnik's own paper. Despite months of legal and parliamentary investigations about who approached and said what to whom, to this day it has not been legally established who was responsible for the manipulation. Many puzzles remain, such as who authorized the intrusion into the legislative process and the activities of prominent individuals.[37]

The allegedly proposed deal never quite materialized. Still, somewhere in the neverland of state and private was the elusive, albeit real "group of power holders" whose mechanisms of influence were stronger than the government's.

Appropriating the State

One way to observe the influence of institutional nomadic groups and less well-organized networks is to examine the state budget. To see a big impact, one need only look at the destination of significant sums of taxpayer money. The record of 1990s Russia and Ukraine—of massive looting of the state and the transfer of national treasures to Western banks and tax havens—is by now well established. But even Poland, a transition "success story," legislated many opportunities for private players and organizations to not only appropriate public resources to their own purposes, but to do so legally and even to expand the realm of the state in the process. The culprits, organizations known as "agencies" (*agencje*) and "targeted funds" (*fundusze celowe*), at times have consumed as much as a quarter of the state budget, with some of these public funds going it's-not-clear-where. The defining feature of these entities, as sociologist Antoni Kamiński has explained, is their unclear responsibility and functions. They do not have the same legal status as state bodies, but they use and allocate state resources, rely on the coercive powers of the state administration, and have broad prerogatives supported by administrative sanctions. NIK, Poland's rough equivalent of the U.S. Government Accountability Office (GAO), reported that, as recently as 2006, these entities continued to result in losses to the state budget. Until the latter 2000s, by which time they had been substantially reined in by government regulation, the entities were subject to limited public accountability.[38]

The boom of these entities in postcommunist Poland is steeped in paradox: They are not communist holdovers, for it was the first Solidarity governments that enacted legislation to enable their creation and proliferation. Although these entities fuel under-the-table dealings in the gray zone of state and private, they are legal. At the same time, they aren't official bodies, but they are vehicles of potential enlargement of the state sphere, despite the privatization of other parts of the same state.

While a few analysts, journalists, and, notably, committed public servants at NIK have tracked these entities, their workings have been largely hidden from public view. I took an interest in them in the mid-1990s, following up information that began coming to light about their existence by talking with people affiliated with them, as well as investigators tracking them. Among my informants was the director of NIK, Lech Kaczyński, whom I interviewed in 1999, with frequent interruptions from his twin, Jarosław. (Six years later Lech Kaczyński took office as president of Poland; his brother became prime minister at the same time.) Lech acknowledged that, with *agencje* and *fundusze celowe*, "much taxpayer money flows to private hands on a large scale." In fact, despite the country's success-story reputation, the number of these bodies grew through the 1990s.[39]

The ability to set up and empower such bodies with one's own creates a perfect vehicle for institutional nomadic groups and less organized networks to achieve their private agendas and make money for themselves. A 2000 NIK report characterized *fundusze celowe* as "corruption-causing." The auditing body substantiated the "lack of current controls" over their activities and concluded that they enjoy "excessive discretion" in their use of public resources—considerably more than that of state organizations. One example is that of PFRON, the Fund for the Rehabilitation of Disabled People, set up to subsidize the employment of handicapped individuals. Considerable discretion was built into every level of decision making, from whether a particular workplace was subsidized and the amount of the subsidy to whether that workplace used the funds to benefit its disabled employees.[40]

Agencje also had a lot of leeway. As provided for by law, *agencje* are set up by state officials, attached to their ministries or state organizations, and funded by the state budget. The minister typically appoints an *agencja's* supervisory board, often basing his choices on political connections, according to a legal analyst and expert on the bodies. Piotr Kownacki, NIK's deputy director, told me in 1999 that *agencje* were created in all ministries with control over property, including transportation, economy, agriculture, treasury, and defense, and that they also dominated coal mining and arms. The coal industry, for example, was governed by a group of institutional nomads whose members organized themselves to cover all the bases by holding or having their fingers in as many influential government, business, and political positions relevant to their success in the industry as possible, regardless of which political parties were in power. Agricultural *agencje* were another case in point. With so much property under their control, including cooperative farms inherited from the communist past, *agencje* began "to represent [their] own interests, not those of the state," as Kownacki put it. He observed that "most of the money is taken by intermediaries" and the state has very little control over this process.[41]

This "privatization of the functions of the state" signals "areas of the state in which the state is responsible but has no control," Kownacki said. The discretion afforded these entities has enabled them to maintain a life of their own: At times, the state authorized them to conduct commercial activities (and keep the profits), manage foreign-aid funds, invest in the stock market, start companies, and even spawn new organizations. It is as if the U.S. secretary of commerce were to set up a baseball-promotion "foundation" within the department using taxpayer funds, employ his friends and family in it, invest in the stock market, and then offer the profits to the foundation's "employees" and to the president who appointed him. Legally. [42]

Such unaccountability is self-proliferating. In setting up organizations that are easily appropriated by networks of associates, yet still part of the state sphere, the result may be the state's *enlargement.* The players involved not only privatize policy; they also can help expand an unaccountable state. Antoni Kamiński argues that postcommunist legislative initiatives facilitated "an indirect enlargement of the dominion of the 'state' through founding of institutions that in appearance are private, but in fact are part of the [appropriated] public domain." This larger, less accountable state is made up of parts that are run by informal groups and networks that conflate state and private agendas and, in their roles as officials, help distance the state from responsibility and accountability to the public. In theory such a state, however self-enlarging, is responsible for the use of its resources and the well-being of its citizens. Yet in practice, as the state widens, accountability slips ever further away from its citizens. This aspect of the state is not altogether dissimilar from an evolution that can be tracked in the United States, there with contracting out of government work as a key propeller.[43]

Poland in the 1990s is an important case, for it developed a market democracy—despite this substantial appropriation of the state and the institutional nomads and other networks that underwrote it—and avoided the excesses in these dimensions that characterized many countries further east during the same period. Moreover, Poland so far this century offers some examples of harnessing earlier excesses. Journalists and public-minded servants at institutions such as NIK have played no small part.[44]

◊ ◊ ◊

LIKE MAMA AND ELA skillfully dealing with the 1982 search of Mama's apartment, people who rise to become such effective players are extraordinarily accomplished at dealing with the unexpected. Their interactions with guardians of the system allow them to adeptly toy with it. During the search, many features that would later characterize the top players and flexians of the

coming era were on display: versatility, quick-wittedness, improvisational talent, propensity to personalize relationships, and shrewdness in swiftly selecting and adopting appropriate roles.

On a systemic level, signature features of both communism and postcommunism would find steady footing in the new system of power and influence that began to crystallize in the early to mid-1990s. The personalization
of bureaucracy; the lack of loyalty to official institutions; the performance of
overlapping roles that fuse state and private power; and the scarcity of should-
be public information available to the public and the snaring of it by private
players—all these features, among others, displayed themselves as the system
ensconced itself widely in both the East *and* the West. In fact, nowhere else
in the developed world would the four transformational developments, and
the new system of power and influence they ushered in, ensconce themselves
more thoroughly than in the United States, infecting the heart and mind—
perhaps even the soul—of its governing.

CHAPTER FOUR

U.S. Government, Inc.

IN AUGUST 2008, ABOVE THE FRONT DOOR OF THE SPRAWLING Health and Human Services headquarters in Washington, D.C., hung a giant streamer proclaiming: CONGRATULATIONS HHS / FOR OUTSTANDING PERFORMANCE ON THE PRESIDENT'S MANAGEMENT AGENDA / GREEN ACROSS THE BOARD (green being the highest performance category). George W. Bush instituted the President's Management Agenda in 2001. One of its hallmarks was "competitive sourcing," which mandates competition with the private sector and encourages the outsourcing of government work.[1]

The agency's Web site bragged that, in 2004, HHS was "one of the first of three agencies to receive a green status score for the Competitive Sourcing Initiative" (later renamed Commercial Services Management Initiative), a key component of the Agenda. At first glance, the HHS streamer recalls the annual May Day ritual in communist countries, where banners applauded diligent workers. But at least the communists' banners celebrated what workers themselves had supposedly accomplished. What does it mean when the government's highest performance award is given to an organization for handing work off to others?[2]

Competitive sourcing has redefined the notion of "government work." Government agencies are now faced with justifying *not* contracting out a government program, project, or function, rather than the other way around. How could an institution be *less* encouraging of loyalty and commitment to itself?

HHS's award followed a 2003 Bush administration initiative that was even more stunning in its willingness to deplete government of government. That directive, buried in an Office of Management and Budget circular, ate away at the long-established norm that "certain functions are inherently Governmental in nature, being so intimately related to the public interest as to mandate performance only by Federal employees." The new mandate, in a subtle language shift, fundamentally weakened the definition of "inherently governmental" functions, going from activities requiring "the exercise of discretion in the application of government authority," to "the exercise of *substantial* discretion" (emphasis added). In effect, the directive expanded the definition of commercial activity and established the legal basis for more contracting. It thus provided justification for practices that were already routine: private companies performing inherently government functions, including crafting and practically directing policy. [3]

While some might perceive these initiatives as mere excesses of the Bush years, tectonic movement in the state-private relationship began long ago and continues under the Obama administration. This movement, whatever its pace, has been largely invisible to the public. For many Americans, the first inkling of governing beyond government happened when reports surfaced about the extent to which private companies were prosecuting the war in Iraq. In fact, the slow overhaul of American federal governing has been taking place for years, speeding up over the past decade and a half. And while companies like KBR Halliburton (the two split in 2007) and Blackwater (which changed its name to Xe in 2009) have come to symbolize the perils of contracting out, these firms, whatever their excesses, have largely provided routine services.[4] Meanwhile, corporations like Booz Allen Hamilton, Science Applications International Corporation (SAIC), Raytheon, and Lockheed Martin routinely stand in for the U.S. government in making policy and performing inherently government functions, sometimes even *becoming*, for all practical purposes, the government. This is far more threatening to the national and public interest than farming out supply and security services.[5]

Today, a host of nongovernmental players do the government's work, often overshadowing government bureaucracy, which sometimes looks like Swiss cheese: full of holes. The Clinton and Bush II administrations took this trend to new lengths through such means as contracting out and quasi-government boards. The financial crisis has caused the Obama administration to intensify this interdependency of state and private power as financial and political policy deciders "coincide" at the highest echelons of power. The result is that, in the established democracy of the United States, who and what constitutes "the government" has become murkier. New institutional forms of governing join the state and the private, permeating virtually all arenas of government. The economic arena now vies for the "excellence in blurring" prize with intelligence, military, and "homeland security" enterprises, where so much action has taken place since 9/11. Ironically, grand narratives exulting democracy, free markets, and the information revolution that accompanied the four transformational developments help obscure these new forms. Meanwhile, private players are afforded fresh opportunities to make governing and policy decisions without meaningful government involvement. Whether for profit or to advance an agenda, they can privatize policy beyond the reach of traditional monitoring systems. These changes are so systemic and so sweeping that they cannot simply be rolled back. The institutional forms that intertwine state and private are the body and soul of federal governing today—the ground upon which any future changes will occur.

Some changes in federal government that contribute to the current institutional landscape are quantifiable and well documented: the great upsurge in contracting government work, including crucial government functions; the rise in awarding contracts without competition; the climbing number of contractors (who are subject to more lax conflict-of-interest regulations than government officials) with proportionately fewer civil servants to monitor them; the proliferation of quasi-government organizations and advisory boards; the fortification of executive power. Other changes pertaining to mutated processes, such as newly convoluted or nonexistent chains of command, also are well documented. Other trends are evident in new popular terms, such as the "blended workforce." Certain other changes are more difficult to document systematically but have been identified by long-term government observers: the greater politicization of parts of government, as well as a drain of brains, information, prestige, and authority away from government. Still other trends are even more difficult to pin down, yet they are undeniably part of the culture. Notable among them is "performing for the public," which makes reliable information harder to sift out. Specific government programs are trotted out by their sponsors—bureaucrats and contractors alike—as "success stories" and provide subject matter for upbeat "show and tells" for government and congressional overseers.[6]

These changes help a variety of actors, including our new agents, to wend their way through state and private domains. These operators help organize the interrelations between state and private (as did their counterparts in 1990s transitional central and eastern Europe), and thereby bring about new institutional forms of governing and of power and influence. Adept at performing, and with ambiguity often surrounding their roles, they slip through the accountability cracks. Observers become more reliant on what the players themselves *say* they are doing, further removing public decision making from the citizens' purview.

Who Is the Government?

Defining just who the government "is" is more difficult in the United States than perhaps in any other developed country. This isn't a question of Republican versus Democrat or independent, or federal versus state or local administration. Instead, the question gets at the array of actors who do much of the actual work of government.[7]

The American model of governing builds on the nation's rich tradition of voluntary associations playing a role in public and civic life; the participation of a plethora of entities in governing can be considered not only as a natural outgrowth but also as a strength of the American system. In 1969, in *The End of Liberalism*, political scientist Theodore J. Lowi foresaw government being administered more and more by the private sector and its lobbyists—and he was prescient in understanding the implications. Not only are policymaking and implementation today scattered among many actors—official, shadow, and quasi-governmental—but the burgeoning quantity and roles of private sector entities vis-à-vis government are fraying the whole system of accountability.[8]

Over roughly the past six decades, but especially since the end of the Cold War, the architecture of much of federal governing has transformed. A major pillar of this structure is the shadow government (briefly described in Chapter 2) that today comprises the companies, consulting firms, nonprofits, think tanks, and other nongovernmental entities that swell the ranks of contractors. These private actors are interdependent with government, involved in all aspects of governing and negotiating "over policy making, implementation, and enforcement," as one legal scholar has noted. Where once federal employees executed most government work, today upwards of three-quarters of the work of federal government, measured in terms of jobs, is contracted out. Although this practice is not new, it has accelerated and assumed new incarnations, most notably since the early days of the Clinton administration.[9]

According to the U.S. Congressional Research Service (CRS), "government" today encompasses mixed state-private entities, which have proliferated and play a greater role than ever. They take several forms. One is the hybrid, or "quasi-government" organization, defined by the CRS as "federally related entities that possess legal characteristics of both the governmental and private sectors." In recent decades these organizations have boomed not only in numbers but also in import. They run the gamut from the National Science Foundation to RAND to certain venture capital funds designed and managed almost as if they were in the private sector. Another form comprises federal advisory committees that provide guidance to more than fifty government agencies, whose members have grown in numbers from some 52,000 in 2000 to 65,000 in 2008. The GAO has called the committees the "fifth arm of government" for their "important role in the development of public policy and government regulations" in arenas ranging from defense, homeland security, and space exploration to food safety and stem cell research.[10]

These mixed state-private entities, along with a host of other actors on the governmental stage, have revamped governing. So altered is the landscape that the term "governance," a relative newcomer to the vocabulary that refers to rule by a combination of bureaucratic and market entities, now often substitutes for "government." The shadow government, which devises and implements so much policy and forms the core of governance, warrants close examination. It is the elephant in the room.

The Overshadowed Government

I asked the well-known conservative thinker and publisher Alfred S. Regnery, who had just given a book talk on the importance of limiting the size of government, what he made of the fact that three-quarters of employees doing the work of the federal government are now contractors and that the federal budget for services increases by the day. He was taken aback. It was immediately apparent that the subject was not on his radar. The façade of small government—so effective as political rhetoric espoused by Republicans and Democrats alike—appears as a perennial ruse in American public discourse despite the enduring reality that de facto federal government has long been growing.[11]

The story is best understood in the larger historical context stretching back to the end of World War II. According to Dan Guttman, coauthor of the 1976 book *Shadow Government*, U.S. reformers decided to use contractors to "grow" government after the war. While politicians and pundits of nearly all stripes were decrying "big government" and endorsing its containment, shadow government was becoming evermore firmly entrenched.[12] The *redesign of governing* that championed the privatization and deregulation of government (the first transformational development) gave shadow government a huge push. But many of the most dramatic alterations have occurred since the end of the Cold War (the second transformational development), particularly during and since the Clinton administration. The *advent of evermore complex technologies* (the third transformational development), which gave birth to information technologies upon which society now relies and which the U.S. government largely outsources, tipped the balance even further. The result is that many inherently government functions now find a comfortable home outside government.

Underlying the growth of shadow government is the effort to cap or even reduce the number of civil servants, which has been making headway for some sixty years. The shadow government is the creature of these attempts to curb official government. While it may be the elephant in the room, we know little about the nature of the beast. Government scholar Paul C. Light compiles the most reliable available figures on contractors, but these are inexact. The number of contract workers as compared with civil servants, uniformed military personnel, and postal service employees increased steadily over the last two decades. In 1990 roughly three of every five employees in the total federal labor force (including contractors) worked indirectly for government—in jobs created by contracts and grants, as opposed to jobs performed by civil servants, uniformed military personnel, and postal service workers. By 2002, two of every three employees in the federal labor force worked indirectly for government and, by 2008, the number was three out of four. Phasing out official government grows the shadow government: The very necessity of upholding the façade of contained government in fact begets the opposite.[13]

An even more reliable barometer of the growth of shadow government is the U.S. federal budget. Under Bush II, shadow government, driven in part by the increase in demand for military, nation-building, and homeland security services after 9/11, captured record levels of procurement (or contract) spending. The cost of services alone (not counting goods) provided by contractors soared from some $125 billion in 2001 to an estimated $320 billion plus in 2008. Nearly 90 percent of NASA's and the Department of Energy's budgets go to contracts. The American federal government today is the world's largest customer for goods and services. Where once the government procured mainly manufactured goods from the private sector, a huge and rising portion of government purchases is now for work that would once have been performed by the civil service.[14]

The Department of Defense is the federal government's biggest buyer of services. In 1984, nearly two-thirds of the Pentagon's shopping budget was for products as opposed to services. But by the early 1990s the figure was even. And by fiscal year 2003, the figure was 56 percent, weighted in favor of services over products. In fiscal year 2006, the department obligated upwards of $151 billion to service contracts, an increase of 78 percent since 1996.[15]

In recent years, both the Department of Defense and the new Department of Homeland Security, the megabureaucracy cobbled together from twenty-two government agencies in 2003, recorded colossal increases in contract spending (for both goods and services), with Defense accounting for nearly three-quarters of the total federal procurement budget in 2008. Moreover, about 70 percent of the budget of the U.S. intelligence community is devoted to contracts, according to the Office of the Director of National Intelligence, an office created in 2005 that supervises sixteen federal agencies. Contract employees make up an estimated one-quarter of the country's core intelligence workforce, according to the same office. The director both heads the U.S. intelligence community and serves as the main adviser to the president on national security matters.[16]

Joan Dempsey, a former CIA deputy director, has referred to the consulting giant Booz Allen Hamilton, headquartered in McLean, Virginia, as "the shadow intelligence community." With more than 19,000 employees (13,000 in the Washington area alone), the company is one of the region's biggest employers and suppliers of services to government. Booz was named 2003 Government Contractor of the Year in the $500 million plus annual revenue category. That such an awards category exists is revealing in its own right. Departments that contract with Booz Allen Hamilton include Homeland Security, the Department of Defense, the Internal Revenue Service, and the Department of Health and Human Services. For Defense alone, during the five-year period from 1998 to 2003, Booz Allen was awarded contracts worth more than $3 billion, 26 percent of them with no open bidding process.[17]

In theory, these contracts and contractors are overseen by government employees who would guard against abuse. But as the capacity of government oversight has been diminishing—a lessening that seems to flow directly from the need to maintain the façade of small government—this is less and less true. A look at trend lines is illuminating. The number of civil servants who could potentially oversee contractors fell during the Clinton administration and continued to drop during the subsequent Bush administration. The contracting business boomed under Bush, while the "acquisition workforce"— government workers charged with the conceptualization, design, awarding, use, or quality control of contracts and contractors—has remained virtually constant. In 2002, each federal acquisition official oversaw the disbursement of an average of $3.5 million. In 2006 the workload expanded to $7 million, while also demanding increasingly complex contracting skill. Thus the façade of keeping government small is revealed for the sham that it is, as is that of government invariably being in control. It has too many holes in it for that to be the case.[18]

The paucity of oversight leads large procurement operations to be identified by the U.S. Government Accountability Office (GAO) as "high risk" due to "their greater susceptibility to fraud, waste, abuse, and mismanagement." In 1990 the GAO began periodically issuing reports identifying high-risk areas. The list of such areas has, since 1990 or 1992 (depending on the specific area), included the large procurement operations of the Departments of Defense and Energy, as well as NASA. The high-risk designation means that the agency may well lack "the ability to effectively manage cost, quality and performance in contracts," according to U.S. Comptroller General David M.

Walker, longtime head of the GAO. When these deficiencies play out on the ground, as they have done, for instance, in Iraq, they can lead to serious consequences. In 2006 the GAO found that "problems with management and oversight of contractors have negatively impacted military operations and unit morale and hindered DOD's ability to obtain reasonable assurance that contractors are effectively meeting their contract requirements in the most cost-efficient manner." The inspector general of the Department of Homeland Security concluded in 2005 that a dearth of oversight has exposed that department to the proverbial fraud, waste, and abuse in procurement too.[19]

Another effect of the trend is ambiguity regarding who constitutes the government day to day. This ambiguity is most obvious in what has come to be called the "blended" or "embedded" workforce: government employees and private contractors who work side by side, often sitting next to each other in cubicles or sharing an office and doing the same or similar work (but typically with markedly different pay scales). Their interactions help forge new institutional forms of governing wherein state and private are, in practice, enmeshed.[20]

A class of service contracts, used primarily in the defense arena, called SETA (Systems Engineering and Technical Assistance) furthers this ambiguity. SETA contractors advise government officials as they evaluate contractors' bids, oversee other contractors, or act as an interface between government and contractors. An individual contractor can actually have a different status (government official or contractor) depending on the entity he's interacting with at the moment—"flex" is built into the job description. A SETA contractor working for the Department of Homeland Security told me that different entities he deals with on a daily basis treat him differently: To the Department of Defense and the contractors he oversees, he is a government official; to the State Department he is still a contractor, not allowed to represent DHS as an official. Thus is "flex" institutionalized.[21]

The shift to contractors and to flex-ability highlights the redesign of governing. This redesign threatens both the accountability of government and the competition of the private sector—all the while hiding behind the grand narratives of democracy and free markets that accompanied the end of the Cold War. Of course, contracting itself, especially of simple services, is not necessarily corrosive and can even be beneficial. For instance, a contractor with access to people at all levels of an organization can correct misimpressions held by people at the top about what is going on at the bottom and vice versa—something a regular employee is ill-positioned to do. But contracting gone wild widens the de facto base of government power in which new institutional forms of governing can flourish. The outsourcing of inherently governmental functions reveals the significance of these new forms—and makes the façade that government is in charge even more damaging.

Government Without Soul

Gone are the days when government contractors primarily provided services such as printing, serving food, or landscaping. Contractors long ago invaded the realm of "inherently governmental" functions—those activities that involve "the exercise of sovereign government authority or the establishment of procedures and processes related to the oversight of monetary transactions or entitlements." The nineteen "inherently governmental" functions historically on the books include the following eight:

- The command of military forces, especially the leadership of military personnel who are members of the combat, combat support or combat service support role.
- The conduct of foreign relations and the determination of foreign policy.
- The determination of agency policy, such as determining the content and application of regulations, among other things.
- The determination of Federal program priorities or budget requests.
- The direction and control of Federal employees.
- The direction and control of intelligence and counter-intelligence operations.
- The selection or non-selection of individuals for Federal Government employment, including the interviewing of individuals for employment.
- The approval of position descriptions and performance standards for Federal employees.[22]

Because these functions focus largely on designing and directing policy, it is mostly in this realm that the potential exists for private players to reorganize the interrelations between state and private in the service of their own policy agendas—and to forge new institutional forms of power and influence. Moreover, the very idea of inherently governmental functions, as well as the notion that certain activities should remain the responsibility of government alone, is controversial. Some voices from industry, academe, and think tanks argue that the notion of these functions—not consistently defined across the government—should be scaled back or replaced with "core capabilities" or "competencies." This view is but one expression of the movement away from stable bureaucracy and toward flexibility. It is also the predictable culmination of more than a half century's worth of thinking that much of the government's work can be done more efficiently and cost effectively outside the government superstructure of bureaucracies and employees. Beginning as early as 1955 with the Eisenhower administration, the U.S. government has issued guidelines to federal agencies regarding its policy vis-à-vis private contractors. These guidelines have been revised periodically as industry has ratcheted up the pressure for service contracts.[23]

The Clinton administration gave contracting a major push with its Federal Activities Inventory Reform (FAIR) Act of 1998. FAIR supplied the legislative mandate for Bush II's "competitive sourcing" and compels agencies to inventory their civil service work and assess which functions are "commercial" and thus subject to outsourcing to the private sector, and which are "inherently governmental" and therefore not eligible. The Bush administration subsequently attacked inherently governmental functions head-on with its 2003 directive.

A close look at inherently governmental functions reveals that contractors are today firmly implanted in them. For instance, contractors:

- Manage—and more—federal taxpayer monies doled out under the stimulus plans and bailouts. The government enlisted money manager BlackRock to help advise it and manage the rescue of Bear Stearns and the American International Group (AIG). BlackRock also won a bid to help the Federal Reserve, an institution which itself combines state and private power, to evaluate hard-to-price assets of Freddie Mac and Morgan Stanley.[24] As the *Wall Street Journal* noted, "Black-Rock's multiple hats put it in the enviable position of having influence on setting the prices of both the assets it is buying and selling."[25] With regard to the fall 2008 $700 billion bailout, also known as the Troubled Asset Relief Program (TARP), the Department of Treasury hired several contractors to set up a process to disburse the funds.[26]

- Choose other contractors: The Pentagon has employed contractors to counsel it on selecting other contractors. The General Services Administration (GSA) enlisted CACI, the Arlington, Virginia–based company, some of whose employees were among those allegedly involved in the Abu Ghraib prisoner abuse scandal in Iraq, to help the government suspend and debar (other) contractors. (CACI itself later became the subject of possible suspension/debarment from federal contracts.)[27]

- Oversee other contractors: The Department of Homeland Security is among the federal agencies that have hired contractors to select and supervise other contractors. Some of these contractors set policy and business goals and plan reorganizations. The Departments of Defense and Homeland Security enlist "lead systems integrators" (contractors or teams of contractors) to carry out large, complex programs, develop systems, and hire subcontractors to work under their supervision. Defense contractors also "improve thought leadership and change management services." And, in the National Clandestine Service (NCS), an integral part of the Central Intelligence Agency (CIA), contractors are sometimes in charge of other contractors.[28]

- Control crucial databases: In a megacontract awarded by the Department of Homeland Security in 2004, Accenture LLP was granted up to $10 billion to supervise and enlarge a mammoth U.S. government project to track citizens of foreign countries as they enter and exit the United States. As Asa Hutchinson, undersecretary for Border and Transportation Security at the Department of Homeland Security under Bush II, remarked, "I don't think you could overstate the impact of this responsibility, in terms of the security of our nation."[29]

- Draft official documents: Contractors have prepared congressional testimony for the Secretary of Energy. Web sites of contractors working for the Department of Defense have also posted announcements of job openings for analysts to perform functions such as preparing the Defense budget. One contractor boasted of having written the Army's Field Manual on "Contractors on the Battlefield."[30]

- Run intelligence operations: In more than half of 117 contracts let by three big agencies of the DHS (the Coast Guard, the Transportation Security Administration, and the Office of Procurement Operations) and examined by the GAO, the GAO found that contractors did inherently governmental work. One company, for instance, was awarded $42.4 million to develop budget and policies for the DHS, as well as to support its information analysis, infrastructure protection, and procurement operations. At the National Security Agency (NSA), the number of contractor facilities approved for classified work jumped from 41 in 2002 to 1,265 in 2006. A full 95 percent of the workers at the very secret National Reconnaissance Office (one of the sixteen intelligence agencies), which runs U.S. spy satellites and analyzes the information they produce, are full-time contractors.[31]

- Execute military and occupying operations: The Department of Defense is evermore dependent on contractors to supply a host of "mission-critical services," including "information technology systems, interpreters, intelligence analysts, as well as weapons system maintenance and base operation support," according to the GAO. U.S. efforts in Iraq illustrate this. As of July 2007, some 160,000 soldiers plus several thousand U.S. civilian employees were greatly reliant on the 180,000 U.S.-funded contractors, of which some 21,000 were Americans (about 43,000 foreign contractors and 118,000 Iraqis made up the rest). As of early 2008 the figure was more than 190,000 contractors. This is in sharp contrast to the 1991 Persian Gulf War: The 540,000 military personnel deployed in that effort greatly outnumbered the 9,200 contractors on the scene.[32]

The government is utterly dependent on private contractors to carry out many inherently governmental functions. As the Acquisition Advisory Panel, a government-mandated, typically contractor-friendly task force made up of representatives from industry, government, and academe, acknowledged in its final 2007 report: "many federal agencies rely extensively on contractors in the performance of their basic missions. In some cases, contractors are solely or predominantly responsible for the performance of mission-critical functions that were traditionally performed by civil servants." This trend, the report concluded, "poses a threat to the government's long-term ability to perform its mission" and could "undermine the integrity of the government's decision making." Contractors are so integrated into the federal workforce that proponents of "insourcing"—transferring work back to the government—acknowledge they face an uphill battle.[33]

As inherently governmental functions are outsourced, Swiss-cheese bureaucracy develops even more holes. Because the number of government contracts and contractors has risen, while the number of civil servants available to supervise them has proportionately fallen, thus decreasing the government's capacity to oversee the process, even when government officials sign on the dotted line, they are sometimes merely rubber stamping the work of contractors. New institutional forms of governing have gathered force. Yet not only the public but even government officials who should be in the know are often left out of the information loop.

The Information Revolution?

This is the information era, right? The age of Web 2.0, smartphones, and twenty-four-hour news cycles. But one of the most important dangers in contracting government functions is that information that is supposedly of and for government often ends up, and remains, in private hands. When contractors have superior information, they have the edge over their government overseers.

Government sometimes lacks the specific information it needs to carry out its work—let alone to monitor the entities that work for it. The GAO has examined contracts government-wide with this issue in mind. Katherine Schinasi, a top GAO official, reports that, in many cases, government deciders scarcely supervise the companies on their payrolls. As a result, she observes, they are unable to answer simple questions about what the firms are doing, whether they have performed well or not, and whether their performance has been cost effective. In April 2002, eleven months *before* the war in Iraq, the army reported to Congress that its best guess was that it directly or indirectly employed between 124,000 and 605,000 service contract workers—a discrepancy of half a million workers.[34]

Lest one think it inconsequential whether the army or any other arm of government gathers information on its contractors, consider Defense's meager ability to monitor contractors who work with classified information, as detailed by the GAO. In a report revealingly titled *Industrial Security: DOD Cannot Ensure Its Oversight of Contractors Under Foreign Influence Is Sufficient*, the GAO warned that the agency "cannot ensure that its oversight of contractors . . . is sufficient to reduce the risk of foreign interests gaining unauthorized access to U.S. classified information." The report elaborated that Defense "does not systematically collect information to know if contractors are reporting certain foreign business transactions," which would enable Defense to learn when a contractor has come under foreign influence and determine "what, if any, protective measures are needed to reduce the risk of foreign interests gaining unauthorized access to U.S. classified information." For example, one foreign-owned contractor appeared to have had access to U.S. classified information for at least six months before a protective measure was implemented. Moreover, Defense neither centrally collects information to determine the magnitude of contractors under foreign influence nor assesses the effectiveness of its oversight so it can identify weaknesses in its protective measures and make necessary adjustments. In 2007 the GAO added a new category to its high-risk list: "ensuring the effective protection of technologies critical to U.S. national security interests."[35]

Further eroding government is the practice of outsourcing oversight itself— to contractors who are enmeshed with government. The BlackRock case cited earlier is one example. Another is known as SWIFT. Following the 9/11 terrorist attacks, one of the surveillance efforts undertaken by the U.S. government was a systematic program used to track money flowing into and out of the United States, transactions abroad and, in a small portion of cases, financial transactions within the United States. The "SWIFT" case takes its name from the Belgium-based Society for Worldwide Interbank Financial Telecommunications, a "member-owned cooperative" that processes international financial transactions. Through SWIFT the U.S. Treasury Department sought and gained access to large numbers of financial and communication records. Treasury then established the Terrorist Finance Tracking Program, run out of the CIA, to analyze the SWIFT data and later shared it with the CIA and FBI. It also hired Booz Allen as an "independent" auditor, which, along with SWIFT, reviewed Treasury's logs of information searches. When the surveillance program was exposed amid controversy in 2006, a key question was how Booz Allen could be impartial given its record as a government contractor and the close ties of its executives to high government officials, and considering the fact that some of these executives are themselves one-time intelligence officials. As Barry Steinhardt, Director of the ACLU's Technology and Liberty Project, put it: "It is bad enough that the administration is trying to hold out a private company as a substitute for genuine checks and balances on its surveillance activities. But of all companies to perform audits on a secret surveillance program, it would be difficult to find one less objective and more intertwined with the U.S. government security establishment."[36]

To sum up that interaction: A private company, given "government" access to sensitive and private data about citizens of the United States and other countries, not only worked alongside government to analyze the data, but then also (supposedly) oversaw the process.

While blended state-private power is busily governing, government officials are absent with leave. Conversations with officials and contractors, as well as those monitoring them (such as GAO investigators) and interacting with them (such as congressional staff) yield records of countless instances in which contractors vastly outnumber government officials in "government" meetings—or in which officials are altogether absent.[37]

In some cases we see a disturbing role reversal, with vital information in the hands of the contractors rather than those of the relevant government officials, putting the contractors firmly in the driver's seat. In one instance, the GAO, in its typical bureaucratese, warned that the practices of the Department of Homeland Security encourage "the risk that government decisions may be influenced by, rather than independent from, contractor judgments." The result might be the DHS's loss of control over decision making.[38]

Companies also sometimes drive policy, rather than the other way around. Or they draft rules that benefit themselves. Conversations with government officials and contractors reveal that this happens frequently. To offer just two examples, both from the huge government contractor SAIC: The company suggested the idea of a biosurveillance shop in a study it conducted for DHS. The agency subsequently bought the idea of such an operation, decided to contract it out, and awarded SAIC the contract. In a separate instance, SAIC, while advising the Nuclear Regulatory Committee (NRC) on rules regarding the recycling of radioactive materials, also worked as a contractor on such a recycling project and concealed that fact, a federal jury found, even as the firm's recycling business could benefit from its NRC consulting. Moreover, a top SAIC official also helped manage an association that promoted favorable nuclear recycling standards as the company was embarking on a venture that would be subject to the very rules it was helping to write, according to Department of Justice documents. While these stories have come to light, consider what others, given how much is outsourced, remain hidden.[39]

The outsourcing of information technologies themselves also touches practically every area of government operations. While contracting much information technology (IT) such as computer network services may be unproblematic or even desirable, it often can't be separated from other vital operations like logistics that are integral to an agency's mission. Contractors perform most of the federal government's IT work: An estimated upwards of three-quarters of governmental IT was outsourced even before the major Iraq war–related push to contract out. For companies in search of federal business, IT is "the new frontier," according to Thomas Burlin, who is in charge of IBM Business Consulting Services's federal practice. With evermore complex technologies always on the horizon, the outsourcing of IT only stands to grow. As Burlin observes, "What has really changed today in this market is . . . that line where the traditional IT services and best practices are blended with the mission." In fact, in 2004, Dan Guttman speculated that, with regard to IT, "contractors are not simply the shadow government, but may become the primary government."[40]

Government that literally doesn't know what it's doing can scarcely be operating effectively. Moreover, it becomes vulnerable on all fronts.

Emasculated Government

Wrapped up with the shifting balance and transfer of functions from state to private is not only the privatization of should-be official information, but also the privatization of legitimacy, expertise, institutional memory, and leadership, which, in turn, relegates information to private hands. It is telling that, nowadays, not only are salaries and perks for comparable jobs typically greater in the private sector, but, often, so is prestige (though benefits are often inferior).

The draining of official government appears to be widespread, and it is depriving the government of crucial in-house expertise and institutional memory. Take, for example, the Department of Homeland Security. During fiscal years 2005 and 2006, according to the GAO, more than half the senior employees at the department's headquarters either resigned or transferred to another executive branch department. DHS's Federal Emergency Management Agency, even before hurricanes Katrina and Rita, lost the services of demoralized professionals. This and the recruitment of government talent by private industries are a general problem. CIA director Michael Hayden complained in 2007 that his agency had begun "to look like the farm system for contractors around here." In response, agency officials banned some companies from soliciting in their cafeteria.[41]

The problem is not that intelligence and military professionals are switching between the state and the private sector, a pattern that accompanied the ascent of the military-industrial complex. As a reporter who has investigated the issue observes: "What we have today with the intelligence business is something far more systemic: senior officials leaving their national security and counterterrorism jobs for positions where they are basically doing the same jobs they once held at the CIA, the NSA and other agencies—but for double or triple the salary, and for profit. It's a privatization of the highest order, in which our collective memory and experience in intelligence—our crown jewels of spying, so to speak—are owned by corporate America."[42]

Is government losing its soul? While it may be strange to mention "soul" and government in the same breath, linking the quintessentially personal with the quintessentially bureaucratic and impersonal, a government procurement lawyer described the state of affairs as the "ebbing away of the soul of government."[43]

Perhaps it is not only government that is losing its essence and edge. Think of the companies that work mainly or exclusively for government. When a contractor becomes, for all practical purposes, another branch of Government, Inc.—just a little further out on the Beltway—what happens to its competitiveness, risk, innovation, and dynamism, private sector qualities that are supposed to make it attractive and beneficial to government? Booz Allen, for instance, separated its government business (which has thrived with new megacontracts since 9/11) from its commercial business (which has not) in 2008. The split was prompted by the diverging directions of its government and commercial units as evidenced in differing cultures, employees, and retention practices, according to the head of the new management consulting company, Booz & Co. While the commercial unit tends to recruit business school graduates and either promote them quickly or discard them, the government unit recruits from government, military, and engineering entities and retains employees in the same positions for years. When companies or units thereof dedicate themselves wholly to government business, those private sector qualities that supposedly justified contracting in the first place may not apply.[44]

The marriage of bureaucracy and business may be mutually profitable, and the two members of the couple may look more and more alike, but there are significant differences. Each is fundamentally constrained and enabled by different incentives and laws. This is especially obvious when it comes to the blended workforce. Whether they perform as a government official or a private contractor, individuals not on the government payroll are subject to more relaxed (or ambiguous) rules governing conflicts of interest and ethics than are civil servants. Whether the rules that apply to civil servants should pertain to contractors is an area of active policy discussion. Be that as it may, the official workforce is governed by a host of statutory provisions that do not concern contractors.[45]

The disparity in the application of regulations to civil servants and to contractors performing the same work raised concern even in some quarters of the executive branch of the Bush II administration, which prided itself on its record of contracting out. In August 2002, the Office of Government Ethics, a small, independent, federal government agency, sent a letter to attorneys and ethics officials in nineteen government agencies inviting comment on "whether federal contractors raised conflicts of interest problems or concerns and, if so, whether such problems can best be solved by applying regulations" to the contractors. Amy Comstock, the Office of Government Ethics director (a Clinton appointee serving a fixed term), noted, "In many agencies, federal employees and contractor personnel work side by side [in official office space] on the same projects. Yet there are different 'ethics' rules for these employees." Then she inquired: "Does this make sense?"[46]

The underlying reality is that, even as government and business try to accomplish common tasks, the two have inherently divergent purposes. While companies are expected to make money for their shareholders, and have a fiduciary duty to do so, government is supposed to be accountable to the public. Companies, unlike government, have no obligation to "stay the course" when the going gets tough.

Such an uneasy relationship spawns arenas of the state where it is responsible but has little control. This can hardly bode well for the efficacy of federal governing.

"Competition" Without Competing

So far we've seen who comprises government and who controls it—in short, the architecture of the system. A look at the reforms instituted during the Clinton administration helps explain how new institutional forms of power and influence have gathered force with this evolving architecture as the backdrop. Again, the privatization of information is basic to the emasculation of government, from the depletion of information away from its agencies to the removal of information about contracts and the contracting process from the public.

The administration of President George H. W. Bush did little to expand the role of contractors (and in fact presided over a number of contract oversight investigations). But the opposite is true of the Clinton administration, which introduced regulations and statutes in the procurement system that ushered in noncompetitive network-friendly practices that are substantially hidden from government overseers and accountability. Contracting rules established under Clinton paved the road for the actions of his successor. A top government procurement official whose tenure spanned the administrations of George H. W. Bush, Bill Clinton, and George W. Bush, said it succinctly: "Clinton laid the framework and set the speed limit at 500 miles per hour but never drove the car past 250. Bush tested the limit."[47]

The crux of the story is this: Under the rubric of "reinventing government" and deregulation, the Clinton administration transformed contracting rules with regard to oversight, competition, and transparency. Here the activities of Steven Kelman, the flexian and government contracting guru (who coined the term the "evolving door"), are important. Kelman worked with industry associations, including the Acquisition Reform Working Group and the Professional Services Council, as well as Congress, particularly with Democratic Leadership Council supporters and Republicans, to make government purchasing faster for the agencies and "friendlier" for contractors. Many of these industry-energized reforms were embodied in the Federal Acquisition Streamlining Act (FASA) of 1994 and the Federal Acquisition Reform Act (FARA) of 1996.[48]

FASA and FARA removed many of the traditional competition and oversight mechanisms that had been in place for decades and provided the statutory basis for new kinds of megacontracts, such as the "Multiple Award" Indefinite Delivery/Indefinite Quantity (IDIQ) system, under which an estimated 40 percent of all federal government contracts are now awarded in areas ranging from computer support to analysis of intelligence. (In some functional areas this proportion is much higher. For instance, nearly all contractors in Iraq are working under IDIQ contracts.) Like the euphemisms of politicians obscuring their intentions, the language of these awards is telling: "contracts" that aren't really contracts; "competitions" without real competition; "task" orders that may sound like small potatoes but can net billions of dollars for the contractor.[49]

The stated intention of the "reforms" was a streamlined procurement process that would reduce the time, costs, and bureaucracy incurred in separate purchases and make contracting more efficient. As a result, over the past decade and a half, small contracts often have been replaced by bigger, and frequently open-ended, multiyear, multimillion- and even billion-dollar, and potentially much more lucrative (IDIQ) contracts with a "limited pool of contractors," as the Acquisition Advisory Panel put it. The changes may, in part, have simplified bureaucracy, but with players on this terrain personalizing bureaucracy, they also reinvented it and helped bring about new institutional forms of governing in which government and business cozily intertwine. The IDIQ contracting system substantially removes public information and transparency from the contracting process and creates conditions that encourage network-based awarding of contracts, off-record deal making, and convoluted lines of authority—all ingredients in the personalization of bureaucracy.[50]

Legally, IDIQ contenders engage in "full and open competition." But IDIQ contracts are not traditional contracts, they are agreements to do business in the future, with the price and scope of work to be determined. "Competitions" for open-ended contracts preapprove contractors for almost indeterminate periods of time (five to ten years, for instance) and money ranging into billions of dollars. When so anointed, contractors' names appear on a list maintained by a government agency. That agency, and usually other agencies, can turn to the chosen contractors, who now possess what has been called a "hunting license," to purchase everything from pens to services. The old system required publicly announcing—through posting in the *Commerce Business Daily*—each solicitation for government work over $25,000, and then allowing companies to compete for it. Under today's IDIQ system, only competitions for hunting licenses are required to be announced in advance (by posting on a government Web site).

What comes next—after the award of a megacontract—takes place behind closed doors and constitutes a virtual revolution in government procurement. Under the old system, overseers could document the amount of the contract because the amount was, more or less, clear when the contract was awarded. Under the current system, services are contracted in the form of "task orders," minicontracts that specify particular work assignments. There is no public posting of task orders, so the ability to obtain sub-rosa information is crucial to success. Issuances of task orders occur on an ad hoc basis without prior announcement. For instance, in July 2007, the government awarded a telecommunications IDIQ contract worth $50 billion to twenty-nine companies. Such awards are only the beginning of the day at the hunt. No open bidding will divvy up those billions. With competition off the books, rather than through bureaucratically monitored processes, the deciders are afforded more discretion and subject to less oversight than in the past. Who you know and who you owe are more likely to be decisive. Not surprisingly, since the institution of the IDIQ system, an entire support industry has taken off, replete with trade publications (such as *Washington Technology, Federal Computer Week,* and *Government Computer News*) that highlight new business opportunities and "networking events" that bring together companies and government officials. There, contractors lobby officials who select the contractors they want to do the work. A company can say good-bye to competition for years while collecting millions or even billions of taxpayer dollars. All of this exists mostly out of public view.[51]

Not only has the process of determining who gets what been banished to the basement, with only those involved having the facts to question it. But the new system also requires little to be disclosed: Neither the company nor the government agency must make any public announcement or report transactions involving task orders, except that which is reported on a long list in the Federal Procurement Data System (FPDS)—a resource friendly only to government procurement wonks—sometimes months after the fact, long after deals are done.

For example, by August 2008, the Federal Procurement Web site that lists transactions had not posted any transactions for 2007. Thus, not only are important goings-on substantially behind the scenes, but one cannot be sure that reliable data will be made available. The current practices are largely beyond monitoring, let alone real-time accountability.[52]

Another practice that has risen sharply over the past decade and a half that makes monitoring even more difficult is the use of IDIQ contracts for interagency acquisition of services. IDIQ contracts are the primary form of interagency contracts. In an interagency contract, the agency that actually needs the contractor's services, and with whom the contractor will work most closely, isn't necessarily the legal contracting entity or legally responsible for monitoring the contractor.

The contractor CACI, whose employees allegedly participated in Abu Ghraib prisoner abuse, was working under such a contracting agreement. When the Defense Department, in the midst of a war for which it wasn't fully prepared, needed personnel, CACI, which had a long collaboration with the department, was well positioned to supply them. CACI officials told GAO investigators that they "marketed their services directly to Army intelligence and logistics officials in Iraq because of relationships they had developed over time." Contractors such as CACI are not legally authorized to sell goods or services not provided for in their contract. Yet, with relationships often trumping contracts, that rule is often breached. During their investigation, the inspector general of the Department of Interior (legally, CACI's monitoring authority) and the General Services Administration (the government agency that manages government properties and purchasing) found that the contract under which CACI supplied interrogators was for technology, including computer integration and data processing work: CACI was not approved to provide interrogation services.[53]

The personalization of bureaucracy in the awarding of contracts and task orders is only the beginning. Interagency contracts are vulnerable to diffusion of authority and responsibility, helping to create the mother of all Swiss-cheese bureaucracies. While the Defense Department enlisted the services of CACI and CACI worked for Defense in Iraq, Defense was not legally responsible for CACI. The Department of Interior, an agency better known for its management of national parks, was. (Interior manages some Defense contracts in exchange for a fee.) Interior, not surprisingly, had little capacity to monitor CACI. Moreover, Defense relied on the absentee Interior Department not only to manage the contract but to issue individual task orders. Clearly, the official operational control that would apply through a government chain of command does not necessarily apply to contractors. One result, clearly, is the obfuscation of authority.[54]

Information, or its lack, is an essential component: The government personnel with particulars about a given project have no contractual monitoring responsibility, while the contracting officer—without those specifics—is responsible. With regard to CACI, the GAO determined that the army officials who were supposed to oversee CACI "for the most part, lacked knowledge of contracting issues and were not aware of their basic duties and responsibilities in administering the orders." The result was de facto governing by contractor. CACI "effectively replaced government decision makers in several aspects of the procurement process," the GAO concluded.[55]

With much of the work in government contracting of services done under IDIQ contracts, many of them also interagency ones, CACI is unlikely to be an aberrant case. Moreover, the dearth of manpower and expertise in government, thanks to caps on or reductions in the number of civil servants, leaves still more contractors to fill the holes.

Another complex (but not unusual) case, this one involving compensation to nuclear weapons workers via interagency contracting, was first brought to light by Richard Miller, former senior policy analyst at the Government Accountability Project, a public-interest NGO, in 2004. In this case, the Department of Energy outsourced responsibility to a well-connected IT firm called Science and Engineering Associates, which was hired under a GSA contract through an interagency agreement with the Navy). In the process, the work to be done transmuted from an IT contract into a contract for workers' compensation claims development and processing. The entity chosen to do the job had scant qualifications, experience, or in-house knowledge for it, and contracting arrangements were convoluted and nearly impossible to track. As Miller summarized the case: "An IT contract issued through the GSA morphed into a completely different scope of work and ballooned in size. Meanwhile, the contractor failed to perform. No federal agency was willing to accept responsibility for the circle of mismanagement. Ultimately Congress was forced to strip the Energy Department of the program, restructure it, and offload it to the Labor Department." A slew of congressional hearings and press reports followed Miller's revelations about the case. When GAO investigators tried to hold agencies accountable for who contracted with whom for what and why—not to mention the results produced—each agency rejected culpability. The buck stopped nowhere and a circular firing squad formed. Not surprisingly, in 2005 the GAO added the "management of interagency contracting" to its high-risk list. A clear chain of command and real-time oversight are lost in such a contracting system.[56]

Real-time monitoring may not be in the cards, but what of after-the-fact sanctions? The CACI and Energy Department examples, unusually, culminated with in-your-face excesses that eventually hit the press, with little consequence to the entities involved. Once the General Services Administration initiated an investigation into whether CACI had broken federal contracting rules, the results of which could have resulted in its being barred from further government work, CACI retained the services of powerful Washington lob-byists. CACI was cleared in July 2004, and, that August, awarded a contract without competitive bidding—this time for interrogation services.[57]

While a substantial portion of government contracting was being drained of its accountability lifeblood, competition among businesses—supposedly the free market's signature feature—was also diminishing. Now, for the first time on record, most federal procurement contracts are conferred either without competition or through the use of IDIQ contracts to a limited set of contractors. Industry consolidation (defense is a case in point) has produced fewer and larger firms. This development, the Acquisition Advisory Panel notes, results in more opportunities for organizational conflicts of interest, in which, for instance, one section of the organization bids on a project that the other section designed.[58]

Although IDIQ contracts help maintain the façade of government effi-ciency, the reality is that favored contractors sometimes make the list be-cause they have personal connections with government officials. For instance, huge, noncompeted awards, justified on national security grounds, have been granted for work in Iraq. Defense companies linked to senior members of the Bush administration's inner circles were the beneficiaries of some of these awards. Audits conducted by the inspectors general for the departments of Defense and Interior found that more than half of the con-tracts inspected were granted without competition or without checking to see that the prices were sensible. And in the aftermath of hurricanes Katrina and Rita, FEMA initially contracted with four large companies to provide housing by using noncompetitive procedures. Some government procure-ment specialists have also argued that the supposedly cost-saving IDIQ sys-tem has often kept government contracting officials from getting good deals for their agencies. In fact, in the few cases in which government agencies have "insourced," they have done so after calculating they would save sig-nificant amounts of money. The money salvaged through competitive sourc-ing is also overstated, according to the GAO. So much for competition and the free market.[59]

When on-the-books competition gives way to off-the-books "competi-tion," rational bureaucracy to personalized bureaucracy, and chains of command to Swiss-cheese bureaucracy, it is not hard to see how contractors can become de facto government officials and accountability vanishes.

Ambiguous Authority

Swiss-cheese bureaucracy, government by contractor, and emasculation of government are not the only developments that have created opportunities for private players to sway public policy while serving their own interests. Ambiguous institutional arrangements provide additional playgrounds for them by enabling greater discretion or making it difficult to establish where authority resides.

Consider first the Coalition Provisional Authority (CPA), the U.S. occupation authority in Iraq under L. Paul Bremer (from May 2003 until June 2004). Although the CPA was short-lived (and the United Nations and representatives of other governments also participated in its governance structure), it was created and funded as a division of the U.S. Department of Defense, and Viceroy Bremer reported directly to the U.S. defense secretary. Until its dissolution, the CPA was vested with executive, legislative, and judicial authority over Iraq. During its reign, the CPA transferred billions of U.S. taxpayer dollars to contractors. Power clearly lay with U.S. authorities. Yet the CPA's murky status enabled contractors under its authority to wheedle out of accountability. In response to a case brought by former employees of a U.S. contractor in Iraq, the U.S. Department of Justice ruled in 2004 that the CPA was beyond the purview of U.S. authority. In response to the same charges, a federal judge ruled in 2006 that "the CPA was not a U.S. government entity, and therefore employees of the CPA were not working in their official capacity as employees or officers of the United States government." Only in April 2009, six years after the creation of the CPA, did a U.S. Court of Appeals panel dismiss the argument that the contractors were not working for the CPA. While ambiguity in this case merely enabled contractors (allegedly) to misuse millions of taxpayer dollars (not to privatize U.S. policy), the issue the case raises is crucial: To whom were the contractors answerable, if not to the U.S. government?[60]

Second, on American soil a host of institutional arrangements generate opportunities for private players, supposedly engaged in public service, to

infuse the agendas of their companies, networks, or selves in government policy, and for this to be hidden from governmental overseers and the public.
These institutional arrangements include the quasi-government organizations and federal advisory committees mentioned earlier, which have grown
in quantity and significance, along with task forces of ambiguous standing.
Many of these bodies make invaluable contributions by bringing the expertise of scientists and other specialists to bear on public policy issues. And getting the relevant and competing players together in the room may enhance the
possibility that they will keep each other honest. But not every member of
these organizations or committees is engaged simply in public service or ré-
sumé building; members not only find out what is going on but can gain entrée to the people who are helping it go on. The information and access these
bodies provide can make the difference between being an influencer, or not,
in the service of one's company, network, or self, rather than the public's. And
how would we know? Federal advisory committees can operate in a less-than-
transparent way because, under the Federal Advisory Committee Act (FACA),
to which they are subject, so-called "task force," "subcommittee," or "working
group" meetings (less than full FACA meetings) do not have to be open to
the public. The Center for Public Integrity has concluded that these committees "sometimes are tainted by financial conflicts of interest, needless secrecy,
industry dominance and outside interference." The information, access, and
government imprimatur that the entities provide their members with may
help them serve private agendas, rather than public ones.[61]

Overlap between government advisory boards and companies that do
business in the same arenas is hardly unusual. Ten current or previous members of the influential Defense Policy Board (since 1997) and twenty-five
members of the authoritative Defense Science Board serve or served as an
executive, board member, consultant, or lobbyist for one of the top twenty
government contractors. The story of Richard Perle, privy to classified information as a member of the Defense Policy Board, is a case in point. His chair-
manship of (and later membership on) the Defense Policy Board was one of
many roles he occupied during the run-up to the Iraq war. While his tenure
on the board ended following a conflict-of-interest controversy entailing his
concurrent role as consultant for a defense contractor, his board position
helped him wield policy influence at a crucial moment. In a "coincidence" of

(his) interests, he used the information, access, and stature afforded him by the board to agitate for policies long pushed by his group.[62]

Such coincidences abound. While serving on a government advisory board, a member who also works for a contractor may use information to which he has access for his own and the contractor's advantage (a possible conflict of interest), but may also merge the agenda of the government and the contractor in a coincidence of interests, by, say, recommending the same program or need to both entities. While supposedly acting on behalf of the public, he can instead help craft "public" policies to benefit himself or his group.

The role of task forces in making public policy also has raised controversy—and legal questions. When federal task forces involve private citizens as members (as opposed to being composed exclusively of federal employees), the task forces are subject by law to the Federal Advisory Committee Act. Two task forces in particular have received much scrutiny in recent years from public interest watchdogs and congressional and public critics. Some of these bodies' members and dealings are steeped in might-be-private, might-be-public ambiguity.[63]

President Clinton's Task Force on National Health Reform, to which he appointed First Lady Hillary Rodham Clinton as chair, is famous among them. While the task force's recommendations and the role of a policy-involved first lady were touchy, of interest here is the nebulous status of the group. The standing of the first lady herself in this unusual role was particularly contentious. She was appointed by the president to the post but was she, or was she not, a "government official"? If not, and were she merely a private citizen, then the task force would be subject to FACA, meaning its proceedings generally would have to be open to the public and minutes made available to interested parties. The controversy surrounding the task force set off litigation. Although the U.S. Court of Appeals for the D.C. Circuit eventually rendered the Clinton task force not subject to FACA, it was widely criticized for operating behind closed doors, and under public pressure the White House complied with a GAO investigation.[64]

The Bush II White House was even less forthcoming when it came to Vice President Dick Cheney's energy task force, officially the National Energy Policy Development Group. Bush appointed Cheney to chair the group within weeks of taking office, and many observers understood it to be developing a national

energy policy. However, Cheney's office never did turn over its records for public scrutiny. The informal consultations that the vice president and relevant officials and staff held with energy industry representatives prompted
investigations by the GAO, in addition to legal challenges from the Sierra Club
and Judicial Watch. The GAO found that the task force personnel had "met
with, solicited input from, or received information and advice from nonfederal
energy stakeholders, principally, petroleum, coal, nuclear, natural gas, and electricity industry representatives and lobbyists." GAO head David Walker told
one interviewer that the GAO's inability to obtain the task force documents
raised the issue of "a reasonable degree of transparency and an appropriate degree of accountability in government." He said it was the first case since 1998,
when he assumed his position, that the GAO was kept from doing its job and
putting out a report worthy of government auditing standards. Ultimately, a
2004 Supreme Court ruling concurred with Cheney's office that the task force's
deliberations need not be released to the public.[65]

The way that Cheney's office handled the disclosure—or nondisclosure—
of events and people connected to the task force fits in with the trend toward
personalization, networking, and behind-the-scenes transactions. Cheney in-
formalized the policy process and kept records from the eyes of the public
and government and legal investigators, and got away with it. The usual channels to force transparency, including congressionally ordered investigations
and the courts, proved impotent. At one point in a fit of flex-like bravado,
Cheney tried to have his cake and eat it too. After claiming executive privilege,
he provoked derision from many quarters, in 2007, when he asserted that his
office was not an "entity within the executive branch."[66]

Public policy institutions are more often partisan than neutral. Think
tanks, for example, which sometimes carry out government projects but more
often are simply engines of influence, once enjoyed a greater reputation for
scholarly distance from politics. Think-tankers often present themselves as
public intellectuals. Some of them indeed are. (The New America Foundation, with which I have been affiliated as a fellow while writing this book, con-
ducts programs known for creating policy proposals not predictable or easily
pegged in terms of left or right, Democratic or Republican.) Part of the usefulness of think tanks, from the point of view of their affiliates, is that they
provide a veneer of neutrality and objective study. But this may be more pub-

lic relations than reality. An authoritative survey of trends in American think tanks documents "an increase in partisan politics, from which a corresponding rise in partisan organizations and institutions that produce analysis along partisan lines has been identified." (This trend recalls many of the "think tanks," foundations, and NGOs of the 1990s' transitional central and eastern Europe that acted as [unregistered] political parties or simply personal springboards for their founders.)

While purporting to be scholarly and disinterested, think tanks can issue findings that are either ideologically based or crafted to serve the ends of specific companies or industries. A think tank funded by energy concerns can create confusion over the facts surrounding climate change for the benefit of the industry. Those funded by the defense industry can likewise cloud the issues. Meanwhile, they can smooth the passage of policy ideas from industry to public discourse or legislation, or they can quash attempts to change more objectively derived policies. Think-tankers can pose as objective analysts for a public that is often unaware of sponsors' vested interests. The press, sometimes equally uninformed, quotes these "experts" without disclosing when the think tanks are bankrolled by companies whose profits are crucially linked to the views offered by the experts. The environment of truthiness, which allows people to play with how they present themselves to the world regardless of fact or track record, can keep critical questions at bay. The survey of think-tank trends concluded that: "the omnipresent media with its focus on sound bites rather than sound analysis is driving think tanks to respond to its time and content parameters by producing quick, pithy analysis that is quotable and accessible." These trends and others, the author writes, "combine to pose great challenges for the sustainability of think tanks as independent, reliable providers of sound public policy advice in the future."[67]

The trends we see in the think tank world are consistent with more general ones: the movement away from neutrality, the emphasis on sound bites, and the shift toward partisanship and politicization. Think tanks, then, are but one illustration of the way in which the distinctions among government, business, and other institutions have become less clear. Built-in institutional ambiguity creates fertile ground for those who would pursue coincidences of interest. And, of course, this elevates these players beyond the reach of traditional monitoring.

The End of Loyalty to Institutions?

The HHS banner congratulating employees for handing agency work to outsiders is emblematic. Waning loyalty of institutions to people and of people
to institutions (congruent with the flex-ability inherent in ambiguous authority and Swiss-cheese bureaucracy filling in for shadow government) goes
hand in hand with the proliferation of people's roles. Both parties have greater
expectation that the employee will perform multiple jobs and projects simultaneously, and less expectation of long-lasting affiliation and loyalty.[68]

An employee working for a small international development consulting
firm that receives contracts from the U.S. Agency for International Development (USAID), the government's foreign aid arm, describes what he calls
a "lack of demonstrated loyalty to the company by independent consultants."
He reports:

> Because ours is a small firm, the vast majority of the people that work
> on the company's projects in the field are independent consultants. The
> consequence of this relationship is that once the consultant's assign-
> ment is over, there is no guarantee of additional work—or money.
> Therefore, when implementing assignments in the field, consultants
> tend simultaneously to be looking for their next assignment, which
> often involves brownnosing with competitors of the company that are
> working in the same country. Also, because they have no real ties to our
> company, these consultants usually do not go out of their way to help in
> the long run, by, for example, giving us notice of an upcoming project
> that they have heard about through the local U.S. expatriate gossip mill.
> This negatively affects the company because having advance notice of
> a project gives us time to pre-recruit. If we do *not* have the same ad-
> vance notice as our competitors, by the time the Request for Proposals
> is formally released by USAID, all the best people have already been re-
> cruited by the other firms that did have advance notice, which makes
> winning a project significantly more difficult.
>
> An example of this type of situation involves Mr. G., who was hired
> by our company to lead a rule of law project in Jordan. He has been
> there for about 10 months now. Last month, we saw a publicly posted

Request for Proposals from USAID for work in that country that was right up our and Mr. G's alley. We had been unaware that USAID planned to fund such a project. When one of our employees asked Mr. G. about it, he said: "Yes, I knew it was coming but didn't think you'd be interested." This was clearly a lie because it was exactly the type of project on which we always bid. Over the course of the next week, we found out that Mr. G. was in negotiations with another firm about working on the project. That firm had approached Mr. G., saying that if he went with them and if they won the contract, they would pay him much more than we were paying. This made it more lucrative for Mr. G. to withhold information about the upcoming project from us and to help the other firm win it.

As a short-term consultant, it behooves Mr. G. to adopt multidimensional professional roles, rather than the one-dimensional roles of an earlier era. Through Mr. G. we see but one example of how loyalty to institutions no longer is as wise as it once was. In fact, the GAO has found that "compared to direct-hire staff, personal services contractors generally do not have the same level of agency commitment . . . [and] are not subject to the same degree of accountability." Clearly this observation applies to such contractors no matter the government agency.[69]

Because people play more professional roles than in the past, players are better able to actively structure their roles to suit themselves amid declining loyalty to institutions. Today, top government posts seem like stepping stones on the career path to the private sector gravy train, and the "big boys" who have held these posts and now perform for big ticket contractors carry great cachet and legitimacy in policy and influence circles. Following Steven Kelman's "evolving door," these influencers move in and out of institutions along their career paths, never permanently fixed to any. Like many other high-powered players, they are apt to ensconce themselves, at least temporarily, in think tanks and consulting firms, and more likely to work for more than one institution at a time or move among them in more rapid succession or with more alacrity than in the past.

Officials go to companies and then back to government, but the landing spots that supply the big bucks, and with them the influence and stature, are often those held by former government officials now in an industry perch. Although there are rules to address the revolving door syndrome, companies with significant government contracts are often headed by former senior officials of intelligence- and defense-related government agencies.[70] For instance, William Studeman, former director of the National Security Agency (NSA), where outsourcing has grown rapidly, is now a vice president of Northrop Grumman, the defense giant. Three of Booz Allen's current and former vice presidents previously served as intelligence agency directors, including James Woolsey, a Neocon core member who headed the CIA during the Clinton administration. And a number of former defense and intelligence officials, including defense secretaries Melvin R. Laird and William J. Perry, CIA directors John M. Deutch and Robert M. Gates, and NSA director Bobby R. Inman, have either worked for or served on Booz Allen's board.[71]

Means of accountability have not evolved accordingly. While conflict-of-interest laws and regulations are well established, rules and practices designed to address coincidences of interest are not. And, when government contractors hire former directors of intelligence- and defense-related government agencies, they are banking on coincidences of interest between their hires and their hires' former (government) employers. In these coincidences, "The Intelligence Community and the contractors are so tightly intertwined at the leadership level that their interests, practically speaking, are identical," as one intelligence expert put it.[72]

Coincidences of interest, together with sagging institutional loyalty, employees who come and go, a fading ethos of public service, and unsecured databases, among other phenomena, introduce fundamental vulnerabilities into an institution, whether governmental or business. And when these vulnerabilities exist in the realm of national security and foreign policy, one can only wonder about the nation's sovereignty.[73]

Enhanced Executive Power

While today's influencers busily pursue coincidences of interest and move quickly to plug holes in Swiss-cheese bureaucracy, they also take advantage of executive power. Its intensification and concentration in the United States, again, has largely occurred under the radar. Enhancing executive power is not new, but it is another feature of the governing landscape that heightens the influence prospects of strategic players, who not only work across the system, but also from the top down. They avail themselves of opportunities to take over public policy agendas in pursuit of their own interests and operate beyond the reach of the checks and balances that Americans earlier enjoyed.

The U.S. presidency, which had been intensifying its power throughout the twentieth century, stepped up this process in the wake of 9/11. (Indeed, in countries throughout the world, executive power has grown as a result of the post-9/11 adaptation of international security law. In addition to their rearranging bureaucracy through the empowerment of shadow government, Presidents Clinton and Bush II took several means of exercising executive power to new levels. One means was the toolbox of unilateral power that includes executive orders, proclamations, and other instruments. Another means, the presidential "signing statement," has been used in ways that directly challenge the system of checks and balances laid out in the Constitution, as the American Bar Association and presidential scholars have argued.[74]

A signing statement is a pronouncement about a provision of a law passed by Congress and signed by the president. Presidents beginning with James Monroe have occasionally issued such statements. Once they tended to be only rhetorical and usually demonstrated presidential backing of the legislation in question. Recent statements, however, have been used to challenge or reinterpret the provisions of the law, and in some cases, to function as a virtual veto of the law or provisions of it. President Reagan greatly escalated the number of signing statements and suggested he might not be duty-bound to enforce parts of the law with which he disagreed.[75] While Presidents Carter, Bush I, and Clinton all signaled their objections from time to time through constitutional challenges contained in signing statements, Bush II increased the number of such challenges more than tenfold compared with Clinton. By the end of his second term, Bush II had issued more than 1,100 constitutional challenges to provisions of law. Further, he employed them in an unprecedented way: to effectively curtail the power of the legislative branch by threatening (via the challenge) to not enforce a law passed by Congress. In effect, Bush claimed to accomplish what the Supreme Court has deemed unconstitutional—a line item veto. Just as presidents have been afforded leeway during wartime in the interest of protecting the nation, Bush used 9/11 as

justification to expand presidential powers, often keeping the legal justifica-
tions secret.[76]

Such precedents leave an enduring legacy, which may be why in early 2007 a distinguished panel of the American Bar Association determined that the ways that signing statements were used by Bush II are "contrary to the rule of law and our constitutional system of separation of powers." This strengthen-ing of executive power, of course, corrodes the system of checks and balances.[77]

Executive power has also been enhanced through the increasing exposure of civil servants to politicization. The rules that have governed civil servants for the better part of a century have come under attack. Bush II, for instance, relaxed the application of long-standing civil service rules in the Departments of Defense and Homeland Security on a limited basis and slated other de-partments to follow suit. At the same time, the work of civil servants may have become more open to network- and politics-influenced decision mak-ing. According to Paul Light, who studies the presidential appointment process, a "thickening" occurred under the Bush administration in which po-litical appointees filled more management layers in government. One related practice for federal employees, says Light, was "very tight coordination from the White House on down to the political appointees."[78]

How President Obama will use the various tools of executive power and the precedents he has inherited, as well as the extent to which the civil serv-ice will continue to be politicized, remains to be seen. The tendency, of course, would naturally be not to relinquish such power when one is its beneficiary.[79]

Privatizing Policy

While the grand narrative that followed the end of the Cold War trumpeted the worldwide triumph of democracy and free markets, it is ironic that the United States has led the developed world in its unannounced merging of state and private, thus rendering government less accountable and relevant markets less competitive—all the while emulating transitional eastern Europe in this regard and perhaps even eroding its own sovereignty. Many building blocks of the new forms of intertwined state-private power are reminiscent of that region: from the heightened discretion afforded American bureaucrats in the contracting process and politicization of think tanks, to the dearth of loyalty to institutions. Equally ironic is enhanced executive power. So is the privatization of information, expertise, and institutional memory and the advent of truthiness when we are in a supposed era of access to information. When information, expertise, and institutional memory are relocated more to corporate America than government—and when players can perform their way out of the reach of accountability—sovereignty is surely challenged.

Meanwhile, today's premier operators can co-opt policymaking and ultimately alter regulations and government structures in ways that generate both the policies they prefer and those that provide them with a favorable environment. In reorganizing relations between state and private, bureaucracy and market, they help forge new institutional forms of power and influence—forms that take on a life of their own and enable players to further concentrate power and influence. Not unlike their institutional nomad and clan cousins of transitional eastern Europe, these footloose operators pursue coincidences of interest, travel through the evolving door, and master the art of flex, in the process helping to fashion ambiguous authority and institutions.

Who or what can slow the players down? The mechanisms to hold them accountable to either democratic or free-market principles that applied not long ago largely do not effect these players' machinations. Moreover, they are attractive because they get things done: Swiss-cheese bureaucracy needs networks to shore it up and "get the ball rolling"—in short, to be personalized. Flexians and flex nets do that in spades, and they appeal to authorities and the public because they are effective and their appearances of the moment are taken at face value.

As new institutional fusions are invented and replayed when bureaucrats and contractors collaborate to get things done, these players put the lie to the façade of limited government. They also test the idea that outsourcing mobilizes competition, that signature feature of the free market, so heralded with the so-called "end of history." Moreover, they challenge the contention that the reforms necessarily spring from concern about efficiency.

Meanwhile, unaccountable government grows its base, and the playing field becomes evermore open to the operators who fuse state and private power to achieve their own agendas.

CHAPTER FIVE

The Privatizers

THE CITY WAS MOSCOW, THE YEAR 1994, AND THE PLANS GRAND: to transform the new Russia. The old communist system lay in ruins, but the new capitalism existed only in hectic possibilities amid a high-octane world of hope. The myth of the "Evil Empire" was officially dead, felled by the breakup of the vast Soviet state at the end of 1991. America nurtured a new myth about its former adversary: Russia was reforming into a vibrant market democracy, one the West could do business with. Of course, we in the West were helping—not only with aid and loans, but also with our indispensable expertise.

I had been invited to sit in on what was billed as a routine "closed" meeting about the West's aid: nine or ten people, most already acquainted with one another, mapping the next phase of a particular privatization effort. We sat around an oblong table in a nondescript conference room, presided over by an American in his early thirties, Jonathan Hay. I had heard Hay's name probably a dozen times in Moscow that summer. Barely out of law school, he was a consultant to the "Harvard project," a U.S. government-funded brainchild of the Harvard Institute for International Development (HIID) whose stated mission was to reform Russia's economy. The other Westerners in the room were consultants—mostly high-priced senior associates with the "Big Six" accounting firms—whose companies were also paid by Western assistance.

By comparison, Hay was a kid with little experience. Though outwardly unrefined and boyishly energetic, Hay was clearly comfortable with his own authority. During the meeting, the elder consultants readily deferred to him. He had also been more difficult to reach than senior consultants and harder to pin down for an interview. In Poland I had watched visionary, inexperienced young men morph from lives of dissidence to power virtually overnight, as an unprepared Solidarity took over the government in 1989. But Hay wasn't a local leader. He was an American in Russia, merely working on a U.S.-sponsored project like many others. Why did he command so much attention and authority, I wondered?

Hay's authority was but one clue as I set out to understand the workings of economic reform aid to Russia. Another lay in Hay's obvious closeness to the Russian I sat across from at the meeting: Dmitry Vasiliev, an understated official in his late twenties. Vasiliev was one of a dynamic group of young men led by the redheaded Anatoly Chubais, himself only in his midthirties. Boris Yeltsin, president of the new Russia, had brought Chubais to Moscow from his hometown of St. Petersburg. The *New York Times* called them the "Young Reformers." Hay and Vasiliev seemed like fellow missionaries, with Hay appearing to be more than a mere adviser. The more interviewing I did, the more the senior consultants' deference to Hay began to make sense. Hay's role as Vasiliev's cohort became clearer, as did the fact that my interviewees kept mentioning their names in conjunction with a variety of activities, no matter the stated purpose of the reform project at hand.

While I have told the story of these Russian and American players before as it pertains to foreign aid, I have since come to see them and what they pulled off as an example of the new system of power and influence in the making. As early forgers of new institutional forms of fused official and private power, these transnational players were able to shape the course of one of the most crucial projects of the twentieth century—remaking Russia—as well as break new ground in outsourcing U.S. government functions. With these new forms all but impervious to old means of accountability, up to a dozen players show us how a small flex net can make a big impact, far from the input of publics or the reach of monitors. The Young Reformers and their American counterparts constituted pieces of an intricate puzzle. It took me years to assemble but its picture is now coming clear, even as some pieces are still missing.[1]

Transnational Togetherness

In 1994, Moscow was the place for any bigshot international consultant to make his mark. Fact-finding missions, and scores of consultants from the International Monetary Fund, the World Bank, and governments ranging from the United Kingdom to Germany to Japan, not to mention would-be investors, jacked up hotel and restaurant prices to make Moscow the second most expensive city in the world (after Tokyo). Jeffrey Sachs, the Harvard wunderkind credited with turning around entire national economies, was already on the scene. Touted by *The Economist* as one of the world's most important economists, the peripatetic Sachs had come to symbolize shock therapy—radical economic change in which the state releases price and currency controls, removes subsidies, and often privatizes its assets—and even reform itself, as he offered his services throughout the former Eastern Bloc.

The aid story in Russia, I thought, would resemble the scene I had witnessed in central Europe in the late 1980s and early 1990s, where I had earlier set out to examine the effects of the aid effort on the ground. I had interviewed many players in Poland, Hungary, and Czechoslovakia—which the West had deemed most willing of the former Eastern Bloc countries to enact economic reforms and thus most worthy of assistance. As consultants and "experts" rushed to the region, they were greeted by legions of local brokers who rose up to assist and use the often naïve outsiders. Poles dubbed them the "Marriott Brigade" because they encamped at the Marriott, Warsaw's only five-star hotel at the time. Some were paid by foreign aid monies—either through their companies or personally—to advise local people, which is a form of aid known as "technical assistance." Because technical assistance was the largest chunk of aid supplied by Western governments, West-East people-to-people encounters significantly shaped the aid process.

As in central Europe, the goals of economic reform aid in Russia were to construct a market economy through privatization, and to establish institutions such as capital markets and stock exchanges. These were supposed to be accomplished largely through Western-supplied technical assistance. And while Moscow did see its version of the Marriott Brigade with the hottest consultants parachuting in and out, a new dynamic also revealed itself. Over and over I heard the names of the *same* individuals. I cast a wide net and sought out a range of people—donor representatives, embassy functionaries, local officials, consultants, participants in or targets of foreign aid projects—engaging them over drinks and dinners, in formal and informal meetings, and at social and professional events. Yet my net did not yield the wide catch of participants it had in central Europe. I wondered why. Sachs had brought along some of his Harvard associates, and their names kept coming up in my interviews. One was Hay, who had worked as a World Bank consultant and played a minor part in a Jeffrey D. Sachs and Associates project funded by the Finnish government. Another was Andrei Shleifer, a thirty-something tenured Harvard economist, who had emigrated from Russia in his teens, and had played a central role in Sachs's project. These were the names I kept hearing in connection with economic reform organizations underwritten by Western sponsors. These organizations, some of them bodies of the Russian state, others nongovernmental organizations, if only formally—at least one was jointly created by the board of directors of Harvard University and Russian governmental decree—had names like the State Property Committee, the Russian Privatization Center, the Federal Securities Commission, the Institute for Law-Based Economy, and the Resource Secretariat. They were supposed to help build the new economy and society by doing things like carrying out privitization and legal reform efforts and developing capital markets. My interviewees, often English-speaking Russians, gave me glossy brochures describing the organizations' missions that had obviously been designed specially for foreign consumption.[2]

Yet when people talked offhandedly about each organization—Who runs it? Who initiated it? Who is on the board of directors? Whose word counts?— they repeatedly named the same individuals. For example, while Chubais chaired the State Property Committee, Vasiliev was its deputy chairman, Hay was its senior legal adviser, Shleifer was an adviser, and another Chubais Clan member, Maxim Boycko, was an economic adviser (later chief economic adviser). While Chubais chaired the Russian Privatization Center's board of directors, Vasiliev was its deputy chairman, with Hay and Shleifer board members, and Boycko its CEO. While Chubais chaired the board of the Federal Securities Commission, Vasiliev served as its executive director and deputy chairman of the board, and Shleifer as a USAID-paid adviser to it. Hay

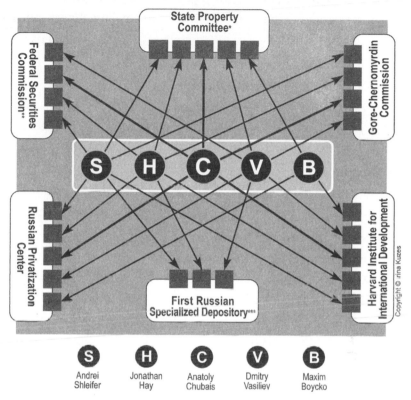

CHUBAIS-HARVARD PLAYERS
Interconnections of Key Actors through Organizations
(Early 1990s)

State Property Committee*

Federal Securities Commission**

Gore-Chernomyrdin Commission

S H C V B

Russian Privatization Center

Harvard Institute for International Development

Copyright © rina Kuzes

First Russian Specialized Depository***

S	H	C	V	B
Andrei Shleifer	Jonathan Hay	Anatoly Chubais	Dmitry Vasiliev	Maxim Boycko

* The Russian acronym is the GKI.
** The Federal Securities Commission is also known by Americans as the "Russian SEC."
*** This depository maintains the records of mutual fund investors' holdings.

had an office in the Commission and headed the U.S.-supported Institute for Law-Based Economy, which funded the Commission.[3]

The more interviewing I did, the more I saw that, despite the participants' different titles and the slick brochures outlining the organizations' different functions, the same people ran the show. Even the sponsors and funders were largely the same. The dynamic seemed to lie in *who*, not *what*. The *who* was reflected in how the Chubais-Harvard players had personalized the bureaucracy. They worked in and through organizations, both governmental and non-, doing what was necessary to advance their goals, with the organizations as a resource for their collective efforts.

◊ ◊ ◊

TIES BETWEEN THE Chubais and the Harvard associates were forged in the late 1980s as the Soviet Union was coming undone and the world was wondering just where Mikhail Gorbachev's glasnost and perestroika would lead. It was natural for these players to gravitate toward one another. They had similar personal qualities: energy, ambition, and youth. They saw eye to eye on matters of economic ideology and policy. All were top-flight players in their own milieus. The Harvard set was well connected in the prestige- and resource-rich world of international economic policy, international financial institutions, and premier economic associations. The Chubais Clan was bravely testing the waters, introducing subversive free-market ideas in their hometown of Leningrad (now St. Petersburg).

While a university student in economics during the Gorbachev years, Chubais courageously started a club called Reforma. The club's risky discussions of market economics attracted hundreds of people eager for change— people whose life experience and only real point of reference was the stagnant communist system. Chubais and Reforma helped transform Leningrad into a model of reform by crafting platforms for local and national elections, drafting legislation, and eventually helping to lead its government. The Chubais associates would come to be known in Russia as the St. Petersburg Clan or Chubais Clan. Like any clan, it had "no registered structure" and was "based on informal relations between its members," as Olga Kryshtanovskaya explains clans. Its members were "united by a community of views and loyalty to an idea or a leader."[4]

Sachs, rainmaker of the nascent transnational network, brought together chosen economists from West and East, amassed resources—from the New York–based Ford Foundation to the Japanese Sasakawa Foundation—and spawned projects in various iterations. Through Sachs, Andrei Shleifer met Chubais. Shleifer in turn introduced Boycko, a Muscovite, to the Russians from St. Petersburg, Shleifer told me. Amid an environment shifting by the minute, these transnationals traded ideas about how to fix the ailing economy.[5]

In 1991, as the Soviet state was collapsing, Boris Yeltsin summoned Chubais from his post as deputy mayor of the newly rechristened St. Petersburg to help guide the nation through this epochal transition. Yeltsin, then president of what was still Soviet Russia, was putting together his team of economic advisers. Chief among them were Yegor Gaidar—the first "architect" of economic reform in postcommunist Russia, with whom Sachs had been working—and Chubais, who was part of Gaidar's team and later would replace him as the "economic reform czar." Unlike the unkempt, less-appealing Gaidar, Chubais was suave and well spoken. He presented an impressive figure to a Western audience. The Chubais Clan assumed a national role.

Meanwhile, across the Atlantic, with high hopes for a favorable relationship with the new Russia, the U.S. Congress allocated funds to the U.S. Agency for International Development (USAID), the U.S. government's chief foreign aid body, to promote Russian reform. The effort could scarcely be more urgent: Economic reform was crucial, and the "window of opportunity" to effect change narrow. Guiding that reform was a United States foreign policy and assistance priority. Who better to pull off this high-stakes international-relations and nation-building feat than the Harvard "Best and Brightest" and the up-and-coming Young Reformers?

Sachs put together an institutional vehicle for what would become the USAID-funded Harvard project. He "packaged HIID as an AID consultant," arranging for the decades-old Harvard Institute for International Development to receive U.S. foreign-aid monies to support the reform efforts, according to an administration insider. No one really knew how to reform economies out of central planning. It was something that had never been done on such a huge scale before. So the Harvard Institute's appeal to an insecure USAID is not hard to understand. USAID was depleted of in-house expertise after decades of contracting out and had no experience in Russia, yet was under an obligation to carry out congressional spending mandates. The consultants, on the other hand, besides carrying the Harvard imprimatur, emanated self-confidence. Their already robust access to resources and social-professional connections made them all the more attractive. And, crucially, they had ties to the forward-thinking Chubais associates.[6]

Enter Larry Summers

It is highly unlikely that the Chubais-Harvard partners could have pulled off what they did on the American side without their friend Lawrence (Larry) Summers being so well placed in the U.S. government. Earlier a Harvard faculty member, later president of Harvard (and still later, head of President Obama's National Economic Council), Summers became perfectly positioned to be the partners' patron and protector when Bill Clinton took office in 1993. Having served as chief economist of the World Bank from 1991 to 1993, Summers held the posts of undersecretary, deputy secretary, and, finally, secretary of the Treasury through much of the 1990s. At Treasury, Summers played a principal role in designing U.S. and international economic policies. Even as undersecretary for international affairs, Summers was directly responsible for designing Treasury's country-assistance strategies and for formulating and implementing international economic policies.[7]

Andrei Shleifer was a protégé of Summers and on intimate terms with him. Their relationship began in the 1970s with Summers as Shleifer's mentor and professor (Shleifer credits Summers with inspiring him to study economics), and continued in walks on the beach at Truro on Cape Cod, where their families vacationed together. In addition to being close friends, the two were coauthors, joint grant recipients, and faculty colleagues and allies at Harvard. Shleifer's wife, Nancy Zimmerman, a specialist in the high-finance area of global, fixed-income securities markets, was frequently consulted by Summers and David Lipton. (Lipton was Summers's deputy at Treasury responsible for eastern Europe and the former Soviet Union, and earlier Sachs's sidekick and vice president of Jeffrey D. Sachs and Associates.) Summers reportedly dubbed the quartet "our little world."[8]

In 1992 Shleifer became project director of the Harvard Institute's Russia project. When rivalry between Sachs and Shleifer ended their working relationship, to hear observers tell it, the Harvard project became Shleifer's baby, while Sachs continued his association with Gaidar. Meanwhile, in 1991 Hay had been named a senior legal adviser to Russia's new privatization agency, the State Property Committee, and the following year he became the Harvard Institute's on-site director in Moscow, and the institute's public face there. From here on, Shleifer and Hay were the key drivers of the project.[9]

The Harvard players' ready access to Summers and other top Harvard-connected officials in the Clinton administration eased open the aid spigot for themselves and their Russian associates. Step by step, with the support of Summers, the Harvard players acquired control of a crucial U.S. policy portfolio—economic reform aid to Russia—which was almost completely outsourced to a private entity, with that entity handed management authority over virtually the entire portfolio. This scenario was tailor-made to provide opportunities for coincidences of interest for the players who presided over it.

To bypass all the established practices and procedures, the Harvard players employed their flexian skills of personalizing bureaucracy and relaxing rules. With the help of Summers et al., the Harvard Institute sidestepped competitive bidding and was granted special permission that enabled it to legally engage in "the conduct of foreign relations and the determination of foreign policy," an "inherently governmental" function (as discussed in Chapter 4). The Institute largely circumvented the usual bidding process for aid contracts through waivers to competition supported by Summers and other benefactors in the administration, according to veteran U.S. government procurement officers and officials from the GAO. This was unusual, and so, also, was the justification given for the waivers: "foreign policy considerations." That is, the national security of the United States.[10]

In another departure from established practice at the time, management and oversight functions over the economic reform aid portfolio were substantially relinquished to the Harvard Institute, providing (legal) opportunities for its various roles to influence each other. One coincidence is that Harvard recommended U.S. policies while being itself a chief recipient of aid. From 1992 to 1997, the Harvard Institute helped steer and coordinate USAID's $300 million reform portfolio in grants to the Big Six accounting firms and other companies such as the public relations firm Burson-Marsteller, in addition to the $40 million the institute received directly. In another coincidence, the Harvard Institute "served in an oversight role for a substantial portion of the Russian assistance program," according to the GAO, helping supervise other contractors that were its competitors. And this oversight had teeth because governmental oversight didn't: In its customary management-speak, the GAO concluded that USAID's management and oversight over Harvard was "lax."[11]

While the United States had long contracted out foreign aid projects to consulting firms, NGOs, and universities, putting a project like Russian economic reform—one of the most important foreign policy initiatives of the era—in the hands of a private entity was a departure from accepted practice at the time. To hear U.S. government investigators tell it, both the contracting process and the wide influence and authority Harvard was afforded were highly irregular, if not unprecedented, in the annals of aid contracting. The Government Accountability Office (then called the General Accounting Office) was asked by Congress to investigate in 1996 after complaints to congressional offices had begun piling up. It found that the Harvard Institute had "substantial control of the U.S. assistance program."[12]

Treasury official Summers served as indispensable backer, indeed guarantor, of not only Shleifer and the Harvard team but also of Chubais and his clan, which he dubbed the "Dream Team."[13] Economic reform aid was personalized and used to boost Chubais's political position. Both the Chubais and Harvard players themselves and their U.S. sponsors made this explicit. In a book published by Shleifer, Boycko, and a coauthor at the height of the reform fervor, the authors baldly stated: "Aid can change the political equilibrium by explicitly helping free-market reformers to defeat their opponents. . . . Aid helps reform . . . because it helps the reformers in their political battles." They defined the goal of U.S. assistance to "alter the balance of power between reformers and their opponents" and confirmed that "United States assistance to the Russian privatization has shown how to do this effectively." Top USAID officials, too, made this clear. When I asked USAID Assistant Administrator Thomas Dine whether USAID helped propel Chubais into top positions in government, he admitted that it did. Richard Morningstar, the Department of State's top aid official, supported this politicization overtly. "When you're talking about a few hundred million dollars, you're not going to change the country, but you can provide targeted assistance to help Chubais," he told me.[14]

With such all-important boosts, the Chubais Clan acquired broad powers, ostensibly to carry out the complex tasks of economic reform, and controlled the ministries responsible for privatization and the economy. Its reach also extended to a host of other arenas: Chubais served as Yeltsin's chief of staff and headed his reelection campaign, even as he performed other political activities. At the same time he held sway in such domains as "relations with regions (including the organization of the gubernatorial elections) and what was called 'the propaganda work' in Soviet times," as Kryshtanovskaya observed. The Chubais team's comparative advantage in Russia was neither ideology nor even reform strategy but precisely its standing with and ability to attract resources from the West. As Kryshtanovskaya explained in 1997, "Chubais has what no other elite group has, which is the support of the top political quarters in the West, above all the USA, the World Bank and the IMF, and consequently, control over the money flow from the West to Russia. In this way, a small group of young educated reformers led by Anatoly Chubais turned [itself] into the most powerful elite clan of Russia in the past five years." Indeed, Chubais's cozy relations with Western power and resource brokers bolstered his clan's standing as Russia's chief representative to Western aid and financial institutions. Hay meanwhile served as a key link between the clan and the aid bureaucracy, while also assuming power over contractors, policies, and program specifics. He told me that his role included helping Chubais and others to prepare requests to the leadership of USAID that communicated what the Russian government wanted to do.[15] Project director Shleifer traveled frequently to Moscow.

Blessed by Summers and anointed in the quarters that mattered, the Chubais-Harvard partners presided not only over hundreds of millions of dollars from Western governments, but over Russian economic reform and crucial aspects of U.S.-Russia relations. Nonetheless, Shleifer and Hay showed up on the organizational charts as mere consultants for a private entity, with no one above them in the chain of command.

Guardians of the Gates

Far more loyal to each other than to any governmental, corporate, sponsoring, national, or international entity, the Chubais-Harvard players formed *an intricate spine*—the first defining feature of flex nets—and *personalized bureaucracy* to achieve their goals—the corresponding defining feature of flexians. The Chubais Clan's loyalty to the Harvard set and vice versa was of *strategic* value. Allegiance to the other amplified each set's potential influence and reach, helped solidify its image, and garnered for each set and the transnational team as a whole evermore legitimacy and advantages in Western policy and aid circles.

Transnational loyalty as a strategy entailed two essential components. First, the Chubais associates and the Harvard consultants each shared their own unique access to information, resources, and contacts with their counterparts. For instance, members of the intertwined Chubais-Harvard network appointed each other to visible binational posts in economic, energy, and high-tech areas. They arranged for each other to be well represented on the high-level Gore-Chernomyrdin Commission (the binational body created in 1993 and chaired by vice presidents in the Clinton and Yeltsin administrations), which helped to facilitate cooperation on U.S.-Russian oil deals and the Mir Space Station, among other issues. The Commission's Capital Markets Forum, established to "play a key advisory role to the Russian government," according to the SEC, was chaired by Chubais and Vasiliev on the Russian side and, on the American side, by the SEC's Arthur Levitt Jr. and Treasury Secretary Robert Rubin. Summers, then deputy treasury secretary, exalted the Forum's mission, "assisting Russia in the development of its capital markets," as "a top priority" of the department. Shleifer was named special coordinator of the forum's four working groups and the only representative to all of them. Vasiliev appointed Elizabeth Hebert, Hay's girlfriend (now wife) and head of her own financial company, to serve on at least one of these groups. Others represented on the groups were CEOs from Salomon Brothers, Merrill Lynch, and other powerful American-based investment houses.[16]

The second essential component of the strategy was that the transnational players, in addition to sharing information and resources with their opposite numbers, kept a lock on their influence. They did this by serving as each other's gatekeepers with their own countrymen and bureaucracies, and edging out potential competitors. The Chubais Clan was the Harvard team's avenue to Russia, crucial to its clout and contacts with the Russian government. In turn, the Harvard team was the clan's conduit to the eyes and ears of U.S. policymakers. For instance, Harvard's Hay arranged entrée to Russian officials for U.S. officials, even those as important as the USAID director in Moscow, Jim Norris, who oversaw its Russia operations from 1992 to 1995, during the height of the reform period.[17]

With loyalty and gatekeeping as core practices, the Chubais-Harvard partners had found a recipe for their own rise to influence.

Branding Conviction

The Chubais Clan and their Harvard brethren also had in common an almost zealous devotion to radical and rapid economic reform and a commitment to seeing themselves emerge as central players in Russia's reform processes. This *shared conviction and action*—the Chubais-Harvard partners' common view of the world and of their role in it, the second feature of flex nets—eased their move forward in a self-propelling team. Their partnership crystallized around the privatization effort in 1991 and 1992, when Russian economic reform activities were centralized in the State Property Committee, the primary headquarters of privatization activities in those early days. Denationalization or privatization of the nation's wealth and state-owned enterprises was their signature belief, goal, and practical project.

Presented in the West as a fight between enlightened Reformers trying to move the economy forward through privatization, and the retrograde Luddites who opposed them, this story misrepresented the facts. The idea or goal of privatization was not controversial, even among the communists. In the summer of 1991, shortly after Yeltsin became the elected president of the new Russia, the Russian Supreme Soviet, a communist body, passed two laws laying the groundwork for privatization. Opposition to privatization was rooted not in the idea itself but in the *particular* privatization program that was implemented, the opaque way in which it was put into place, and the use of executive authority to bypass the parliament. The 1991 legislation specified personal privatization accounts as the vehicle of privatization that would prevent corruption and create a degree of equality in the process of denationalization. But during a parliamentary recess in August 1992, Chubais quietly and without public discussion pushed through a decree (using Yeltsin's emergency powers) that enacted an entirely different scheme, one in which "vouchers" would be distributed among citizens. The Harvard partners participated in this endeavor and mobilized multiple sponsors for their work. Sachs's company reported to one of its sponsors, "The [Sachs] team has had an extensive interaction with the [Russian] State Committee on Privatization and has helped in the design of the mass privatization program." The documents boast that "Professor Sachs, Dr. [David] Lipton and Professor Shleifer have worked with Deputy Prime Minister Chubais and the staff of the Russian State Committee on Privatization." Shleifer, in particular, "played a central role in the formulation of the Russian privatization program."[18]

As the head of the State Property Committee (beginning in 1991), Chubais drew up plans to privatize thousands of state enterprises. The Chubais-Harvard team not only designed but also coordinated the signature mass-voucher privatization program, launched in November 1992, in which citizens were granted certificates or vouchers that they could use either to acquire shares in state-owned companies or to sell for cash. Harvard's Shleifer and Chubais's Boycko describe themselves as "members of the team that put it [privatization] together." USAID, for its part, spent $58 million to underwrite privatization, including its design, implementation, and promotion via public relations firms Sawyer Miller and Burson-Marsteller.[19]

As the Chubais-Harvard players went about their work, they had at their fingertips inside information that was difficult to obtain independently. Their success depended on their ability to get, guard, and craft information for public consumption—in short, to *privatize information*, while also *branding (their) conviction*—the second defining feature of flexians. They could use the information for purposes that were both difficult to detect and less than in the public interest, while controlling the message to keep their game going. They were the near-exclusive guardians of the information. And they had virtually no incentives to share it.

Potemkin Privatization

The players' success depended on promoting their branded conviction that they were the only legitimate reformers and that their reforms were transforming Russia for the good. But without independent information, how could the public know what they were actually doing? To ensure that their claims and brand would be the most credible, the Chubais and Harvard players each burnished the reputations of their counterparts in their own national and international circles. In Russia, the Chubais Clan promoted the Harvard advisers as the best foreign economic experts. In the United States, the Harvard group touted Chubais as the voice of Russia, and it helped advertise the Chubais team as the Young Reformers. It is no coincidence, then, that the Western media built up the clan's mystique and overlooked other qualified and reform-minded players in Russia. The mainstream American media, having bought into the myth of the Young Reformers and the Harvard Best and Brightest, exhibited little curiosity about the reality on the ground.

But from the point of view of the Russian public, away from whom information had been privatized, the reform was a fiasco. Privatization had been touted as a way that citizens would become property owners and shareholders in the economy. (Yeltsin's rallying cry was "We need millions of owners, not a few millionaires.") But the program that Chubais implemented fostered the concentration of vouchers and property in a few hands (through unregulated voucher investment funds, for instance); managers retained control over most industries and investors wound up owning very little. The outcome rendered privatization "a de facto fraud," as one economist put it, and the parliamentary committee that had judged the Chubais scheme to "offer fertile ground for criminal activity" was proven right. Making matters worse was the privatization to end all privatizations: the Chubais-approved "loans for shares" scheme, involvement in which depended entirely on access to private information and informal dealing. Masterminded in 1995 by Chubais associate Vladimir Potanin, the oligarch and one-time deputy prime minister for economic affairs, the scheme transferred control of many of Russia's prime assets for token sums to seven preselected bank chiefs. These quintessential insider deals crystallized the ascendancy of a breed of oligarchs, who would fundamentally configure the nation's politics, economics, and society for years to come, and further intertwined state and private authority and resources.[20]

All told, privatization encouraged looting, asset stripping, and moving money into Western bank accounts and offshore havens. E. Wayne Merry, who had a bird's-eye view of the process as chief political analyst at the U.S. Embassy in Moscow, later observed: "We created a virtual open shop for thievery at a national level and for capital flight in terms of hundreds of billions of dollars, and the raping of natural resources."[21] Russians, struggling to survive severe economic hardship,[22] dubbed privatization "the great grab," for its confiscation rather than creation of wealth. While privatization may have signaled growth to Westerners, to Russians it simply meant that others had the money—and weren't sharing it. Even Yeltsin, with his popularity severely waning as he stood for reelection in 1996, recognized that Russians were right to blame Chubais for the personal losses they had incurred and the fire sale of state enterprises, saying that "[Chubais] sold off big industry for next to nothing; we cannot forgive this."[23]

Despite the meltdown associated with privatization, "reform" continued as the clarion call of the Chubais-Harvard players. The myth of the Reformers prevailed in the eyes of U.S. officials and opinion makers. In 1997 *The Economist* described Chubais as "the antithesis of the hatchet-faced apparatchik" and predicted he would be president of Russia by 2010. Chubais flourished as the quintessential enlightened mastermind of the nation's economic transition.[24]

Personalizing Reform

The Harvard Institute's portfolio of tricks in Russia encompassed not only privatization but also legal reform, capital markets, and the development of a Russian securities and exchange commission. Many of these endeavors depended on changes in law, public administration, or mindsets, and required working with the full spectrum of legislative and market participants, not with just one preapproved group or clan. But, to the detriment of true reform, *personalizing bureaucracy* and *privatizing information*—essential arrows in the quiver of the Chubais-Harvard partners' exclusionary modus operandi—pervaded these reform arenas as well. The Chubais-Harvard players sometimes not only failed to design programs that required broad-based stakeholder participation and support, but also blocked the successful implementation of those that did.

This ranged from the petty, as when the Harvard players declined to work with Stanford University and then managed to maneuver an award from USAID for the same project, to the far more consequential, as when they obstructed reform efforts that originated from outside their approved circle. For instance, when the Chubais-Harvard players failed to receive as many USAID funds as they sought, they blocked legal reform activities in title registration and mortgages—programs that were launched by agencies of the Russian government, according to interviews with USAID-paid consultants and GAO officials. As GAO's lead investigator looking into the Harvard project told me, the Harvard people wanted "to keep power within their own structure." This compulsion put the players at cross purposes with their own, and the U.S. government's, purported aim of fostering markets.[25]

Excluding other players often did not serve the cause of true market reform, which would mean including—or at least not excluding—people who just wanted to be participants in Russia's market system in the making. A case in point is USAID's showcase effort to reform Russia's tax system and to establish clearing and settlement organizations (CSOs), an essential ingredient in a sophisticated financial system. Those efforts failed primarily because they were put largely into the hands of the Chubais-Harvard group, which declined to work with other market participants. In Moscow, for example, many Russian brokers were excluded from the process and declined to use the CSO. The GAO called the CSO effort "disappointing."[26]

Personalizing Resources

All around them, people were on the take. The Chubais-Harvard players had enormously lucrative opportunities—the spoils of an unraveling resource-rich state—right under their noses. And they had near-exclusive access to insider information in venues where some of these spoils could be found. They were playing on a new field in which their potential monitors often lacked the information they had, let alone the means to hold them accountable. They could use the information in ways unbeknownst to their sponsors and to the nations that they, when performing official roles, purported to serve. As gatekeepers of access, they could engage in a coincidence of interests—structuring overlapping or ambiguous roles for themselves—and serve their own goals. They could cover it all up by branding their activities as high-minded reform, for how would we know better?

It is precisely the Harvard players' hold on privileged information and their use of it for personal gain in Russian markets that led them into legal trouble and, allegedly, to open themselves to classic conflicts of interest. In 1997 the U.S. Justice Department began investigating the Harvard project after complaints circulating among on-the-scene consultants and in the U.S. aid and diplomatic community in Moscow came to the attention of the new Moscow USAID director. One of the U.S.-funded assignments of the Harvard advisers was to help create the regulatory infrastructure in the image of Western institutions such as the U.S. Securities and Exchange Commission, one of the functions of which is to detect and prosecute illegal insider trading. But at the same time the advisers were supposedly creating this infrastructure, they invested in the lucrative securities market; equities, aluminum, oil, and other companies (including Gazprom); real estate; and mutual funds.[27] These areas "were within the scope of their [Harvard's] economic and legal advice on behalf of USAID," according to the U.S. Department of Justice, which brought a $120 million lawsuit against Harvard University, Shleifer, Hay, and their wives (later dismissed from the case) in 2000, following a multiyear investigation into alleged wrongdoing. Justice concluded, "Harvard's actions, instead of fulfilling their intended purpose of fostering trust and openness in the nascent mutual fund market, in fact involved exactly the type of favoritism and perceived and actual barriers to entry and success that the United States was spending hundreds of millions of dollars to dispel."[28]

The same contradiction between supposed goals of reforms and other goals the players pursued lies at the heart of a suit brought against Shleifer, Hay, and Harvard University by an American mutual funds firm working in Russia. When the company filed suit in fall 2000, Harvard spokesman Joe Wrinn called its claims baseless. Two years later, however, Harvard and its two codefendants quietly settled with the company, agreeing to a payment but denying any misconduct.[29]

Through all this, the Chubais-Harvard players were backed by an incurious, and often complicit, American mainstream media. As Russia scholar Stephen F. Cohen observed: "Most journalists writing for influential American newspapers and news magazines believed in the Clinton administration's crusade to remake post-Communist Russia." Partly as a result, the Chubais-Harvard players had little trouble spreading their own version of reality in the West. For example, as the unpopular Yeltsin sought reelection after the Communists won the parliamentary election in late 1995, fears of a Communist comeback were stoked to justify privatization at all costs—however inequitable, unpopular, or undemocratic. The Reformers were hailed as heroes. Shleifer, Boycko, and Robert Vishny (Shleifer's business partner and a professor of economics at the University of Chicago who worked with the Chubais-Harvard team), pushed this happy little story in their book *Privatizing Russia*. This volume (funded by the Harvard Institute) was found on the desks of many USAID officials. As they told it, a "large class of owners" had been "created"—a claim that was patently untrue.[30]

American media and opinion-setters consumed the Chubais-Harvard story. Many U.S. officials also drank the Kool-Aid peddled by Harvard's reputedly brilliant technical specialists now producing simplistic, rosy narratives. As late as 1997, when the U.S. Justice Department began investigating the Harvard project, the response of USAID officials was telling. "We had even more than usual confidence in them [the Harvard advisers]," said USAID Deputy Administrator Donald Pressley. As one U.S. investigator confided:

"The [Clinton administration's] excuse [for any alleged impropriety] always was: those [Harvard] guys, we need them; they're the experts." The players did everything in their power to keep their own dominance and influence intact (as well as that of their Chubais counterparts), investigative attention at bay, and government officials, policymakers, and the mainstream media largely swallowing the prevailing myths.[31]

Strategic Legerdemain

The game of *juggling roles and representations*—the third defining flexian feature—helped the players build and reinforce these myths, not only with the media, but with governments and international institutions. Of course, such juggling was facilitated by the lack of information independent of the players. With information in the possession of the most involved players, and with little opportunity for independent verification until after the fact, if at all, their accounts could easily be taken at face value. This, of course, enhanced the players' influence and authority, while demanding little accountability.

For the Chubais-Harvard players to maintain their leading positions and squelch potential opposition, they had to promote the myths with the media that mattered. Anders Åslund was one of their prominent storytellers. A former Swedish envoy to Russia whose connections to Chubais and associates went back to the late 1980s, Åslund worked with Sachs and Gaidar and served as a member of the boards of multiple Chubais-Harvard-run, foreign-aid-sponsored organizations. Those are but a few of his many links to the players. He was intimately involved on many sides and flexed his various roles to suit the situation. To name four: Chubais's personal (unofficial) envoy (as he was understood to be by some Russian officials in Washington); a "private" citizen of Sweden who played a leading role in Swedish policy and aid toward Russia; a participant in high-level meetings at the U.S. Treasury and State Departments about U.S. and IMF policies; and a person engaged in business in Russia (and Ukraine, where he also operated). (While Åslund denies business activity in Russia, he had "significant" investments there, according to the Russian Interior Ministry's Department of Organized Crime.) Yet, when writing for publication, Åslund always mentioned only a fifth role—that of a (presumably independent) analyst affiliated with Washington think tanks.

(Flexians, of course, adopt the most prestigious and neutral of their various roles when in the public eye.) Writing frequently for the *Washington Post*, London's *Financial Times*, *Foreign Affairs*, and other influential publications, Åslund was also among the most quoted analysts of the Russian economy by Western journalists. While presenting himself as a detached think-tanker, Åslund steadfastly promoted Chubais and the Reformers. But as their (unofficial) envoy, he can hardly be regarded as a disinterested analyst.[32]

Åslund was by no means alone. His Chubais-Harvard teammates were equally adept at presenting the most appropriate of their roles to meet any given situation. To best serve their own objectives (though not necessarily those of the nations and efforts they supposedly represented), they donned all manner of government, political, business, NGO, and university hats, performing overlapping, shifting, or ambiguous roles to achieve their goals. The Chubais-Harvard players distinguished themselves, at least in the recent history of developed states, by their readiness and ability to exchange roles—even to the extent of representing a different nation from their own. Key players switched the side they represented back and forth depending upon their purposes. Such activity is not wholly new. But it can achieve more in today's world, when "nonstate" actors standing in for states, and with exclusive access to official information, brand their activities as they like for an unsuspecting audience.[33]

Take Jonathan Hay. In addition to being Harvard's chief representative in Russia, with management authority over other U.S.-funded contractors, Hay was appointed by members of the Chubais Clan to, in essence, *be* a Russian. According to documents I obtained from officials of the Chamber of Accounts (Russia's rough equivalent of the Government Accountability Office), Hay was given signature authority, empowering him to approve or veto some privatization decisions of the Russian state. Thus did Hay, an American citizen and consultant to a private entity, represent the Russian state.[34]

In roles that overlapped and blurred, Hay represented Russia, the United States, his girlfriend Elizabeth Hebert's company, and the business interests of himself and his associates. He could play these roles interchangeably or simultaneously, the sum of all of them becoming greater than any one by itself. He became, in effect, his own institution. No wonder higher-status Americans and Brits, whose titles and track records were weightier than Hay's, deferred to him.

Such juggling is not inherently bad or unethical. It does, however, illustrate why flexians are so difficult to hold to account. For instance, when asked by U.S. authorities to explain his privatization or aid directives, Hay could legitimately argue that he had made those decisions as a Russian, not an American. His multiple roles afforded him an "out"—or at least wiggle room. For he could always claim to have been playing another role. While Hay's multiple roles could be rationalized as efficient, they can hardly be judged to be immutably accountable to organizations, funders, or countries, let alone reflect clarity of loyalty, except, notably, to his fellow players.[35]

Power of the Collective

Players like Åslund and Hay, who were so very adept at juggling their roles and representations, greatly compound their advantages when they work as part of a flex net. This allows them to create *a resource pool,* the third feature of flex nets, from which they can draw. By aggregating their various roles and financial resources, such players gain collective effectiveness.

The Chubais-Harvard players engaged each other in a variety of venues, keeping each other apprised of valuable information, and making deals on behalf of each others' spouses and associates. They became evermore intertwined. Take, for instance, just two individuals, Hay and Vasiliev. In addition to their ties to each other via the State Property Committee, the Russian Privatization Center, and the Federal Securities Committee (as detailed earlier), they enlisted each other in transactions to further their own purposes. For instance, Vasiliev fixed several matters for Elizabeth Hebert, arranging for her participation in the Gore-Chernomyrdin Commission's Capital Markets Forum. More important, as head of the Federal Securities Commission, Vasiliev arranged for Hebert's company, a little-known mutual fund, to be the first licensed fund in Russia—ahead of Credit Suisse First Boston (now Credit Suisse) and Pioneer First Voucher, both high-powered investment firms. This decision displeased the much larger and more established financial institutions. Vasiliev even put Hebert's company in charge of an important Russian government fund (financed by the World Bank) that was set up to compensate victims of pyramid schemes that had defrauded many citizens. Vasiliev's decision was taken not only without a competitive tender, it further disadvantaged the already disadvantaged victims.[36]

CHUBAIS-HARVARD PLAYERS
Multiple Roles of Two Key Actors
(Early 1990s)

Gore-Chernomyrdin
Commission

Chairman

appointment

State Property
Committee*

Legal
Adviser

Deputy
Chairman

Elizabeth
Hebert

Jonathan
Hay

Dmitry
Vasiliev

Board
Member

Deputy
Chairman

Mutual
Fund

Institute
for
Law-Based
Economy

Russian
Privatization Center

Deputy
Chairman
&
Executive
Director

funding

licensing

Federal
Securities Commission**

Copyright © Irina Kuzes

 * The Russian acronym is the GKI.
** The Federal Securities Commission is also known by Americans as the "Russian SEC."

This account of Hay's and Vasiliev's roles (illustrated above) conveys the connectedness of just *two* players. Imagining up to a dozen players—all strategically placed and interlinked like these—gives a glimpse of how the Chubais-Harvard flex net was afforded wide-ranging influence by pooling roles. The greater the positioning in roles that matter and the more the potential for the roles to influence each other when the players enact them, the more influence the players can wield.

In pooling roles, the Chubais-Harvard players also spun themselves through what I call a "collective revolving door" to keep the right people in the right positions to ensure continuity of goals—and to evade culpability. The players appear to have carefully coordinated their roles as they placed themselves in government and nongovernmental entities for maximum influence. The Chubais Clan moved its members around as they fielded accusations of corruption. Take the State Property Committee, headed by a succession of Clan members, including Chubais himself, Maxim Boycko, and Alfred Kokh. In 1997 Kokh was fired as head of the committee after it hit the press that he had accepted a $100,000 payment from a company that had received preferential treatment in a privatization scheme. Kokh was also charged with embezzlement of state property; the case was closed after Yeltsin granted him amnesty. The once U.S.-underwritten Kokh was denied entry to the United States in December 1999, though later he was allowed in. Boycko took Kokh's place, only to be fired himself, also for accepting money for a privatization favor. The collective revolving door enabled the players to maintain a façade of respectability while retaining power.[37]

This juggling of roles allowed the players to weave an economic base that afforded them independence. In addition to the aid-sponsored organizations and the hundreds of millions of aid dollars that the Chubais-Harvard partners managed, Chubais, with the involvement of Boycko and Kokh, set up several "foundations" with names like the Center for the Protection of Private Property and the Civil Society Foundation. While these entities were not much more than money-moving operations, and there is little to suggest that they played a role in policy, they bolstered the base of Chubais et al.[38]

A flex net pools resources and positions players to expand its capacity for influence. When its players represent more than one country and can make decisions on behalf of one or another country, as did the Chubais-Harvard partners, the potential for influence without accountability is more easily achieved. These players' ability to claim that they were making decisions on behalf of either nation, while in fact serving their transnational flex net, bolstered their influence and facility to serve their own agendas.[39]

Institutionalized Ambiguity

The Chubais-Harvard players accomplished many of their goals through organizations that they set up and ran, ostensibly to carry out economic reform. These "flex organizations" (not to be confused with an informal flex net) help

a flex net, whose members empower them, to amass information and resources, and to wield influence beyond accountability. The organizations not
only harbor individuals whose multiple roles overlap and may be ambiguous;
as entities, they are themselves ambiguous, neither clearly official nor private,
but exhibiting features of both.[40]

An archetypal flex organization was the donors' flagship, the Russian Privatization Center, underwritten by a panoply of government and private
sources, from the international financial institutions and the European Union
to the United States, Germany, Japan, and the United Kingdom. Its work included policymaking on major macroeconomic issues, as well as negotiating
loans with international financial institutions. Under its umbrella was a network of "local privatization centers" charged with developing restructuring
plans for enterprises and advising local governments on policy questions.[41]

Was the Center a state or a private entity? Legally, it was a nonprofit NGO
set up by the Harvard Corporation, the university's board of directors. (Center documents state that Harvard University was both a "founder" and "Full
Member of the Center"—in fact, the "highest governing party of the Center.")
But perhaps it was a state entity, for the Center was mandated by Yeltsin's
presidential decree, and its U.S. sponsors (notably USAID) sometimes treated
it as a government agency. USAID's Tom Dine told me that he thought his
agency saw the Center as a government organization and that Maxim Boycko,
its longtime CEO, was a "government employee." The international financial
institutions, too, treated the Center as a government agency, negotiating with
and lending it hundreds of millions of dollars, including from the World Bank
($59 million) and the European Bank for Reconstruction and Development
($43 million). A World Bank official told me that "we [the Bank] didn't give
[the loan] to [the Center] as a private organization but as an agent for the government of Russia . . . the government of Russia is responsible for paying it
back." Indeed, funding a nongovernmental entity is unusual for the bank,
which typically negotiates with governments.[42]

But while the Center seemed to have the rights of a government entity (in
the eyes of some institutions), did it have the responsibilities of one? And
while a slew of outside funders were underwriting the Center because it functioned as a state body, another slew of donors underwrote the Center for the
opposite reason: It was an NGO. The Center received hundreds of millions of

dollars from Western foundations and governments, many of which support NGOs because they regard them as building blocks of "civil society." The Center's flex quality helped it attract diverse funding. For the donors, it was a one-stop shop.

While the standing of the Center seesawed and was ambiguous, just who had influence wasn't: Chubais served as chairman of the board of directors; Vasiliev, deputy chairman; Shleifer, Hay, and Åslund, members of the board; and Boycko, CEO. Members of the clan appointed one another to serve in the founding, governing, and management structure of the Center. During the height of the reform period it was the epicenter of much policy action and implementation, powered by the Chubais-Harvard net.[43]

Flex organizations are also one-stop shops for the players themselves, providing convenient bases from which players can enact their less-than-official activities, often involving money. For instance, Hay was the subject of a civil suit under U.S. racketeering laws alleging that he used the Institute for Law-Based Economy (the USAID- and World Bank–created and funded flex organization run by the Chubais-Harvard team, and Hay specifically) to engage in fraud and money laundering involving a Russian bank. And how would anyone know this? Only because the allegedly defrauded party filed a lawsuit.[44]

In part because their participants are so effective at personalizing bureaucracy and privatizing information, flex organizations themselves have little power or influence independent of their flex net. In fact, if members depart, they take their capacities with them. It is not an institution that is left behind, but an empty shell. This is but one reason why flex organizations must not be confused with static hybrids like the United Kingdom's quangos or the United States' Fannie Mae or Freddie Mac.

Supplanting the State

The Chubais-Harvard players achieved their aims by creating their own methods and vehicles (like flex organizations), to bypass or override official ones—or to simply stand in for the state. They also operated through presidential decree. These means undermined bureaucracy's role in policymaking and implementation and helped the players *relax rules* at the interstices of official and private institutions—the fourth defining feature of flexians.

Flex organizations do more than enable their players to worm out of accountability through their might-be-state, might-be-private status; they supplant the state. The private Russian Privatization Center, for instance, had at its disposal sensitive information, "state" funds (supplied by international financial institutions), and other privileges of a state body, but without the accountability of one. Tellingly, this ostensible NGO was put in charge of the postprivatization restructuring of enterprises. Such a task would be a major responsibility of a denationalizing country, yet no government agency was charged with this mission. Through its network of satellite offices strategically placed around the country, the Center collected sensitive business and political information. It acquired more access to inside information about privatized companies and regional economic and political goings-on than did any governmental entity (except possibly state security bodies) or the relevant parliamentary committee. At the same time, the Chubais associates had their own political agendas for gathering such information, according to aid-paid consultants I talked with who helped set up and man the satellite offices. The local (Russian) directors of these offices were handpicked by Boycko, and, as one consultant remarked, "they did what Maxim wanted."[45]

The Center had the rights but not the responsibility of the government in still other ways. The loans it accepted from the international financial institutions were not ratified by the democratically elected parliament; neither the parliament nor the government had decision-making authority or control over the ways Center monies were spent. Yet the government (read: taxpayers) was responsible for paying them back. As a Russian representative to an international financial institution observed, "The same people who approve the loans use the money."[46]

The Center not only bypassed parliament, but also the State Property Committee during the brief period (November 1994 to January 1995) when it was not run by a Chubais Clan member. According to documents I obtained from Russia's Chamber of Accounts, the nongovernmental Center wielded more influence over certain privatization matters than did the State Property Committee, the government agency responsible for privatization. The Center, then, had the best of each world: the authority of government, but without responsibility to parliament or government auditors.[47]

In supplanting the state, yet beyond its accountability, flex nets diminish checks and balances through still another means: operating through executive authority. Eschewing legislative and judicial bodies that might encumber or oppose their activities, the Chubais-Harvard players realized many of their goals through top-down decisions in the executive branch. They organized the issuance of many presidential decrees—their chief strategy for legal reform. Hay and his associates themselves drafted decrees for President Yeltsin's signature. According to a consultant who worked with the Harvard team and shared an office with Hay during the period of intense reform from 1992 to 1996, most of the legislation that was pushed by Yeltsin and Chubais was written by Hay. As the consultant explained it, "Jonathan bypassed the whole system. . . . Jonathan would draft a law or decree, [Chubais Clan member Albert] Sokin, a pretty good lawyer, would Russify it, and [then Jonathan] would just messenger it over to Chubais. If he [Chubais] liked it, he walked it down the hall to Yeltsin [for signature]."[48]

Achieving legal change by decree was a departure from Harvard's contract with the U.S. government, which specified passing laws through the legislature. This modus operandi further diverged from stated U.S. policy regarding establishing democratic and legal institutions and consolidating Russian democracy, as well as voices in the aid community who supported those goals. USAID's Washington Office of Democracy Assistance for Russia had an agenda and a sensibility not so easily seduced by the rapid-privatization-at-all-costs mentality (while neglecting the creation of a legal and regulatory backbone) of the USAID economic reform people. That office opposed the use of decrees, expressing that they were inconsistent with democratic purposes. But these voices seemed not to stand a chance. With the Harvard flexians personalizing bureaucracy and with Summers as their sponsor, the officials who prevailed were those who turned a blind eye as the Chubais-Harvard partners made end-runs around the parliament, reorganized official bodies for their own ends, and engaged in other not-so-democratic processes.[49]

Through these activities, the Chubais-Harvard players helped to create in Russia *a hybrid habitat*—the fourth, corresponding feature of flex nets. They contributed to the development of the clan system and the "clan-state" in the 1990s. With the clan monopolizing foreign aid and running segments of government related to the economy, competing clans had equivalent ties with other segments of government such as the "power ministries" (the ministries of defense and internal affairs, and the security services) or the energy ministry (of which the energy giant Gazprom is a part). Collectively, these clans made up the clan-state, in which there is little separation of the clan—with its own political and economic agendas—from the state: The same people with the same agenda undertaking the same activities constitute the clan and the relevant state authorities. The clan-state is democracy-challenged: It lacks visibility, accountability, and means of representation for those under its control. The only real counter to a clan's influence comes from a competitor clan, as when one clan sics law enforcement and prosecutorial authorities on a rival one.[50]

That, in Russia, the Chubais-Harvard players helped forge the working rules of the emerging order may not be so very surprising amid the political, legal, administrative, economic, and societal flux that accompanied the undoing of an authoritarian system. The players' ability to relax rules and fashion a hybrid habitat was obviously extensive. But the Harvard players also did so in the United States. And while they did so to much less wholesale effect, what they achieved was a portent of things to come. The amounts let to the Harvard Institute in uncompeted awards may today seem trivial (think the Iraq war). But the model they crafted broke new ground, both in structural terms: a private organization directing a momentous policy arena and carrying out inherently governmental functions, while managing itself and its competitors; and in operational ones: private players monopolizing official information, policy, and implementation and thereby fashioning new institutional forms of power and influence, largely invisible and scarcely accountable to citizens.

More Transnational Togetherness

Noting who stood (and stands) up to defend the Chubais and Harvard players in response to their public troubles offers opportunities to glimpse the larger network that helped sponsor and also benefited from the players' activities. Media accounts of the reform efforts gone bad and of Harvard advisers run amok or "gone native"—the way the tale was told on the few occasions when it did attract mainstream press attention—focused on corruption, greed, or a few bad apples who enriched themselves. This focus misses a crucial operational feature: the solidarity and self-propelling quality of the flex net, as well as the wider network that was invested in their success. The Harvard players required such a network through which to secure privileges and resources in the United States—and this network also had a stake in the players' semicloaked financial and business success in Russia.[51]

Clues into the interests of this wider network may be found in the fact that the endowment funds of two Ivy League universities, Harvard and Yale, gained access to valuable investments through networks inhabited by the Chubais-Harvard associates. Shleifer's wife, the currency trader and hedge fund manager Nancy Zimmerman, was front and center. She had worked in the 1980s for Robert Rubin at Goldman Sachs (also a sometime board member of the Harvard Management Company, which oversees Harvard University's investments) and remained close to him when he was secretary of the treasury and Larry Summers's boss (until Summers was himself promoted to the post).[52]

Zimmerman managed a portion of the Yale University endowment. Her investment company traded in short-term Russian government bonds (GKOs) and repatriated the profits to the United States beyond the allowable limits set by Russian law. Zimmerman was ideally placed to time these highly lucrative transactions because her husband, Shleifer, advised the Russian official making decisions regarding the government's backing of GKOs. Meanwhile, Harvard's endowment—the Harvard Management Company—benefited from some of the most valuable privatization deals, to which it received entrée through networks occupied by the Chubais-Harvard nexus. The deals were officially closed to foreign investors.[53]

The players' responses to allegations of "corruption" leveled against them illuminate the self-protecting quality of the network. There was plenty to do on both sides of the Atlantic. Summers shielded both Shleifer's job at Harvard and his reputation. When Summers became Harvard's president, he was even better positioned to protect Shleifer, and not surprisingly, Shleifer and Zimmerman lobbied for his appointment. As the legal proceedings of the government's lawsuit heated up, Summers is credited with keeping his friend's job intact. Summers did recuse himself from the school's managing of the case, but he asked the relevant dean to protect Shleifer.[54]

Summers was equally indispensable as a patron of Chubais et al. While corruption played differently in Russia than in the West, in the latter it was important for Chubais's continued good standing to explain away allegations. Members of the Chubais Clan—Summers's "Dream Team"—were consistently under investigation by Russian authorities. Documented reports abound, which the Chubais players do not deny, of their taking money in return for favors in the privatization process. In one incident, Chubais and several members of his clan each received $90,000 (or more) from a Swiss firm not normally engaged in publishing, but controlled by a company that had received privatization favors, explained after the fact as an advance for a book on the history of Russian privatization. Summers consistently led the charge not only to safeguard Chubais's reputation, but to keep him in power. While Yeltsin in 1996 had fired Chubais—in the midst of an uproar over privatization—from his post as first deputy prime minister (to which he had additionally been named in 1994), in March 1997, amid Western support and political maneuvering, Yeltsin catapulted Chubais back to the post of first deputy prime minister—and added the portfolio of minister of finance. Although again fired by Yeltsin in March 1998 along with the entire government of Prime Minister Viktor Chernomyrdin, Chubais was reappointed in June 1998 to be Yeltsin's special envoy in charge of Russia's relations with international lending institutions.[55]

In times of special crisis, Summers sought to ensure Chubais's continued top billing. When the issue of "Russian" corruption began to capture American headlines in 1998 and the Bank of New York money-laundering scandals hit the press in 1999, Treasury Secretary Summers rushed to the defense of Chubais and other key players. Chubais admitted to a newspaper that he had "conned" from the IMF a $4.8 billion loan installment in July 1998, the details of that deal having been worked out in Summers's home over brunch—a meeting that the *New York Times* deemed crucial to obtaining release of the funds. In testimony before the U.S. House of Representatives Committee on International Relations, for example, Summers stoutly defended Chubais and asked that Chubais's prepared statement (titled "I Didn't Lie")—be placed in the Congressional Record. Less than a year later, allegations began surfacing of the alleged involvement of Chubais and clan member Alfred Kokh, a one-time minister of the State Property Committee, in laundering billions of dollars through the Bank of New York and other Western banks.[56]

Whether or not Chubais lied, the protective network he and his clan enjoyed, together with their Harvard cohort, indisputably aided their ability to virtually determine American foreign policy in at least one crucial area of U.S.-Russia relations. At a time when the Russian people were suddenly freer than ever before, the players also did the same with Russian domestic economic policy and significant aspects of state building.

And who or what was capable of stopping them? The Chubais-Harvard partners were members of a flex net that was its own entity—to all intents and purposes, answerable to little outside itself.

Fruits of the Flex Net

The Chubais-Harvard players can be seen as employing an emergency modus operandi (personalizing bureaucracy, revising rules, privatizing information, and so on) in response to a onetime historical event that called for dramatic action. But as the aftermath of 9/11 in the United States has made clear, emergency measures have a way of becoming more permanent.

Just a few short years after these icons of enlightened social engineering set out to transform Russia, a lot had not gone quite as planned. As the era of reform came to a crashing close (made undeniable by the collapse of the Russian ruble in August 1998), Russia was far from a stable and prosperous democracy. The rapprochement that was supposed to usher in a new era seemed like a distant memory. While the American triumphalism—and Russian acquiescence—of the immediate post–Cold War period could not last forever, the fact that U.S.-sponsored "reform" left many Russians worse off materially than they had been under communism did not help America's standing. The United States lost the moral authority with which many Russians had earlier credited it. A clan-state was in evidence, with the reform strategy having helped birth it. Oligarchies—in which instant billionaires such as Boris Berezovsky and Mikhail Khodorkovsky acquired fortunes virtually overnight while much of the rest of the population was left impoverished— had been created through the privatizations and mass looting of the 1990s. Progress toward building the checks and balances and other institutions of a democratic state was difficult to detect. In short, the Russian order that the Chubais-Harvard players helped forge in the 1990s went in a direction that was decidedly other than the one that had been anticipated. While blame cannot be laid solely at the feet of Chubais and the Young Reformers and their Western underwriters (and while we can't know what other scenarios might have developed without their involvement), ample responsibility for what did happen is theirs.

Tellingly, Russia turned to more decisive leadership. In the next decade President Vladimir Putin set out to rein in the oligarchs, as well as those who opposed his rule. As he hobbled his adversaries, he entrusted control over gas, oil, and weapons reserves and industries to clans of industrial elites and former KGB functionaries. The form of governing introduced by Putin pro- duced a state with a democratic façade, but it is one lacking in genuine rep- resentative democracy.

Three paradoxes leap out from this experience: First, the reforms and the activities of the reformers who were supposed to usher in a democratic system actually hindered that development and facilitated the expansion of an unac- countable state. Second, while they were entrusted with creating a competitive market economy—complete with a legal and regulatory backbone—to replace the failed communist system, the "reformers" not only served as a powerful example of noncompetitive dealing within a closed circle, they facilitated the very opposite of their stated goal: a corrupt bureaucracy that virtually pre- cluded the development of a free market economy. Finally, they ended up as practitioners—and high-level ones—in the new authoritarian state.

Unflagging Flexians

What has become of the members of the Chubais-Harvard flex net who made such an impact in the 1990s? Generally, their fortunes have risen. The Young Reformers have become technocrats making money in an authoritarian state. Anatoly Chubais is the poster boy among them. From 1998 to 2008 he was chairman of Unified Energy Systems, Russia's electricity monopoly, a powerful post that placed him at the center of the nation's economic life. In 2008, President Dmitry Medvedev appointed Chubais head of the state-run Russian Corporation of Nanotechnologies, another powerful post. That same year J. P. Morgan Chase named him to the firm's International Council. For his part, Dmitry Vasiliev had been recruited a year earlier by J. P. Morgan to lead its Russian investment branch. Vasiliev landed there from a top job in Moscow's huge energy conglomerate—a position he had received thanks to Chubais.[57]

Not surprisingly, Chubais has earned a reputation for taking care of his friends—including not only Vasiliev, but Boycko and Kokh as well. Kokh has used his former status and continued closeness to Chubais for investments in the energy sector.

The American players in this story are similarly or better known today—and largely without negative overtones. Jeffrey Sachs has reinvented himself several times since his "shock therapy" days. Despite the claims made in his project documents regarding his personal involvement in Russian reforms, when they began to get less-than-favorable reviews in the West, Sachs quickly distanced himself from responsibility. As a journalist summed it up: "The economic collapse of Russia was, in his [Sachs's] calculation, the fault of the World Bank, the International Monetary Fund, the first Bush administration and the Clinton administration, and European governments for failing to deliver promised billions in aid." As a celebrity activist whose endeavors enlist movie stars and other "personalities," Sachs pursued an anti-AIDS campaign and later recast himself as an antipoverty expert. The latter effort, which he has pursued since 2002, now as head of Columbia University's Earth Institute, looks like old hat to this veteran observer of Sachs's modus operandi, replete with might-be-official, might-not-be-official self-presentations that characterized his activities in eastern Europe.[58]

The existing means of curbing the coincidences of interests and forms of power and influence forged by movers in the Harvard project, and Harvard University itself, seem largely impotent. Even exposure in the press proved of little effect. In the mid- to latter 1990s articles about the role of the U.S.-funded

Harvard advisers in Russia's economic reforms began to reveal their web of interconnections. But the Harvard players' maze of high-powered networks enfeebled the multiple investigations of their activities.[59]

And there has been no dearth of inquiries. The various governmental and business investigations into the handling of U.S. assistance for Russian economic reforms entrusted to Harvard began as early as 1996. Although the GAO report published that year went only so far as to call USAID's oversight over Harvard's Russia project "lax," its original draft report (a copy of which was given to me by GAO staff) was far more critical.[60]

The U.S. government tried to penalize the Harvard players for their purported conflicts of interest and alleged (mis)use of government monies, but it was slow to act. In 1997 the Justice Department embarked on its investigation, and later sued Shleifer, Hay, and Harvard University on the grounds that they had conspired to defraud the government. But it was eight years before the case culminated, and that was merely with a negotiated settlement. The 2005 settlement required the university to pay fines to the U.S. government of $26.5 million, Shleifer to pay $2 million, and Hay between $1 and $2 million. The lawsuit against the same players brought by the American mutual funds firm was settled out of court. The civil suit brought against Hay over an alleged fraud and money-laundering scheme was apparently not resolved in his favor, although it seemed to do him little harm. At least one other investigation was initiated, then suspended.[61]

While these probes were in process, Shleifer's star was steadily rising. He consulted as an anticorruption expert and testified before a congressional committee on the same topic. No mention was made that Shleifer himself was the target of a government investigation. Shleifer, again as an expert on corruption, also published articles in reputable journals. *Foreign Affairs* printed his piece on the supposed success of Russian "reforms"—without mentioning his role in crafting them. In 1999 he was awarded the American Economic Association's John Bates Clark Medal, a coveted prize for the top economist under forty, with Summers's fingerprints on the selection process. In 2003, the same association appointed him editor of its *Journal of Economic Perspectives*. Despite Harvard's having to pay a record settlement, largely because of Shleifer's activities, he has been (and remains) a full professor there.[62]

The U.S. government and its investigators proved no match for Harvard University and its powerful network. To name one example, under pressure from GAO lawyers, themselves under pressure from Harvard's lawyers, GAO staff were forced to dilute the strength of their report. Not only did Harvard do little to look into activities conducted in its name, but in 2001 the Harvard Corporation, with sole authority to hire and fire the Harvard president, tapped Summers to serve as president of the university, despite all the information on record about his entanglements. Only after Harvard settled the government lawsuit did Summers resign (in 2006) amid public relations troubles within and outside the university. In true flexian fashion, he landed well, as a university professor at Harvard, a part-time managing director of the investment and technology development firm D. E. Shaw & Co., and columnist for the *Financial Times*. He has since landed even more smoothly. While fallout from his unpopular performance as Harvard president may have kept him from being renamed treasury secretary and confirmed by Congress, he is now back in the saddle as a crucial economic adviser to President Obama. Not only did his Harvard and Russia track records not keep him from a White House post, his past advice and promotion of deregulation—which has come back to haunt the financial system of the United States, indeed the world—did not deter Obama from appointing him.[63]

Hay, for his part, was employed between 2002 and 2005 as an associate in the London office of Cleary Gottlieb, a law firm, and today works for a real estate development company in Ukraine. Unlike Chubais, Sachs, and Shleifer, Hay never had a big media or academic profile. But his legal troubles don't appear to have derailed his career.[64]

For both Shleifer and Hay, these troubles have amounted to little more than a slap on the wrist, albeit a costly one. Any damage to the reputation of Shleifer, the much better known of the two, seems to be inconsequential in the circles that matter. As Harry R. Lewis, professor and former dean at Harvard, opined in 2006, "Most of Shleifer's economist colleagues [have] gathered around him supportively. . . . In fact, no one seems ashamed of this affair at all."[65]

While Shleifer and Hay had to pay settlements and legal fees, it is too late for the Russian people, who, instead of wise guidance, got a corrupt, vastly inequitable system. Shleifer's defense in the Justice Department's lawsuit is emblematic of flexians' and flex nets' evasion of responsibility: Although U.S. prosecutors charged that his investments violated federal conflict-of-interest regulations, defense lawyers maintained that he was a "mere consultant," and thus not subject to these rules. Yet as director of the project, the buck stopped with him.

Harvard University, for its part, is not on record as having publicly apologized or publicly acknowledged responsibility, while paying millions of dollars in fees for legal settlement.

◊ ◊ ◊

THE GRAND PLANS never worked out, reform is dead, and even the idea of reform has been badly battered. But the new institutional forms blending official and private power that the players fashioned are alive and well.

To the extent that the Chubais-Harvard players were vulnerable to sanction from legal and media quarters, it was almost invariably due to their alleged conflicts of interest, not the coincidences of interest they structured for themselves as they fused official and private power. Yet it is precisely their coincidences of interest that afforded them vast power and influence, beyond the input of citizens and the reach of monitors. Today it seems that their coincidences of interest, and the new forms of governing that they escort, have ricocheted back to the United States.

CHAPTER SIX

The Commandeers

RICHARD PERLE, PAUL WOLFOWITZ, DOUGLAS FEITH. IT SEEMS THE world has moved on and left these neoconservatives—prime movers behind the war in Iraq—in the dust. The flex net that I call the Neocon core, a tight-knit dozen or so key players clustered around Richard Perle, are out of power and favor with the Obama administration. But in their longtime quest to re-make American foreign policy according to their own vision, they have put an indelible stamp on the shape of the Middle East. And in doing so, they have pioneered ways of engaging in governing and policy in the United States—forging new fusions of official and private power—that are far from the eye of publics and reach of government monitors, yet have gained a certain accept-ability. Their policy endeavors have not always met with success, but in their means of exercising power and influence, they have consistently been one step ahead of transformational global and American developments under way. That is why, even though they may be largely out of favor with the current administration, the story of their profound impact is such an important tale to tell. As one observer close to the Neocon core put it to me, "Where they were successful, they out bureau-cratted the bureaucracy."

A running example of the conduct of Perle, Wolfowitz, and Feith—their run-ins with government authorities over several decades, propensity to skirt bureaucracy and breach regulation, and skill in bailing each other out—provides a few of the clues to the reasons for their success.

In 1973 Richard Perle, then in his early thirties and a senior staff mem-ber to Senator Henry "Scoop" Jackson, a Democrat and cold warrior from

NEOCON CORE
Mutual Protection of Three Key Players Over Time

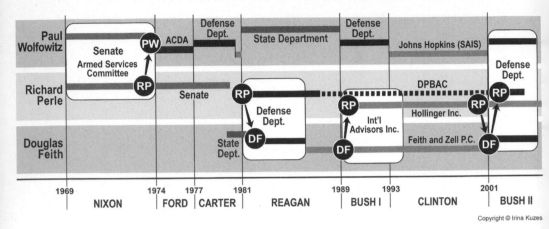

Copyright © Irina Kuzes

ACDA -- Arms Control and Disarmament Agency
DPBAC – Defense Policy Board Advisory Committee

Washington state and a member of the Senate Armed Services Committee, helped Wolfowitz, then an assistant professor at Yale, find employment in the Arms Control and Disarmament Agency (ACDA). Five years later, Wolfowitz was investigated for passing a classified document to an Israeli government official through a go-between, according to Stephen Green and other sources. Green is a retired journalist who has written for two decades about Israeli espionage in the United States, and in recent years has been interviewed multiple times by the FBI about long-ago activities of these and other members of the Neocon core.[1]

Also in 1978, still working with the Senate Armed Services Committee, Perle was caught in a security breach by CIA director Stansfield Turner, who urged that Senator Jackson fire him. Perle received a reprimand but was kept on staff, according to the *Washington Post*. In another instance, Perle was questioned by the FBI after a wiretap picked him up talking with an Israeli Embassy official about classified information (which he said he obtained from a National Security Council staff member).[2]

In 1982, as an assistant secretary for international security policy in President Reagan's defense department, Perle hired and later promoted Douglas Feith, who had come into the Jackson fold in 1975 when Perle enlisted Feith as an intern (he was Perle and Wolfowitz's junior by at least a decade). Perle promoted Feith after Feith had been fired from his post as a Middle East analyst at the National Security Council. Feith was fired, Stephen Green found, because he was the subject of an FBI inquiry into whether he had supplied classified material to an Israeli embassy official.[3]

After leaving the Pentagon in 1987, Perle became a highly paid consultant for a lobbying firm, International Advisers, Inc., that Feith established in 1989. By serving as a consultant only, Perle—who had supervised U.S. military assistance to Turkey while at Defense—was able to bypass federal regulations prohibiting anyone from representing a foreign government right after leaving American government employment.[4]

The mutual assistance among these three men continued into the new millennium. In 2001, Perle and Wolfowitz championed Feith for the position of undersecretary for policy in the Pentagon. In that post, Feith in turn selected Perle as chairman of the Defense Policy Board. (Perle resigned as chairman in March 2003, amid allegations of conflict of interest, and from the board altogether a year later.)[5]

Perle, Wolfowitz, and Feith have been under frequent investigation for alleged misuse of classified information for a quarter century. Stephen Green told me: "I was asked extraordinarily detailed questions about Paul Wolfowitz, Richard Perle, Douglas Feith, Michael Ledeen" and other members of the core group.[6] Ledeen is a Neocon core member long associated with those three.

For several decades, members of the Neocon core have honed their modus operandi as radicals in the vanguard: They have socially engineered into action their disdain for bureaucracy, distrust of official information, and disregard for government (and professional) expertise and rules—working from inside and out during presidential administrations from Gerald Ford to George W. Bush. They have done so to achieve their own higher goals. And although their foreign policy endeavors have not always met with success, the success they have enjoyed is because they practice what they preach: It is largely thanks to their skills at, say, personalizing policymaking and governing processes, marginalizing the role of bureaucratic procedures in them, and creating their own bodies of expertise and information to substitute for or override those of government. Thus members of the Neocon core have been agents of some of the systemic changes abetted by the four transformational developments—such as waning loyalty to bureaucratic and professional authority—and, through their activities, have helped some of them gain ground in the United States. And although these changes often nudge policy and governmental decisions further behind the scenes, they enjoy broad approval as forward-looking innovations, and are even embraced by reformers whose politics and ideologies could hardly be more different (and who see the Neocon players as bad guys).[7]

Let me walk you through highlights of the Neocon core's journey, its members' heartfelt causes and policy aims, and the ways and means they have honed to see them adopted.

Building the Neocon Core

To date, interest in and research on neoconservatives has been focused primarily on their history and thinking, or on their actions as onetime incidents of history. I set for myself the different task of describing the modus operandi of the tiny activist subset centered around Richard Perle.[8]

This "Neocon core" must not be confused with the much larger and far more amorphous array of leaders and followers of neoconservative philosophy. But it is crucial to understand the social and intellectual context in which this set of committed adherents arose. The roots of neoconservatism lie in 1930s New York with a small group of intellectuals of mostly east European background—Trotskyists who disagreed with the course of Soviet communism and later rejected socialist ideology completely. They spurned social liberalism, became passionately anticommunist in the 1950s, and disdained the 1960s counterculture. The movement's founding fathers include Irving Kristol, managing editor (from 1947 to 1952) of *Commentary*, the movement's flagship magazine, and Norman Podhoretz, editor in chief of the publication for thirty-five years (1960 to 1995) and now editor at large. Neoconservatism first arrived as a force on the American political scene in the late 1960s and early 1970s.[9]

While neoconservatives and neoconservative thought have been concerned with both domestic and foreign policy, the Neocon core, with Perle at the center, has devoted itself to foreign policy. Members of the core have been interlinked, some for more than three decades, through government, think-tank, business, and advocacy roles, as well as family ties. Journalist Jacob Heilbrunn writes in his book about neoconservative ideology and experience that "neoconservatism was turned into an actual movement by Irving Kristol and Norman Podhoretz. Even today, the neoconservative movement is best described as an extended family based largely on the informal social networks patiently forged by these two patriarchs." But the Neocon core did not arise full blown. How did members of this subset begin to team up?[10]

Connections made by them date back to the late 1960s. A key to many of the core's connections was Albert Wohlstetter, a major source of inspiration and a catalytic force for Perle and Wolfowitz. A mathematical logician by training, Wohlstetter held positions at the University of California and the University of Chicago, and became an influential defense strategist at RAND, the think tank that took its name from "research and development." Wohlstetter posited, as Jacob Heilbrunn outlines, "that there was no real distinction between defense and offense. He set up the doctrinal basis for justifying preventive war. The begetter of much neoconservative defense thought, Wohlstetter had a profound impact as a military theorist.[11]

Richard Perle met Wohlstetter through Wohlstetter's daughter, his high school classmate. Perle stayed in touch with Wohlstetter and, in 1969, became acquainted with Paul Wolfowitz through Wohlstetter. As Perle tells the story: "Albert Wohlstetter phoned me one day. I was still a graduate student at Princeton . . . and he said, could you come to Washington for a few days and interview some people and draft a report on the current debate shaping up in the Senate over ballistic missile defense, which was a hot issue. . . . And he said, I've asked somebody else to do this too, and maybe the two of you could work together. The someone else was Paul Wolfowitz. So Paul and I came to Washington as volunteers for a few days, to interview people, and one of the people we interviewed was Scoop Jackson and it was love at first sight. . . . I was there for eleven years."[12]

Jackson himself had been influenced by Wohlstetter. While a liberal on social issues, the intensely anti-Soviet Jackson supported a strong national defense; he was even labeled the "Senator from Boeing" by those who disapproved of his unrelenting support for weapons systems. During Perle's tenure with Jackson (until 1980), several other neoconservative figures—who would become members of the Neocon core—joined Jackson's staff: these included Elliott Abrams, Norman Podhoretz's stepson-in-law, who served as special counsel to Jackson (from 1975 to 1976); and Frank Gaffney, an aide to Jackson in the late 1970s on issues of defense and foreign policy.[13]

These neoconservative activists, and others, came into their own during the Reagan administration; the 1980s were their ideological heyday. Reagan's foreign and security policies were in sync with the Wohlstetter-Jackson mindset: American military superiority and, to a lesser extent, economic strength should unashamedly assert itself in the world. These young men now had the opportunity to put some of their ideas into action; their interconnectedness and network grew as they secured positions in the Pentagon and the Department of State.[14]

Perle was posted to the Pentagon as assistant secretary of defense for international security policy (from 1981 to 1987). Feith served as a special counsel to Perle from 1982 to 1986, and was later named deputy assistant secretary of defense for negotiations policy. Perle and Feith were joined in the Department of Defense by Frank Gaffney. After working under Perle for several years, Gaffney was named assistant secretary of defense for international security policy when Perle left the Reagan administration.[15]

At the State Department, Wolfowitz was appointed to its policy planning staff (and was its head from 1981 to 1982). Joining him at State were Elliott Abrams and Michael Ledeen. Abrams worked for Reagan in several positions. Ledeen, for his part, worked for both the State and Defense departments, as well as serving as a consultant to the National Security Council. Abrams and Ledeen would become important players in the Iran-Contra affair.

The Power of the Collective

Given the neoconservatives' Trotskyist heritage, albeit one generation removed (Perle and his age cohorts are part of the "second" or "younger" generation)—and their repudiation of that past—it is both fitting and not, I suppose, to think of the Neocon core as a collective. Despite their wholesale reversal, the core seems inspired, perhaps unconsciously, both by their collective ideology and the closeness of a Trotskyist cell. Accordingly, the core forms *an intricate spine*—an intertwined, exclusive, and self-protecting network—the first feature of flex nets. Neocon core member Meyrav Wurmser, who has organized seminal activities with Perle and Feith, put it thusly: "You have a story here about ideas, and love among people, and it's true and I'm not being cynical about it, it's real fundamental love and power because some of those ideas make policy and some of the people in the group are policy makers, and we function and we view ourselves as a group, and we will all stand for each other in defence of each other all the way."[16]

Having a leader helps such a group maintain its "love and power" and "defence of each other." Not unlike in a Russian clan, Perle has been the group's linchpin since the beginning. His centrality is widely recognized by both insiders and outsiders. Officials at the Israeli embassy in Washington even reportedly refer to this collection as the "Perle group." Perle has served as a mentor to Abrams, Feith, Ledeen, and Gaffney (among others), all of whom worked for Jackson. As Feith described him: "Richard for sure is a godfather. He would actively work to help anybody he had worked with and liked and admired and who he thought was useful to the overall cause of U.S. national security as he saw it." Perle is at the nexus of a plethora of efforts and seemingly always ahead of the game; I could well have written about him as an archetypal flexian in Chapter 1. Perle connects people, brokers deals—circumventing bureaucracy via informal contracts like a Russian blatmeister—and holds salons in his home to discuss issues about which he and his circle are passionate.[17]

To achieve their agendas, members of the Neocon core engage in complementary activities, in and outside of government, advocacy, and think-tank type organizations (many of which they helped set up), and they play multiple roles in relation to each other. As evidenced by Perle, Wolfowitz, and Feith's mutual-aid round robin, flex nets gain influence in part by the members' quietly boosting one another, promoting one another for influential positions, and covering for one another. And these three are but a sample of the larger Neocon core of roughly a dozen or so players, many (if not most) of whom are equally intertwined with other members, via long, multiple, and intense associations with one another. While working together to achieve a mutual agenda extends a flex net's capabilities, this coordination of effort is not a conspiracy. Unlike conspirators, who keep secret their activities (and, often, the very existence of their group and its purpose), members of a flex net are open about their acquaintanceships. Some of a flex net's activities are kept close to the chest, such as Perle, Wolfowitz, and Feith bailing each other out of trouble. Others, however, are not only in the open—standard policy-input efforts such as writing briefing papers or testifying before congressional sub-committees—they invite media attention and may even be crafted by public relations specialists. Witness the massive and concerted "information" effort conducted by the Neocon core and their associates, with crucial participation from certain columnists and reporters, that was essential in taking the United States to war in Iraq.

Pursuing mutual goals implies a division of labor; not everyone does the same thing. For instance, while Wolfowitz and Feith promoted the Iraq war from within government, Perle helped cultivate and propagate information that served the Neocon core cause from behind the scenes and appeared in the media as an expert. He did this first as a member (for a time, head) of a governmental advisory board and, later, as a private citizen. Visibility does not necessarily equate with influence: Like members of clans, those operating under the radar sometimes wield more influence than those in the spotlight.

Although one can identify a cluster of Neocon core activists, accomplishing open, shared goals in a complex governing system entails some fluidity in a flex net's boundaries; to further specific causes, members sometimes join with close associates and political allies. Ever evolving, the flex net doesn't have a hard boundary but rather a gravitational core. And, of course, all members of the Neocon flex net have not been equally important at all times. Some, especially on the periphery, have moved in and out as needed, as the network mobilizes to achieve its goals.[18]

"Stand[ing] for each other in defence of each other all the way" is but one reason the Neocon core, like other flex nets, is not quite an interest group, whose members have common interests but not necessarily shared interpersonal histories and activities. Standing for each other entails both the benefits of disciplined coherence and the costs of dissent; the cost of "unfriending" a fellow member of the core is likely to be high for all involved.

Conviction and Continuity

The Neocon core's shared interpersonal histories and activities are also at the heart of the second feature of flex nets—their *shared conviction and action*. They are bound together by their common view of the world and their role in it. Like fervent adherents of religious or political-philosophical movements, members of the core have passionately pursued certain policy goals according to their own vision: first to ensure American strength vis-à-vis the Soviet Union, and, after the end of the Cold War, to transform the Middle East (and the world) via U.S. power. Those goals are part of an organized set of ideas that offer an ideal model for society—and can be summed up as an ideology.[19] In that ideology, which is global in scope (and goes from general to specific, not the other way around), world events are interconnected. Fitting into philosopher Hannah Arendt's hypothesis about "objective enemies," the neoconservative ideology posits an absolute "objective enemy" that lacks specific content. Such enemies need not be suspected of actual wrongdoing.[20]

How did this objective enemy come about? The thinking of neoconservatives about foreign policy was significantly shaped by their interpretation of World War II, America's role in it, and the age of American preeminence that followed. Richard Perle put it thusly: "For those of us who are involved in foreign and defence policy today, my generation, the defining moment of our history was certainly the Holocaust. It was the destruction, the genocide of a whole people, and it was the failure to respond in a timely fashion to a threat that was clearly gathering. We don't want that to happen again; when we have the ability to stop totalitarian regimes we should do so, because when we fail to do so, the results are catastrophic."[21]

The neoconservatives' sense that constant vigilance is necessary to avert the next Nazi-type threat mandates that it is America's right—even duty—to export organized violence in the service of U.S. interests. And as victory over fascism was achieved far from U.S. soil, without the trauma of war at home, so can America triumph in war abroad without endangering security at home. The post–World War II experience of American dominance, buoyed by notions of progress and democracy, further honed the view that America can, and should, refashion the world. Neoconservatives thus promote a defense strategy that prefers military intervention—indeed, preemption—and confrontation with enemies. Journalist Jim Lobe, a longtime student of the neoconservatives, sums up the role of the past in the neoconservatives' present as follows: "The Nazi Holocaust . . . lies at the core of the neo-conservative worldview that has animated and given coherence to much of the Bush administration's post-9/11 foreign policy that itself is changing the world."[22] Enmeshed with this worldview is an investment in defending the state of

Israel, manifested in a commitment to a particular faction in Israeli politics and society: the right-wing Likud Party, as represented, say, by Benjamin Netanyahu.[23] Likewise, certainty that their approach is correct: As an Israeli embassy official in Washington told his U.S. government liaison, "They [the Perle group] think they know what's good for Israel better than we."[24]

Where once the first objective enemy for the neoconservatives was world communism, currently it is world terrorism. This enemy is, as Wolfowitz put it when he was deputy defense secretary, "a fascist totalitarianism not fundamentally different from the way it was in the last century—no more God-fearing than [the Nazis and communists] were." The aim of this enemy, in the eyes of a senior fellow at the Center for Security Policy, a Neocon core-powered organization founded by Frank Gaffney, is: "Global domination and the destruction of the U.S." It is, she writes, the "ultimate aim" of "jihadists" (encompassing Al Qaeda and Iran), who constitute a single "enemy." Thus, as Perle concludes in his coauthored 2004 book, *An End to Evil: How to Win the War on Terror*, "For us, terrorism remains the great evil of our time, and the war against this evil, our generation's great cause. . . . There is no middle way for Americans: it is victory or holocaust."[25]

The response to this all-or-nothing worldview is made clear in the writings of Perle and Feith, who single out bureaucracy and professional expertise for bruising. CIA and State Department operations and expertise are particularly derided. Railing against bureaucracy, civil service, and the law, Perle's *An End to Evil* not only resembles a revolutionary tract but stands as an explicit endorsement of many of the trends in American governing that I laid out in Chapter 4. In a section titled "Organizing for Victory," Perle and coauthor David Frum say we must "overhaul the institutions of our government to ready them for a new kind of war against a new kind of enemy." The list of should-be-overhauled institutions begins with the FBI, the CIA, the armed forces, and especially the State Department, but doesn't stop there.[26] Decrying the "byzantine bureaucracy" at the Department of State, Perle and Frum suggest "eliminating the regional bureaus" to "streamline" government's "ponderous bureaucracy" and recommend that "we should increase sharply the number of political appointees in the State Department and expand their role."[27] On this point, Feith is adamant, equating more political appointees with more democracy. "The cult of professionalism," which holds that bureaucrats should run things because they are competent professionals, "is very anti-democratic," Feith told me. "My view is that the American system is a good hybrid of professionalism and democracy. The people who are the democracy part are the political appointees."[28] The problem, as an observer close to the Neocon core emphasizes, is bureaucrats who fashion themselves "guardians of the national interest" and constitute a "new nomenklatura."[29]

In this view of government, centralizing and intensifying executive authority at the expense of checks and balances are necessary. With regard to paramilitary operations, for instance, Perle and Frum suggest "bring[ing] all these secret warriors into a single paramilitary structure ultimately answerable to the secretary of defense, the man responsible for running America's wars." They write that "even a nation of laws must understand the limits of legalism."[30]

What course of action follows from these views? Mobilization: a permanent state of emergency, with suspension of standard process and formal/legal procedures to manage the perceived crisis. Daniel Patrick Moynihan, the late senator from New York and onetime neoconservative, suggested that this kind of suspension of rules and processes was what motivated him to part ways with the movement in the 1980s: "They wished for a military posture approaching mobilisation; they would create or invent whatever crises were required to bring this about."[31]

It is this mentality of crisis that members of the Neocon core have brought to their engagement in foreign policy. In the endeavors they undertook beginning in the mid-1970s, they employed methods ranging from the creation of alternative intelligence; to might-be-authorized, might-not-be authorized diplomacy; to setting up pressure groups; to suspending standard government process, always contesting government information, assessments, and expertise. These methods—perfected over the years—would be deployed in full force in the Neocon core's effort to take the United States to war in 2003.

Larger groups of political beings were also in full force and useful to the Neocon core in pushing the United States to war in Iraq. The core had fashioned alliances on selected issues with two powerful coalitions in particular: the Christian Right, beginning in the late 1970s; and what have been called "assertive nationalists" (also "hyper-nationalists" or "aggressive nationalists"), who believe American action should be unconstrained, who favor preemption versus deterrence and militarism versus diplomacy, and who share a distrust of the U.S. intelligence community and the State Department. Here the Neo-con core found common ground and pursued overlapping efforts with other ideological sometime soul mates, including proponents of missile defense (with whom their funding from defense contractors also overlapped), and with prominent figures such as Dick Cheney, Donald Rumsfeld, and John Bolton.[32]

The Neocon core's sense of urgency—no matter the cost or external con-ditions—has helped it sustain itself, even as organizational and political en-vironments change. Ironically, the core's crisis mentality has propelled it to employ staples of flexian behavior, such as personalizing bureaucracy and re-laxing rules, that recall the very communism the neoconservatives loathed: communist systems, of course, subordinated formal/legal procedures to the whims of their authorities. In the post–Cold War age of truthiness and ever-more complex information technologies, the Neocon core has adopted addi-tional flexian practices, privatizing information while branding conviction and juggling roles and representations, that place it on the cutting edge.

Let's not confuse such a flex net with "Wise Men" or "kitchen cabinets." The Neocon core outdoes them by the combination of its supreme intercon-nectedness, collective zeal, and mentality of mobilization to push along—through thick and thin, favorable presidential administration or not—shared do-or-die goals. This self-propelling quality, motivated by members' ideology and marked by promotion of their worldview, is not only a hallmark of the Neocon core. It has played a more than supporting role, sometimes even a driving one, in major episodes of American foreign policy.

Sidelining Bureaucracy

In the mid-1970s, two key members of what would become the Neocon core joined with a larger group of assertive nationalists who were involved in the first of several efforts to change American foreign policy by producing and promoting alternative intelligence assessments. These assessments, it was hoped, would sideline those generated by U.S. government agencies, help jus-tify the alternative foreign policy courses their supporters advocated, and sway decision makers to change course accordingly. The effort presented a challenge to professional authority, not only bureaucratic authority. Under pressure from critics on the right, CIA Director George H. W. Bush (appointed by President Gerald Ford) authorized a group of non-intelligence specialists—officially the Strategic Objectives Panel of the President's Foreign Intelligence Advisory Board—to conduct an independent intelligence appraisal of the Soviet threat.³³ Paul Wolfowitz was a member of (and Richard Perle was involved in) this 1976 first alternative intelligence exercise, which would be employed and seen as a model known to participants and detractors alike as "Team B"—a counterpoint to the CIA's ostensible Team A.

The impetus for the effort arose from distrust of the policy of containment and a belief that the U.S. intelligence community was underplaying the Soviet threat. Albert Wohlstetter provided intellectual justification in two (1974 and 1975) *Foreign Policy* articles that took issue with the CIA's assessment of the Soviet Union's defense capability contained in its yearly National Intelligence Estimate (NIE). The agency routinely underassessed Soviet missile deployment, Wohlstetter wrote, and he warned that the United States risked being outdone militarily.³⁴ This was fuel for the neoconservative view that America should be the prevailing military might.

The panel's task was to evaluate the data and prepare its own report. The panel would be granted unprecedented entrée to highly sensitive CIA data pertaining to Soviet military capacity.³⁵

Enter Richard Perle. He had no formal part in Team B, but, as an aide to Senator Jackson, he had his fingerprints on the effort. Jackson recommended Harvard professor Richard Pipes, an eminent scholar of Russian history and a foremost critic of détente, to head Team B. This came about because, as Perle told me: "I was a talent scout, if you will. . . . I was aware of Pipes and his work and suggested he would be a good person."³⁶ Pipes's understanding of current events was shaped by his perspective on the evolution of the Russian state and society. Pipes chose Wolfowitz, then perched at the Arms Control and Disarmament Agency, to be on the panel because, as Pipes told me, "Perle suggested to me his friend Wolfowitz."³⁷ While Perle was not on the panel and its conclusions were classified, he told me he knew everyone on Team B. "We were friends and colleagues, we talked all the time . . . and in detail."³⁸

Although the Strategic Objectives Panel was supposedly unbiased, the makeup of Team B was weighted toward the conclusion that the CIA underestimated the Soviet threat. As Paul Warnke, an official at the ACDA around the time of the Team B effort, later wrote: "Rather than including a diversity of views . . . the Strategic Objectives Panel was composed entirely of individuals who made careers of viewing the Soviet menace with alarm."[39] Pipes himself appeared to agree. "We were to be a counterpoint to Team A," he told a journalist. "In other words, the authorities said, 'We are getting the same story all the time from the CIA. . . . Let's get another group who have a different view, give them access to all of the evidence and see what they come up with.' So, this was deliberate. We were not to balance Team A, but come up with the strongest possible argument to prove they are right or they are wrong." Team B, of course, found them wrong.[40]

Although Team B's findings were supposed to be secret, they were leaked to the media. They were used as ammunition by cold warriors and kept vital through op-ed pieces and media interviews of panel members, as well as a media campaign conducted by the (second) Committee on the Present Danger. (That advocacy group, resurrected from its 1950s predecessor while Team B was at work, shared many members over the years with those in and close to the Neocon core.) However one judges the conclusions of the panel, the exercise had a decided impact. As Richard Pipes told me: "Carter's nuclear strategy adopted Team B's point of view."[41]

Team B had a lasting legacy. It set a precedent for alternative intelligence assessments grounded in gauging an adversary's motives more than its actual capacities. The NIE, concluded the panel's fifty-five-page report (two-thirds of which dealt with Soviet "objectives" rather than actual capacities), "substantially misperceived the *motivations* behind Soviet strategic programs, and thereby tended consistently to underestimate their intensity, scope, and implicit threat" [emphasis added]. This misperception, the report argued, "has been due in considerable measure to concentration on the so-called hard data." By contrast, the authors acknowledged, the Team B report focused "on what . . . the Russians are striving for, without trying to assess their chances of success."[42] Team B, as Paul Wolfowitz later summed it up, "demonstrated that it was possible to construct a sharply different view of Soviet motivation from the consensus view of the [intelligence] analysts."[43] Favoring appraisal of motives over fact- and capacity-based analysis, the exercise helped construct a counterreality.

Team B had other ways of persisting, as embodied in key players, in the modus operandi of the Neocon core and, more generally, as a model for doing business. As journalist James Mann, author of an authoritative history of George W. Bush's war cabinet, has written, after Team B, "whenever members of Congress believed that the CIA was minimizing the seriousness of a foreign policy problem, there were calls for a Team B to review the intelligence and make its own independent evaluation."[44]

Indeed, constructing views diverging from the intelligence community—and employing means that would see them adopted as policy—would be a perennial project of the Neocon core.

Unauthorized, Yet Somehow Authorized

Whereas Paul Wolfowitz et al. had created alternative intelligence assessments via Team B a decade earlier, the players in the Iran-Contra affair created alternative governing structures and processes, this time to circumvent not only the standard bureaucracy but also the checks and balances of Congress, which had outlawed their activity. Simultaneously they were also enjoying the tacit approval of the president of the United States, Ronald Reagan, who had secretly blessed the operations.[45] These structures and processes, although substantially embedded within government bodies and often carried out by officials, were off the books: They skirted bureaucratic and chain-of-command structures and enabled the players to carry out illegal operations in secret, thereby derailing official U.S. foreign policy. Thus was policy privatized and relations with certain countries relegated to might-be-official, might-not-be-official diplomacy carried out by "private operatives."[46]

My purpose here is not to rehearse the details of Iran-Contra, but to highlight the overall modus operandi that made it successful, as well the roles of those who became part of the Neocon core. For the core would build on those means; indeed, the modus operandi employed by the protagonists seemed a portent of things to come.

Many players other than those mentioned here took part in the events that led to the scandal. The names we know best—Oliver North, the telegenic former Marine, Vietnam veteran, and self-styled patriot made famous during congressional hearings; Richard Secord, a retired Air Force major general who had met North in the military; and Albert Hakim, an arms dealer—are not associated with the Neocon core. But certain of its members, including Elliott Abrams and Michael Ledeen, were centrally involved in the affair.

The Iran-Contra players arrived onto the world scene as the Cold War was about to draw down. The basic contours of the affair (in reality, two separate operations whose principal operatives and funding sources became intertwined), which burst into the headlines of mainstream media in 1986, were as follows: Operatives in and around the fervently anticommunist Reagan executive branch secretly sold arms to Iran. Iran was not only an enemy of the United States but also was complicit in the five-year detention of American hostages in Iran after the nation's 1979 revolution. In return for the arms, the players got two things: an assurance that Iran would influence the Lebanese terrorist group Hezbollah to release the American hostages they were holding, and revenue to support their agenda half a world away. With the profits from the arms sales, the operatives underwrote the Contras, the anti-Sandinista Nicaraguan rebel group to which aid had been prohibited by Congress. These activities were derailed after a plane crash in Central America involving a lone survivor and CIA operative (and a news article published a month later detailing President Reagan's approval of the sale of missiles to Iran) led reporters to a trail of clandestine activities.[47]

To achieve their own agendas—a combination of ideological, foreign policy, and personal financial goals—players in the "Enterprise," as they referred to their operation, expertly evaded scrutiny as they functioned counter to many U.S. laws and policies.[48] North was at the center of the Enterprise, which connected seemingly disparate efforts, intermediaries, finances, companies, and otherwise unrelated people both from within and outside government. It masked players' unofficial and often illegal activities in titles that could not begin to convey what they were actually doing. A mere National Security Council (NSC) staffer on the organizational charts, North had direct access to CIA Director William Casey. Further circumventing the chain of command, North worked directly with NSC Advisor Robert McFarlane, and, later, NSC Deputy Director John Poindexter when he replaced McFarlane. North's unique and seemingly indispensable role in the NSC was underscored by the direct access he was given to both men.[49]

Key functions in Iran-Contra were performed not only by operatives in the bureaucracy who flouted the organizational structure, but also by operatives outside it. Consider the following job sketch:

- Secretary of state of the United States long enough to negotiate a clandestine deal.
- No confirmation necessary.
- No responsibility or answerability possible because no one outside a secret circle knows there is an acting secretary.

This unwritten position description belonged to Albert Hakim, the Iranian-born, California-based arms merchant eager for U.S. government contracts, who was a friend and business associate of Richard Secord. The United States had no diplomatic relations with Iran. Yet Hakim (sometimes together with McFarlane, Secord, or others) made trans-Atlantic trips in which, presenting themselves as U.S. envoys, he and they met with Iranians and arms dealers to discuss weapons sales and the possible release of the American hostages. This diplomacy was, of course, unofficial, as was the maze of Swiss bank accounts set up by Hakim and Secord in their own names to receive, transfer, and make payments on behalf of the Contras, Israelis, and Iranians. (Hakim personally received more than $2 million as a result of the operation.) North, who was himself unauthorized (yet somehow authorized) to do so, dispatched Hakim to meet with an Iranian delegation in Frankfurt to work out the details of the clandestine agreement to sell weapons to Iran. Hakim negotiated the deal with Iran with not a single real U.S. official present. Hakim later told Senate investigators, who suggested that he had played secretary of state, that his role was better than the actual secretary because he did not have to get confirmed by Congress. And, he added insightfully, "I can achieve more, too."[50]

Two members of the Neocon core, Elliott Abrams and Michael Ledeen, were also high achievers. Abrams blended a variety of roles—official and legal, unofficial and not-so-legal, and public relations—in the service of Iran-Contra. While assistant secretary of state for Inter-American Affairs beginning in 1985, Abrams was integral to Oliver North's Central American activities. It was not just that he knew about the illegal work and allowed it to go on. Abrams, together with the heads of crucial CIA operations, sanctioned blending legal U.S. humanitarian aid to the Contras with illegal shipments of arms and supplies. He encouraged U.S. officials to work in their official capacities on behalf of the Enterprise via a high-level interagency working group on Latin American policy. In yet other important roles, in 1985 Abrams became the administration's chief advocate on Capitol Hill to lift the ban on aid to the Contras. He also helped North raise private funds for the rebel group, meeting with potential underwriters of the cause as they toured the White House and were briefed by North and granted photo opportunities with President Reagan.[51]

Ledeen, for his part, would shine as a budding specialist in might-be-official, might-be-unofficial diplomacy. After working for both State and Defense in the early 1980s, he consulted for NSC Advisor McFarlane from 1984 to 1985. At the NSC, Ledeen briefed McFarlane on Defense Intelligence Agency reports. He also was assigned to work with North on counterterrorism activities. According to Independent Counsel Lawrence Walsh, appointed by the attorney general to investigate the Iran-Contra affair, Ledeen "persuaded McFarlane to permit him to approach [Israeli Prime Minister Shimon] Peres, ostensibly to take advantage of Israeli intelligence in formulating a policy for dealing with Iran after [Ayatollah] Khomeini's death." In 1985, on an official trip to Israel, Ledeen and Peres discussed potential weapons sales to Iran. According to Walsh, Ledeen acted as a "conduit for information between Israeli officials, Israeli and Iranian arms brokers, and the NSC staff." As the unofficial intermediary between McFarlane and the Israelis, as well as between the Israelis and the Middle Eastern arms merchants, Ledeen carried out covert activities that both excluded the intelligence community and the State Department and engaged foreign operatives to conduct might-be-authorized, might-not-be-authorized U.S. relations with foreign nations. These foreign operatives, including Manucher Ghorbanifar, a secret police official under the Shah of Iran turned arms dealer, and Adnan Khashoggi, a Saudi investor, were key brokers of arms sales and relations with Iran. According to Independent Counsel Walsh, Ledeen did not inform North of all his activities with leaders in the Middle East—a breach even of the unofficial chain of command. That is because Ledeen, Walsh speculates, was making money from weapons sales. Many questions remain. As Walsh wonders: "Had he [Ledeen] simply been an amateur welcoming a chance to help formulate presidential policy, while the professional diplomats were excluded from the process? Had he been a cat's paw for McFarlane's ambition for a historic breakthrough to Iran? Had he been paid off by Ghorbanifar or the Israeli arms merchants?"[52]

The roles of the Enterprise players were so improvised and diverse that it is difficult to tease them out of the snarl of camouflaged titles, activities, and events. As Jack Blum, a special counsel leading one of the Senate Foreign Relations Committee's investigations, told me: "I can't even begin to tell you how to categorize those people, because the roles aren't clean, and they play in and out and off and around each other. And then there are people who are go-betweens."[53]

The players' elusiveness, of course, facilitated their effectiveness—helping them personalize policy and diplomacy and skirt democratic checks and balances as they capitalized on executive power and the tacit blessing of the chief executive. This might-be-authorized, might-not-be-authorized setup also helped its operatives enfeeble legal repercussions. Ultimately, though, the ability to evade sanction would come with the exercise of executive power by one Enterprise abettor: Bush I. As president, he pardoned those convicted. Thus, while some of the players were slapped on the wrist, involvement in the scandal scarcely hampered their later success. Moreover, some two decades later, in the Bush II administration, key players in Iran-Contra would resurface as key players in the conduct of unofficial, yet-might-be-official American foreign policy.[54]

Sidelining Expertise

Another neoconservative, as well as assertive nationalist, cause—ballistic missile defense—would spur innovation in ways and means of influence-wielding to affect U.S. foreign and defense policy. It is logical that ballistic missile defense, commonly and first known as "Star Wars," would be taken up as a project by neoconservatives—staunch advocates of the use of military force to promote U.S. interests abroad. While missile defense is by no means a cause exclusive to the Neocon core, some of its members and associates have been among its most steadfast influencers. For a quarter of a century, missile defense proponents have sought to keep the project alive. They have done this through thick and thin—and there has been plenty of thick, especially with the elimination of the Soviet threat and the end of the Cold War.[55]

Ballistic missile defense made its splash as a signature of the Reagan administration's strong-on-defense, tough-on-the-Soviets posturing. It was supposed to shield against nuclear attacks on American cities and included both ground-based and spaced-based components. While this might have seemed like a good idea in principle, scientists and investigators have, since the program's inception, almost uniformly challenged the viability of major aspects of it. Many have also questioned the staggering cost. Yet, while the efficacy of missile defense remains largely undemonstrated to this day and its original raison d'être has been relegated to history books, the program has persisted—morphing variously from the Strategic Defense Initiative (SDI) into the Ballistic Missile Defense Organization (BMDO) and the Missile Defense Agency (MDA), with ever changing government commissions and task forces administering it. What accounts for the longevity of Star Wars?[56]

The role of a set of advocates working in venues related to the cause deserves close attention. These key supporters, powered by private organizations, conservative funders, and industry sponsors, have shepherded it through numerous mutations. Eyeing the rosters of names associated with the project shows striking continuity—with certain individuals playing key roles for more than a quarter century, even when those roles shift (say, from undersecretary or deputy assistant secretary in the Department of Defense to a perch in a think tank, academia, or industry—or vice versa). While their organizational venues may change, a constellation of players has, unswervingly, cradled the Star Wars cause.

Although the effort boasts indispensable backers who are not part of the Neocon core, including some who were active in Team B, certain core members also have been crucial players. Recall that it was the issue of missile defense that prompted Albert Wohlstetter to introduce Richard Perle to Senator Jackson in the late 1960s.[57]

While Perle championed the project since its inception and Wolfowitz has played a supporting role, Neocon core members Frank Gaffney, Douglas

Feith, and R. James Woolsey, Jr.—director of the CIA under Clinton turned vice president of Booz Allen Hamilton—have done more heavy lifting. So have Neocon core allies Stephen Cambone, undersecretary of defense for intelligence under Bush II, and Dov Zakheim, missile defense company official turned comptroller of the Department of Defense under Bush II turned U.S. government adviser and vice president at Booz Allen.[58]

While Star Wars boosters have used traditional means of wielding influence such as lobbying Congress, they have employed additional approaches including establishing think tanks and foundations, as well as enlisting unofficial diplomats to sway decision makers in foreign lands. Crucially, they also have built on the Team B model. Star Wars advocates primarily have been civilians, according to Pulitzer Prize–winner Frances Fitzgerald, who writes that civilian promoters of the project have been much more enthusiastic about it than its military custodians. And in the spirit of Team B, they have disparaged the efficacy of U.S. military and intelligence expertise, produced their own assessments, and helped create and staff government commissions to help legitimize those assessments.[59]

Beginning in the 1980s, Star Wars proponents set up or mobilized several pressure organizations to influence the opinion of decision makers and the public—and thereby, policy. William D. Hartung, an expert on the economics of the defense industry and arms issues, gives think tanks much of the credit for keeping missile defense alive after the end of the Cold War. While most of these organizations were not Neocon core strongholds, the core-powered Center for Security Policy, founded by Gaffney in 1988, played a "coordinating role" in the effort. Gaffney himself is credited with having pulled off an important feat: He reportedly convinced Dick Armey, the congressman from Texas who served as Republican conference chairman, to include missile defense as the sole plank dealing specifically with foreign policy in the 1994 "Contract with America." A handful of additional think-tank-style organizations also have buoyed missile defense through the years, their major priority being the production and propagation of expertise.[60]

From the point of view of Star Wars' supporters, the beauty of think tanks and academic institutes is that they provide a veneer of neutrality and objective study. As William Hartung put it, by providing a buffer between industry and public policy, think tanks are "almost like money launderers." The mega-billion-dollar industry that is missile defense helps keep itself fed by funding these organizations. Industry-underwritten think tanks not only help drum up support for policies (and policy shifts) that benefit their business; they are sometimes drivers of policies that open up new arenas of business.[61]

Star Wars advocates have helped engineer into existence, and then filled the ranks of, Team B–type undertakings, this time in the form of government-sponsored commissions. At the urging of such groups as Gaffney's Center for Security Policy, Representative Curt Weldon (R-PA)—a member of Gaffney's advisory board and chair of the military procurement subcommittee of the House Armed Services Committee in the Republican-controlled Congress—introduced an amendment in the Defense Authorization bill of 1997 allocating funds for an independent commission to assess the menace to the United States posed by ballistic missiles.[62]

The result was one commission and eventually a second, related commission, authorized under a separate amendment. Both were chaired by Donald Rumsfeld, with Stephen Cambone as staff director, and both commissions provided clout and intellectual justification for missile defense. The apparent goal of these commissions, funded by taxpayer dollars, was to compel the administration to beef up the military budget and introduce new weapons programs.[63]

While the director of central intelligence initially took issue with the conclusions of the report generated by the first commission, more than a year later, in September 1999, the CIA issued a new National Intelligence Estimate that was notably more "alarmist" than its earlier NIE. Weldon expressed pleasure with the new threat assessment, calling it "the largest turnaround ever in the history of the [intelligence] agency." Said Weldon, a main sponsor of the Rumsfeld commission, "I was part of making it happen." The recommendations of the second commission, released in January 2001, on the military uses of outer space, also had an effect on policy outcomes.[64]

When Rumsfeld became secretary of defense in the Bush II administration, missile defense got a boost via at least two developments. The first was bringing into the Pentagon members and others involved in the Rumsfeld commissions, including Wolfowitz as deputy secretary of defense, Feith as undersecretary of defense for policy, Cambone as undersecretary of defense for intelligence (a position created for him by Rumsfeld), and Zakheim as comptroller general, as well as Woolsey and other Neocon core allies as members of the Defense Policy Board chaired by Perle.[65]

The second development, an initiative set up explicitly to enable the circumvention of bureaucracy, could not have been friendlier to the antibureaucracy Neocon core. Dubbed the "Freedom to Manage" initiative, the program exempts missile defense programs from standard checks and balances, that is, regulations pertaining to system requirements, timelines, costs, and independent assessments by the Pentagon's testing office. Rumsfeld justified his action with this statement: "The special nature of missile defense development, operations, and support calls for nonstandard approaches to both acquisition and requirements generation."[66]

Although much has changed over the past quarter century, including the names of the Star Wars program, the geopolitical context in which it is promoted, and the organizations and commissions involved in it, the movers and shakers behind it are strikingly constant. So is their skepticism of U.S. intelligence expertise. A 2007 symposium I attended on "Ballistic Missile Defense: Where We Are and Where We Need to Be" summed up this sentiment. It was sponsored by the Jewish Institute for National Security Affairs (JINSA), a Neocon core–associated think tank (paying special attention to missile defense), with representatives of the defense industry in the audience. One of the speakers said: "I don't put much stock in what the NIE [National Intelligence Estimate] says."[67]

This distrust of government expertise and intelligence assessments—and the players' countermeasures to them, such as their sponsorship of industry-supported pressure groups to promulgate "independent" assessments, and their promotion of alternative government findings—would again be reflected in the Neocon core's signature effort to date: the toppling of Saddam Hussein.[68]

Pursuing Personalized Policy

By the time George W. Bush entered office in January 2001 and the Neocon players maneuvered themselves into roles of influence, both within and outside of formal positions in the administration, they had spent the better part of a decade advocating the overthrow of Hussein. Wolfowitz and others had long maintained that the elder Bush had made a grave mistake by not un-seating the dictator during the first Gulf War in 1991. Brick by brick members of the Neocon core put together the building blocks that would attempt to correct that mistake and reorder the Middle East according to their own vi-sion. They spawned a proliferation of initiatives and organizations under-pinned by collections of roughly the same set of players.

In 1996, during the Clinton years, Perle chaired a study group that issued a report aimed at balancing power in the Middle East in Israel's favor. Neo-con core member David Wurmser, husband of Meyrav Wurmser, directed the effort from a Jerusalem-based think tank, with the involvement of his wife, Feith, and others.[69] The report, *A Clean Break: A New Strategy for Securing the Realm*, called for "removing Saddam Hussein from power," among other pre-scriptions to rearrange the region. Perle personally delivered the report, in-tended to influence the policies of the new Likud-led government, to Prime Minister Benjamin Netanyahu.[70]

Before long, Perle and other members of the Neocon core were pressing the Clinton administration to pursue the same objectives. In 1998, in an effort known as the Project for the New American Century, core members Perle, Wolfowitz, Woolsey, and Elliott Abrams (who would serve Bush II as deputy assistant to the president and deputy national security adviser for global democracy strategy, and additionally as Middle East adviser), as well as core ally John Bolton (who would serve as undersecretary of state for arms con-trol), were among the signatories of a letter to President Clinton calling for the removal of Hussein. Clinton sought regime change in Iraq, mostly through sanctions imposed by the United Nations. But the neoconservatives consid-ered sanctions ineffective. Signatories of these two documents would later overhaul this approach from their posts in the Bush II administration.[71]

Familial NGOs

To move the U.S. government to undertake policies its members did consider effective, the Neocon core worked through a host of organizations, many of which it created in the 1990s and after 9/11, to further its agenda in the Mid-dle East. In the process, members of the core and their allies were at the fore-front of a trend in American governing: the uptick in politicized think-tank-type organizations, as described in Chapter 4. Moreover, they added their own organizational innovation: the steel-girded framework of their network, which bolstered their capacity for coordination of resources and influence.

Members of the core started and were prime movers in a series of organizations of influence variously pegged as think tanks, educational associations, policy conveyors, and the like—including Gaffney's Center for Security Policy and JINSA. They also populated the decades-old American Enterprise Institute (AEI), which has long served as a primary launching and landing pad for members of the core and other neoconservatives. This is the think tank where Richard Perle, Michael Ledeen, and David Wurmser hang (or have hung) one of their hats, and where Wolfowitz and Bolton landed after their Bush II administration gigs.

In addition, members of the Neocon core were instigators and signatories of "letterhead organizations" (LHOs), albeit influential and landmark ones such as the Project for the New American Century, as well as the Committee for Peace and Security in the Gulf, the Committee for the Liberation of Iraq, and the U.S. Committee for a Free Lebanon, among others. Although letterhead organizations may sound inconsequential, in fact their significance is often in their founding and the buzz their founders create. A series of LHOs enables the same collection of individuals to appear under different guises and to create the impression that their reach is ever widening—bolstering the impact of truthiness. For, as Jim Lobe assesses, these organizations function as "a vast echo chamber for one another and for the media."[72] This same set of individuals also played lesser roles in small, but often well-endowed shops of wider (or somewhat different) circles set up for similar purposes.[73] These organizations support the core's activities in, among other efforts, drafting policy papers and publicizing them, raising money and media attention, and lobbying policymakers and members of Congress.

These inbred organizations are a different animal from think tanks (in the model of the Brookings Institution or the Center for Strategic and International Studies, or CSIS), from foundations (in the mold of Ford or Rockefeller), and from lobbying organizations (such as the National Organization for Women or the National Rifle Association). The Neocon-associated organizations are anchored in the network. They have drawn on or been energized by a handful of participants—participants who, for the most part, had

NEOCON CORE[1]
Players' Interconnections Through Organizations[2]
(Ideological and Think-Tank Only)

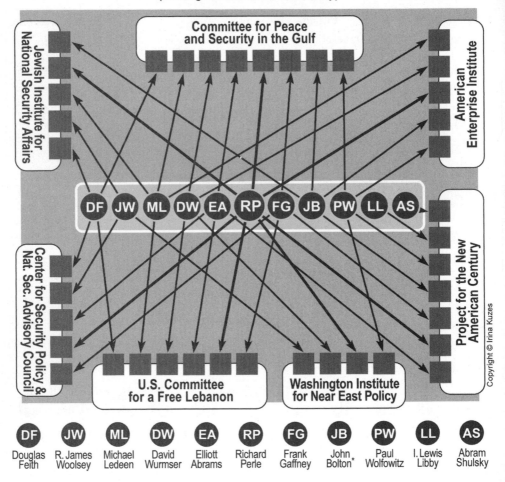

DF — Douglas Feith
JW — R. James Woolsey
ML — Michael Ledeen
DW — David Wurmser
EA — Elliott Abrams
RP — Richard Perle
FG — Frank Gaffney
JB — John Bolton[*]
PW — Paul Wolfowitz
LL — I. Lewis Libby
AS — Abram Shulsky

Copyright © Irina Kuzes

1 This graphic provides a sampling of organizations (circa 1979 to 2008) empowered –and mostly set up by– members of the Neocon core. The list is not comprehensive.
2 This graphic includes membership only; it does not capture other forms of involvement. Players were not always involved in these organizations at the same time.

* John Bolton comes from a different rightwing tradition than do neoconservatives, but is closely allied to the Neocon core.

a past with each other and were already connected via other endeavors. Douglas Feith, for example, is a founding member of the Center for Security Policy's board of advisers and former chairman of its board of directors.[74]

Many members of the Neocon flex net have moved and shaken several of the handful of organizations they created. Here the intricate spine of their exclusive, intertwined network (flex net feature one) is especially in evidence.

NEOCON CORE
Official Positions in Government and Governmental Boards/Commissions
(Administration of George W. Bush)

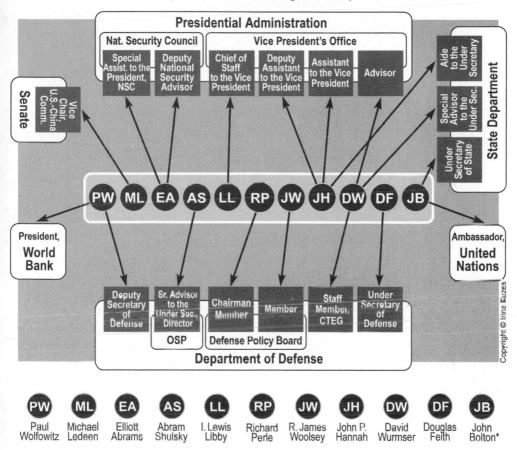

CTEG -- Counter Terrorism Evaluation Group
OSP -- Office of Special Plans
NSC -- National Security Council

* John Bolton comes from a different rightwing tradition than do neoconservatives, but is closely allied to the Neocon core.

In addition to their many other roles vis-à-vis each other in and around government, business, and community, members of the core connect with each other through leadership in these entities, as illustrated on page 172. A sociologist who conducted a network analysis of memberships in neoconservative-associated organizations found that "the activities of fourteen organizations were coordinated by individuals who comprised a web of interlocking memberships." For instance, the Center for Security Policy had twelve membership links to the Project for the New American Century, seven to the Defense Policy Board, six to JINSA, four to the Committee for the Liberation of Iraq, and five to the American Enterprise Institute, among others.[75] As a consequence, the players' network configurations resemble those of the Chubais-Harvard set explicated in Chapter 5.

As well, the Neocon core organizations are not so very different from the NGOs of transitional eastern Europe that emerged from the understructure of communism as it became undone. The first prerequisite to belonging to such an NGO—and belonging is an apt term—was already to be in the network. Typically, only those with common social background, pedigree, and shared experience could qualify. (The paradox for building civil society, however, is that it needs to attract members based on common interests.) Likewise, the Neocon core–established organizations are loyalty- and network-based associations with an extended-family flavor.[76]

Of course, these organizations are powered by fierce ideological commitment, the quality of throwing oneself into goals deemed almost as crucial as survival itself. In terms of organization, committedness, and "us versus them," this quality recalls early Communist Party cells and the Trotskyist past of the neoconservative founding fathers. Both these aspects—a resilient network and do-or-die commitment—fortify them in and against an American environment in which the prevailing attitude often is "I'll go with whoever pays me the most."

◊ ◊ ◊

FORMING AN *INTRICATE SPINE* and employing *shared conviction and action* (the first two features of flex nets) rendered the Neocon core a formidable force in empowering pressure organizations and publicizing their cause. But it would not be enough to achieve the core's goal of overthrowing Hussein. The chief decider would have to be on board: The core could scarcely have attained its goal without a presidency favorably disposed toward parts of its agenda. It was also crucial to have core members in key government posts vis-à-vis U.S. policy toward the Middle East. Richard Perle said as much to journalist George Packer when Packer interviewed Perle for his book *The Assassins' Gate: America in Iraq*. Perle observed, "If Bush had staffed his administration with a group of people selected by Brent Scowcroft and Jim

Baker . . . which might well have happened, then it could have been different, because they would not have carried into it the ideas that the people who wound up in important positions brought to it."[77]

Further, to achieve their longstanding goals once in those positions, members of the Neocon core would have to put their modus operandi to work: to form *a resource pool* and forge *a hybrid habitat*—the third and fourth features of flex nets. This time, they could capitalize on their most hospitable environment to date, one shaped by trends such as the explosion of private entities filling in for Swiss-cheese government; the rising number and influence of government advisory boards, think-tank styled organizations, and personal envoys helping to create and carrying out public policy; and the drift of governmental authority, legitimacy, expertise, and prestige to private partners (consistent with the general loss of exclusive claim to expertise by traditional institutions) that would help them do so. Still, members of the Neocon core would need to reorganize relevant governing structures and processes, infusing them with their own personalistic, network-based ones, in order to manufacture and market their own intelligence assessments to decision makers and the media. They would need to override reservations from relevant communities in government, including some within intelligence units and the State Department. Their strategic alliances with assertive nationalists and the Christian Right would also serve their cause.

All these were necessary, but not sufficient, conditions to get American troops to Baghdad. The environment would have to be receptive. September 11, 2001, helped create that receptivity. Without the emergency atmosphere it generated—a shaken population and a government lacking experience with demonstrated threats to its own shores—it would have been much more difficult, perhaps even impossible, for the Neocon core to achieve its objective during the Bush II years. This crisis atmosphere, friendly to urgent measures and improvisation writ large, helped push along the intensification of executive power, the upswing in contracting out of government functions, and the greater number of political appointees in management positions, among other measures.

Perle's Homemade Policy

In *The Assassins' Gate*, Packer recounts that, "When I half jokingly suggested that the Iraq War began in Scoop Jackson's office, Perle said, 'There's an element of that.'" Packer calls Perle the "impresario" of the Iraq war, "with one degree of separation from everyone who mattered."[78]

In the run-up to and after the invasion of Iraq, private meetings reportedly took place, some of them in Perle's home, in which both Iraq policy and media messages were discussed and even coordinated. These meetings included Neocon core members in formal government, as well as some outside it such as think-tankers and pundits. While details of these meetings are not available (and, of course, core members deny any hint of collaboration), the neoconservatives' massive and concerted public relations operations around the war effort are clear, with obvious coordination of information, judging from the match of message and vocabulary. Also revealing is the fact that the same neoconservative-oriented public relations firm, Benador Associates, founded in the aftermath of 9/11, helped coordinate the media relations for Neocon core members Perle, Gaffney, Ledeen, and Woolsey, as well as neoconservative *Washington Post* columnist Charles Krauthammer and other first-rank neoconservative players and proselytizers. *New York Times* reporter Judith Miller, who would emerge at the very least as an enabler of the Neocon screed, at most a propagandist, was also a client. The firm is run by Eleana Benador, a "Swiss-American publicist," who served as an adviser to the Middle East Forum, a neoconservative-associated Philadelphia think tank. While many people helped to disseminate the rush-to-war message, the core was crucial in creating, organizing, and providing the raw materials for it. So were Neocon core–nourished brokers.[79]

As early as Iran-Contra, members of the Neocon core cultivated, and were cultivated by, brokers to help accomplish their goals with foreign nations or entities. In this case, the key figure was Ahmed Chalabi, the Iraqi-born businessman and exile living in the UK. Chalabi, founder and president of the Iraqi National Congress (INC), was a key player in helping take the United States to war. While Chalabi did not belong to the Neocon core, they shared mutual interests: They wanted to overthrow Hussein and he wanted to be the president. Perle and company helped Chalabi secure many millions in U.S. taxpayer dollars beginning in the 1990s and hoped to install him as president of the new Iraq. Chalabi would feed vital "information" to the administration, the U.S. Congress, and the public—information that would play a winning role in the campaign to sell the war.[80]

Personalizing the Pentagon, the Vice Presidency, and the Process

A good part of that campaign would be waged by the Neocon core within government bureaucracy, and won, thanks to their skill at bypassing and personalizing it, according to a wealth of accounts from inside officials. Neocon core members put their antibureaucratic views into practical action and marshaled past experience, drawing on the core's staples—Perle as ringleader; loyalty- and ideology-based recruitment at the expense of professional expertise; the supplanting of official intelligence and information—while substantially innovating government processes. Members of the Neocon core and their allies thwarted both bureaucratic and professional authority, creating within government personalized practices and network-based structures while circumventing standard ones and marginalizing officials who were not part of their network. A chorus of insiders variously placed in the bureaucracy under Bush II is strikingly unified in their outrage and irritation at what they observed. Lawrence B. Wilkerson, who participated in the policy process as chief of staff to Secretary of State Colin Powell from 2002 to 2005, is one of them. As he put it to me: "We were up against a ruthless machine that had its people in every corner of the bureaucracy, with a vision and a strategy for carrying out the vision."[81]

The upshot is that the decision to go to war clearly was made—but we don't know where. When I asked Wilkerson how the decision was reached, he replied without hesitation. "I don't know. I can point to no document, to no point when a decision was made to go to war." Paul R. Pillar, a veteran CIA officer in charge of coordinating the intelligence community's assessments regarding Iraq, was equally adamant: "There was no process. . . . No one has identified a single meeting, memorandum, showdown in the situation room when the question was on the agenda as to whether this war should be launched. It was never discussed. . . . That is the respect in which this case is markedly different from anything I've seen in the past. . . . There's well established machinery for this . . . : For the decision to go to war in Vietnam there was meeting after meeting, policy briefing after briefing. The Iraq war was qualitatively different in that there was no such process. . . . In Iraq such machinery never got used."[82]

One of many aberrations in the run-up to the Iraq War is that the vice president's office played a key role. War policy and conduct traditionally is in the Pentagon's purview, with the National Security Council, located in the White House, also advising the president on national security and foreign policies. A substantial role for a vice president's office in national security policy, let alone such a huge one as that of Cheney's shop, is virtually unprecedented in U.S. history, according to a number of scholars and observers.[83]

Cheney's office was successful because it undermined bureaucracy and expertise. It operated through an "alternate national security staff" that undercut the actual National Security Council, according to Wilkerson. He speaks of a covert "cabal" constructed by Cheney and Secretary of Defense Rumsfeld, with the agendas led by key Neocon core members in those offices and with "insular and secret workings" that were "efficient and swift—not unlike the decision-making one would associate more with a dictatorship than a democracy." I. Lewis "Scooter" Libby, who had gotten his start as a student of Wolfowitz, later worked for him in Reagan's State Department, and in Bush II's White House was an embedded Neocon core member—serving simultaneously as Vice President Cheney's chief of staff and his national security adviser—ran this informal national security operation. (Libby resigned, of course, after being indicted in 2005 in the Joseph Wilson/Valerie Plame CIA "outing" case.) As Wilkerson concludes: "Many of the most crucial decisions from 2001 to 2005 were not made within the traditional NSC process."[84]

Sources from within the Bush NSC concur. Flynt Leverett, a senior staff member, told me: "I have no objection to people who have different views than I do working through the system. But the neocons worked around processes in ways I thought were illegitimate. There were constant efforts to pressure the intelligence community to provide assessments that would support their [the neocons'] views. If they couldn't get what they wanted out of the intelligence community, they simply created their own intelligence." Libby, together with the vice president, helped assemble discredited claims that were used to make the case for invading Iraq.[85]

With regard to decision making in the Pentagon, Wolfowitz, deputy secretary of defense, and Feith, undersecretary of defense for policy, were well placed to influence and justify the decision to go to war. They and other members of the Neocon core contend that the intelligence community had seriously underestimated threats to the security of the United States. Feith was entrusted with devising a strategy for executing Bush's "war on terror." To facilitate the mission, members of the core set up alternative structures: two secretive offices in the Pentagon that dealt with policy and intelligence after September 11—the Counter Terrorism Evaluation Group, established in October 2001, and the Office of Special Plans, founded in September 2002. Duplicating job descriptions of existing government units, they exerted influence, at least in part, by bypassing or altering standard government entities and workings, such as intelligence-gathering and decision processes, and supplanting them with their own. Feith oversaw both offices.

With relationships the nuts and bolts of personalized bureaucracy, Perle, ever the ringmaster, helped recruit staff for these offices. Loyalty, as determined by being in or close to the Neocon core network, appears to have been the principal guideline for staffing these offices, as well as for parts of the existing bureaucracy. As Perle himself explained, underlining the longtime Neocon theme of questioning the efficacy of government expertise, the reason for the Office of Special Plans was to "bring in people with fresh eyes to review the intelligence that the CIA and other agencies had collected." Feith's offices, along with the Near East South Asia directorate (NESA), which spawned the Office of Special Plans (OSP), marginalized professional civil servants and brought in neoconservative-affiliated staff. Feith put into policy his view that government should have more political appointees and fewer bureaucrats. Thus the replacements were not only not bureaucrats or experts on the Middle East, but people from "agenda-bearing think tanks," as U.S. Air Force Lieutenant Karen Kwiatkowski has put it. She worked for NESA, located next to OSP, and, upon her retirement after more than twenty years of active-duty service, became a vocal critic of Feith's operations and a valuable source of inside-the-Pentagon information. The OSPs' eighteen or so staff members consisted of a cadre of "neocon-friendly appointees or contractors," as Kwiatkowski described them, who overshadowed the others—several military personnel and professional civil servants who were made "largely invisible . . . and dispensable," as she has described it.[86]

W. Patrick Lang, who earlier served stints as both a Defense intelligence officer for the Middle East, South Asia and Counter-Terrorism and a director of Defense HUMINT (human intelligence collection) for the Defense

Intelligence Agency, recalls a revealing conversation he had with Feith in his office in early 2001. When Feith learned that Lang is an Arabist, he asked him "Is it really true that you really know the Arabs this well, and that you speak Arabic this well? Is that really true?" When Lang replied in the affirmative, Feith responded "That's too bad." As Lang observed, the neoconservatives typically employed "people who were not intelligence professionals. Rather, they hired people brought in because they thought like [the neoconservatives]." Here we see disregard both for bureaucratic and professional authority. [87]

With trusted people in replacement units created by Neocon core members, both could be sidelined. Paul Pillar, the CIA officer in charge of coordinating the intelligence community's assessments regarding Iraq, wrote that "The administration's rejection of the intelligence community's judgments became especially clear with the formation of a special Pentagon unit," the Counter Terrorism Evaluation Group. As well, the Office of Special Plans replicated (and sometimes overrode) some functions performed in other parts of the Pentagon. One of these was war planning and execution, typically in the hands of "combatant commanders" who report to the secretary of defense. Yet a senior State Department official confirmed that he had seen a number of documents on war planning that had been assembled by the Office of Special Plans, according to reporter Jane Mayer.[88]

Another task undertaken by the Office of Special Plans, the preparation of talking points, is typically the prerogative of the intelligence agencies that collect and analyze the data on which talking points should be based. But the mission of the Office of Special Plans was "developing propaganda and pushing . . . an agenda on Iraq," in Kwiatkowski's words, and desk officers had to quote Office points in materials compiled for senior officials and for anyone outside the Pentagon.[89] Saddam Hussein's use of chemical weapons, the supposed connection between Hussein and Al Qaeda, Hussein's alleged aid to the Palestinians, and signs that his nuclear program was viable and that he was planning to use nuclear weapons (thus making him a serious threat to the United States)— all were talking points designed to help sell the war.[90] By late 2002, the Office of Special Plans eclipsed the CIA and the Pentagon's own Defense Intelligence Agency, becoming the administration's primary source of intelligence on Iraq's alleged WMDs (weapons of mass destruction) and Hussein's alleged Al Qaeda ties, as journalist Seymour Hersh has written.[91]

Whether to the Pentagon or the NSC, Ahmed Chalabi and his Iraqi National Congress were core suppliers of such intelligence. This took place despite Chalabi being long distrusted by the CIA and the State Department and being wanted for allegedly defrauding the Jordanian government in the 1980s to the tune of $200 million. His operation, which had in the past run a forgery shop, was seen by many in the intelligence community as providing questionable information at best.[92] Nonetheless, both the Counter Terrorism Evaluation Group and the Office of Special Plans had a special relationship with Chalabi and his group. Both offices assessed intelligence based on information supplied by these sources—assessments typically not shared with or vetted by counterparts in relevant government quarters.[93]

In one arrangement brokered by Perle, Chalabi and his INC staff supplied intelligence "information" to the Counter Terrorism Evaluation Group. This unit was manned by two longstanding Perle associates: core member David Wurmser and Michael Maloof, with whom Wurmser had coauthored the "Clean Break" report. The two combed the voluminous influx of daily intelligence reports on terrorism, looking for documentation of connections between terrorist organizations and their potential state sponsors. They were to dispel the common view in the intelligence community that such groups did not work together. The men did not disappoint. They indeed posited links between Al Qaeda and Saddam Hussein's Iraq—findings that did not square with those of other intelligence units and agencies.[94]

Nonetheless, it was "news you can use." Maloof briefed Perle, who had security clearance through the Defense Policy Board, in his suburban Washington home. Maloof and Wurmser also briefed senior Bush administration officials, including Rumsfeld and Director of Central Intelligence George Tenet, as well as Wolfowitz, Stephen J. Hadley (who had worked under Wolfowitz in Reagan's defense department), Bolton, and Libby. The Office of Special Plans, for its part, was charged with gatekeeping: approving the exact wording to be used by other officials when discussing Iraq, weapons of mass destruction, and terrorism. Kwiatkowski said that she "witnessed neoconservative agenda bearers within [the Office of Special Plans] usurp measured and carefully considered assessments, and through suppression and distortion of intelligence analysis promulgate what were in fact falsehoods to both Congress and the executive office of the president." To show that Saddam

Hussein presented an imminent threat, she noted, the office "developed pretty sophisticated propaganda lines which were fed throughout government, to the Congress, and even internally to the Pentagon." One such (leaked) report, titled "Assessing the Relationship Between Iraq and al Qaida" and prepared either by the Counter Terrorism Evaluation Group or the Office of Special Plans, is marked as a briefing paper for the NSC and Office of the Vice President.[95]

This "intelligence" was used to help sell intervention in Iraq. Jim Lobe reports that "the offices fed information directly and indirectly to sympathetic media outlets, including the Rupert Murdoch-owned *Weekly Standard* and FoxNews Network, as well as the editorial pages of the *Wall Street Journal* and syndicated columnists, such as Charles Krauthammer."[96]

In time, prewar intelligence activities orchestrated by Feith and other Neocon core members came under investigation. Feith, who left his post as defense undersecretary in August 2005, became the subject of review by the Pentagon's inspector general. In 2007, the IG found that the Office of Special Plans had "developed, produced, and then disseminated alternative intelligence assessments on the Iraq and al Qaida relationship, which included some conclusions that were inconsistent with the consensus of the Intelligence Community, to senior decision-makers" and that Feith's intelligence briefings to the president presented "conclusions that were not fully supported by the available intelligence." The Senate Select Committee on Intelligence had already established that the unit exaggerated the Iraqi threat to justify the war in its first report of July 2004, which focused primarily on prewar assessments of the intelligence community. In a second report, issued in June 2008, the Committee found that Feith's office conducted sensitive intelligence activities without the intelligence community or the State Department knowing about them. While the vice chairman of the committee characterized Feith's operation as an illegal "private intelligence" one, the Pentagon's inspector general concluded that his operation was "inappropriate" but not illegal. Indeed, that it wasn't illegal is a key point. It did not have to be illegal to be highly effective in the influence game.[97]

Through it all, the Neocon core marginalized officials who were not part of their group and operated through a cross-agency clique that enabled them to limit information and activities to their associates. In interagency discussions, Feith and his two special offices, for instance, were in touch with members of their own network in the other agencies instead of their official counterparts in other agencies, even the Pentagon's Defense Intelligence Agency, according to Kwiatkowski. Instead of interfacing with the State Department's Bureau of Intelligence and Research or its Near Eastern Affairs bureau, for example, they worked through people in their network such as Undersecretary of State for Arms Control and International Security Bolton. At the National Security Council they dealt primarily with Deputy National Security Advisor Stephen Hadley (who had worked under Wolfowitz in Reagan's defense department) and then with Elliott Abrams of Iran-Contra fame, when he became the NSC's chief Middle East aide in December 2002. Kwiatkowski says that she "witnessed several cases of staff officers being told not to contact their counterparts at State or the National Security Council because that particular decision would be processed through a different channel." True flexians, members of the Neocon core and their allies personalized bureaucracy while revising rules in pursuit of their joint mission.[98]

Organizing Truthiness

Following 9/11, the case had to be made to the public that Iraq posed a serious threat to the United States. Invading the cradle of civilization was not only justified, but necessary.

While discussion about whether to go to war was stunningly absent in the bureaucracy, discussion about how to sell it was ubiquitous, according to many insiders. As Paul Pillar summed it up: "The discussion was only about the message to the public. It was all about what will persuade the public. It was all selling. In the past, getting public support was important, but this was all-consuming."[99]

In an atmosphere of federal governing carried out to a large extent by private entities, in which the state and the private sector each have a part and each reinforces the other, who best to sell the effort? Richard Perle and the Neocon core, of course, itself composed of players on both the outside and inside, as well as those individuals who bridged and blurred the state-private divide. Accordingly, members of the Neocon core helped organize a band of collaborators in the media, friendly think tanks, and political organizations.

These players formed an overlapping effort with another group of long-time neoconservative activists who mostly made their mark as public intellectuals and pundits. Many of them constitute a parallel collection. Front and center are the political commentator William Kristol, son of the elder Kristol, who edits the *Weekly Standard* (which he founded in 1995 together with John Podhoretz, son of the elder Podhoretz), and Robert Kagan, cofounder and codirector of the Project for the New American Century and a *Washington Post* columnist. As journalist John Judis expounded, "the neoconservatives were part of a broader network of writers, editors, academics, and activists that gave them access to the *Wall Street Journal*'s editorial page, Murdoch's Fox News, *The New Republic*, the *Washington Post* editorial page, and a host of friendly conservative publications including the *National Interest*, *Policy Review*, *Commentary*, and *National Review*, as well as conservative talk radio." To make the war happen, these neoconservative public intellectual activists relentlessly graced the airwaves and op-ed pages, advocating for and defending the invasion of Iraq.[100]

It goes without saying that Perle was ubiquitous. He claimed on the airwaves that there were "substantial links" between Iraq and al Qaeda. He told the British House of Commons that the U.S. would attack Iraq even if UN weapons inspectors found nothing.[101] In fact, quasi-government official Perle (head of the Defense Policy Board) gave talks all over Europe promoting the war. Wilkerson's boss, Secretary of State Powell, privately grumbled that "Perle is doing a lot of proselytizing around the world." Powell instructed Wilkerson to compile a dossier of Perle's speeches and activities, of what he was saying and to whom. As Wilkerson expressed: "He was making remarks as if he were an official inside the U.S government. The Germans, French, Brits, and Japanese perceived him as an official purveying official U.S. policy. . . . He was giving speeches about the need to take out Saddam Hussein, the reliability of Ahmed Chalabi, Saddam Hussein's intent to use nuclear weapons. He was also pitching the argument for preemption [preemptive war]. . . . I had to bring on an extra staff person to keep up [the dossier]. It turned into five notebooks . . . and they were big notebooks too! One was four-inches thick," he said.[102]

Helping to advance the marketing effort, both in the run-up to the war and in its early years, was Benador Associates, which represented many neoconservatives. The firm ran a well-coordinated and targeted campaign. Often more than once a day, Benador sent out an e-mail titled "Eleana's Choice" or "Latest Articles by Our Experts" to some 4,000 journalists and other subscribers.[103] The 24/7 campaign not only included articles, say, promoting and defending the war in Iraq, but a minute-by-minute chronicle of neoconservative responses to critics, ranging from the failure to find weapons of mass destruction in Iraq to American military abuse of prisoners. Benador's efforts were often rewarded quickly. For example, in the *National Review Online* of April 30, 2004, Frank Gaffney refuted the claims of an April 27, 2004, *New York Times* article detailing the workings of Feith's two Pentagon shops.[104]

The *New York Times's* star reporter Judith Miller turned out to be that paper's leading handmaiden for the neoconservatives. Out of her unusual access to Chalabi, Libby, and others came riveting front-page stories of Iraqi weapons of mass destruction and the threat they posed to the United States.

The "echo chamber" reverberated. Like their communist forebears, the neoconservatives are very skilled at framing issues, creating front organizations, and planting and propagating stories. Jim Lobe has tracked several stunning cases of neoconservative media orchestration. One, right after 9/11, introduces the idea that organized governments (read Iraq) are supporting terrorists, and that they must be held to account. The run of stories begins on September 12, 2001, with Perle quoted in the *Washington Post*, through Kristol on National Public Radio and Fox News with a like message, and extends to the September 20 publication of a letter signed by thirty-seven people, primarily neoconservatives, printed in several publications.[105]

Another example of orchestration documented by Lobe goes as follows: Chalabi planted a story with Judith Miller about Saddam Hussein having an active nuclear weapons program, which appeared in the *New York Times* on December 20, 2001. James Woolsey repeated it on MSNBC's *Hardball with Chris Matthews* that same evening, giving it further attention. Perle gave it ultimate credibility by publishing an op-ed piece in the *New York Times* a week later. Then, with this story having been test driven, at a pivotal moment, when Cheney needed to discredit Joseph Wilson, the vice president picked it up several months later.[106]

Throughout this echo chamber, the medium was the message and the message was managed. Libby and Hadley were part of the White House Iraq Group (WHIG), a secret organization founded to persuade the American public that the war in Iraq was necessary by any means possible, including by leaking intelligence to the media. According to an authoritative study by media scholars Charles Lewis and Mark Reading-Smith of speeches, briefings, interviews, and testimony in the run-up to the war, also pivotal in rousing public opinion was the meticulously coordinated and overlapping misinformation campaign conducted by President Bush and seven top administration officials.[107]

Truthiness helped enable the successful march to war. Of course the "facts" that make up the "truthy" picture are really images—resilient ones, oft repeated, from the mushroom cloud and supposed terrorist training ground in Iraq to the supposed meeting between the 9/11 terrorist Mohamed Atta and an Iraqi official.[108] And it doesn't really matter if the mushroom cloud or training ground are real or the meeting took place, the images stick, and we believe the image, thus producing the "reality." (The Senate Intelligence Committee concluded that President Bush and his advisers exaggerated claims of Iraq's weapons and terrorist ties by suggesting an Iraq and Al Qaeda partnership that was not corroborated by intelligence.[109])

The acceptance of truthiness is made all the more insurgent by the institutional backdrop it partially plays on: the devaluation of knowledge and the blurring of boundaries between punditry and journalism (recall General Barry McCaffrey and the other retired high-ranking military professionals retained by major television networks as ostensibly neutral commentators) and the parallel decline in the institution of investigative reporting.

And the dearth of memory. Practitioners of truthiness know that the truth of the present moment may not be that of yesterday. Our neoconservative protagonists have mastered this art around the Iraq war, constantly revising history as needed. Thus, for instance, Perle can say with a straight face: "Huge mistakes were made, and I want to be very clear on this: They were not made by neoconservatives, who had almost no voice in what happened. . . ."[110]

Mission Accomplished

Perle's remarks notwithstanding, the extent to which the Neocon core influenced the rush to war is well established. Core members were so intimately enmeshed in advocating, executing, and justifying the war, from so many complementary, interconnected, and influential positions—in government, consultancy, and quasi-governmental posts, NGOs, and media—that it is difficult to imagine the decision to invade Iraq without the involvement of the flex net. To do so, they not only revived, but pressed into full service, their methods from the 1970s, 1980s, and 1990s—including gathering and disseminating alternative intelligence to supplant government processes and findings; manipulating around bureaucratic and legal rules; improvising and obfuscation of roles; working through pressure groups and quasi-governmental positions; and use of might-be-authorized, might-not-be-authorized American envoys, as well as foreign brokers as go-betweens with foreign nations. They thrust themselves to the top of their influence game not only via these practices, but as flexian innovators in personalizing bureaucracy, privatizing (official) information while branding conviction, and revising (official) rules. Their great achievement is perhaps best summarized by the words of Meyrav Wurmser on a program aired by the BBC in 2003. In introducing Wurmser and other neoconservatives, the host called the moment of the fall of Saddam Hussein "a dream that Meyrav Wurmser and her husband David, now at the State Department, had cherished as long as anyone in Washington." Meyrav responded: "We actually opened a bottle of champagne. This was a moment we waited for, for many, many years. I mean we've been working on freedom for Iraq for the past 9 years maybe. My personal feeling was doing an incredibly good deed by pushing this war because, you know . . . people got their freedom out of it."[111]

And Yet, They Still Go On and On . . .

The entrance of a new administration into the White House is unlikely to change the players' ways and means of operating, not to mention their long-held beliefs, even if they no longer occupy key government posts. While the exact extent of their influence on the new administration remains to be seen (some neoconservatives see their future more with Democrats than with Republicans, as Jacob Heilbrunn documents), one thing is certain: They will continue to employ their proven modus operandi—to the extent they are able to get away with it.[112]

Iraq was only the first stop. Iran, and, to a lesser degree Syria, have long been on the Neocon core's wish list.[113] Members of the core have long advocated "regime change" in Iran via U.S. interference. Their aim is baldly articulated by intellectual neoconservatives such as Norman Podhoretz, who wrote in a 2007 *Commentary* article: "As an American and as a Jew, I pray with all my heart that he [President George W. Bush] will [bomb Iran]."[114] Michael Ledeen, longtime holder of the "Freedom Chair" at the AEI (now Freedom Scholar at the Foundation for the Defense of Democracies, where Perle and Gaffney are advisers and Woolsey is a member of the Leadership Council), has been a steadfast, vocal advocate for regime change. In a forum at the AEI featuring his book *The Iranian Time Bomb: The Mullah Zealots' Quest for Destruction*, Ledeen emphasized that the debate should focus on "the nature of the Iranian regime," not on Iran's potential acquisition of nuclear weapons.[115]

His activities saturated with ambiguity, Ledeen appears to be the Neocon core's point person on Iran. In 2006 a new Iranian directorate was created inside the Pentagon's policy shop where the Office of Special Plans had been housed. Three veterans from the earlier office, including Neocon core member Abram Shulsky (who had worked for Perle in Reagan's Pentagon and headed the OSP), were tapped to advise or staff the new directorate. In leading the charge on Iran, Ledeen has revived brokers with whom he worked in the Iran-Contra affair. He arranged two secret meetings in 2001 and 2003 with Manucher Ghorbanifar, the expatriate Iranian arms dealer, the goal of which was to put U.S. officials in touch with Iranian dissidents, according to Ledeen. Also participating in the meetings was Lawrence A. Franklin, a Pentagon employee who worked in Feith's Office of the Undersecretary of Defense for Policy, as well as in his Office of Special Plans, and was later convicted of passing classified documents about Iran to Israel via officials of AIPAC (the American Israel Public Affairs Committee), the pro-Israeli lobbying group. The Senate Intelligence Committee investigated these meetings and found, in the words of journalist Laura Rozen, "that the Pentagon meetings with Ghorbanifar were inappropriate, but neither unauthorized nor illegal. Indeed, it found that the meetings had been authorized by Stephen Hadley, and then deputy defense secretary Paul Wolfowitz, among others."[116]

◊ ◊ ◊

WHAT TO MAKE of the Neocon core? This web of state-private players, of course, does not fit neatly into standard categories. They are clearly much more than an "issue network" or assortment of like-minded activists or pundits. They have never been top-tier official "deciders": They have exerted influence either from second-tier positions in government or from outside (and working together from these varying venues and posts). Because they are not simply government officials, they are often not within reach of government oversight. They cannot be reduced to lobbyists or interest groups, which operate mostly from outside government, or Wise Men, who serve as in-house advisers. They are not covert or intelligence operatives who, by definition, lie outside the public eye (though aspects of their activities may well be covert).[117]

The Neocon core is effective because they practice the modus operandi of a flex net. Bringing coordination to sometimes convoluted government, flex nets can be attractive to an administration and the public. For instance, the perseverance, unity, and modus operandi that has made the Neocon core effective in achieving many of its goals can make it an asset to a president. But these same qualities can also make it a liability, because the group has its own power and interests, which may at times diverge from the president's or reflect badly on him if the policies turn out to be unpopular.

In fact, it seems, unpopular policies are more likely to reflect badly on the president than they are on themselves. One of the features of flexians is their propensity to skirt not only legal and regulatory rules, but avoid career and reputational damage as well.

Whether the Neocon core is successful in getting its policies implemented or not, its members' success as personalities seems well established. Once Bush II was reelected in 2004, members of the Neocon core fared well, despite the Iraq debacle. Paul Wolfowitz, deputy defense secretary in the first term, was promoted to be the new president of the World Bank (though he later resigned for "personal reasons"). John Bolton moved to the United Nations, despite the U.S. Congress's unwillingness to confirm him. Douglas Feith, who announced his resignation as undersecretary of defense for "personal reasons," continued to work on the Pentagon's Quadrennial Defense Review (an unprecedented role for nonofficials), joined the faculty at Georgetown University, and later moved to a think tank.[118]

More important, none, save Scooter Libby, has suffered serious consequences for his actions. Libby was convicted of felonies in March 2007 including obstruction of justice and perjury in the Plame-CIA case, but his
sentence was quickly commuted by President Bush. Libby soon found a perch
at the conservative Hudson Institute (where Feith and Meyrav Wurmser are
now also affiliated).[119] And one can rest assured that his fellow core members
will continue to help rehabilitate his reputation and ensure him a comfortable livelihood; after all, they created a multimillion-dollar fund to aid in his
defense.[120]

Chalabi, their buddy, is a veritable Energizer bunny. While the Neocon
core failed to install him as president of the new Iraq, Chalabi has played a
number of formal roles there, from member of the Iraqi Governing Council
to head of the services committee, a consortium of service ministries, and
two Baghdad municipal posts. No doubt many of Chalabi's informal roles
have yet to come to light. Through it all, Chalabi has floated in and out of U.S.
administration grace, but to date has always come back. In 2004 the FBI undertook an investigation after respected U.S. intelligence sources concluded
he was a double agent for Iran. Tellingly, while still under active investigation
by the FBI for alleged espionage during a November 2005 visit to Washington, he was apparently not interrogated by its agents. Instead he had audiences with Vice President Cheney, Secretary of State Condoleezza Rice,
Secretary of Defense Rumsfeld, National Security Advisor Hadley, and other
high officials, despite allegedly then being out of Bush-administration favor.
Through it all, he was publicly backed by Perle. During this same visit, I heard
Chalabi speak at AEI, the same platform from whence two and a half years
earlier he had called for the removal of Saddam Hussein. Chalabi was received as a respected statesman, even as he claimed, fantastically, that the
Iraqi "government has stopped 95 percent of the corruption." Democracy
and transparency are taking hold in the country, he declared. In October
2007 Malaki's naming of Chalabi as head of the services committee prompted
the spokesperson for General David Petraeus, the highest U.S. military com-
mander in Iraq, to say that Chalabi "is an important part of the process."[121]
By May 2008, however, U.S. officials in Baghdad once again announced they
had severed ties with him.[122]

While the track record as experts of members of the Neocon core and their trusted brokers is weak, to put it generously (having been wrong about everything from the existence of WMD's in Iraq to American troops being greeted as "liberators" to the creation of democracy in Iraq), for the most part their status as players remains strong.

The fact that they identify themselves as fellows at neutral-sounding think tanks, and exude an aura of intellectual expertise and objectivity in their writings and public appearances, helps make these players more convincing than if they were to present themselves as current or former operatives. Even now, the public is frequently exposed to Perle's "analysis" as a supposedly disinterested observer on the Middle East and U.S. foreign affairs on mainstream news programs and in widely respected newspapers.[123]

Not only do the stars of individual Neocon core members and their associates continue to rise. As a group, their influence may appear to wane with the close of the Bush II era, but there is no reason to believe they will stop pushing their agenda forward from whatever perches they organize. What, then, does the story of the Neocon core tell us about the ability of U.S. government to operate in the public interest and to push back in the face of such effective fusions of state and private power? What does it mean when individuals can no longer be embarrassed or shamed? In the next chapter, we shall explore these questions.

CHAPTER SEVEN

Accountability in the Age of Flex Nets

THE NEW SYSTEM OF POWER AND INFLUENCE AND THE PLAYERS who thrive in it have transformed our world. The consequences are well illustrated by the global economic meltdown that became incontrovertible in the fall of 2008. At the root of the crisis and the heart of the new system is a decline in loyalty to institutions. This decline is reflected in the proliferation of players who swoop in and out of the organizations with which they are affiliated—who operate in them, but are not of them—and create "coincidences of interest" that serve their own goals at the expense of their organizations and the public. The greed that Wall Street high fliers symbolize is merely an egregious expression of such lack of loyalty and disdain for the public good— outcomes of the four transformational developments at work. This recalls the cross-pollinating institutional nomads of Poland and especially the plundering clans of 1990s Russia. In such a moral universe, ethics becomes a matter of individual choice, with the only real control being social pressure exerted by the network. Ethics are disconnected from a larger public or community and detached from the authority that states and international organizations, boards of directors, and even shareholders once provided. With the players removed from the input and visibility of these institutions, not to mention that of voters, the consequences to the public are multiple and serious.

As the political economist Susan Strange astutely observed more than a decade ago, "In a world of multiple, diffused authority each of us shares

Pinocchio's problem: our individual consciences are our only guide." While Strange lived only long enough to observe the fruits of the first two transformational developments, the reinvention of bureaucracy and the end of the Cold War, she saw how they undermined accountability and made the public more reliant on the vicissitudes of individual conscience.[1]

The public is vulnerable because of the greater potential for players who are supposed guardians of official information and public policy to further their own rather than the public interest, and to do so unnoticed. States, international organizations, and all manner of institutions face a daunting responsibility: ascertaining the allegiances of the consultants and even the executives who work for them. The problem is that these are the very institutions that are diluted by divided loyalties and undermined by flex activity.

Think back, for instance, to the retired military professionals retained by major television networks as ostensibly unbiased commentators on the war in Iraq. The quintessential example is General Barry McCaffrey. They presented themselves, and were presented by the media, as impartial analysts. Yet they had overlapping roles as undisclosed beneficiaries of exclusive Pentagon briefings and perks, which they had incentives to avail themselves of because of their potential usefulness in their business consulting—as well as for enhancement of their status. These benefits afforded them other incentives to maintain their access and good standing with the Pentagon. Their coincidences of interest could well have affected their ability to call the facts as they saw them. Yet how could the public, trying to understand events in Iraq, know that their information was coming from commentators of questionable objectivity? No institution—from the Pentagon to its contractors to the media—had an incentive to be anything but complicit. While the military men's activities might not pass a smell test, they were mostly beyond the reach of auditors. (Government auditors, adhering to their specified narrow focus, looked into certain activities under their jurisdiction involving money and possible conflicts of interest and found no wrongdoing.)

Conversely, the episode also shows journalism at its best. We know about the generals' multiplicity of roles because the *New York Times* underwrote an investigation for which the reporter won a Pulitzer. But these facts were not unearthed until long after American public opinion had already been swayed.

Existing means of holding de facto public decision makers accountable to the public are far too inflexible for the maneuverings of today's premier influencers—flexians and flex nets—who are, above all, wielders of influence on public issues. Not only do government audits harken back to a world with clearer demarcations that depend on the existence of a definite state-private divide. They also have limited jurisdiction and are not typically charged with tracing influence across organizations, but rather with how government spends taxpayers' money.

There are other problems, too. The very institutions that are supposed to mind the store may be occupied by players working on behalf of themselves and their networks, not the institutions. Enron, the now defunct energy giant, whose CEOs and CFOs kept key information from their board of directors and forsook shareholders in favor of their own spoils, famously illustrates the shortcomings. Communist managers pale in comparison: Although they vastly underreported profits—in their case, merely to make the system work (and under postcommunism, to conceal income and shrink tax liability)— the top officials of Enron grossly overreported profit in order to rake in millions for themselves.

Moreover, at the same time that the accounting firm Arthur Andersen (formerly among the Big Six) was auditing certain units of the company, top executives at Enron were maneuvering across the whole, concealing money-making schemes by creating entities that enabled those schemes. These executives used Enron stock as collateral for new partnerships, which they used to hide Enron losses and keep the company's balance sheets looking better and better. (Tellingly, flexlike overlapping roles enabled these partners-in-crime to hide many of their money-making schemes.) Meanwhile, not only did Arthur Andersen auditors (let alone Enron's board of directors or shareholders) not know the true nature of these schemes, they avoided the hard questions because Arthur Andersen had cozy relations with Enron executives and the auditing company had a unit dedicated to servicing Enron exclusively. "Cross pollination" of employees between the firms was routine. There were few incentives to do much actual auditing. As the lawyer and fraud investigator Jack Blum told me: "There's an understanding between the audited and the auditor. Each piece without context is okay. And people at the top are paid to sit with paper bags over their heads." The Enron executives were masters of performance, demolishing any reporter or industry analyst who dared to question the efficacy of their statements. Business journalist John Cassidy argues that such corporate scandals arise in part from "the culture of auditing."[2]

Arthur Andersen's complicity and issuances of clean bills of health eventually contributed to its own demise, as well as Enron's. Observance of institutional goals went missing in both companies. While Enron's top executives greatly enhanced their personal wealth, they devastated the incomes and future pensions of their employees, and the equity of the stockholders whose financial well-being they were duty-bound to protect. When signature firms like Arthur Andersen go down in flames, auditing institutions as a whole lose authority. As Dipak Gyawali, an international development specialist and one-time cabinet member of Nepal, put it: "Because of auditing scandals such as that of Arthur Andersen . . . , audit reports do not inspire much confidence and serious doubts crop up in many minds asking whether garden-variety audit reports have left much still undiscovered."[3]

While the case of Enron and Arthur Andersen is in the realm of American finance, some of which, as of late, has distinguished itself as ethically challenged to say the least, the fact is that the prevailing approach to "accountability" can enable flex activity to go on behind the veneer of the auditors' clean bill of health.

Auditing the Audit

A brief look at the recent history of oversight and evaluation practices shows how ill suited they are to monitor the activities of today's top influencers. In the past several decades, accountability has become associated with specific auditing practices in the United States, the United Kingdom, and other neoliberal havens. These practices disconnect it from loyalty to and trust of the institution being audited and sever it from its original spirit. In the go-go 1980s, when Thatcher and Reagan were at the helm in the United Kingdom and the United States, the goal of refashioning the state in the image of the private sector motivated the migration of audits from their original association with financial management to other areas of working life.

The result was, as Michael Power, an experienced chartered accountant, as well as a professor at the London School of Economics, charts, the idea of audits exploded throughout society and permeated organizational life as the chief method of controlling individuals. The tools and approaches of accountancy became the means through which "the values and practices of the private sector would be instilled in the public sector," as several anthropologists studying the subject have assessed. For instance, the UK's Audit Commission, created in 1983 to ensure that local authorities used resources efficiently, took audit functions beyond the traditional role of financial accounting to encompass such tasks as monitoring "quality" and "performance," and identifying "best practice." Ensuring "value for money" through measuring performance outputs and the "effectiveness of management systems" became hallmarks of "good government." The new definition of audit was soon applied widely: Audits were employed in public sector arenas such as education to evaluate employees, training, curricula, and research. In the United States, although cost-benefit analysis and similar management models were introduced into the Defense Department in the 1960s, it was not until the early 1980s that the UK-style audit began to be adopted widely in American government.[4]

Auditing, which derives from accountancy, breaks things down into observable, isolated, and often quantifiable pieces, and then scrutinizes the pieces—typically with little or no regard for the whole. "Audit has thereby become the control of control," as Power writes, "where what is being insured is the quality of control systems, rather than the quality of first order operations." This practice is patterned after the audit's first major application after finance: industry, where the audit employed rigid rules to the quality control and counting of mechanical items, such as nuts and bolts at a factory. Well-defined jobs had a clear list of tasks for which one individual was responsible. The audited performed discrete tasks and were not expected to know how the pieces fit together.[5]

Let's take a look at how that approach worked in just one instance of the elaborate maneuverings of Richard Perle, consultant, businessman, pundit, think-tanker, and government adviser—and Neocon core ringleader. As we saw in Chapter 6, while serving as chair (later member) of the Defense Policy

Board in the first term of George W. Bush, Perle used that position as a platform from which to call for the overthrow of Saddam Hussein and pushed
"information" manufactured by Ahmed Chalabi through state and private
channels to help make the case for war. In his extensive operations abroad, he
left many listeners with the impression that he spoke for the U.S. government.
He also allegedly used state information for nonstate purposes, offering his
defense-related clients sensitive information. In one instance, according to
the *Los Angeles Times*, Perle advised clients of Goldman Sachs on investment
activities in postwar Iraq soon after he and other board members had been
briefed by the Defense Intelligence Agency and other classified sources. Also
while on the board, Perle represented two companies in their dealings with
the U.S. government: A major American satellite manufacturer retained him
to help counter U.S. government allegations that the firm had illegally transferred technology to the Chinese, and a telecommunications company retained him to advise it on deals with China that the FBI and the Defense
Department opposed for national security reasons.[6]

Following an investigation of these activities, the Pentagon's inspector general concluded that Perle "arguably represented" two firms in issues "pending
in the department or agency of the government in which such employee is
serving," and he therefore may have violated two federal laws. But because
Perle was classified as a "special government employee," with his job entailing only an estimated eight days of annual service (as opposed to the sixty
days required to breach the law), he was not in violation. While auditors were
busy counting the number of days instead of looking at the big picture, much
more was at stake, namely, the mission of the organization that Perle was supposedly serving (in this instance meaning the Pentagon, not the contractor)
and the country's national security.[7]

Flexians' skill at skirting the rules and getting away unscathed fits nicely
with the neoliberal approach to accountability. It is substantially removed
from the internal ethics of community to which it is supposed to apply and
goes hand-in-hand with the waning allegiance of people to institutions. "Accountability" is imposed from the outside—without the engagement of the
"moral community"—a community "that shapes (and is shaped by) the expectations, rules, norms and values of social relationships," as a scholar who
studies the history of the concept of accountability has explained. This

moral community approach lies at the heart of governing "in contexts where there is a sense of agreement about the legitimacy of expectations among community members." The prevailing accountability approach, however, doesn't address people's investment in an institution's mission. Except in egregious cases, it can scarcely assess whether the public trust is being served or violated.[8]

When information is broken up into bits so that essential pieces are separated from each other, knowledge, wisdom, and institutional memory are sidelined. Appearances are what matter. Nowadays one performs for the external evaluators, whether that be Enron's top executives announcing amazing profits while the company is actually going down the tubes; Perle reporting his number of days on a project; or a report listing the titles and number of workshops held or performance goals met. As practiced today, "accountability" encourages performance that showcases accountability, but not necessarily that is accountable. The result is reminiscent of centrally planned communist systems in which bureaucrats who must—but can't—meet production targets construct alternate realities for the central planners. As Power writes: "There is a sense that the tail of audit is increasingly wagging the dog of accountability, and there are doubts about whether audits really empower the agents which they are intended to serve." Likewise, today's accountability performers often pull the wool over the eyes of the auditor. The embrace of truthiness can only deepen this tendency.[9]

Getting away with "performing" is made all the more easy for the players when they work in a network or across borders. Accountability practices evaluate individuals, not group actions. Groups are scarcely subject to investigation unless they fall under organized crime or terrorism, and even then it is only individuals who can be held to account. But members of flex nets, who dominate influential roles across governmental and nongovernmental organizations, sidestep accountability systems and evade culpability precisely through their collective and flexible role playing. Recall how Perle, Wolfowitz, and Feith helped each other evade consequences of breaches of government security rules. Such players, finally, can advance laws and regulations on their own behalf and create a playing field that is designed for their activities. This is plain to see in the financial world. And, crucial to bear in mind, the vast majority of the influence-wielding activities of flex nets, although far removed from democratic oversight and input, is not illegal, so is not even subject to legal scrutiny.

Flex nets, those self-propelling teams that pool resources, are skilled at wriggling out of trouble while still privatizing policy and following their goals. Both the Chubais-Harvard and Neocon flex nets did exactly this when members of their network were investigated or had their reputations damaged and thus needed to be removed from a government post or revived so they could get one.

Vacuums of accountability are exacerbated when players operate across countries and cultures, encountering disparate laws, information, norms, standards, and enforcement. "Nonstate" actors who today often possess information once reserved for official organizations can also play off the rules of any particular country in which they operate against the rules of others. Moreover, when a flex net is made up of players representing more than one nation or party, as was true with the Chubais-Harvard partners, members can play one off against another. For example, Jonathan Hay, Moscow representative for Harvard's U.S.-underwritten economic reform program, could legitimately argue that his input was offered as a Russian, not an American; he was given signature authority by Russian members of his flex net, some of whom doubled as officials, on privatization decisions of the Russian state. Such overlapping roles can be rationalized as "efficient," but they can scarcely be judged to be accountable; nor do they embody clarity of loyalty, except, notably, to fellow players.[10]

Flexians and flex nets are too peripatetic for a fixed accountability system. In the old world, when roles and responsibilities were more clearly defined, the audit served a purpose because it could break things down and observe where people stepped over boundaries. Today, we have fewer tidy boundaries. Flexians can breezily outmaneuver the system, evade culpability, and get away with it—playing one role today and another role tomorrow (or both simultaneously today), while an auditor typically has jurisdiction over a limited number of roles. These players have expanded their repertoires of roles, which they can keep separate, merge, combine, and otherwise manipulate to achieve their goals. Flexibly employing their repertoires affords them deniability and thereby also diminishes the ability of auditors to hold them to account because the means of monitoring are not integrated.

For instance, Gaston L. Gianni, a former inspector general with more than forty years of government auditing experience and a former vice chairman of the President's Council on Integrity and Efficiency, an umbrella organization for IGs (now called the Council of the Inspectors General on Integrity and Efficiency), notes that the typical U.S. government approach to auditing is to "take policy already made and look to see how well it's being implemented, if it's achieving the results intended, if it's efficient, and if it's effective. . . . Auditors generally don't get into the arena of who influences policy. The flexians you describe are coming in when policy is being made. . . . There are no processes in place to monitor [them]. If we find out what's going on at all, . . . then it's too late to do anything about it." Monique Helfrich, an energy specialist who has been on both sides of the regulatory aisle, as a staff engineer and an external regulator working as a technical specialist for the Defense Nuclear Facilities Safety Board, asserts that "External regulation comes out of an environment in which you know who the groups are and what their mission is. We've moved into a world in which groups change; you can't regulate them because you can't find them. The regulators are in a constant game of catch up and never have the chance to implement a standard regulatory scheme."[11]

Really holding flexians to account would be a daunting enterprise. To know what individual players are up to, the astute observer would need a bird's-eye view, synthesizing the players' various roles and discrete functions and seeing how they interrelate. In fact, this enterprise would require a team of investigators and public servants, tracking flexians' activities, networks, and funding sources over time: reporters connecting the dots; attorneys and regulators picking up on their work and subpoenaing documents that reporters cannot; and legislators dedicated to passing laws to reflect changes in the environment and hold culprits to account. Because the potential influence and "corruption" of flexians and members of flex nets is interrelated, that would involve a holistic approach, one that considers all the components collectively and how they interact. Helfrich adds that there must be at least an element of self-regulation because "the people doing it need to own it." But, she says, external regulation should also play a role. "The external entity doing regulation needs to be fluid and flexible." By examining the interconnectedness of flexians' activities, their individual pronouncements would be more transparent in terms of who and what they represent: coordinated pieces of a whole strategy, rather than isolated individual initiatives. That way, such players could not so easily get away with compartmentalizing their activities and projecting a false image of themselves that is readily accepted at face value.[12]

Some information about these players' activities can potentially be dug up, and investigatory bodies, journalists, and public interest watchdogs can publish these findings, which can reside on their Web sites and even become common knowledge among a small sliver of society. The question is, Does it matter? Players like McCaffrey and Perle can be investigated by, say, the Pentagon's inspector general, one of the many institutions they've touched. But even if such investigations are not covered up (in the case of the former, it reportedly was), they have little effect. Players like Perle, scarcely slowed, leave behind a dust cloud of investigations almost without consequence or result. The incentives that led the Pentagon to open its access to high-ranking retired military officers-cum-pundits, the media to put them on the air, and contractors to hire them are very much alive and well. These incentives will continue to be at work as other issues arise, in other incarnations and venues. Perhaps most important, once flexians' activities are exposed, the damage usually has already been done.

Moreover, few have the power and influence to bring the new players of power and influence to light. The authority of journalism is waning. Investigative reporting is dying a swift death, as the institution of journalism itself undergoes massive gutting, newspapers fold right and left, and dwindling resources are available for investigative reporting of the kind that enabled the *Washington Post* to break the Watergate story. To make matters worse, flexians and their networks are skilled at warding off efforts to illuminate their methods or activities. They respond immediately and aggressively to criticism by putting out their own stories, attacking the messenger, and enlisting all possible allies in the antimessenger campaign to highlight their integrity and good works. Perle and other members of the Neocon core specialize in this strategy.

Finally, even when people can be named, can they be "shamed"? Truthiness not only facilitates flexians' ability to appear in the moment without burden of track record; it also draws in institutions and the public, rendering them active participants in blessing the flexians. So we have Harvard professor Andrei Shleifer presenting himself as an anticorruption expert while he's under investigation or being sued for conspiracy to defraud the U.S. government, continuing, undaunted, to deliver testimony before congressional committees as a scholar of corruption, and writing for *Foreign Affairs* on the success of Russian "reform"—without disclosing his role in it and nary a mention by anyone. It is perhaps why that flagship journal can be equally mum on all these issues.

The flexians' success is greatly enhanced by the fact that no one is minding the store as a whole—even as we can't answer the most basic of questions: Who does the player represent, who are his associates and sponsors, and with whom is he affiliated? Where do his loyalties lie and to whom is he ultimately answerable? When these questions are difficult, if not impossible, to answer for so many of today's influencers, it follows that the prevailing means of keeping them in check are outmoded.

Serving Multiple Masters

The new system may have provided the conditions for the current global economic crisis, but that does not mean that the responses to it will unravel the system. In fact, they may well exacerbate it. There has been a multitude of responses so far on the part of governing institutions, from states, regional governments, and international financial institutions to local governments. But whether they are getting to the root of the problem remains in question. Calls for regulation and re-regulation cannot address the underlying dynamics—the span and speed of the players' ability to flex the walls between bureaucracy and business.

Still, regulation, particularly of the financial system, can help. The hollowing out of the regulatory functions of the state—enabled by financial legerdemain that privatized profit for a megawealthy handful while socializing risk for the rest—bears considerable responsibility for the crisis. But there are limits to regulation. The more regulation is introduced, the more loopholes are often opened up for flexians to squirm through. Regulation has to be smart and anticipate people's reactions to it; for, not unlike under a rigid communist system, regulation that doesn't do so only encourages the most skilled players to dance around it. These are the very players who often double as the rule makers. And flexians are not only dancers, they are choreographers, adept at performing their way out of trouble and thriving amid chaos.

Financial wizards who operate globally are doing just that. Moisés Naím, who wrote a book about illicit global trade, now outlines a "shadow financial system." Commenting in April 2009 on the effects of the economic crisis on this system, he predicted that it will not only not go away, but that it will grow. Shadow financiers, he noted, are "very important players with lots of money, lots of energy, and lots of relationships. . . . Those who understand how to play the regulations system and exploit gaps will flourish and operate even more opaquely than in the past."[13]

We've also seen, in response to the crisis, the creation of new institutional fusions of state and private power. What today in the United States is symbolized by "Government Sachs" does not appear altogether different from the merging of state and private power that characterized both communism and postcommunism. Such fusions, of course, are a crucial feature of the very system that helped bring about the crisis. In the United States, these mergers are not only in governing, where an interlocking handful of Wall Street–government "evolvers" create not only the financial architecture of the future, backed by the power and billions of the state, but new relationships among bureaucracy and market more generally, including new ownership structures. Via mega bailouts, the government has become a significant owner of mega companies: President Obama is now the shareholder-in-chief of three companies across economic sectors: the insurance behemoth AIG, the banking-financial conglomerate Citigroup, and the big-three automaker Chrysler. With inside information and power confined to a few actors who cozily intermingle with the beneficiaries of many of the bailouts, it is hard to get more "efficient." This state of affairs provides even more opportunities for these deciders to further reinforce both their influence and the fusion of state and private power, and to do so with minimal public input or even notice. Gone are the messy disagreements and competing interests and involvement of a diversity of actors that is the democratic process. New institutional forms of power and influence, forged by a smattering of state-private actors, many of them invisible to the public, become not only the norm, but are ever further removed from public input.

◊ ◊ ◊

ALTHOUGH THE NEW SYSTEM occasioned the crisis, it will adapt to the still newer, sometimes hostile circumstances that arise partly as a result—from regulation, political volatility, and cultural developments, to deepening economic turmoil. The challenge for the public is to try to preserve the accountability and transparency that is needed in a democratic society.

The world still has some hope for tracking the shadow elite. But existing means are far from being sufficient or able to cover the traveling bases of the players, who operate largely above public input, knowledge, and visibility. While new modes of dealing with some of the most obvious abuses will likely emerge (though not necessarily in the most opaque arenas such as finance), the problems presented by the new breed of players can't be solved by going back to traditional means of accountability. Few are the champions of boundaries in today's world.

My goal here has been to lay out the problem and identify patterns so that, at the very least, we can comprehend the new phenomenon. To change something, you must first understand it. I have written this book so that others can use the same lens to identify the players to which the transformational developments of the last quarter century have given rise. Their numbers and influence are sure to multiply in the coming years.

The rise of the shadow elite warrants revisiting age-old thinking on corruption. In the New Testament, the author of the Gospel of Matthew wrote, "No one can serve two masters; for a slave will either hate the one and love the other, or be devoted to the one and despise the other" (Matthew 6:24). This is corruption at its most basic—a violation of public trust. Flexians and flex nets pursue the ends of their own ideological masters, which often contradict the other masters they supposedly serve. The challenge for policymakers and readers, now that the problem has been laid out and the animal named, is to work toward recovering that public trust.

NOTES

Notes to Chapter 1

1. Anthropologist Aihwa Ong discusses "flexible identities" in Aihwa Ong, *Flexible Citizenship: The Cultural Logics of Transnationality* (Durham and London: Duke University Press, 1999).

2. Intelligence expert Steven Aftergood has employed the term "coincidence of interest" in this meaning, as cited in Tim Shorrock, "Former High-ranking Bush Officials Enjoy War Profits," Salon.com, May 29, 2008, http://www.salon.com/news/excerpt/2008/05/29/spies_for_hire/index1.html.

3. The *New York Times* article reference is David Barstow, "One Man's Military-Industrial-Media Complex," *New York Times*, November 30, 2008, http://www.nytimes.com/2008/11/30/washington/30general.html.
Defense Solutions is the name of the company on whose behalf McCaffrey contacted Petraeus.

4. Ibid.

5. The earlier piece in the *Times* appeared in April 2008. David Barstow, "Behind TV Analysts, Pentagon's Hidden Hand," *New York Times*, April 20, 2008, p. A1, http://www.nytimes.com/2008/04/20/washington/20generals.html. The *Times* characterization of the call for an investigation is from David Barstow, "Inspector General Sees No Misdeeds in Pentagon's Effort to Make Use of TV Analysts," *New York Times*, January 16, 2009, http://www.nytimes.com/2009/01/17/washington/17military.html.

The Pentagon's inspector general report is, Department of Defense, Office of Inspector General, *Examination of Allegations Involving DoD Public Affairs Outreach Program*, January 14, 2009, Report Number IE-2009–004, http://www.dodig.mil/Inspections/IE/Reports/ExaminationofAllegations InvolvingDoDOfficeofPublicAffairsOutreachProgram.pdf. Responding to the report, the *Times* found striking factual errors in the DoD's investigation, including that several military analysts who have easily documented affiliations with defense contractors are listed as having no such relations. The *Times* also pointed out inherent weaknesses in the DoD's investigative approach (Barstow, "Inspector General Sees No Misdeeds . . . "). For McCaffrey's response to the *Times*, see http://www.reuters.com/article/press-Release/idUS70468+17-Jan-2009+PRN20090117, and for response from McCaffrey's consulting company, as well as a friend, see http://www.mccaffreyassociates.com/pages/news.htm. For response by the *Times*'s ombudsman to these points, see Clark Hoyt, "The Generals' Second Careers," *New York Times*, January 25, 2009, http://www.newsombudsmen.org/cgi-bin/ono_article.pl?mode=view&article_id=1232910801.

For information on steps taken (and not taken) by the Obama administration with regard to the Pentagon Inspector General's report, see Frank Rich, "Obama Can't Turn the Page on Bush," *New York Times*, May 17, 2009, p. WK12. See also Glenn Greenwald, "The Ongoing Disgrace of NBC News and Brian

Williams," Salon.com, November 30, 2008, http://www.salon.com/opinion/greenwald/2008/11/30/mc-caffrey/ (accessed April 15, 2009), and Glenn Greenwald, "NBC and McCaffrey's Coordinated Responses to the NYT Story," Salon.com, December 1, 2008, http://www.salon.com/opinion/greenwald/2008/12/01/mccaffrey/ (accessed April 15, 2009). In addition to the Pentagon's inspector general, the Government Accountability Office and the Federal Communications Commission also initiated investigations of the Pentagon's program. In July 2009 the GAO found that the Pentagon did not violate propaganda laws. See: GAO, "Department of Defense—Retired Military Officers as Media Analysts," July 21, 2009, p. 2, http://www.gao.gov/decisions/appro/316443.pdf.

6. Jon Stewart's *The Daily Show*, January 26, 2005, http://www.thedailyshow.com/video/index.jhtml?videoId=113523&title=headlines-the-rice-storm&byDate=true.

7. The political-legal scholars here quoted are: Yves Dezalay and Bryant Garth, *The Internationalization of Palace Wars: Lawyers, Economists, and the Contest to Transform Latin American States* (Chicago: University of Chicago Press, 2002), pp. 11, 10.

8. For mention of Schroeder having negotiated the deal as chancellor and other facts, as well as commentary, see: BBC, "Schroeder attacked over gas post," December 10, 2005, http://news.bbc.co.uk/2/hi/europe/4515914.stm. For *Washington Post* editorial, see: Editorial, "Gerhard Schroeder's Sellout," *Washington Post*, December 13, 2005, p. A26, http://www.washingtonpost.com/wp-dyn/content/article/2005/12/12/AR2005121201060.html.

9. See, for instance, Ian Traynor, "Poland Recalls Hitler-Stalin Pact Amid Fears over Pipeline," *The Guardian*, May 1, 2006, http://www.guardian.co.uk/world/2006/may/01/eu.poland.

10. Information provided by a Russian journalist who heard about the deal in April 2005.

11. The Russian sociologist here quoted is Olga Kryshtanovskaya, interviewed by Pavel Zhavoronkov, "Proiskhozhdenie VIPov. Bogatstvo v Rossii Ostaetcia Privilegiei Nomenklatury" (The Origin of VIPs: Wealth in Russia Remains the Nomenklatura's Privilege), *Kompania*, May 15, 2003, http://maecenas.ru/doc/2004_5_6.html.

Gazprom monopolized (and still monopolizes) the gas sphere, including its international aspects conducted in the interest of the Russian state, not a private corporation. (Gazprom remains a strategic organization of the Kremlin, in which the power of the Kremlin clearly resides. It is in complete control of prospecting, transport, sale, distribution, pricing, and international activities.) Gazprom was born in 1989 in the Soviet Union's dying days when entire resource-rich ministries (in this case, the Ministry of Gas [the official translation is Soviet Ministry of Gas Industry]) were transformed into state enterprises under the personal control of members of the *nomenklatura*. While Gazprom was turned from a state ministry into a so-called private corporation in 1993 (after first being converted into a joint-stock company under the leadership of the prime minister, Viktor Chernomyrdin), the state owns more than 50 percent of its stock. (In November 1992, Russian president Boris Yeltsin signed decree #1333 "On the transformation of the state gas concern Gazprom into Russian joint-stock company 'Gazprom.'" See, for example, Elena Ivanova, "Gazovaia Industriia" [Gas Industry], *Vlast*, no. 47 [November 27, 2001], http://www.kommersant.ru/doc.aspx?DocsID=295883. See also "Theft of the Century: Privatization and the Looting of Russia. An Interview with Paul Klebnikov," *The Multinational Monitor* 23, nos. 1, 2 [Jan/Feb 2002], http://multinationalmonitor.org/mm2002/02jan-feb/jan-feb02interviewklebniko.html.)

12. For Schroeder's position, see see: Craig Whilock and Peter Finn, "Schroeder Accepts Russian Pipeline Job," *The Washington Post*, December 10, 2005, http://www.washingtonpost.com/wp-dyn/content/article/2005/12/09/AR2005120901755.html.

13. In the fall of 2008, after the failure of Lehman Brothers brought credit markets to their knees, banks found political connections more precious than ever. With American investment banks in free fall, the most politically connected seemed to land on the padded mattress of the TARP program, while their competitors received the concrete blow of forced mergers. Thomas B. Edsell of the *Huffington Post* is among those who have pointed out that it was a Lehman competitor, Goldman Sachs, that benefited most from the bailout of the insurance giant American International Group (AIG). Goldman Sachs was the largest beneficiary of AIG's government sponsored life support—$12.6 billion. The key decision maker on these matters was Treasury Secretary Henry Paulson, the former CEO of Goldman Sachs. In fact, Goldman has taken significant advantage of government funds. As Edsell has written: "On November 25, 2008, Goldman became the first bank in the nation to benefit from the Federal Deposit In-

surance Corp.'s Temporary Liquidity Guarantee Program (TLGP) . . . All told, Goldman has issued a total of $20 billion in government-guaranteed debt under TLGP. In their dealings with banks, both Treasury and the Fed have been subject to relatively minimal disclosure, in order to protect the proprietary interests of financial institutions, especially to prevent rumors of illiquidity or excessive debt from threatening a bank's viability." Thomas B. Edsall, "AIG Bonus Bombshell Raises New Questions about Goldman Sachs," *Huffington Post*, April 2, 2009, http://www.huffingtonpost.com/2009/03/17/goldman-sachs-goes-for-th_n_175638.html. See also Lila Rajiva, "Three-Card Capitalists: The Financial Disappearing Act of 2008," LewRockwell.com, October 1, 2008, http://www.lewrockwell.com/rajiva/rajiva11.html.

14. Investigative reporter John B. Judis has unearthed many of the facts of Jackson's activities. See John B. Judis, "Minister Without Portfolio," *The American Prospect, Inc.* 14, no. 5 (April 30, 2003), http://www.prospect.org/cs/articles?article=minister_without_portfolio. See also Jackson's bio at the Project for the New American Century, http://www.newamericancentury.org/brucejacksonbio.htm.

With regard to Lockheed Martin as the largest federal contractor, as of 2006, the company was the largest defense contractor by revenue (http://www.defensenews.com/static/features/top100/charts/rank_2007.php?c=FEA&s=T1C) and "the largest provider of IT services, systems integration, and training to the U.S. Government," according to the company (http://www.lockheedmartin.com/aboutus/index.html). See also Scott Shane and Ron Nixon, "In Washington, Contractors Take on Biggest Role Ever," *New York Times*, February 4, 2007, p. A1; and Dana Hedgpeth, "Balancing Defense and the Budget After Eight Boom Years for Spending on Military Equipment, Contractors Expect a Slowdown," *Washington Post*, October 13, 2008, p. D01, http://www.washingtonpost.com/wp-dyn/content/article/2008/10/12/AR2008101201724_pf.html. Lockheed Martin's Web site states: "As a global security and information technology company, the majority of Lockheed Martin's business is with the U.S. Department of Defense and the U.S. federal government agencies. The remaining portion of Lockheed Martin's business is comprised of international government and some commercial sales of our products, services and platforms." See http://www.lockheedmartin.com/aboutus/index.html.

15. Judis, "Minister Without Portfolio." For perspectives on costs faced by new entrants to NATO, see John Laughland, "The Prague Racket," *The Guardian*, November 22, 2002, http://www.guardian.co.uk/comment/story/0,3604,845129,00.html.

For signatories of the original (June 3, 1997) statement of principles of the Project for the New American Century, see: http://www.newamericancentury.org/statementofprinciples.htm. For Jackson's role as project director, see http://www.newamericancentury.org/aboutpnac.htm.

16. For Jackson's congressional testimony, see Bruce Pitcairn Jackson, "Testimony before the Senate Foreign Relations Committee," April 1, 2003, http://www.globalsecurity.org/military/library/congress/2003_hr/jacksontestimony030401.pdf. See also F. William Engdahl, "The Emerging Russian Giant Plays its Cards Strategically," *Geopolitics–Geoeconomics*, http://www.engdahl.oilgeopolitics.net/Geopolitics_Eurasia/Russian_Giant/russian_giant.html. The "Vilnius Ten" consisted of Albania, Bulgaria, Croatia, Estonia, Latvia, Lithuania, Macedonia, Romania, Slovakia, and Slovenia. The text consists of a "Statement of the Vilnius Group Countries in Response to the Presentation by the United States Secretary of State to the United Nations Security Council Concerning Iraq," February 5, 2003. See "Vilnius Group Response to Powell UNSC Presentation on Iraq," America.gov, February 7, 2009, http://www.america.gov/st/washfile-english/2003/February/20030207173228lfenner@pd.state.gov0.5013697.html. The source of Jackson's role is Judis, "Minister Without Portfolio." In 2003, Jackson shut the doors of both the Iraq and NATO committees. However, in the same set of offices, he and his colleagues launched a new undertaking, the Project on Transitional Democracies, another neoconservative-sponsored organization. See Engdahl, "The Emerging Russian Giant."

17. For Kelman's "evolving door," see, for example, Steven Kelman, "Evolving Door," *Government Executive Magazine* 36, no. 4 (March 16, 2004), http://www.govexec.com/features/0304/0304view.htm. For a profile of Kelman, see Forbes.com, "Steven Kelman Profile," http://people.forbes.com/profile/steven-kelman/38757.

18. Kelman also led support for the Federal Acquisition Streamlining Act of 1994 (FASA) and the Federal Acquisition Reform Act of 1995 (FARA). See "Steven Kelman," http://www.hks.harvard.edu/about/faculty-staff-directory/steven-kelman.

For Kelman's views, see, for instance, the front flap of his 1990 book, as follows: "Requirements intended to promote competition in contracting have made the performance of government worse, not better, according to Professor Kelman. Using federal procurement of computer systems as his model, Kelman shows the devastating effects of practices designed to prevent collusion between vendors and officials." Steven Kelman, *Procurement and Public Management: The Fear of Discretion and the Quality of Government Performance* (Washington, DC: American Enterprise Institute Press, 1990).

19. The advisory body Kelman sat on was the Defense Science Board Task Force. The press release is from the Bureau of National Affairs, "Gansler Asks Defense Science Board Group to Identify DOD Policies and Practices That Weaken Health, Competitiveness of U.S. Defense Industry," *Federal Contracts Report* 73, no. 4 (Jan. 25, 2000), p. 105. The board's final briefing is available at Defense Science Board Task Force, "Preserving a Healthy and Competitive U.S. Defense Industry to Ensure our Future National Security," November, 2000, http://www.dtic.mil/cgi-bin/GetTRDoc?AD=ADA399865&Location=U2&doc=GetTRDoc.pdf.

The name of the company referred to here is GTSI Corporation. For information about Kelman's role with GTSI, see "Investor Relations—Corporate Governance Biography," http://investor.gtsi.com/phoenix.zhtml?c=116604&p=irol-govBio&ID=58294. According to GTSI's Web site, "GTSI has provided technology products, professional services, and IT infrastructure solutions to federal, state, and local government." For GTSI company information, see "About GTSI," http://www.gtsi.com/cms/aboutgtsi/aboutdefault.aspx?ShopperID=36238be2–88b0–4856–8e7a-64993d5ec6fc. For GTSI's annual sales, see their Securities and Exchange Commission Form 10-K, GTSI Corp. Commission File Number 0–19394, for the fiscal year ending December 31, 2008, Part I, http://www.sec.gov/Archives/edgar/data/850483/000136231009003216/c82046e10vk.htm#101. See also Forbes.com, "Steven Kelman Profile," http://people.forbes.com/profile/steven-kelman/38757.

20. Information on *Federal Computer Week*'s audience and circulation is from its publisher, 1105 Media, Inc., http://certcities.com/pressreleases/release.asp?id=2. Kelman's column, "The Lectern," can be found at http://fcw.com/blogs/lectern/list/blog-list.aspx. For an example of Kelman presenting himself as a Harvard professor and former OFPP administrator, while failing to disclose his paid company connections yet advocating policies that benefit that company, see, for instance: Steve Kelman, "A Pair of Misguided Bills," *Federal Computer Week*, September 18, 2000, http://fcw.com/articles/2000/09/18/a-pair-of-misguided-bills.aspx.

21. Under Share in Savings contracting, contractors finance on behalf of the government certain capital improvements—typically information technology or energy equipment (such as heating or cooling systems)—in return for which the contractor receives a "share of the savings," a largely hypothetical calculation of what the government agency "would have spent" but for the contractors' contributions to capital improvement that led to "savings." Anitha Reddy, "Sharing Savings, and Risk: Special Contracts Appeal to Cash-Strapped Agencies," *Washington Post*, Business section, February 16, 2004, p. E01, http://pqasb.pqarchiver.com/washingtonpost/access/545898301.html?dids=545898301:545898301&FMT=ABS&FMTS=ABS:FT&fmac=&date=Feb+16%2C+2004&author=Anitha+Reddy&desc=Sharing+Savings%2C+and+Risk.

At the time of the *Post* article, Kelman was a registered lobbyist for Accenture Ltd., one of the largest beneficiaries of Share in Savings contracts, as well as a board member of FreeMarkets, Inc. Accenture's primary business model employs Share in Savings techniques (see GAO report, http://www.gao.gov/htext/d03327.html). The *Washington Post*'s original article and correction are available at http://www.washingtonpost.com/ac2/wp-dyn/A44259–2004Feb15?language=printer. Following such incidents and letters to editors demonstrating that Kelman had failed to disclose relevant industry affiliations, he began doing so in his Federal Computer Week column.

22. Kelman's op-ed can be found at Steve Kelman, "The IG Ideology," *Washington Post*, April 4, 2007, p. A13. Information from the Project on Government Oversight can be found at "Gutting Government Oversight: The Steve Kelman Ideology," POGO Web site, April 30, 2007, http://pogoblog.typepad.com/pogo/2007/04/gutting_governm.html.

23. With regard to members of flex nets being united by shared activities and interpersonal histories, in social network terms, members have "multiplex" ties vis-à-vis each other, meaning that they play multiple roles vis-à-vis their fellow members. Their ties are also "dense" in that each person in the group

knows and can interact with every other person independently of any intermediary. Social network analysis is a long-standing method and theoretical perspective that focuses on social relations among actors, rather than the characteristics of actors. Pioneers in the field were John Barnes, Clyde Mitchell, and Elizabeth Bott, all associated with the Department of Social Anthropology at Manchester University in the 1950s. They saw social structure as networks of relations and focused on "the actual configuration of relations which arose from the exercise of conflict and power." John Scott, *Social Network Analysis: A Handbook* (London, UK: Sage Publications, 1991), p. 27. With respect to interest groups, some scholars have defined them broadly. In his summary analysis of the literature, political scientist Grant Jordan defines "interest groups" (the term typically used by American authors) and "pressure groups" (used by British authors) simply as "organizations that seek to influence public policy." Adam Kuper and Jessica Kuper, eds., *The Social Science Encyclopedia*, 3rd ed., vol. I: A-K, New York: Routledge, 2004, p. 514. The category typically encompasses labor unions, professional associations, and voluntary associations founded to further a common interest, such as, to name some of the more powerful American groups, the National Organization for Women (NOW), Common Cause, the American Association of Retired Persons (AARP), the American Israel Public Affairs Committee (AIPAC), or the National Rifle Association (NRA).

24. Lenin said: "Without revolutionary theory there can be no revolutionary movement." Vladimir Lenin, quoted in Doug Lorimer, *The Birth of Bolshevism* (Resistance Books, 2005), p. 106, http://books.google.com/books?id=B0q8emwoTncC. Political scientist Theodore J. Lowi elaborates on this point. See Theodore J. Lowi, *The Politics of Disorder* (New York: Basic Books, 1971), especially chapter 2 and pp. 42–47.

25. Ideology and intense interconnectedness in multiple roles and venues distinguish flex nets from "issue networks," as defined by government scholar Hugh Heclo. Heclo coined the concept in 1978 to describe the "partnerships of groups or individuals" who organize around particular policy issues and attempt to influence policy development (James P. Pfiffner, interview with Hugh Heclo, "The Institutionalist: A Conversation with Hugh Heclo," *Public Administration Review*, May/June 2007, p. 421). When it suits their cause, these working groups of individuals form loose alliances with interest groups, nongovernmental organizations, and economic actors (Heclo, "Issue Networks and the Executive Establishment," *The New American Political System* [Washington, DC: American Enterprise Institute, 1978], pp. 87–124). Today, says Heclo, "Issue activists are . . . increasingly important in all aspects of governing and political campaigning" (Pfiffner, "The Institutionalist").

With regard to the crucial role of information, as anthropologist Annelise Riles points out, information has replaced capital as an organizer of social groups (Annelise Riles, *The Network Inside Out* [Ann Arbor, MI: University of Michigan Press, 2001], especially pp. 92–94).

26. For these reasons, among others, flex nets are not simply cliques, core groups whose members contact one another for multiple purposes and advance their own interests; see Jeremy Boissevain, *Friends of Friends: Networks, Manipulators and Coalition* (Oxford, UK: Basil Blackwell, 1974). Although flex nets can be seen as a *type* of clique (see Jacek Kurczewski, ed., *Lokalne Wzory Kultury Politycznej* [Warsaw: Wydawnictwo Trio, 2007]), cliques do not typically possess key features of the flex net modus operandi that define its operations. Similarly, flex nets also are not merely political elites. While elites in many contexts exert power and control, as anthropologists (see, for instance, Cris Shore and Stephen Nugent, eds., *Elite Cultures: Anthropological Perspectives* [New York: Routledge, 2002]; and Mattei Dogan, ed., *Elite Configurations at the Apex of Power* [Leiden-Boston: Brill, 2003]) have shown, flex nets—small, mobile, and with a certain modus operandi—mean something much more specific than political elites.

Flex nets also are not Mafias. While flex nets, like Mafias, work at the interstices of state and private (see Anton Blok, "Mafia," in *International Encyclopedia of the Social and Behavioral Sciences*, vol. 13 [Amsterdam: Elsevier, 2001], p. 9126), pursue common goals, and share rules of behavior, they should not be confused with Mafias (which, in the classic usage, are a type of patronage system, run by family enterprises, that developed in Sicily and Calabria, Italy.) Unlike flex nets, which primarily seek to influence policy, Mafias pursue illegal transactions to gain power or wealth and employ violence to achieve their objectives. Federico Varese, "Mafia," *The Concise Oxford Dictionary of Politics*, eds. Iain McLean and Alistair McMillan (Oxford, UK: Oxford University Press, 2003).

27. The political scientist cited here is Simon Reich. See my joint article with Simon Reich, "Conspiracies, Clubs, Competitors, and Cliques: The Changing Character of American Politics," forthcoming. The study cited of American political power from the Civil War to the New Deal is by Philip H. Burch, Jr., *The Civil War to the New Deal* (New York: Holmes & Meier Publishers, Inc., 1981). C. Wright Mills's *The Power Elite* was first published in 1956 (New York: Oxford University Press). Following Mills, G. William Domhoff, in *Who Rules America?* (New York: Prentice-Hall, 1967), asserted that a few rich Americans control the nation. See also Morton Keller's *America's Three Regimes: A New Political History* (New York: Oxford University Press, 2007), which argues that the endurance of American political institutions lies at the heart of its success, and that such endurance depends upon a degree of continuity and exclusivity among political leaders.

28. Author's interview with Jack Blum, November 2, 2004.

Notes to Chapter 2

1. The quote is contained in an e-mail sent by Steve Clemons, director of the American Strategy Program at the New America Foundation. Addressed to "Dear Friends and Colleagues," the message refers to a recent "note to my regular friends and colleagues around the world."

For discussion of how players both make and mirror the environment, or, put another way, how behavior changes the environment—what has been called "coevolution"—see the work of political scientist Robert Jervis, such as, *System Effects: Complexity in Political and Social Life* (Princeton, NJ: Princeton University Press, 1997), pp. 48–58.

2. Author's interview with Ešref-Kenan Rašidagić, June 1, 2006.

3. Author's conversations with Greg Callman, 2006.

4. Comments of Paul Stubbs, Conference on "Multi-Level Governance: Emerging Transnational Governmentality in South East Europe: Intermediaries and Translation in Interstitial Spaces," Institute of Economics, Zagreb, Croatia, April 30, 2006. In his work on donor programs and development in Bosnia-Herzegovina, Stubbs suggests the "need to explore the complexities and the rise of more flexible and rather unstable practices." Paul Stubbs, "Flexible Agencification on the Sovereign Frontier: Poverty Reduction and Development Strategies in Bosnia-Herzegovina," Paper prepared for the Association for the Study of Nationalities, 2007 World Convention, New York, April 2007, Introduction.

5. Comments of Ana Devic, Conference on "Multi-Level Governance: Emerging Transnational Governmentality in South East Europe: Intermediaries and Translation in Interstitial Spaces," Institute of Economics, Zagreb, Croatia, April 30, 2006.

6. With regard to the baby boomers, the Department of Labor also reported that "job duration tends to be longer the older a worker is when starting the job." U.S. Bureau of Labor Statistics, "Number of Jobs Held, Labor Market Activity, and Earnings Growth Among the Youngest Baby Boomers: Results from a Longitudinal Survey," *Economic News Release*, USDL 08–0860, June 27, 2008, p. 2. With regard to workers aged 33 to 37 years old, 42.8 percent ended their employment in a particular job in less than one year, while 80.6 percent ended it in less than five years. When first interviewed in 1979, participants in the study were ages 14 to 22; in 2006–2007, they were ages 41 to 50. United States Department of Labor, Bureau of Labor Statistics, "Table 2. Duration of employment relationships with a single employer for all jobs started from age 18 to age 42 in 1978–2006 by age at start of job, sex, race, and Hispanic or Latino ethnicity." *Economic News Release*, June 27, 2008, http://www.bls.gov/news.release/nlsoy.t02.htm. Job tenure has been falling in the United States. Since the 1970s, "job tenure and the incidence of long-term employment have declined sharply," according to data analyzed for the National Bureau of Economic Research (Henry S. Farber, "Job Loss and the Decline in Job Security in the United States," Princeton University, Industrial Relations Section, Working Paper No. 520, September 2007). See also David Neumark, "Changes in Job Stability and Job Security: A Collective Effort to Untangle, Reconcile, and Interpret the Evidence," NBER Working Paper No. 7472, January 2000.

With respect to new flexibility demanded of workers, see, for example, Anthony Giddens, *Runaway World: How Globalization is Reshaping Our Lives* (London, UK: Taylor and Francis, 2003); Robert Jay

Lifton, *The Protean Self: Human Resilience in an Age of Fragmentation* (New York: Basic Books, 1993); and Emily Martin, "Flexible Survivors," *Bipolar Expeditions: Mania and Depression in American Culture* (Princeton, NJ: Princeton University Press, 2007), especially chapter 1.

7. With regard to flexible identities, see Aihwa Ong's *Flexible Citizenship: The Cultural Logics of Transnationality* (Durham and London: Duke University Press, 1999).

8. The source for David Osborne and Ted Gaebler's quote is Osborne and Gaebler, *Reinventing Government: How the Entrepreneurial Spirit is Transforming the Public Sector* (Reading, MA: Addison Wesley, 1992), pp. 11–12.

9. Political scientist Susan Strange elaborates on the development of the neoliberal project by delineating five crucial political choices, made mostly by the United States from 1971 to 1985, which propelled the neoliberal financial agenda. Strange's five choices are the following: (1) the "extreme withdrawal" on the part of the United States "from any intervention in foreign exchange markets"; (2) the false but convincing claim that monetary reform remained a serious issue on the international policy agenda; (3) the U.S. "confrontational strategy of an oil-consumers' coalition armed . . . with strategic stockpiles against any repetition of the 1973 oil price rise"; (4) the "stonewalling strategy . . . against the Conference on International Economic Cooperation," which followed from the failure to negotiate with the Organization of Petroleum-Exporting Countries; and (5) the "positive" bolstering of "cooperation between central banks in their dual role as bank regulators and lenders of last resort" in response to two notable bank failures. Susan Strange, *Mad Money: When Markets Outgrow Governments* (Ann Arbor, MI: University of Michigan Press, 1998), pp. 6–7.

10. Deregulation actually began in 1978 under President Jimmy Carter. See Susan J. Tolchin and Martin Tolchin, *Dismantling America: The Rush to Deregulate* (Boston, MA: Houghton Mifflin Company, 1983), especially pp. 45–56, 60, 107, 272. "The key to Reagan's regulatory policy," explain Tolchin and Tolchin, "was a three-pronged attack, consisting of a regulatory rollback, budget cuts, and the appointment of key personnel dedicated to the Reagan philosophy of 'getting the government off the backs of the people'" (p. 41). The Tolchins' work on deregulation describes not only the breadth of Reagan's deregulation regime and its capture of the regulators but also presciently lays out the consequences.

11. Geographer Wendy Lerner notes that "neoliberalism" is used to describe vastly different political projects across the global North and South—from welfare state restructuring to structural adjustment programs. Lerner observes that "neoliberalism doesn't necessarily travel in the directions we assume, take on the forms we expect, or have the consequences we expect." She clarifies that, while neoliberalism should not be confused with "neoconservatism" (a movement that began in the United States roughly four decades ago), neoliberal and neoconservative concepts are sometimes intertwined. See Wendy Lerner, "Situating Neoliberalism: Geographies of a Contested Concept," presented at the workshop on "Transnational Governmentality in South East Europe: Translating Neo-Liberalism on the Sovereign Frontier," Rabac, Croatia, cosponsored by the Institute of Economics, Zagreb, Croatia, and the Friedrich Ebert Stiftung, June 1, 2007.

For reviews of perspectives on neoliberalism, see, for instance, Dieter Plehwe, Bernhard J. A Walpen, Gisela Neunhöffer, eds., *Neoliberal Hegemony: A Global Critique* (New York: Routledge, 2005), and Justin B. Richland, "On Neoliberalism and Other Social Diseases: The 2008 Sociocultural Anthropology Year in Review," *American Anthropologist* 111, no. 2 (June 2009), pp. 170–176.

12. On the issue of bureaucracy: It is important to keep in mind that the regulation of bureaucracy through formal, impersonal structures does not imply a lack of personal networks or personalized relationships. As governance scholar Hugh Heclo showed in 1977, "life at the top of the government bureaucracy is far different from the strict procedures, written orders, and rigid hierarchies generally associated with the term 'bureaucracy.'" See Hugh Heclo, *A Government of Strangers: Executive Politics in Washington* (Washington, DC: The Brookings Institution, 1977), p. 2.

On the issue of Japan, see the work of American political scientist Chalmers Johnson. In his 1982 *MITI and the Japanese Miracle,* he argued that Japan's economic "miracle" in the second half of the twentieth century could largely be explained by the nation's close cooperation between government and business. This miracle manifested itself in rates of economic growth unprecedented in Japan's history, and, more specifically, growth in industrial production. Chalmers Johnson, *MITI and the Japanese Miracle* (Stanford, CA: Stanford University Press, 1982). See especially chapter 1, "The Japanese

'Miracle.'" See also Clyde Prestowitz, *Trading Places: How We Allowed Japan to Take the Lead* (New York: Basic Books, 1988). For later reflections on the subject, see, for instance, Edward W. Schwerin, "Japan's Economic Crisis: The Role of Government," *Managing Economic Development in Asia: From Economic Miracle to Financial Crisis*, Kuotsai Tom Liou, ed. (Westport, CT: Praeger Publishers, 2002), p. 43. For a description of East Asian government-business relationships and the variety of models, see Manuel Castells, *The Rise of the Network Society*, 2nd ed. (Malden, MA: Blackwell Publishers, 2000), pp. 188–195.

13. With regard to the goals of contracting out, see Dan Guttman, "Contracting, an American Way of Governance: Post 9/11 Constitutional Choices," in Thomas H. Stanton, ed., *Meeting the Challenge of 9/11: Blueprints for More Effective Government* (Armonk, NY: M. E. Sharpe Publishers, 2006), p. 230. With regard to the participation of nongovernmental actors in governing, see, for example, Lester M. Salamon, *The New Governance: Getting Beyond the Right Answer to the Wrong Question in Public Sector Reform*, School of Policy Studies, Queen's University: The J. Douglas Gibson Lecture, delivered February 3, 2005, p. 5.

14. The quote from Reagan is from Ronald Reagan, "To Restore America," March 31, 1976, http://reagan2020.us/speeches/To_Restore_America.asp, accessed June 24, 2006.

The quotes from Gore are from Al Gore, "Remarks by Vice President Al Gore, Opening Session of International REGO Conference," International Reinventing Government Conference, January 14, 1999, http://clinton2.nara.gov/WH/EOP/OVP/speeches/interego.html, accessed April 14, 2007.

The ideas about injecting business principles into government are set out in David Osborne and Ted Gaebler, *Reinventing Government: How the Entrepreneurial Spirit is Transforming the Public Sector* (Reading, MA: Addison Wesley, 1992). Berating bureaucracy is a crucial component here. David Osborne even wrote a book (with Peter Plastrik) titled *Banishing Bureaucracy: The Five Strategies for Reinventing Government* (Reading, MA: Addison-Wesley Publishing Company, Inc., 1997).

15. Author's interview with Graham Scott, December 10, 2006.

16. On "performing for the public," see the work of John Clarke, "Performing for the Public: Doubt, Desire and the Evaluation of Public Services," *The Values of Bureaucracy*, Paul Du Gay, ed. (Oxford, UK: Oxford University Press, 2005).

17. Daniel Guttman and Barry Willner, *The Shadow Government: The Government's Multi-Billion-Dollar Giveaway of Its Decision-Making Powers to Private Management Consultants, "Experts," and Think Tanks* (New York, NY: Pantheon, 1976).

18. For evidence regarding the outsourcing of inherently governmental functions and dearth of contract oversight, see chapter 4 of this book. As legal scholar and governance expert Dan Guttman wrote 30 years after coauthoring *The Shadow Government*, "The evidence that the official workforce can no longer be presumed to have capacity to account has long gone well beyond anecdote; red flags counseling due diligence are omnipresent; they include high level official admissions of systematic deficiency, years of Government Accountability Office findings of agency-wide deficiencies, and continuing failures of third party oversight in sensitive and showcased programs." Dan Guttman, "Contracting, an American Way of Governance: Post 9/11 Constitutional Choices," Thomas H. Stanton, ed., *Meeting the Challenge of 9/11: Blueprints for More Effective Government* (Armonk, NY: M. E. Sharpe Publishers, 2006), p. 231.

The first quote from the inspector general in this paragraph is from Department of Homeland Security, Office of Inspector General, *Improvements Needed in the U.S. Coast Guard's Acquisition and Implementation of Deepwater Information Technology Systems*, OIG-06–55, August 2006, p. 1. The Government Accountability Office earlier found that "the key components needed to manage the program and oversee the system integrator's [that is, the Lockheed/Northrop team's] performance have not been implemented." Government Accountability Office, *Coast Guard's Deepwater Program Needs Increased Attention to Management and Contractor Oversight*, GAO-04–389, March 2004, p. 3. The inspector general cited in the *Wall Street Journal* is found in Bernard Wysocki Jr., "Is U.S. Government 'Outsourcing Its Brain'?" *Wall Street Journal*, March 30, 2007, p. A1. Information on the continuing involvement of the companies can be found, for example, in Renae Merle and Spencer Hsu, "Coast Guard to Take Over 'Deepwater,'" *Washington Post*, April 17, 2007, p. D01. The length of time it will take to refederalize the operation is from my interview with a staff member responsible for oversight, United States House Committee on Energy and Commerce, May 24, 2007.

19. The neoliberal ethos holds that handing government functions to nongovernmental entities merely improves management (or, in the case of NGOs delivering services, responsiveness and citizens' participation). On NGOs and citizens' participation, see, for instance, Jennifer R. Wolch's *The Shadow State: Government and Voluntary Sector in Transition* (New York, NY: The Foundation Center, 1990) in which she argues that state-sponsored voluntary organizations comprise a "shadow state."

With respect to American-trained economists playing leading roles in implementing neoliberal policies, see Yves Dezalay and Bryant G. Garth, *The Internationalization of Palace Wars: Lawyers, Economists, and the Contest to Transform Latin American States* (Chicago, IL: University of Chicago Press, 2002). With regard to local economists trained in the United States playing leading roles, the "Chicago Boys" in Chile are but one (albeit important) example. See, for instance, Juan Gabriel Valdes, *Pinochet's Economists: The Chicago School in Chile* (Cambridge, UK: Cambridge University Press, 1995). But neoliberal policies did not always have their origins in such networks. Johanna Bockman notes, for instance, that Yugoslav socialism and experts played a role in Chilean and Peruvian neoliberalism ("The Origins of Neoliberalism between Soviet Socialism and Western Capitalism: 'A Galaxy Without Borders,'" *Theory and Society* 36, no. 4 [2007], pp. 343–371.)

With regard to the policies that became standard international development fare in the 1980s, the International Monetary Fund (IMF) and the World Bank tied "structural adjustment programs" (SAPs) with loans to countries burdened by debt. These international financial institutions offered SAPs to nations as varied as El Salvador, Bangladesh, Ecuador, Argentina, Thailand, and Tanzania—and new loans to implement them. The goal typically was to contain inflation, stabilize currencies, promote export-led growth, and make government more efficient. For an analysis of the effects of SAPs, see the work of William Easterly, for instance, "The Effect of IMF and World Bank Programs on Poverty," World Bank, December 2000, http://papers.ssrn.com/paper.taf?abstract_id=256883, and *The White Man's Burden: Why the West's Efforts to Aid the Rest Have Done So Much Ill and So Little Good* (New York: Penguin Press, 2006).

Certain notable states, such as China and India, have demonstrated more autonomy from many policies of the international financial institutions. This is not to say that they have skirted neoliberal policies; homegrown forms of neoliberalism can be found. See, for example, Wang Hui's *China's New Order: Society, Politics, and Economy in Transition* (Cambridge, MA: Harvard University Press, 2003), especially pp. 44, 96–115, 118–199; and Aradhana Sharma's *Logics of Empowerment: Development, Gender, and Governance in Neoliberal India* (Minneapolis: University of Minnesota Press, 2008).

With respect to states demonstrating autonomy from international financial institutions, see, for instance, John Ralston Saul, *The Collapse of Globalism and the Reinvention of the World* (Toronto: Viking Canada, 2005), pp. 232–233. As Saul writes, the International Monetary Fund, the World Bank, and other organizations were created by the West a half century ago "to monitor a continued evolution along the same path among non-Western countries" (p. 232).

Democracy-challenged countries into which neoliberal policies were introduced include, for instance, Nicaragua, El Salvador, Somalia, and Zaire, which the two superpowers had turned into Cold War battlegrounds through their support of opposing dictators and military groups.

Governance scholars Laura S. Jensen and Sheila S. Kennedy challenge the neutrality of neoliberal-style reforms, arguing: "It remains to be seen how the new governance can achieve efficiency and effectiveness without sacrificing the democratic norms of equity, accountability, and due process that are fundamental to our political order and constitutional culture." Laura S. Jensen and Sheila S. Kennedy, "Public Ethics, Legal Accountability, and the New Governance," *Ethics in Public Management*, H. George Frederickson and Richard K. Ghere, eds. (Armonk, NY: M. E. Sharpe, 2005), p. 235.

For a list of various Cold War interventions, see Easterly, *The White Man's Burden*, pp. 314–316. For analysis of regimes installed by the United States, see Jonathan Kwitny, *Endless Enemies: The Making of an Unfriendly World* (New York: Congdon & Weed, Inc., 1984).

On the issue of neoliberal reforms occasioning the reorganization of government and society, see the work of anthropologist Carol Greenhouse (forthcoming volume on *Politics, Publics, Personhood: New Ethnographies at the Limits of Neoliberalism*, Carol Greenhouse, ed.); and legal analyst Alfred C. Aman, Jr., *Democracy Deficit: Taming Globalization through Law Reform* (New York: New York University Press, 2004).

20. The concept of "quasi-nongovernmental organization" was coined by Alan Pifer in 1967. Alan Pifer, "Letter: On Quasi-Public Organizations; Whence Came the Quango, and Why," *New York Times*, September 5, 1987, http://query.nytimes.com/gst/fullpage.html?res=9B0DE2D61030F936A3575AC0A961948260.

21. The term "privatization revolution" is from P. W. Singer's *Corporate Warriors: The Rise of the Privatized Military Industry* (Ithaca, NY: Cornell University Press, 2003), especially pp. 66–68.

Data on the privatization explosion and its rate of increase in the 1990s are from Martin Van Creveld, *The Rise and Decline of the State* (Cambridge and New York: Cambridge University Press, 1999), p. 375–377, and Adrian T. Moore, ed. *Privatization 98: 12th Annual Report on Privatization* (Los Angeles, CA: Reason Public Policy Institute, 1998).

The quote about elites' view of privatization is from Harvey Feigenbaum and Jeffrey Henig, "Privatization and Political Theory," *Journal of International Affairs*, no. 50 (Winter 1997), p. 338.

Ian Thynne and Roger Wettenhall investigate the nature and diversity of privatization activities and observe a range of state-private mixes. See, for instance, Roger Wettenhall and Ian Thynne, *The Asia Pacific Journal of Public Administration* 27, no. 2 (December 2005), pp. 111–116.

For documentation and details regarding Western-underwritten privatization in central and eastern Europe, see Janine R. Wedel, *Collision and Collusion: The Strange Case of Western Aid to Eastern Europe* (New York: Palgrave, 2001), especially chapter 2.

22. The quote on bureaucracy is by Jan Aart Scholte: Jan Aart Scholte, *Globalization: A Critical Introduction* (New York: St. Martin's Press, 2000), p. 5.

23. Francis Fukuyama's *The End of History* made this view popular. Francis Fukuyama, *The End of History and the Last Man* (New York: The Free Press, 1992).

24. For analysis of the increased role of nonstate actors, see, for example, Susan Strange, *The Retreat of the State* (Cambridge, UK: Cambridge University Press, 1996); Jessica Mathews, "Power Shift," *Foreign Affairs* 76, no. 1 (January/February 1997), pp. 50–66; and Anna-Marie Slaughter, *A New World Order* (Princeton, NJ: Princeton University Press, 2004). Slaughter outlines governance through a web of global networks that are governed by a variety of entities, including NGOs, segments of states, and international organizations.

On transnational networks promoting new policies and practices, see Diane Stone, "Transfer Agents and Global Networks in the 'Transnationalization' of Policy," *Journal of European Public Policy* 11, no. 3 (June 2004), p. 546. On transnational advocacy networks, see Margaret E. Keck and Kathryn Sikkink, *Activists Beyond Borders: Advocacy Networks in International Politics* (Ithaca, NY: Cornell University Press, 1998). On corporate policy interlocks, see, for instance, William K. Carroll and Colin Carson, "The Network of Global Corporations and Elite Policy Groups: A Structure for Transnational Capitalist Class Formation?," *Global Networks* 3, issue 1 (Abstract, January 2003), p. 29. On international commerce and state and international authority, see, for instance, A. Claire Cutler, Virginia Haufler, and Tony Porter, "Private Authority and International Affairs," A. Clair Cutler, Virginia Haufler, and Tony Porter, eds., *Private Authority and International Affairs* (Albany, NY: SUNY Press, 1999), pp. 3–27.

For an understanding of the darker side of the new sparsely governed arenas, see Moisés Naím, *Illicit: How Smugglers, Traffickers and Counterfeiters are Hijacking the Global Economy* (New York: Random House, Inc., 2006); and R. T. Naylor, *Wages of Crime: Black Markets, Illegal Finance, and the Underworld Economy* (Ithaca, NY: Cornell University Press, 2004).

25. Figures on money laundering are from Moisés Naím, "It's the Illicit Economy, Stupid: How Big Business Taught Criminals to go Global," *Foreign Policy* (November/December 2005), p. 95. See also Moisés Naím, *Illicit: How Smugglers, Traffickers and Counterfeiters are Hijacking the Global Economy*. The quote about illicit activity as taboo is from Raymond Baker, "Dirty Money and Its Global Effects," *International Policy Report* (Washington, DC: Center for International Policy, January 2003). See also Raymond W. Baker, *Capitalism's Achilles Heel: Dirty Money and How to Renew the Free-Market System* (Hoboken, NJ: John Wiley & Sons, Inc., 2005).

26. Many analysts and observers lauded NGOs and other "civil society" actors, even becoming triumphalist in tone, especially in the immediate Cold War aftermath. Some tended to attribute to transnational nonstate actors a positive role in society, such as that of helping to build "civil society" or democracy. Of course, there are many examples of human and indigenous rights and environmental advocacy organizations working effectively and valuably across borders. (One is the Soros-funded East-

East initiative, which funds partners in different postcommunist countries to do joint projects ranging from mini-ecological endeavors such as protecting endangered bird species and cleaning up parts of the Russian far east wrecked by military-industrial installations to organizing vacations for Belorussian children affected by Chernobyl and working with drug and alcohol addicts throughout the region.)

However, a darker side of "civil society," replete with opportunities for actors to mesh state and private power in the service of their own interests, is also part of the reality. See, for example, Bob Clifford, *The Marketing of Rebellion: Insurgents, Media, and International Activism* (New York: Cambridge University Press, 2005); Alexander Cooley and James Ron, "The NGO Scramble: Organizational Insecurity and the Political Economy of Transnational Action," *International Security* 27 (Summer 2002), pp. 5–39; and Sebastian Mallaby, "NGOs: Fighting Poverty, Hurting the Poor," *Foreign Policy* (Sept-Oct 2004), pp. 50–59. Consider, for instance, that the circumstances that enable respected and effective NGOs to work effectively across borders, and the informal networks and local ties that help them cut through bureaucracy, meanwhile may do the same for organized criminal groups. Such groups seldom function without links to the state. See, for example, Phil Williams, "Russian Organized Crime—How Serious a Threat?" *Transnational Organized Crime* 2, no. 2/3 (Summer/Autumn 1996), p. 20, and Roy Godson, "Enhancing Democratic Society through a Culture of Lawfulness," *Trends in Organized Crime* 4, no. 2 (Winter 1998), p. 6.

27. Technology is about manipulating nature, and, increasingly, also the biology of *homo sapiens*. Complex technologies are typically those that cannot be understood in detail by any one expert. Technological complexity can be identified by looking into: the number of components in a product; the cybernetic nature of the systems and subsystems that integrate those components through feedback loops; and the sociotechnical systems that combine product technologies with social processes, in other words, the organizational systems that innovate the products. See Robert Rycroft and Don E. Kash, *The Complexity Challenge.*

On how complex information technologies consolidate power, influence, and commerce, see Barry C. Lynn, *Cornered: The New Monopoly Capitalism and the Economics of Destruction* (New York: John Wiley, forthcoming 2010), ch. 2.

With regard to technology giving government the tools to hide secrets and impede transparency, see Alasdair Roberts, *Blacked Out: Government Secrecy in the Information Age* (New York: Cambridge University Press, 2006). See also James Bamford, *The Shadow Factory: The Ultra-Secret NSA From 9/11 to the Eavesdropping on America* (New York: Doubleday, 2008).

28. With regard to commodity prices, a U.S. government report of April 2009 concludes that, in 2008, due to the influx of financial flows into commodity markets, natural gas and electricity prices were driven far in excess of the levels related to supply and demand. According to the report, "the rise in natural gas prices coincided with a global increase in many commodity prices. This increase in commodity prices occurred as large pools of capital flowed into various financial instruments that essentially turn commodities like natural gas into investment vehicles. Ultimately, we believe that financial fundamentals along with the modest tightening in the supply and demand balance for gas during the first part of 2008 explains natural gas prices during the year," http://www.ferc.gov/market-oversight/st-mkt-ovr/som-rpt-2008.pdf, p. 8.

A U.S. congressional investigation into wheat prices comes to a similar conclusion. See Press Release, "Investigations Subcommittee Releases Levin-Coburn Report on Excessive Speculation in the Wheat Market," Senate Committee on Homeland Security and Governmental Affairs, June 24, 2009, http://hsgac.senate.gov/public/index.cfm?FuseAction=PressReleases.Print&PressRelease_id=5a459e69-e9f9–4550–904c-871a5b6c693a&suppresslayouts=true. With respect to oil prices, the Commodity Futures Trading Commission, as of mid-2009, was preparing a report indicating that speculators helped drive huge swings in oil prices, according to the *Wall Street Journal* (http://online.wsj.com/article/SB124874574251485689.html#mod=djemalertNEW).

With regard to exemption from regulation: "Legal certainty" that derivatives will be exempted from regulation is specified in Section 2(g) and 2(h)(1) of the Commodity Exchange Act. The Commodity Exchange Act, passed in 1936 by the U.S. Government, was last amended in 2008, http://agriculture.senate.gov/Legislation/Compilations/Comex/COMEX.pdf.

With regard to the Bank for International Settlements, see Monetary and Economic Department Bank for International Settlements, "Regular OTC Derivatives Market Statistics" activity in 2005 and 2008, http://www.bis.org/publ/otc_hy0611.htm. The December 2005 figure is at: http://www.bis.org/publ/otc_hy0611.pdf. The June 2008 figure is at: http://www.bis.org/statistics/otcder/dt1920a.pdf.

29. Regarding the Obama administration's position on regulating OTC derivatives, Treasury Secretary Timothy Geithner opposes banning naked credit default swaps (Edmund L. Andrews, "Unresolved Questions After Hearing With Geithner, New York Times, July 11, 2009, http://query.nytimes.com/gst/fullpage.html?res=9E00E2DB123FF932A25754C0A96F9C8B63&sec=&spon=&pagewanted=print). See also http://money.cnn.com/news/newsfeeds/articles/reuters/MTFH43652_2009-07-22_18-14-11_N22324533.htm.

With respect to G-8 finance ministers calling for regulation, see, for instance, Jo Winterbottom, "G8 Finmins Want Curbs on Commodity Speculation," *Reuters*, June 13, 2009, http://in.reuters.com/article/governmentFilingsNews/idINLD42648720090613.

With regard to the political power of the financial services industry, see, for instance, a letter to Henry Waxman, chairman of the House Committee on Energy and Commerce, and Edward Markey, chairman of the House Subcommittee on Energy and Environment, from members of the New Democrat Coalition, which expresses concern about proposed regulation: "We are concerned about provisions related to derivatives and the Over the Counter (OTC) market. Specifically, we are concerned about requiring all OTC derivatives and swaps to be centrally cleared and settled" (June 17, 2009), letter in author's possession.

30. The anthropologist of finance here quoted is Bill Maurer. With regard to offshore finance, the OECD developed a program to try to regulate it. In the spirit (and practice) of democratic participation of all stakeholders, the OECD allowed the trust and estate practitioners to take part. Not only did they merely participate, however, they created new multilateral organizations modeled on the international organizations that were trying to regulate them that then had to also be included in the initiative. This altered the rules of the endeavor and necessitated greater participation by those most affected by the shifts in regulation. Thus island economies with few other choices in the world economy ensured a continued position for themselves *and* got themselves invited. See Bill Maurer, "Re-regulating Offshore Finance?" *Geography Compass* 2, no. 1 (2008), pp. 155–175, http://www.anthro.uci.edu. The quote from Bill Maurer is from my interview with him (July 26, 2009). High finance uses policymakers' purported lack of understanding of financial instruments as "a narrative," according to Bill Maurer—one "that empowers the people who can say, 'listen Congress, listen policymakers, we're the ones who know what's going on. So just back off. There's no way you can understand unless you have a degree in advanced math'" (author's interview with Bill Maurer, July 26, 2009). This "narrative" has been analyzed by anthropologists, geographers, and sociologists of finance. Their research has found that financial traders, while they may have complicated formulas at their fingertips, admit to often making decisions based on intuition without first calculating the numbers. For a review of this area of scholarship, see Bill Maurer, "Finance," *A Handbook of Economic Anthropology*, James G. Carrier, ed. (Northampton, MA: Edward Elgar, 2005), pp. 187–190.

31. The author of *Future Shock* is Alvin Toeffler (New York: Random House, 1970). The passage is from Don Kash, "The Role of Culture in Organizational-Technological Change," Lecture at George Mason University, November 17, 2004.

32. The contractor writing the report was Booz Allen Hamilton. For the report, see Art Fritzson, Lloyd W. Howell Jr., and Dov D. Zakheim, "Military Millennials," *Strategy+Business* magazine (Booz Allen Hamilton, 2008).

33. Robert Rycroft and Don E. Kash, *The Complexity Challenge: Technological Innovation for the 21st Century* (London and New York: Pinter, 1999), p. 5. For further analysis on this point, see also Robert Jervis, "Complexity and the Analysis of Political and Social Life," *Political Science Quarterly* 112, no. 4 (Winter 1997–1998), pp. 569–593; Paul R. Krugman, *The Self-organizing Economy* (Cambridge, MA: Blackwell Publishers, 1996); Woody van Olffen and A. Georges L. Romme, "The Role of Hierarchy in Self-Organizing Systems," *Human Systems Management* 14, no. 3 (1995), pp. 199–206.

34. The quote from Susan Strange is from Susan Strange, *The Retreat of the State* (Cambridge, UK: Cambridge University Press, 1996). The quote from Jessica Mathews can be found in Jessica

Mathews, "Power Shift," *Foreign Affairs* 76, no. 1 (January/February 1997), p. 50. The terms from Anna-Marie Slaughter are found in Anna-Marie Slaughter, *A New World Order* (Princeton, NJ: Princeton University Press, 2004), pp. 12–14. The quote from Michael Hardt and Antonio Negri is from Michael Hardt and Antonio Negri, *Empire* (Cambridge, MA: Harvard University Press, 2000), p. xii. The other political analyst here quoted is John Ralston Saul, *The Collapse of Globalism and the Reinvention of the World* (Toronto: Viking Canada, 2005), pp. 232–233. See also Saskia Sassen's work on the impact of the creation of an economic system focused on global flows and telecommunications on state sovereignty (Saskia Sassen, *Losing Control? Sovereignty in An Age of Globalization* (New York: Columbia University Press, 1996).

35. With respect to the creation of cross-national links with enmeshed state-private executive authorities, see Kim Lane Scheppele, *The International State of Emergency*, forthcoming.

With regard to coziness between the "regulators" and the "regulated" and the financial crisis, see, for instance, columnist Frank Rich, who questions whether Larry Summers, President Obama's chief economic adviser, can "be a fair broker of the bailout when he so recently received lavish compensation from some of its present and, no doubt, future players." Frank Rich, "Awake and Sing!" *New York Times*, April 12, 2009, p. WK8. See also the *New York Times'* exposé of Treasury Secretary Timothy Geithner's embeddedness with Wall Street, Jo Becker and Gretchen Morgenson, "Geithner, as Member and Overseer, Forged Ties to Finance Club," *New York Times*, April 27, 2009, p. A1.

The quote by Barry Lynn is from Lynn, *Cornered*. James K. Galbraith might describe the American order as a "predator state"—"an economic system wherein entire sectors have been built up to feast on public systems built originally for public purposes. . . . The corporate republic simply administers the spoils system." James K. Galbraith, *The Predator State: How Conservatives Abandoned the Free Market and Why Liberals Should Too* (New York: The Free Press, 2008), p. 146.

36. See, for instance, Lisa Adkins, "The New, Economy, Property and Personhood," *Theory, Culture and Society* 22, no. 1 (2005), pp. 111–130.

37. Merriam-WebsterUnabridged.com, accessed July 25, 2008. Stephen Colbert's concept of "truthiness" bears some similarity to the French philosopher Jean Baudrillard's notion of "simulacra." Baudrillard argues that today's society is constructed around "simulacra," which (then) become reality. Simulation, unlike pretense, and like "truthiness," produces real intuitive feelings, emotions, or symptoms in someone, and, therefore, blurs the difference between the "real" and "imaginary." Jean Baudrillard, *Simulacra and Simulation* (Ann Arbor, MI: University of Michigan Press, 1995). The connection between simulacra and truthiness has been made by several other scholars. See, for example, Diane Rubenstein, *This is Not a President: Sense, Nonsense, and the American Political Imaginary* (New York: New York University Press, 2008), p. 12.

38. The quote from Frank Rich appears in Marc Peyser, "The Truthiness Teller," *Newsweek*, February, 13, 2006, http://www.newsweek.com/id/56881/page/3, accessed July 25, 2008. For Manuel Castells's analysis of the new media and new economy, see Manuel Castells, *The Rise of the Network Society*, 2nd ed. (Oxford, UK: Blackwell Publishers, 2000), p. 188.

39. See http://www.broadcaster.com/clip/30543.

40. Dick Meyer observes that "truthiness actually has a long philosophic pedigree. It is called 'emotivism'," a term resurrected in 1981 by the Scottish moral philosopher Alasdair MacIntyre in *After Virtue*. "Emotivism is the doctrine that all evaluative judgments and, more specifically, all moral judgments are *nothing but* expressions of preference, expressions of attitude or feeling," according to MacIntyre. Alasdair MacIntyre, *After Virtue: A Study in Moral Theory*, 2nd ed. (Notre Dame, IN: University of Notre Dame Press, 1984), p. 11. Building on MacIntyre, Meyer explains that "in this view there is no difference between saying 'the death penalty is wrong' and 'I don't like the death penalty'." An "emotive" society lacks objective criteria for evaluating moral truth or judgment. As Meyer points out, "People don't—and probably can't—acknowledge their own emotivism; they think their judgments are fact-based and reasoned, not emotional." Dick Meyer, December 12, 2006, http://www.cbsnews.com/stories/2006/12/12/opinion/meyer/main2250923.shtml.

41. For more on the concept of "post-politics," see, for example, Slavoj Zizek, *The Ticklish Subject* (London, UK: Verso, 2000), pp. 187–190 and 198–200. The philosopher's observations here are those of Ted Kinnaman, personal communication of July 25, 2008.

42. For *New York Times* quote, see Jim Rutenberg and Jacques Steinberg, "That Pundit on Fox News? An Upstart Named Rove," *New York Times*, May 12, 2008, p. A1.

43. This incident was relayed to me off the record.

Note that truthiness is not quite the same as propaganda. During the Cold War, with its ideological conflict between the two superpowers, propaganda on both sides was devised in the service of ideology, whose truth was taken for granted by believers. But the truthiness game is different. If today's policy communicators succeed and people buy their message, it is because, as philosopher Jean Baudrillard might argue, the messengers have built an emotional connection with the recipients by dissolving the difference between "true" and "false," and replacing reality with intuitive "knowing." Indeed, this is the essence of corporate branding, more and more adopted by everyone, including government policy mes- sage-makers. Today's branding is all about creating a look and feel that consumers intuitively identify with, enough to choose to buy into the seller's message, product, or service. Consumers become branded and the brand becomes, ironically, a private reality that generates market share for the corporation while helping construct a public identity that is constantly innovating and recreating itself. In this way it is more subtle—and difficult to detect—than garden-variety propaganda. The work of Jean Baudrillard here cited is *Simulacra and Simulation* (Ann Arbor, MI: University of Michigan Press, 1995).

44. For analysis of President Obama's use of new media, see Virginia Heffernan, "The YouTube Pres- idency: Why the Obama Administration Uploads So Much Video," *New York Times Magazine*, April 12, 2009.

45. The reference to Rich's book is Frank Rich, *The Greatest Story Ever Sold: The Decline and Fall of Truth From 9/11 to Katrina* (New York: The Penguin Press, 2006). The quote from Frank Rich appears in Marc Peyser, "The Truthiness Teller," *Newsweek*, February, 13, 2006, http://www.newsweek.com/ id/56881/page/3, accessed July 25, 2008. The *New York Times* reporter here cited is quoted in Ron Suskind, "Faith, Certainty and the Presidency of George W. Bush," *New York Times Magazine,* October 17, 2004, http://www.nytimes.com/2004/10/17/magazine/17BUSH.html?_r=1&oref=slogin (accessed 11/27/2007).

Notes to Chapter 3

1. János Kornai, *Economics of Shortage* (Amsterdam, The Netherlands: North-Holland Press, 1980).

2. Some prewar residents of Vilnius were resettled to Szczecin in the postwar agreements; German residents of Szczecin were resettled to postwar Germany.

3. Václav Havel, "The Power of the Powerless," *The Power of the Powerless: Citizens Against the State in Central-Eastern Europe*, John Keane, ed. (Armonk, NY: M. E. Sharpe, 1985), p. 31.

4. The sociologist here cited is Adam Podgórecki, "Polish Society: A Sociological Analysis," *Praxis International* 7, no. 1 (April 1987), pp. 57–78.

5. The term "command economy" was coined by economist Gregory Grossman. See "The Structure and Organization of the Soviet Economy," *Slavic Review* 21, no. 2 (June 1962), pp. 203–222.

6. Kornai, *Economics of Shortage*. Informal distribution systems existed throughout Eastern Europe and the Soviet Union. See, for example, Steven Sampson, "The Informal Sector in Eastern Europe, *Telos* 66 (Winter 1986), pp. 44–66; Wojciech Pawlik, "Intimate Commerce," *The Unplanned Society: Poland During and After Communism*, Janine R. Wedel, ed. (New York: Columbia University Press, 1992), pp. 78–94; also in that volume, see Elżbieta Firlit and Jerzy Chłopecki, "When Theft is Not Theft" (pp. 95–109), Joanna Smigielska, "There's the Beef" (pp. 110–121), Stefan Kawalec, "The Dictatorial Supplier" (pp. 128–143), and Piotr Gliński, "Acapulco Near Konstancin" (pp. 144–152); Gregory Grossman, "The Second Economy of the USSR," *Problems of Communism* 26, no. 5 (September-October, 1977), pp. 25– 40; and Alena V. Ledeneva, *Russia's Economy of Favours: Blat, Networking and Informal Exchange* (Cam- bridge, UK: Cambridge University Press, 1998).

While Grossman outlined the phenomenon of the "second economy," other terms employed to de- scribe the same or similar phenomena include "shadow," "black," and "informal" economy. The definition of *blat* is from Alena V. Ledeneva, *How Russia Really Works: The Informal Practices That Shaped Post-Soviet Politics and Business* (Ithaca and London: Cornell University Press, 2006), p. 1.

7. Although not institutionalized, these relationships were regularized and exhibited clear patterns. For further analysis of these relationships, see Janine R. Wedel, ed., *The Unplanned Society*, especially pp. 11–16.

8. Ledeneva, *Russia's Economy of Favours*, pp. 105, 114–119.

9. The day-to-day workings of this informal economy are discussed in Janine Wedel, *The Private Poland: An Anthropologist's Look at Everyday Life* (New York: Facts on File, 1986), pp. 33–117.

10. For analysis of pride and shame, see Wedel, *The Private Poland*, pp. 145–152 and 163–168.

11. Cited in Ilona Morzoł and Michal Ogórek, "Shadow Justice," in *The Unplanned Society*, Wedel, ed., p. 62.

12. Workers distinguished among such practices as theft, lifting, bribery, "arranging," "exchanging services," and "doing favors." These terms—ranging from condemnation to open justification of more or less the same activity—had dramatically different social implications. See Firlit and Chłopecki, "When Theft is not Theft," *The Unplanned Society*, Wedel, ed., pp. 95–109.

13. Joseph S. Berliner, *Factory and Manager in the USSR* (Cambridge, MA: Harvard University Press, 1957), p. 324. See also Stefan Kawalec's "The Dictatorial Supplier," which details how informal mechanisms among state-owned enterprises often rendered central management irrelevant and set the real terms of transactions (in *The Unplanned Society*, Wedel, ed., pp. 128–143). On *pripiski*, see Ledeneva, *How Russia Really Works*, p. 147; and Stephen Shenfield, "*Pripiski*: False Statistical Reporting in Soviet-type Economies," *Corruption: Causes, Consequences and Control*, M. Clarke, ed. (London, UK: Francis Pinter, 1983), pp. 239–258. On *tolkachi*, see Ledeneva, *How Russia Really Works*, pp. 177–178; and Ledeneva, *Russia's Economy of Favours*.

14. Leonid Kosals, "Essay on Clan Capitalism in Russia," *Acta Oeconomica* 57, no. 1 (2007), p. 71. Also author's interview with Leonid Kosals, November 16, 2007. These clans are grounded in longstanding association and incentives to act together, not kinship or genealogical units.

15. The political analyst of networks here cited is Gerald Easter. He elaborates that, "Beneath the formal façade of the monolithic party and the planned economy existed an informal world of cliques, factions, networks and *druzhina* [personal networks surrounding a patron]. Power and status within the state elite derived as much from the workings of these informal groupings as they did from the formal lines of command." Gerald M. Easter, *Reconstructing the State: Personal Networks and Elite Identity in Soviet Russia* (Cambridge, UK: Cambridge University Press, 2000), pp. 46, 173–174. See also Ledeneva, *How Russia Really Works*, pp. 103–105, and John P. Willerton, *Patronage and Politics in the USSR* (New York: Cambridge University Press, 1992).

16. The record of an earlier epoch, the brutal German occupation of Poland (during which one-sixth of the nation's population perished, and city and village alike were bled and battered) may be instructive. Kazimierz Wyka, a renowned literary critic, depicted the "social fiction" of the economy at the time—one "excluded" from and functioning contrary to both the moral fabric of society and the commands of its formidable occupiers. By "fiction," he meant the *illusion* of a "very tight noose" under which an elaborate informal exchange system, often in collusion with corrupted Germans, enabled many Poles to survive starvation rationing and other hardships. The "calamitous psychosocial practices" and "social distortions" of the occupation, as Wyka observed, did not disappear when the conditions that engendered them did. Instead, they persisted into the new era, burdening the new Polish state and becoming a feature of the new system. Kazimierz Wyka, "The Excluded Economy," in *The Unplanned Society*, Wedel, ed., p. 58.

17. Janine R. Wedel, "The Polish Revolution Turns Economic," *The Christian Science Monitor*, February 13, 1989.

18. Paszyński explained his decision to decline the cabinet-level position in an underground (illegal) newspaper.

19. On institutional nomads, see Antoni Kamiński and Joanna Kurczewka, "Main Actors of Transformation: The Nomadic Elites," Eric Allardt and Włodzimierz Wesołowski, eds., *The General Outlines of Transformation* (Warszawa: IFIS PAN Publishing, 1994), pp. 132–153.

20. Quote is from author's personal communication with Grażyna Skąpska, October 14, 2002.

21. The authors of *The Unplanned Society* (Wedel, ed.), a collection of articles by Polish sociologists, writers, and journalists, illustrate the first point of this paragraph. The volume provides a counterweight to many of the assumptions of Western Sovietology, an understanding built considerably on the study of formal institutions such as communist parties, the defense establishment, and central planning—institutions that disappeared with the demise of communist regimes. Without an understanding of the role of informal institutions such as social networks, many scholars found themselves without ready tools for analyzing change. By contrast, the study of informal institutions, either by insiders or outsiders, became evermore relevant. One logic at work was the "virtual economy." See Clifford G. Gaddy and Barry W. Ickes, *Russia's Virtual Economy* (Washington, DC: Brookings Institution, 2002).

22. In theory, two types of outcomes are possible: Informal systems can *support* the development of new institutions and reforms, or they can *thwart* them. Both outcomes burgeoned in different contexts and moments of postcommunism.

On network capital, see Endre Sik and Barry Wellman, "Network Capital in Capitalist, Communist, and Post-Communist Countries," *Networks in the Global Village: Life in Contemporary Communities*, Barry Wellman, ed. (Boulder, CO: Westview Press, 1999), pp. 225–254.

23. Sociologist Vadim Volkov, for example, has written that: "Russia . . . was close to the state of nature, where anarchy rather than hierarchy prevails. Such a diagnosis . . . is empirically correct . . . at least until the very end of the 1990s. The image of the state as one private protection company among others does more justice to the reality in question than a view of the state as the source of public power." Vadim Volkov, *Violent Entrepreneurs: The Use of Force in the Making of Russian Capitalism* (Ithaca, NY: Cornell University Press, 2002), p. 26.

24. Hilary Appel shows how privatization was, above all, an ideologically driven process. See Hillary Appel, *A New Capitalist Order: Privatization and Ideology in Russia and Eastern Europe* (Pittsburgh, PA: Pittsburgh University Press, 2004).

With regard to organized crime in Russia, see, for example, Louise I. Shelley, "Privatization and Crime: The Post-Soviet Experience," *Journal of Contemporary Criminal Justice* 11 (1995), pp. 244–256; and Svetlana P. Glinkina, "Privatizatsiya and Kriminalizatsiya: How Organized Crime Is Hijacking Privatization," *Demokratizatsiya: The Journal of Post-Soviet Democratization* 2 (1994), pp. 385–391.

25. David Stark and Laszlo Bruszt coined the term "restructuring networks." David Stark, "Recombinant Property in East European Capitalism," *American Journal of Sociology* 101, no. 4 (1996), pp. 993–1027, and David Stark and Laszlo Bruszt, *Postsocialist Pathways: Transforming Politics and Property in East Central Europe* (Cambridge, UK: Cambridge University Press, 1998), pp. 142–153.

Katherine Verdery coined the term "unruly coalitions." Katherine Verdery, *What Was Socialism, and What Comes Next?* (Princeton, NJ: Princeton University Press, 1996), p. 193–194.

26. Author's interview with Leonid Kosals, November 16, 2007. See also Leonid Kosals, "Essay on Clan Capitalism in Russia," *Acta Oeconomica* 57, no. 1 (2007), pp. 67–85, and "Interim Outcome of the Russian Transition: Clan Capitalism," *Discussion Paper No. 610* (Kyoto, Japan: Kyoto Institute of Economic Research, January 2006), pp. 1–36.

27. In Ukraine, the struggle over economic resources spurred "dynamic competition" among regional clans and crystallized the clan system by 1996, according to Oleg Soskin, director of the Kiev-based Institute of Society Transformation (author's interview with Soskin, July 9, 1999). Soskin discusses "regional clans as the major factor of the state-monopoly pattern" ("What Socio-economic Model Does Ukraine Choose? On a Difficult Way to the Status of the Central European Country," unpublished paper by Soskin, July 1999) and maintains that "clans determine most of the money flow in Ukraine" (author's interview with Soskin). On the links of clans to political power, see Oleksandr Turchynov, "The Shadow Economy and Shadow Politics," *Political Thought: Ukrainian Political Science Journal* 3, no. 4 (1996), pp. 75–86; and author's interview with Turchynov (July 9, 1999). On competition among clans for power, see Oleg Soskin, "Political System and Institutional Changes in Ukraine: Interrelation and Dependence," unpublished paper by Soskin, July 1999. On how clans shape Ukraine's political economy, see the work of Roman Kupchinsky, coordinator of corruption studies, RFE/RL.

28. Author's interview with Joanna Kurczewska, June 22, 2008, and Antoni Z. Kamiński and Joanna Kurczewska, "Institutional Nomads Fifteen Years Later," forthcoming article.

29. The Kryshtanovskaya quote is from Olga Kryshtanovskaya, "The Real Masters of Russia," *RIA Novosti Argumenty I Fakty,* no. 21 (May 1997), reprinted in *Johnson's Russia List,* http://www.cdi.org/russia/johnson/default.cfm. See also Olga Kryshtanovskaya, "Illegal Structures in Russia," *Sociological Research: A Journal of Translations from Russian* (July-August 1996), pp. 60–80; Olga Kryshtanovskaya, "Illegal Structures in Russia," *Trends in Organized Crime* 3, no. 1 (Fall 1997), pp. 14–17; and Olga Kryshtanovskaya and Stephen White, "From Soviet *Nomenklatura* to Russian Elite," *Europe-Asia Studies* 48, no. 5 (1996), pp. 711–733.

30. Olga Kryshtanovskaya is cited in Andrew E. Kramer, "The Kremlin Flexes, and a Tycoon Reels," *New York Times,* July 8, 2007, Business Section, p. 1. The quote from the 1990s is from Virginie Coulloudon, "Elite Groups," *Demokratizatsiya: The Journal of Post-Soviet Democratization* 6, no. 3 (1998), p. 545. The journalist here cited is Brian Whitmore, "Might Makes Right," *Transitions Online,* October 2, 2000, reprinted in *Johnson's Russia List* #4555, October 3, 2000.

31. Author's interview with Kurczewska; and Kamiński and Kurczewska, "Institutional Nomads Fifteen Years Later."

32. Sources on the statement that Ordynacka counted among its ranks professionals placed in the most important political and economic structures, including banks, political parties, and the media, include: author's interview with Kurczewska, and Kamiński and Kurczewska, "Institutional Nomads Fifteen Years Later."

33. For the market position of Polish Television, see *Television Across Europe: Regulation, Policy and Independence* 2 (New York: Open Society Institute, 2005), http://www.soros.org/initiatives/media/articles_publications/publications/eurotv_20051011/voltwo_20051011.pdf, p. 1082.

34. Information on Ordynacki was gleaned in part through author's interview with Kurczewska, and Kamiński and Kurczewska, "Institutional Nomads Fifteen Years Later."

35. While the final session of the parliamentary commission was held in April 2004 and the last hearing was conducted in November 2003, various prosecutorial investigations continued for several years. The last, conducted by the prosecutor's office in Białystok, was dismissed in January 2008.

For astute analyses of Rywingate, see: Jan Skórzyński, ed., *System Rywina: Czyli Druga Strona III Rzeczypospolitej,* Warsaw: Presspublica, 2003.

36. Observations of Barbara Pomorska recorded in unpublished document sent to Janine Wedel, September 7, 2005.

37. Michnik initiated an investigation by his own paper, ostensibly to try to establish the facts. The article that appeared almost six months later, however, failed to shed new light on the story but instead raised suspicions as to the newspaper's true role in it. It was shortly thereafter that the parliament established a special commission to look into the matter.

38. For documentation about the legislation that expanded opportunities for private players and entities, see Antoni Kamiński, "Corruption under the Post-Communist Transformation: The Case of Poland," *Polish Sociological Review* 2, no. 118 (1997), pp. 91–117; and "The New Polish Regime and the Specter of Economic Corruption," summary of paper presented at the Woodrow Wilson International Center for Scholars, Princeton, April 3, 1996.

The figure "as much as a quarter of the state budget" is from author's interview with NIK official Andrzej Łodyga, July 24, 2002. On losses to the state budget as recently as 2006, see NIK, *Analiza Wykonania Budżetu Państwa I Założeń Polityki Pieniężnej w 2006 Roku* (Warsaw, Poland: Najwyższa Izba Kontroli, June 2007), pp. 109–125. On the same topic regarding conclusions that pertain to several years earlier, see *Report of the Activities of the Supreme Chamber of Control in the Year 2002 (Sprawozdanie z Działalności Najwyższej Izby Kontroli w 2002 Roku)* (Warsaw, Poland: Najwyższa Izba Kontroli, June 2003), p. 127. The NIK report of June 2008 reports that both agencies and targeted funds, unusually, achieved positive financial results (NIK report: *Analiza Wykonania Budżetu Państwa I Założeń Polityki Pieniężnej w 2007 Roku* (Warsaw, Poland: Najwyższa Izba Kontroli, June 2008), p. 115 and p. 123.

39. The quote from Kaczyński is from author's interview with Lech Kaczyński, July 14, 1999. Information on growth of the entities during the 1990s is from: author's interviews with Jan Stefanowicz, legal analyst and expert on these bodies, July 14 and 15, 1999. See also Jan Stefanowicz and Antoni

Z. Kamiński, "Jak Się Buduję Instytucje III Rzeczpospolitej: Ułomne Reguły Gry," *Polska Niezakonczona Transformacja,* Jan Winicki, ed. (Warsaw, Poland: Centrum im. Adama Smitha, 1996).

40. With regard to NIK characterizing *fundusze celowe* as "corruption-causing" and the examples in this paragraph, see NIK, *Zagrożenie Korupcja w Świetle Badań Kontrolnych* (Warsaw, Poland: Najwyższa Izba Kontroli, Departament Strategii Kontrolnej, March 2000), pp. 45, 46. With respect to NIK's anticorruption activities, NIK employee Alina Hussein has been a pioneer not only in introducing anticorruption efforts into the work of NIK, but also in devising innovative anticorruption methods.

41. The legal analyst and expert on the bodies cited is Jan Stefanowicz, author's interviews with Jan Stefanowicz, July 14 and 15, 1999. Information on the coal sector is from Kaja Gadowska, *Zjawisko Klientelizmu Polityczno-Ekonomicznego: Systemowa Analiza Powiązań Sieciowych Na Przykladzie Przeksztalcen Sektora Gorniczego w Polsce* (Kraków, Poland: Uniwersytet Jagielonski, Wydział Filozoficzny, Instytut Socjologii, *Rozprawa Doktorska,* 2000).

Information from Kownacki is from author's interview with Piotr Kownacki, Deputy Director of NIK, July 26, 1999.

42. Quotation from Kownacki is from author's interview with Piotr Kownacki, Deputy Director of NIK, July 26, 1999.

43. The quotation from Kamiński is from: Antoni Kamiński, "The New Polish Regime and the Specter of Economic Corruption," Summary of paper presented at the Woodrow Wilson International Center for Scholars, Princeton, April 3, 1996, p. 4.

44. Since 2005, when a new law on public finance was ushered in, these bodies have been subject to greater financial discipline.

Notes to Chapter 4

1. Executive Office of the President Office of Management and Budget, "The President's Management Agenda," Fiscal Year 2002, p. 17, http://www.whitehouse.gov/omb/budget/fy2002/mgmt.pdf.

2. The quote is contained in information on the President's Management Agenda and the agency's "scorecard" in achieving its goals appeared on HHS's Web site, http://archive.hhs.gov/pma/.

3. The quote is from the 1999 version of the circular, Office of Management and Budget, *Circular No. A-76, Revised 1999,* Washington, D.C., August 4, 1983, http://www.whitehouse.gov/omb/circulars/a076/a076.html. The 2003 version can be found as follows: Executive Office of the President, Office of Management and Budget, *Circular No. A-76 (Revised) to the Heads of Executive Departments and Establishments on the "Performance of Commercial Activities,"* May 29, 2003, http://www.whitehouse.gov/omb/circulars/a076/a76_rev2003.pdf, or http://www.whitehouse.gov/omb/circulars/a076/a76_incl_tech_correction.pdf.

4. For discussion of the companies that constitute "Blackwater," see http://pogoblog.typepad.com/pogo/2008/07/blackwater-more.html.

5. For Halliburton split, see KBR, "Halliburton Announces Commencement of KBR Exchange Offer," March 2, 2007, http://www.kbr.com/news/2007/corpnews_070302.aspx.

6. On the ratio of contractors to government officials, see later statistics in this chapter. See also Elizabeth Newell, "Federal officials strategize on boosting acquisition workforce," *Government Executive,* February 14, 2008, http://www.govexec.com/dailyfed/0208/021408e1.htm.

On "performing for the public" see John Clarke, "Performing for the Public: Doubt, Desire, and the Evaluation of Public Services," *The Values of Bureaucracy,* Paul Du Gay, ed., (Oxford: Oxford University Press, 2005), pp. 211–229.

Although some of the analysis in this paragraph (and chapter) may also apply to state and local government, I limit my examination to the federal level.

7. With regard to defining who the government is being more difficult in the United States, the United Kingdom is a possible exception. While the United States reportedly expends more on outsourced services, the United Kingdom extends a larger portion of its GDP on such services.

Nicholas Timmins, "Outsourcing Covers a Third of Services," *Financial Times*, July 9, 2008, http://www.ft.com/cms/s/e4b000da-4dea-11dd-820e-000077b07658.

8. The reference to Lowi's book is Theodore J. Lowi, *The End of Liberalism: Ideology, Policy, and the Crisis of Public Authority* (New York: W. W. Norton and Company, 1969).

Political scientist Catherine Rudder disputes the common assumption that only the government enacts public policy and shows that private governance and independently formed policy are common in the American political system. See Catherine E. Rudder, "Private Governance as Public Policy: A Paradigmatic Shift," *The Journal of Politics* 70, no. 4 (October 2008), pp. 899–913.

9. The legal scholar here cited is Jody Freeman, "The Private Role in Public Governance," *New York University Law Review* 75, issue 3 (June 2000), p. 548.

The three-quarters figure is from government scholar Paul C. Light. In 2008 he calculated that the contract workforce consisted of upwards of 7.6 million employees, or "three contractors for every federal employee." Paul C. Light, "Open Letter to the Presidential Candidates," *Huffington Post*, June 25, 2008, http://www.huffingtonpost.com/paul-c-light/open-letter-to-the-presid_b_109276.html. See also: Paul C. Light, *A Government Ill Executed: The Decline of the Federal Service and How to Reverse It*, Cambridge, Massachusetts: Harvard University Press, 2008.

10. The CRS report here cited is Kevin R. Kosar, *The Quasi Government: Hybrid Organizations with Both Government and Private Sector Legal Characteristics*, CRS Report for Congress, Washington, DC: Congressional Research Service, updated January 31, 2008, Summary, http://fas.org/sgp/crs/misc/RL30533.pdf. See this resource also for a taxonomy of "quasi-government" entities.

With regard to quasi-government organizations, RAND, created by the Air Force in 1947, was the first Federally Funded Research and Development Corporation (FFRDC). FFRDCs are a type of contracting organization that has a special relationship with a federal government agency. FFRDCs range from longstanding research and development facilities (the majority of FFRDCs are affiliated with the Departments of Defense and Energy) to two much newer entities created by the Department of Homeland Security (Kosar, *The Quasi Government*, pp. CRS-17–19). For a list of FFRDCs, see http://www.nsf.gov/statistics/nsf09300/content.cfm?pub_id=3898&id=6.

An example of venture capital funds is the Enterprise Funds set up with U.S. aid money in Central and Eastern Europe after the fall of communism. For an analysis of how the Enterprise Funds functioned in the region, see Janine R. Wedel, *Collision and Collusion: The Strange Case of Western Aid to Eastern Europe* (New York: Palgrave, 2001), pp. 180–194. See also Kosar, *The Quasi Government*, p. CRS–27.

Federal advisory committees are provided for in the Federal Advisory Committee Act (FACA), which allows most federal agencies to have boards, but only applies to agencies. Boards also can be established by statute. See, for example, GAO, *Federal Advisory Committees: Additional Guidance Could Help Agencies Better Ensure Independence and Balance*, Washington, DC: GAO, GAO-04-328, April 2004; and *Twenty-Seventh Annual Report of the President on Advisory Committees, Fiscal Year 1998*. In 2007 there were 52 agencies with 915 "active" federal advisory committees. GAO, *Federal Advisory Committee Act: Issues Related to the Independence and Balance of Advisory Committees Statement of Robin M. Nazzaro, Director, National Resources and Environment*, Washington, DC: GAO, GAO-08–611T, April 2008, p. 1, http://www.gao.gov/new.items/d08611t.pdf. The number of members sitting on federal advisory committees grew from some 52,000 in 2000 to 67,000 in 2006, while the number of committees oscillated between 900 and 1,000 during the same period. Jim Morris and Alejandra Fernandez Morera, "Network of 900 Advisory Panels Wields Unseen Power: Concerns Raised about Secrecy, Industry Influence and Political Interference," The Center for Public Integrity, March 29, 2007, at http://www.publicintegrity.org/shadow/report.aspx?aid=821 (accessed 8/6/2007). The quote and other information are from the GAO, *Federal Advisory Committee Act: Issues Related to the Independence and Balance of Advisory Committees Statement of Robin M. Nazzaro, Director, National Resources and Environment*, Washington, DC: GAO, GAO-08–611T, April 2008, p. 1, http://www.gao.gov/new.items/d08611t.pdf; and GAO, *Federal Advisory Committees: Additional Guidance Could Help Agencies Better Ensure Independence and Balance*, Washington, DC: GAO, GAO-04–328, April 2004, http://www.gao.gov/new.items/d04328.pdf, p. 14.

11. The exchange with Alfred Regnery was at a book talk and signing event, Washington, DC, August 9, 2008. The book is Alfred S. Regnery, *Upstream: The Ascendance of American Conservatism* (New York: Threshold Editions, 2008).

12. On bipartisan support for shadow government, see Dan Guttman, "Contracting, an American Way of Governance: Post 9/11 Constitutional Choices," *Meeting the Challenge of 9/11: Blueprints for More Effective Government,* Thomas H. Stanton, ed. (Armonk, NY: M. E. Sharpe Publishers, 2006), pp. 233, 236.

13. Regarding efforts to cap or reduce the number of civil servants: From 1940 to 1997, there were 24 pieces of legislation or executive actions to limit the number of civil servants who could be hired, to stop their hiring, or decrease their total number. During the same period, there were only 10 pieces of legislation or executive actions that created the potential to increase the civil service. Paul Light, *The True Size of Government* (Washington, DC: Brookings Institution Press, 1999), pp. 207–209. The number of contractor and grantee jobs as a proportion of the total federal workforce (contractor and grantee jobs plus federal civil servants, uniformed military personnel, and postal service workers) increased steadily over a dozen years, from 59 percent in 1990, to 61 percent in 1993, 63 percent in 1999, and 66 percent in 2002. Paul C. Light, "Fact Sheet on the New True Size of Government," Center for Public Service, The Brookings Institution, http://www.brookings.edu/gs/cps/light20030905.pdf. In 2008, Light calculated that the contract workforce consisted of upwards of 7.6 million employees, or "three contractors for every federal employee." Paul C. Light, "Open Letter to the Presidential Candidates," *Huffington Post*, June 25, 2008. With regard to data predating 1990, comparing 1984 to 1996 (earlier and annual data between these years are not available), the ratio of contractor and grantee workers to civil servants decreased 4.3 to 1 in 1984 to 4.2 to 1 in 1996 (Paul Light, *The True Size of Government*, pp. 198– 199). This relative decrease is attributable to drastic cuts in defense contracting associated with the end of the Cold War. However, when defense jobs are excluded, the ratio of contractor and grantee workers to civil servants increased from 3.5 to 1 in 1984 to 3.9 to 1 in 1996 (Ibid., pp. 41, 198–199.) In recent years defense and homeland security jobs have accounted for a sizeable portion of the growth in government outsourcing.

14. With respect to the rise in federal dollars spent on contractors' services: These figures are calculated from data available on the Federal Procurement Data System (FPDS), at https://www.fpds.gov/. While the FPDS data base shows the 2001 service figures by category, the 2008 data base does not. The total combined figure of goods and services for 2008 is $534 billion. Because procurement spending on services currently accounts for more than 60 percent of total procurement dollars, the $320 billion figure given is 60 percent of $534 (see http://www.fpdsng.com/downloads/agency_data_submit_list.htm). For the assessment that "procurement spending on services accounts for more than 60 percent of total procurement dollars," see *Report of the Acquisition Advisory Panel to the Office of Federal Procurement Policy and the United States Congress*, January 2007, p. 3, http://acquisition.gov/comp/aap/ 24102_GSA.pdf.

The latest FPDS data in which services are compiled by category are for 2006, and the figure for that year is $244.7 billion. See Federal Procurement Data System, "Federal Procurement Report 2006: Section 1 Total Federal Views," pp. 31–32, http://www.fpdsng.com/downloads/FPR_Reports/2006_fpr_section_I_total_federal_views.pdf. The number was calculated by adding total spending on R&D (p. 31), plus total spending on other services (p. 32). No more recent compilation of these numbers is available as of July 2009.

In 2008, the figure for NASA was 88 percent. $15.1 billion in contract spending (http://www.fpdsng.com/downloads/agency_data_submit_list.htm) divided by total NASA budget— $17.1 billion, reported in OMB's 2009 Historical Tables, Office of Management and Budget, "The Budget for Fiscal Year 2009, Historical Tables," p. 105, http://www.gpoaccess.gov/USbudget/fy09/pdf/hist.pdf. The 2008 figure for Energy was 88 percent. $24.6 billion in contract spending (http://www .fpdsng.com/downloads/agency_data_submit_list.htm) divided by total Energy budget ($27.8 billion in appropriated funds before offsetting receipts, http://www.cfo.doe.gov/budget/09budget/Content/ ApropStat.pdf).

With regard to the portion of government purchases now spent on work previously performed by the civil service: The proportion of services, as compared with total procurement (goods and services) went from 39 percent at the end of the Reagan administration (FY 1988) to 46.5 percent at the beginning of the Clinton presidency (FY 1993) to approximately 60 percent in 2006 (see https://www.fpds.gov/). See also Project on Government Oversight, "Pick Pocketing the Taxpayer: The Insidious Effects of Acquisition Reform, Revised Edition," March 11, 2002, http://www.pogo.org/pogo-files/reports/contract-oversight/pickpocketing-the-taxpayer/co-rcv-20020311.html. The 2007 report of the Acquisition Advisory Panel assessed that "procurement spending on services accounts for more than 60 percent of total procurement dollars" (*Report of the Acquisition Advisory Panel to the Office of Federal Procurement Policy and the United States Congress*, January 2007, p. 3, http://acquisition.gov/comp/aap/24102_GSA.pdf).

15. The 2003 information can be found in Larry Makinson, "Outsourcing the Pentagon: Who Benefits from the Politics and Economics of National Security?" The Center for Public Integrity, September 29, 2004, http://projects.publicintegrity.org/pns/report.aspx?aid=385.

The 2006 information is provided in Testimony of John P. Hutton, Acting Director, Acquisition and Sourcing Management, Government Accountability Office, "Defense Acquisitions: Improved Management and Oversight Needed to Better Control DOD's Acquisition of Services," May 10, 2007, p. 2, http://www.gao.gov/cgi-bin/getrpt?GAO-07-832T.

16. With regard to Defense accounting for almost three-quarters of the total federal procurement budget in 2008, these figures are calculated from data available on the Federal Procurement Data System (FPDS), at http://www.fpdsng.com/downloads/agency_data_submit_list.htm. With respect to the percentage of the budget of the U.S. intelligence community that goes to contracts, see Bonnie Goldstein, "Spy Central Slip-Up," Slate.com, June 8, 2007, at http://www.slate.com/id/2168032/entry/2168033/. According to a declassified government document obtained by investigative journalist Tim Shorrock in 2007, some 70 percent of the U.S. intelligence budget is spent on contracts (Tim Shorrock, "Private Spies," *The New York Post*, May 11, 2008). With regard to contract employees making up one-quarter of the core intelligence workforce, see Robert O'Harrow Jr., "Contractors Augment Intelligence Agencies," *Washington Post*, August 28, 2008, p. D01, http://www.washingtonpost.com/wp-dyn/content/article/2008/08/27/AR2008082703142.html.

17. Dempsey was elected vice president of Booz Allen in 2005. The quote from her is from Tim Shorrock, "The Spy Who Billed Me," *Mother Jones*, January/February 2005, http://www.motherjones.com/news/outfront/2005/01/12_400.html. The figure on total number of workers at Booz Allen is found in http://www.boozallen.com/media/file/Booz_Allen_Annual_Report_06-07.pdf. Other facts are provided in Zachary A. Goldfarb, "The New Booz & Co.," washingtonpost.com, May 21, 2008, http://voices.washingtonpost.com/washbizblog/2008/05/the_new_booz_co.html. The award given to Booz Allen, conferred by the Professional Services Council, the Fairfax County Chamber of Commerce, and *Washington Technology* magazine, "recognizes the firm for its outstanding contributions during the past year to its employees, the government contracting industry, and the U.S. government." See http://www.boozallen.com/about/article/658795?1pid=825646. For government departments that contract with Booz Allen, see http://eagle.bah.com/ and http://www.boozallen.com/media/file/Booz_Allen_Annual_Report_06-07.pdf. See http://www.aclu.org/pdfs/safefree/boozallen20060914.pdf. See also Elizabeth Brown, "Outsourcing the Defense Budget," The Center for Public Integrity, July 29, 2004, http://projects.publicintegrity.org/report.aspx?aid=363&sid=200.

18. The size of the federal civilian workforce fell by 426,200 positions between January 1993 and September 2000. (See History of the National Partnership for Reinventing Government Accomplishments, 1993–2000, http://govinfo.library.unt.edu/npr/whoweare/appendixf.html#1.)

With regard to the Department of Defense, the Pentagon reduced its civilian and military workforce after the end of the Cold War, resulting in a disproportionate reduction of defense employees overseeing contractors. In 2000, a Defense Department Inspector General Audit reported that the Department had decreased its acquisition workforce by about 50 percent from 460,516 employees at the end of FY 1990 to 230,556 at the end of FY 1999, while the workload had not shrunk proportionately. The dollar value of Defense procurement underwent a marginal decline (approximately 3 percent) during the period, while procurement actions rose by approximately 12 percent, from about 13.2 million to about 14.8 million (Office of the Inspector General Department of Defense, "Closing Overage Contracts Prior to Fielding a New DOD Contractor Payment System," *Audit Report*, Report No. D-2002–027, December 19, 2001, p. 10, http://www.dodig.mil/audit/reports/fy02/20–027.pdf).

For data on the Bush administration, see Paul C. Light, "The New True Size of Government," August 2006, p. 11, http://wagner.nyu.edu/performance/files/True_Size.pdf. In 2000 there were 57,835 federal officials in five job classifications related to acquisition and contracting, according to a database maintained by the U.S. Office of Personnel Management (Office of Personnel Management, *Central Personnel Data File: Status File*, Sept. 2000). In 2006, the number was 58,723 (Federal Acquisition Institute, *Annual Report on the Federal Acquisition Workforce Fiscal Year 2006*, May 2007). On the expansion of the workload, see United States House of Representatives, Committee on Oversight and Government Reform, Majority Staff, June 2007, *More Dollars, Less Sense: Worsening Contracting Trends under the Bush Administration*, p. 10. For details about the increased skills required on the job, see "Report of the Acquisition Advisory Panel to the Office of Federal Procurement Policy and the United States Congress" (December 2006), at http://www.acqnet.gov/comp/aap/index.html.

19. For the list of high risk areas including the Departments of Defense and Energy, as well as NASA, see GAO, *High Risk Series: An Update*, Washington, DC: GAO, GAO-07–310, January 2007, pp. 6, 7, available at http://www.gao.gov/new.items/d07310.pdf.

The Walker quote is from Comptroller General David Walker, Remarks at the George Washington University Law School Symposium on the Future of Competitive Sourcing, September 15, 2003 (transcript on file with the Public Contract Law Journal). The GAO quote is from GAO, *Military Operations: High-Level DOD Action Needed to Address Long-Standing Problems with Management and Oversight of Contractors Supporting Deployed Forces*, United States Government Accountability Office, GAO-07–145, December 2006, p. 35, www.gao.gov/cgi-bin/getrpt?GAO-07-145. The assessment from the Department of Homeland Security's inspector general can be found at Department of Homeland Security Inspector General, *Department of Homeland Security's Procurement and Program Management Operations*, OIG-0–53, Sept. 2005, p. 8, http://www.dhs.gov/xoig/assets/mgmtrpts/OIG_05-53_Sep05.pdf.

20. The Acquisition Advisory Panel has written: "In many cases contractor personnel work alongside federal employees in the federal workspace; often performing identical functions." Acquisition Advisory Panel, Report of the Acquisition Advisory Panel to the Office of Federal Procurement Policy and the United States Congress, January 2007, p. 392, http://acquisition.gov/comp/aap/24102_GSA.pdf.

21. The SETA contractor here referenced is Glenn Danielson. Author's conversation with Glenn Danielson, November 25, 2008.

22. The definition of inherently governmental functions is from Executive Office of the President, Office of Management and Budget, "Circular No. A-76 (Revised) to the Heads of Executive Departments and Establishments" on the "Performance of Commercial Activities," May 29, 2003, http://www.whitehouse.gov/omb/circulars/a076/a76_rev2003.pdf, or http://www.whitehouse.gov/omb/circulars/a076/a76_incl_tech_correction.pdf.

Legal scholar Paul Verkuil discusses the implications of outsourcing government functions in *Outsourcing Sovereignty: Why Privatization of Government Functions Threatens Democracy and What We Can Do About It* (New York: Cambridge University Press, 2007).

The list of eight inherently governmental functions is contained in Office of Management and Budget, Office of Federal Procurement Policy, Policy Letter 92–1 to the Heads of Executive Agencies and Departments, Washington, DC, September 23, 1992, http://www.whitehouse.gov/omb/procurement/policy_letters/92–1_092392.html. This list also appears in the Federal Acquisition Regulation (FAR), 7.503, March 2005, http://www.acquisition.gov/far/reissue/FARvol1ForPaperOnly.pdf. According to the Foreword to the FAR, "The FAR is the primary regulation for use by all Federal Executive agencies in their acquisition of supplies and services with appropriated funds. It became effective on April 1, 1984, and is issued within applicable laws under the joint authorities of the Administrator of General Services, the Secretary of Defense, and the Administrator for the National Aeronautics and Space Administration, under the broad policy guidelines of the Administrator, Office of Federal Procurement Policy, Office of Management and Budget."

23. With regard to scaling back inherently governmental functions: Law professor Laura Dickinson suggests that "Congress might consider designating such [inherently governmental] functions as 'core' rather than inherently governmental, which would permit outsourcing but at the same time impose lim-

its on the percentage of positions that may be turned over to contractors" (Laura A. Dickinson, Professor, University of Connecticut School of Law, *Testimony Before the United States Senate Committee on Homeland Security and Governmental Affairs*, Wednesday, February 27, 2008, p. 4, http://hsgac.senate.gov/public/_files/022708Dickinson.pdf). An array of think-tankers and analysts advocate privatizing government functions, including intelligence ones (see, for instance, Michael Rubin, "Privatize the CIA," *Weekly Standard Review* 12, issue 20 [February 5, 2007], http://www.michaelrubin.org/1029/privatize-the-cia). Army Special Forces Major Roger D. Carstens and think tank fellows Michael A. Cohen and Maria Figueroa Küpçü (drawing on a panel of experts from industry, government, and academe) prefer to "permit relevant government agencies to have broad discretionary leeway in determining where and how private contractors should be used" (Roger D. Carstens, Michael A. Cohen, and Maria Figueroa Küpçü, *Changing the Culture of Pentagon Contracting* [Washington, DC: A Publication of the Privatization of Foreign Policy Initiative, New America Foundation, October 2008], http://www.newamerica.net/files/Changing%20the%20Culture%20of%20Pentagon%20Contracting.pdf.) See also comments by Harvard Professor Stephen Goldsmith, "What's Left for Government to Do?" *The American* (January/February 2008), http://www.american.com/archive/2008/january-february-magazine-contents/what2019s-left-for-government-to-do/article_print (accessed March 12, 2009), and attorney Tara Lee, "Redefining Inherently Governmental: The Push to Redefine the Function and Its Consequences," *Journal of International Peace Operations* 4, no. 1 (July-August 2008), pp. 9–10, http://www.ipoaonline.org/journal/images/journal_2008_0708.pdf.

With respect to revisions of guidelines: In 1955, the Eisenhower Administration released the Bureau of the Budget Bulletin 55–4; in 1966 the Bureau of the Budget put out the policy as *Circular No. A-76* (Office of Management and Budget, Office of Federal Procurement Policy, "Enhancing Governmental Productivity through Competition: A New Way of Doing Business Within The Government, To Provide Quality Government at Least Cost: A Progress Report on OMB *Circular No. A-76*, *Performance of Commercial Activities*" [Washington, DC: Office of Management and Budget, Office of Federal Procurement Policy, 1988]). The most recent updates are provided in: Executive Office of the President, Office of Management and Budget, "Circular No. A-76 (Revised) to the Heads of Executive Departments and Establishments" on the "Performance of Commercial Activities," May 29, 2003, http://www.whitehouse.gov/omb/circulars/a076/a76_rev2003.pdf, and Congressional Research Service, "OMB Circular A-76: Explanation and Discussion of the Recently Revised Federal Outsourcing Policy," Washington, DC: Library of Congress, September 10, 2003, p. 1, http://digital.library.unt.edu/govdocs/crs/permalink/meta-crs-7717:1. See also FAR Subpart 7.5—Inherently Governmental Functions, (c)—functions considered inherently governmental, and (d)—functions "generally not considered to be inherently governmental." Federal Acquisition Regulation, March 2005, 7.503, http://www.acquisition.gov/far/reissue/FARvol1 ForPaperOnly.pdf.

24. Eric Lipton and Michael J. de la Merced, "Wall St. Firm Draws Scrutiny as U.S. Adviser," *New York Times*, May 19, 2009, http://www.nytimes.com/2009/05/19/business/19blackrock.html?_r=1.

25. Liz Rappaport and Susanne Craig, "BlackRock Wears Multiple Hats," *Wall Street Journal*, May 19, 2009, http://online.wsj.com/article/SB124269131342732625.html.

26. See for example, Eric Dash, "Bank of New York Mellon Will Oversee Bailout Fund," *New York Times*, October 14, 2008, http://www.nytimes.com/2008/10/15/business/economy/15tarp.html?scp=4&sq=bank%20of%20new%20york%20mellon&st=cse.

27. With regard to the Pentagon employing contractors who choose other contractors, see Larry Makinson, "Outsourcing the Pentagon: Who Benefits from the Politics and Economics of National Security?" Washington, DC, the Center for Public Integrity, September 29, 2004, p. 4, http://projects.publicintegrity.org/pns/report.aspx?aid=385.

With respect to CACI, see Project on Government Oversight, "GSA Hired CACI to Process Suspension and Debarment Cases," February 5, 2007, http://www.pogo.org/pogo-files/alerts/contract-oversight/co-gp-20070205.html.

28. With regard to contractors overseeing other contractors in Homeland Security, see GAO-08–142T, Department of Homeland Security: Risk Assessment and Enhanced Oversight Needed to Manage Reliance on Contractors Statement of John P. Hutton, Director Acquisition and Sourcing Management, Wednesday, October 17, 2007, p. 1, http://www.gao.gov/new.items/d08142t.pdf. GAO

reported that "More than half of the 117 statements of work we reviewed included reorganization and planning activities, policy development, and acquisition support—services that closely support the performance of inherently governmental functions according to federal acquisition guidance." See p. 2 for above quote; pp. 8–10 for overall analysis of the issue.

With respect to lead systems integrators, see Valerie Bailey Grasso, *CRS Report for Congress: Defense Acquisition: Use of Lead System Integrators (LSIs)—Background, Oversight Issues, and Options for Congress, Congressional Research Service,* The Library of Congress, February 10, 2009, pp. 1–2, http://www.fas.org/sgp/crs/natsec/RS22631.pdf. For analysis of how the government's use of lead systems integrators raises the risk of organizational conflicts of interest, see Project on Government Oversight, "Stronger Contractor Organizational Conflicts of Interest Regulations Needed," July 18, 2008, http://www.pogo.org/pogo-files/letters/contract-oversight/co-fcm-20080718.html.

The quote about defense contractors is from: David Hubler, "Six to Upgrade DOD Management Processes," *Washington Technology,* December 19, 2008, http://washingtontechnology.com/Articles/2008/12/19/Six-to-upgrade-DOD-management-processes.aspx?p=1.

With regard to the NCS, see: R. J. Hillhouse, "Who Runs the CIA? Outsiders for Hire," *Washington Post,* July 8, 2007, p. B5, http://www.washingtonpost.com/wp-dyn/content/article/2007/07/06/AR2007070601993.html.

29. Anitha Reddy and Sara Kehaulani Goo, "Database on U.S. Visitors Set for Huge Expansion: Reston Firm's Contract Worth Up to \$10 Billion," *Washington Post,* June 2, 2004, p. E01, http://www.washingtonpost.com/wp-dyn/articles/A7961–2004Jun1.html.

30. With regard to the Secretary of Energy, see Paul R. Verkuil, *Outsourcing Sovereignty* (New York: Cambridge University Press, 2007), p. 45.

With regard to the Army's Field Manual, see Dan Guttman, "The Shadow Pentagon: Private Contractors Play a Huge Role in Basic Government Work—Mostly Out of Public View" (Washington, DC: Center for Public Integrity), September 29, 2004, http://projects.publicintegrity.org/pns/report.aspx?aid=386. See also Headquarters: Department of the Army, "Contractors on the Battlefield," *Field Manual No. 3–100.21,* Washington, DC, January 3, 2003, www.osc.army.mil/gc/files/fm3_100x21.pdf.

31. The GAO on 117 contracts is at GAO-08–142T, *Department of Homeland Security: Risk Assessment and Enhanced Oversight Needed to Manage Reliance on Contractors Statement of John P. Hutton, Director Acquisition and Sourcing Management,* Wednesday, October 17, 2007, p. 2, http://www.gao.gov/new.items/d08142t.pdf. Information about the company being awarded \$42.4 million is found in: GAO, *Risk Assessment and Enhanced Oversight Needed to Manage Reliance on Contractors,* October 17, 2007, p. 6, http://www.gao.gov/new.items/d08142t.pdf.

The number of NSA-approved contractor facilities was reported by Shaun Waterman, "Unveiling US Intel Spending and Contractors," Washington (UPI), June 27, 2007, http://www.spacewar.com/reports/Unveiling_US_Intel_Spending_And_Contractors_999.html. The data on the National Reconnaissance Office are from Tim Shorrock. See his "Private Spies," *New York Post,* May 11, 2008, http://www.nypost.com/seven/05112008/postopinion/postopbooks/private_spies_110301.htm.

In another example of intelligence outsourcing, in August 2007 the Defense Intelligence Agency (DIA) announced its plans to contract out upwards of \$1 billion to private companies. These contractors would conduct, in the words of the DIA (as published on a procurement Web site) "operational and mission requirements" that involve "Gathering and Collection, Analysis, Utilization, and Strategy and Support" of intelligence—in other words, some core intelligence functions. Walter Pincus, "Defense Agency Proposes Outsourcing More Spying: Contracts Worth \$1 Billion Would Set Record," *Washington Post,* August 19, 2007, p. A3, http://www.washingtonpost.com/wp-dyn/content/article/2007/08/18/AR2007081800992.html.

32. The GAO information cited is from Testimony of John P. Hutton, Acting Director, Acquisition and Sourcing Management, Government Accountability Office, "Defense Acquisitions: Improved Management and Oversight Needed to Better Control DOD's Acquisition of Services," May 10, 2007, pp. 2, 5, http://www.gao.gov/cgi-bin/getrpt?GAO-07-832T.

The 2007 figures, compiled from State and Defense Department sources, were reported in: T. Christian Miller, "Private Contractors Outnumber U.S. Troops in Iraq," *Los Angeles Times,* July 4, 2007, http://www.latimes.com/news/nationworld/nation/la-na-private4jul04,1,7664713,full.story?coll

=la-headlines-nation. The article states that these figures may underrepresent private security contractors. The 2008 numbers are from Congressional Budget Office, "Contractors' Support of U.S. Operations in Iraq," August 2008, p. 9, http://www.cbo.gov/ftpdocs/96xx/doc9688/08–12-IraqContractors.pdf. The 1991 figures can be found in John M. Broder and James Risen, "Contractor Deaths in Iraq Soar to Record," *New York Times*, May 19, 2007, http:///www.nytimes.com/2007/05/19/world/middleeast//19contractors.html.

33. The Acquisition Advisory Panel report is Acquisition Advisory Panel, *Report of the Acquisition Advisory Panel to the Office of Federal Procurement Policy and the United States Congress*, January 2007, pp. 391–392, 417, http://acquisition.gov/comp/aap/24102_GSA.pdf.

With regard to insourcing, see, for instance, Elise Castelli, "The Case for Insourcing," FederalTimes.com, September 21, 2008, http://www.federaltimes.com/index.php?S=3733576. The article also states that insourcing, which has been done on a limited basis in the Navy, the Army, the Internal Revenue Service, and the Department of Homeland Security, is "rare."

34. Schinasi is cited in Daniel Zwerdling, "Obama To Tackle Explosion In Federal Contracts," National Public Radio, December 1, 2008, http://www.npr.org/templates/story/story.php?storyId=97322339.

The army's guess is reported in Guttman, "The Shadow Pentagon."

35. For Defense's difficulty in monitoring contractors, see GAO, *High Risk Series: An Update*, Washington, DC: GAO, GAO-07–310, January 2007, p. 67, available at http://www.gao.gov/new.items/d07310.pdf. GAO's report on industrial security is GAO, *Industrial Security: DOD Cannot Ensure Its Oversight of Contractors under Foreign Influence Is Sufficient*, GAO-05-681, Washington, DC, July 2005, pp. 3, 5, http://www.gao.gov/new.items/d05681.pdf. For GAO's new high-risk category: GAO, *High Risk Series: An Update*, Washington, DC: GAO, GAO-07–310, January 2007, pp. 25, 6, available at http://www.gao.gov/new.items/d07310.pdf.

36. Press Release, *Booz Allen's Extensive Ties to Government Raise More Questions About SWIFT Surveillance Program*, ACLU, September 26, 2006, http://www.aclu.org/safefree/spying/26808prs20060926.html. For further information about this case, see Josh Meyer and Greg Miller, "U.S. Secretly Tracks Global Bank Data," *Los Angeles Times*, June 23, 2006, p. A1, http://articles.latimes.com/2006/jun/23/nation/na-swift23; Eric Lichtblau and James Risen, "Bank Data Is Sifted by U.S. in Secret to Block Terror," *New York Times*, June 23, 2006, p. A1, http://www.nytimes.com/2006/06/23/washington/23intel.html; and Eric Lichtblau, "Europe Panel Faults Sifting of Bank Data," *New York Times*, September 26, 2006, p. A1, http://www.nytimes.com/2006/09/26/us/26swift.html.

37. To name just one instance, Katherine Schinasi, a top official at the GAO, described a high-level meeting she attended at a military command. Because she did not know any of the participants, she asked everyone around the table who employed them. "There were several people who worked for the military command, but the majority of people sitting at the table worked for contractors," she said. Interviewed by Zwerdling, "Obama to Tackle Explosion in Federal Contracts."

38. GAO-08–142T, Government Accountability Office, Testimony Before the Committee on Homeland Security and Governmental Affairs, United States Senate, Department of Homeland Security: Risk Assessment and Enhanced Oversight Needed to Manage Reliance on Contractors, Statement of John P. Hutton, Director Acquisition and Sourcing Management, Wednesday, October 17, 2007, Executive Summary, http://www.gao.gov/new.items/d08142t.pdf.

39. For details about the biosurveillance shop SAIC suggested, see Robert O'Harrow Jr., "Biosurveillance, Intelligence and Bugs," Government Inc., Blog, August 13, 2007, http://voices.washingtonpost.com/government-inc/2007/08/biosurveillance_intelligence_a_1.html. For details about SAIC writing the rules, see Robert O'Harrow Jr., "As the government hires more contractors, some have helped draft rules that could benefit their businesses. A federal jury cited SAIC in one such case. SAIC sees no conflict." *Washington Post*, August 18, 2008, p. D, D3.

40. The three-quarters estimate was made by the market research firm INPUT in Chantilly, Virginia, and reported in *Government Executive* ("Experiences Give and Take," *Government Executive*, July 1, 2003, www.govexec.com/feature/0603/ots03s4.htm). The Acquisition Advisory Panel similarly assesses that "Most, if not all, agencies have contracted out major portions of their information technology and communications functions" (Acquisition Advisory Panel, *Report of the Acquisition Advisory*

Panel to the Office of Federal Procurement Policy and the United States Congress, January 2007, p. 399, http://acquisition.gov/comp/aap/24102_GSA.pdf). A notable exception to governmental dependence on privately executed IT is government's underwriting of technological advancement, which often is achieved in government laboratories. However, even in this case, government often lacks in-house expertise and capacity and has little choice but to turn to the private sector. Burlin is cited in *Government Executive*, "Experiences Give and Take."

The Guttman quote is from Guttman, "The Shadow Pentagon."

41. Figures on employees in Homeland Security are from GAO, "DHS's Actions to Recruit and Retain Staff and Comply with the Vacancies Reform Act," July 2007, pp. 15–16, at http://www.gao.gov/new.items/d07758.pdf.

Information about the demoralized FEMA professionals is from the nonprofit Partnership for Public Service, whose mission involves the promotion of federal government careers. The professionals were displaced by or did not want to work for the inexperienced political appointees installed under the Bush II administration. The Partnership for Public Service ranked FEMA last among the 28 agencies it studied in 2003. The American Federation of Government Employees, which surveys employees and lists the best places to work in government, found in 2004 that of 84 career FEMA professionals who responded, only 10 of them ranked their agency leaders as excellent or good. Another 28 employees called their leadership fair, while 33 said it was poor. More than 50 employees responded that they would go to another agency if they could stay at the same pay level, while 67 said the agency had become poorer since it merged into the Department of Homeland Security. Spencer S. Hsu, "Leaders Lacking Disaster Experience: 'Brain Drain' At Agency Cited," *Washington Post*, September 9, 2005, p. A1, http://www.washingtonpost.com/wp-dyn/content/article/2005/09/08/AR2005090802165.html.

Hayden is quoted in Katherine Shrader, "CIA Reviewing Use of Contractors," Associated Press, September 18 2006. Response of Agency officials from: Tim Shorrock, "Private Spies," *New York Post*, May 11, 2008, http://www.nypost.com/seven/05112008/postopinion/postopbooks/private_spies_110301.htm.

42. Tim Shorrock, "Former High-Ranking Bush Officials Enjoy War Profits," Salon.com, May 29, 2008, http://www.salon.com/news/excerpt/2008/05/29/spies_for_hire/index.html.

43. Mini Workshop on Public-Private Interfaces, New America Foundation, July 19, 2007.

44. Information on Booz Allen's split is from Zachary A. Goldfarb, "Booz Allen Units to Part Ways: McLean Consulting Firm's Government Division Being Sold to Carlyle Group," *Washington Post*, May 17, 2008, p. D01, http://www.washingtonpost.com/wp-dyn/content/article/2008/05/16/AR2008051 603788.html. Information on government versus commercial units at Booz Allen is from Zachary A. Goldfarb, "The New Booz & Co.," *Washington Post*, May 21, 2008, http://voices.washington post.com/washbizblog/2008/05/the_new_booz_co.html.

45. For a discussion of the tension between accountability and autonomy of "private" government contractors, including legal decisions, see Daniel Guttman's "Public and Private Service: The Twentieth Century Culture of Contracting Out and the Evolving Law of Diffused Sovereignty," *Administrative Law Review* 52, no. 3 (2000), Washington, DC: Washington Law Review, American University, pp. 901–908. The article also outlines the kinds of conflicts of interest that arise between private employees and their public overseers (pp. 896–901).

46. Quoted in Shane Harris, "Ethics Office Launches Inquiry into Procurement Practices," GovExec.com, September 26, 2002, http://www.govexec.com/story_page.cfm?articleid=23972&printer-friendlyvers=1. Angela Styles, former administrator of the Office of Federal Procurement Policy (for the Office of Management and Budget), makes a similar point.

47. For contract oversight investigations under Bush I, see Office of Management and Budget, *Summary Report of the SWAT Team on Civilian Agency Contracting: Improving Contracting Practices and Management Controls on Cost-Type Federal Contracts*, Washington, DC: Office of Management and Budget, December 3, 1992, http://www1.law.nyu.edu/journals/envtllaw/issues/vol2/1/2nyuelj34.html.

48. Kelman's evolving door can be found at Steve Kelman, "Evolving Door," December 5, 2003, http://www.govexec.com/story_page.cfm?filepath=/dailyfed/1203/120803ff.htm. With regard to Kelman's work with industry associations, see, for example, Jeff Shear, "He's the President's Hatchet Man," *National Journal*, March 25, 1996, p. 754. See also Project On Government Oversight, "Pick Pocketing

the Taxpayer: The Insidious Effects of Acquisition Reform," March 11, 2002, http://www.pogo.org/pogo-files/reports/contract-oversight/pickpocketing-the-taxpayer/co-rcv-20020311.html.

The 1996 FARA is also called the Clinger-Cohen Act.

49. The 40 percent figure (for 2005) is provided by the Acquisition Advisory Panel (Acquisition Advisory Panel, *Report of the Acquisition Advisory Panel to the Office of Federal Procurement Policy and the United States Congress*, January 2007, p. 106, http://acquisition.gov/comp/aap/24102_GSA.pdf). Description of IDIQ contracts can be found in the same report on pp. 67–72.

50. The Acquisition Advisory Panel citations are at: Acquisition Advisory Panel, *Report of the Acquisition Advisory Panel to the Office of Federal Procurement Policy and the United States Congress*, p. 405.

51. The government Web site where task orders are posted is http://fedbizopps.gov. On the billions that can be collected in task orders, see, for instance Bob Brewin's blog on http://nextgov.com, "Obama's Transparency Lost on Defense," February 10, 2009, http://whatsbrewin.nextgov.com/2009/02/obamas_transparency_lost_on_de.php.

For information about the telecommunications IDIQ contract, see, for instance, Elizabeth Newell, "GSA Lets 29 Firms in on Massive Tech Services Contract," Governmentexecutive.com, July 31, 2007, http://www.govexec.com/story_page.cfm?filepath=/dailyfed/0707/073107e1.htm.

Some attempts in the Department of Defense have been made to require competition on IDIQ contracts. Congress enacted Section 803 of the National Defense Authorization Act for Fiscal Year 2002. This provision, which applies only to Defense orders exceeding $100,000 for services under IDIQ contracts, requires "fair notice" to contractors holding an IDIQ award before placing an order. The provision is seen by some contract specialists as weak because "fair notice" is defined in the implementing regulations as being satisfied when only three offers are received (see Defense Federal Acquisition Regulation Supplement, § 208.405–70, http://www.dod.mil/dodgc/olc/docs/2002NDAA.pdf). As noted by the GAO (Government Accountability Office Report GAO-04-874, *Guidance Needed to Promote Competition for Defense Task Orders*, July 30, 2004, Executive Summary, http:// www.gao.gov /new.items/d04874.pdf), even these "enhanced" competition requirements were waived by DOD in approximately 50 percent of cases. Ralph C. Nash and John Cibinic report that "There are numerous indications that Contracting Officers are diligent in finding ways to avoid . . . competition . . . In the traditional tug of-war between 'customer satisfaction' (honoring the desire of program and technical personnel to obtain services from knowledgeable and high performance incumbents) and obtaining competition, customer satisfaction appears to be winning by a large margin" ("Competition for Task Orders: The Exception or the Rule?" 18 Nash & Cibinic Rep., ¶ 42, October 2004).

Washington Technology, Federal Computer Week, and *Government Computer News* have either arisen or shaped themselves to fill the government-contractor networking niche.

52. Reporting of task orders on the FPDS is at http://www.fpdsng.com/downloads/agency_data_submit_list.htm. The link to the 2006 report is at http://www.fpdsng.com/fpr_reports_fy_06.html.

Data posting runs a full fiscal year behind and the GAO has complained about this. See http://www.gao.gov/new.items/d05960r.pdf.

53. Like many such consulting firms, CACI has high-powered connections; its board of directors, for instance, has included such bigwigs as Richard Armitage, who went on to become deputy secretary of state under Bush II. Armitage became a CACI director in 1999, when he was a member of the Defense Policy Board. David Isenberg, "A Fistful of Contractors: The Case for a Pragmatic Assessment of Private Military Companies in Iraq," *Research Report* 2004.4, Washington, DC: British American Security Information Council, September 2004, p. 39, http://www.basicint.org/pubs/Research/2004PMC.pdf. For information about high-powered individuals associated with CACI, see Ellen McCarthy, "Intelligence Work Comes to CACI Via Acquisitions," *Washington Post,* July 8, 2004, p. E01, http://www.washingtonpost.com/wp-dyn/articles/A35630-2004Jul7.html.

The CACI quote is from GAO, *Interagency Contracting: Problems with DOD's and Interior's Orders to Support Military Operations, United States Government Accountability Office,* GAO-05-201, April 2005, p. 14, www.gao.gov/cgi-bin/getrpt?GAO-05-201.

The GAO found that the task orders issued were "beyond the scope of the underlying contract," while the Inspector General of the Department of the Interior and the General Services Administration similarly determined that 11 of 12 procurements reviewed were "outside the scope" of the contract. See GAO, *Interagency Contracting: Problems with DOD's and Interior's Orders to Support Military Operations*, United States Government Accountability Office, GAO-05–201, April 2005, Highlights and pp. 7-8, www.gao.gov/cgi-bin/getrpt?GAO-05-201; and United States Department of the Interior, Office of Inspector General, Memorandum to: Assistant Secretary for Policy, Management and Budget; From: Earl E. Devaney, Inspector General; Subject: Review of 12 Procurements Placed Under General Services Administration Federal Supply Schedules 70 and 871 by the National Business Center (Assignment No. W-EV-OSS-0075–2004), July 16, 2004, http://frwebgate.access.gpo.gov/cgi-bin/getdoc.cgi?dbname=interior&docid=f:2004-i-0049.pdf.

54. See GAO, *Interagency Contracting: Problems with DOD's and Interior's Orders to Support Military Operations*, United States Government Accountability Office, GAO-05–201, April 2005, p. 2, http://www.gao.gov/htext/d05201.html. See also: http://www.acquisition.gov/comp/aap/documents/Chapter3.pdf, especially p. 243.

55. Ibid., pp. 3, 14.

56. For documentation that IDIQ contracts are the primary form of interagency contracts, see *Report of the Acquisition Advisory Panel to the Office of Federal Procurement Policy and the United States Congress*, January 2007, p. 247, http://acquisition.gov/comp/aap/24102_GSA.pdf.

For documentation that GAP brought the case forward, see Sylvia Hsieh, "Attorneys Create Niche in Representing Nuclear Weapons Workers," *Lawyers USA*, October 23, 2006, http://www.allbusiness.com/public-administration/administration-economic-programs/4092301-1.html. Regarding hearings after Miller brought the case to light: On March 30, 2004, the Senate Committee on Energy and Natural Resources concluded three hearings on the implementation of the Energy Employees Occupational Illness Compensation Program Act of 2000 (EEIOCPA), http://energy.senate.gov/public/index.cfm?FuseAction=Hearings.Hearing&Hearing_ID=5f9b1f9d-cd1e-4c11-a107-23a85836298a. On October 8, 2004, an amendment to the FY 2005 Defense Authorization Act removed most responsibility for EEIOCPA from the Department of Energy and gave it to the Department of Labor. Government Accountability Project, "GAP – EEOICPA," January 9, 2007, http://www.whistleblower.org/program/domestic.cfm. See Charles Pope, "Sick DOE Worker's Claims Languish," *Seattle Post Intelligencer*, March 29, 2004, http://www.seattlepi.com/local/166744_doecomp29.html. For details and documentation of the case, see General Accountability Office, GAO-06–547, *Department of Energy, Office of Worker Advocacy, Deficient Controls Led to Millions of Dollars in Improper and Questionable Payments to Contractors*, Washington, DC: Government Accountability Office, May 2006, http://www.gao.gov/new.items/d06547.pdf.

For risk in interagency contracting, see: GAO, *High Risk Series: An Update*, Washington, DC: GAO, GAO-07–310, January 2007, p. 6, http://www.gao.gov/new.items/d07310.pdf.

57. For CACI retaining lobbyists, see David Isenberg, "A Fistful of Contractors: The Case for a Pragmatic Assessment of Private Military Companies in Iraq," *Research Report* 2004.4, London: British American Security Information Council, September 2004, p. 40, http://www.basicint.org/pubs/Research/2004PMC.pdf; for CACI being cleared, see Ellen McCarthy, "Government Clears CACI for Contracts," *Washington Post*, July 8, 2004, p. E01, http://www.washingtonpost.com/wp-dyn/articles/A35432-2004Jul7.html; and for CACI's award of an interrogation contract: Ellen McCarthy, "CACI Gets New Interrogation Contract," *Washington Post*, August 5, 2004, p. E05, http://www.washingtonpost.com/wp-dyn/articles/A41215-2004Aug4.html. CACI has subsequently received additional government intelligence and national security contracts. See, for instance, Robert O'Harrow Jr., "Intelligence Spending: CACI Gets More," washingtonpost.com, January 28, 2009, http://voices.washingtonpost.com/government-inc/2009/01/intelligence_spending_caci_get.html.

58. Acquisition Advisory Panel, *Report of the Acquisition Advisory Panel to the Office of Federal Procurement Policy and the United States Congress*, January 2007, pp. 405–406, http://acquisition.gov/comp/aap/24102_GSA.pdf.

59. With regard to Defense companies linked to senior members of the Bush administration's inner circles as the beneficiaries of awards, see, for example, Walter F. Roche Jr., "Nominee's Business Ties Raise Concerns: Defense chief appointee Robert Gates has some watchdogs worried about a revolving door between the private sector and government," *Los Angeles Times*, December 2, 2006, p. A10.

With respect to FEMA's noncompetitive procedures, see Robert O'Harrow Jr. and Scott Higham, "Interior, Pentagon Faulted In Audits: Effort to Speed Defense Contracts Wasted Millions," *Washington Post*, December 25, 2006, p. A1, http://www.washingtonpost.com/wp-dyn/content/article/2006/12/24/AR2006122400916.html; and U.S. Government Accountability Office, *Hurricane Katrina: Ineffective FEMA Oversight of Housing Maintenance Contracts in Mississippi Resulted in Millions of Dollars of Waste and Potential Fraud*, November 2007, GAO-08–106, p. 2, www.gao.gov/new.items/d08106.pdf.

With regard to government contracting officials not getting good deals for their agencies, see Project on Government Oversight, *Pick Pocketing The Taxpayer: The Insidious Effects of Acquisition Reform*, rev. ed., Washington, DC: POGO, March 11, 2002, http://www.pogo.org/pogo-files/reports/contract-oversight/pickpocketing-the-taxpayer/co-rcv-20020311.html.

With respect to insourcing motivated by cost savings, see Elise Castelli, "The Case for Insourcing," FederalTimes.com, September 21, 2008, http://www.federaltimes.com/index.php?S=3733576. The article states that insourcing has been done on a limited basis in the Navy, the Army, the Internal Revenue Service, and the Department of Homeland Security. With regard to money (not) saved through competitive sourcing, see GAO, *Department of Labor: Better Cost Assessments and Departmentwide Performance Tracing Are Needed to Effectively Manage Competitive Sourcing Program*, GAO-09–14, November 2008, Executive Summary, http://www.gao.gov/new.items/d0914.pdf. See also Elise Castelli, "GAO: Agencies Overstate Savings of Competitive Sourcing," FederalTimes.com, November 24, 2008, http://www.federaltimes.com/index.php?S=3834852.

60. The Justice Department's deliberations were in response to a lawsuit under the False Claims Act brought by two former associates of Custer Battles, a Virginia-based contractor. They alleged that the company had defrauded the U.S. government by overcharging the CPA and billing it for work never done, among other abuses. (Matt Kelley, "Lawsuit Says Iraq Security Contractor Defrauded U.S.," Associated Press, October 8, 2004; and Shane Harris, "Ethics Office Launches Inquiry into Procurement Practices," GovExec.com, September 26, 2002. See also National Public Radio, Morning Edition, "Analysis: First Contractor Fraud Case from Iraq to be Unsealed," November 19, 2004, National Public Radio transcripts.) The quote from the federal judge can be found at: Case No. 1:04cv199, *United States of America ex rel. DRC, Inc., v. Custer Battles, LLC, et al.*, August 08, 2006, p. 17. See also Dana Hedgpeth, "Judge Clears Contractor of Fraud in Iraq," *Washington Post*, February 9, 2007, p. D1, http://www.washingtonpost.com/wp-dyn/content/article/2007/02/08/AR2007020801871.html.

In the April 2009 ruling, a panel of 4th Circuit judges allowed the plaintiffs to seek a new trial for additional damages. See Ellen Nakashima, "Court Revives Suit Over Iraq Work," *Washington Post*, April 11, 2009, A09.

61. The Center for Public Integrity quote is from Center for Public Integrity, "Federal Advisory Bodies Wield Unseen Power," March 29, 2007, http://www.publicintegrity.org/news/entry/217/.

The Bureau of Land Management has issued a brochure explaining what operations are subject to the FACA. Bureau of Land Management, "Federal Advisory Committee Act: Summary of What BLM Staff Need to Know When Working With ADR-Based Collaborative Community Working Groups," http://www.blm.gov/pgdata/etc/medialib/blm/wo/Communications_Directorate/general_publications/faca.Par.59707.File.dat/ADR-FACA_Brochure.pdf.

62. With regard to members of the Defense Policy Board and the Defense Science Board, see "The Politics of Contracting," *Project on Government Oversight*, Washington, DC, June 29, 2004, pp. 17–21. With regard to Richard Perle and the Defense Policy Board, see Seymour Hersh, "Lunch with the Chairman," *New Yorker*, March 17, 2003, http://www.newyorker.com/archive/2003/03/17/030317fa_fact. See also Tim Shorrock, "Richard Perle's Corporate Adventures," *The Nation*, April 3, 2003, http://www.thenation.com/doc/20030421/shorrock.

63. Task forces are provided for in the Federal Advisory Committee Act (FACA). See, for example, *Twenty-Seventh Annual Report of the President on Advisory Committees, Fiscal Year 1998*, http://fido.gov/facadatabase/printedannualreports%5C1998-Twenty-Seventh%20Annual%20Report%20Of%20The%20President%20On%20Federal%20Advisory%20Committees.pdf.

64. Exceptions to task force proceedings having to be open to the public are made when discussions involve classified material, proprietary data, or personal privacy. The identities of its committee members

also would be a matter of public record. (GAO, *Federal Advisory Committees: Additional Guidance Could Help Agencies Better Ensure Independence and Balance*, Washington, DC: GAO, GAO-04–328, April 2004, pp. 9, 10 and 29, www.gao.gov/new.items/d04328.pdf.)

The U.S. Court of Appeals for the D.C. Circuit ruled in June 1993 that Clinton's status, though ambiguous, qualified her as a "de facto officer or employee" (United States Court of Appeals for the District of Columbia Circuit, Argued April 30, 1993, Decided June 22, 1993, No. 93–5086, p. 11, http://www.aapsonline.org/clinton/AAPS/APPOPIN.PDF). See also Robert Pear, "Court Rules That First Lady Is 'De Facto' Federal Official," *New York Times*, June 23, 1993, http://www.nytimes.com/1993/06/23/us/court-rules-that-first-lady-is-de-facto-federal-official.html?n=Top/Reference/Times%20Topics/Subjects/F/Finances.

The investigation into the Clinton task force was at the request of Congressional Republicans. In March 1993 the White House turned over "an extensive listing of working group participants drawn from the government and from outside organizations," according to the GAO. Report from Comptroller General of the United State David M. Walker to Rep. J. Dennis Hastert, Speaker of the U.S. House of Representatives, August 17, 2001, p. 5, http:// oversight.house.gov/documents/20040831103937 -54564.pdf.

65. With regard to Cheney's office not turning over its records for public scrutiny, while only federal employees were formal members of the task force, some critics suggested that Cheney's task force violates the FACA. Legal actions brought by the Sierra Club, an environmental membership and lobbying group, and Judicial Watch, a conservative watchdog group, held that the Energy Task Force should be subject to FACA rules because nonfederal employees and lobbyists were de facto task force members in that they consistently and fully participated in the meetings. (*Cheney, Vice President of the United States, et al. v. United States District Court for the District of Columbia et al.*, Certiorari to the United States Court of Appeals for the District of Columbia Circuit, No. 03–475. Argued April 27, 2004— Decided June 24, 2004, p. 2, http://caselaw.lp.findlaw.com/scripts/getcase.pl?court=US&vol=000&invol= 03–475.) Findings of the GAO are at GAO, *Energy Task Force: Process Used to Develop the National Energy Policy*, Washington, DC: GAO, GAO-03–894, August 2003, p. 2, http://www.gao.gov/new.items/ d03894.pdf (accessed 8/20/2007). These confidential meetings (the list of which was leaked to the *Washington Post* years after the fact) brought in such figures as James J. Rouse, then vice president of Exxon Mobil and a major contributor to Bush's inauguration; the Council of Republicans for Environmental Advocacy, started by Grover Norquist and Gale A. Norton, who was appointed Bush's first interior secretary; electric utilities giants, including Duke Energy and Constellation Energy Group; and Kenneth Lay, the later indicted (and now deceased) chief of the energy giant Enron, with whom Cheney met personally. (Michael Abramowitz and Steven Mufson, "Papers Detail Industry's Role in Cheney's Energy Report," *Washington Post*, July 18, 2007, p. A1.) However, neither these meetings, nor the identities of the individuals involved, are the public's business, according to Cheney's office. Invoking the need to safeguard certain executive deliberations, his office denied access to the GAO of "virtually all requested information." (GAO, *Energy Task Force: Process Used to Develop the National Energy Policy*, Washington, DC: GAO, GAO-03–894, August 2003, Executive Summary, p. 2, http://www.gao.gov/new.items/ d03894.pdf.) These records would shed light on the process by which the task force had developed a national energy policy and the role of nonfederal stakeholders in influencing that policy. Quotes and further experience of the GAO in this regard can be found at Mike Allen, "GAO Cites Corporate Shaping of Energy Plan," *Washington Post*, August 26, 2003, p. A1. The GAO's subsequent suit, filed in U.S. District Court, was dismissed on jurisdictional grounds, and the GAO decided not to appeal (GAO, *Energy Task Force: Process Used to Develop the National Energy Policy*, Washington, DC: GAO, GAO-03–894, August 2003, http://www.gao.gov/new.items/d03894.pdf). With regard to the Supreme Court ruling, see, for example, Michael Abramowitz and Steven Mufson, "Papers Detail Industry's Role in Cheney's Energy Report," *Washington Post*, July 18, 2007, p. A1, http://www.washingtonpost.com/wp-dyn/content/article/2007/07/17/AR2007071701987.html. This is the result of legal actions brought by public interest groups.

66. Peter Baker, "White House Defends Cheney's Refusal of Oversight," *Washington Post*, June 23, 2007, p. A2, http://www.washingtonpost.com/wp-dyn/content/article/2007/06/22/AR200706220 1809.html. Also House Committee on Government and Reform, "Vice President Exempts His Office

from the Requirements for Protecting Classified Information," June 21, 2007, http://oversight .house.gov/story.asp?id=1371.

67. The survey of think tanks cited is James G. McGann, *Think Tanks and Policy Advice in the US* (Philadelphia, PA: Foreign Policy Research Institute, 2005), p. 23.

An example of a defense industry-driven "think tank" is the Lexington Institute, which receives funding from the defense contractors who stand to benefit from the programs their experts are asked to assess. See Sean Reilly, "Analyst's Switch Stirs Tanker Talk," *Mobile Register*, June 9, 2008, http://www.al.com/news/press-register/index.ssf?/base/news/121300295470260.xml&coll=3.

The quote at the end of the paragraph is from McGann, *Think Tanks and Policy Advice in the US*, pp. 23, 24.

68. Allegiance to institutions is now often seen as retrograde. As government scholar Hugh Heclo reflects: "Thinking institutionally is about a larger sense of loyalty and mission and all those old-fashioned words that have tended to drop out of our thinking about public administration, as well as American organizational life in general." James P. Pfiffner, Interview with Hugh Heclo, "The Institutionalist: A Conversation with Hugh Heclo," *Public Administration Review* (May/June 2007), p. 421.

See chapter 2 for analysis of job security trends.

69. GAO, *Foreign Assistance: Strategic Workforce Planning Can Help USAID Address Current and Future Challenges*, August 2003, GAO-03–946, p. 10, http://www.gao.gov/new.items/d03946.pdf.

70. With regard to rules addressing the revolving-door syndrome, see, for instance, http://www .doi.gov/secretary/speeches/012609_speech.html.

With regard to government officials going to industry: For instance, David Kay moved from being a United Nations weapons inspector to a vice president at SAIC (1993 to 2002) to being hired by the CIA to head the effort in search of weapons of mass destruction in Iraq (2003). Likewise, William B. Black Jr. retired from the NSA in 1997, worked at SAIC for three years, and then went back to the NSA as deputy director in 2000. SAIC subsequently was awarded $282 million to oversee the latest phase of the agency's overhaul of its eavesdropping systems. Scott Shane, "U.S.: Uncle Sam Keeps SAIC On Call For Top Tasks," *Baltimore Sun*, October 26, 2003, Telegraph, p. 1A. See also André Verlöy and Daniel Politi, *Advisors of Influence: Nine Members of the Defense Policy Board Have Ties to Defense Contractors*, Center for Public Integrity, May 28, 2003, http://www.publicintegrity.org/articles/entry/374/, accessed 16 August, 2008.

The Project on Government Oversight provides excellent analysis of the problem of service contractor personal conflicts of interest (see, for example, The Project On Government Oversight, "Strong, Consistent Federal Contractor Conflict of Interest Regulations Needed," July 17, 2008, http://www .pogo.org/pogo-files/letters/contract-oversight/co-fcm-20080717.html).

71. For William Studerman and Booz Allen vice presidents, see Tim Shorrock, "The Spy Who Billed Me," *Mother Jones*, January/February 2005, http://www.motherjones.com/politics/2005/01/spy-who-billed-me. See also Booz Allen's Web site, at http://www.boozallen.com/about/people. For SAIC board members, see Shane, "U.S.: Uncle Sam Keeps SAIC On Call," p. 1A; and Siobhan Gorman, "Little-known Contractor Has Close Ties with Staff of NSA," *Baltimore Sun*, January 29, 2006, Telegraph, p. A13.

72. Intelligence expert Steven Aftergood, quoted in Tim Shorrock, "Former High-Ranking Bush Officials Enjoy War Profits," Salon.com, May 29, 2008, http://www.salon.com/news/excerpt/2008/ 05/29/spies_for_hire/index1.html.

73. For additional material on privatization, waning institutional loyalty, and the relationship between them, see Cullen Murphy, *Are We Rome? The Fall of an Empire and the Fate of America* (New York: Houghton Mifflin Company, 2008), especially chapter 3.

74. With regard to enhanced U.S. executive power in the twentieth century, see James P. Pfiffner, *The Modern Presidency*, 5th ed. (Belmont, CA: Thompson Wadsworth, 2007), p. 141.

With respect to the growth of executive power via the adoption of international security law, see Kim Lane Scheppele, *The International State of Emergency*, forthcoming.

John L. Comaroff and Jean Comaroff discuss "law laundering," a form of licensed corruption that can be used to bolster executive power (John L. Comaroff and Jean Comaroff, "Introduction," *Law and Disorder in the Postcolony*, John L. Comaroff and Jean Comaroff, eds. [Chicago, IL: University of Chicago Press, 2006].)

William G. Howell lays out the unilateral tools available for presidents. William G. Howell, "Unilateral Powers: A Brief Overview," *Understanding the Presidency*, 4th ed., James P. Pfiffner and Roger Davidson, eds. (New York: Person-Longman, 2007), pp. 367–382. With regard to signing statements, see, for example, author interview with James Pfiffner, September 5, 2007; and James P. Pfiffner, *Power Play: The Bush Administration and the Constitution* (Washington, DC: Brookings, 2008).

75. With regard to Reagan's use of signing statements, see James P. Pfiffner, *The Modern Presidency*, p. 157. With the Carter and Ford presidencies, issuing such statements gained recognition as a way of putting on record reservations about the constitutionality of a particular law; see also Pfiffner, *Power Play*.

76. On constitutional challenges issued via signing statements by Presidents Carter, Bush I, and Clinton, see Pfiffner, *Power Play*, pp. 194–202. The number of constitutional challenges contained in signing statements rose from 24 issued by Carter to 71 by Reagan and 146 by George H. W. Bush, declined to 105 under Clinton, and jumped to 1,168 (as of October 15, 2008) under George W. Bush. Christopher S. Kelley, "'Faithfully Executing' and 'Taking Care'—The Unitary Executive and the Presidential Signing Statement," paper presented at the American Political Science Association annual convention, 2002. The number of Bush II constitutional challenges is from the Web site of Christopher S. Kelley, a political scientist who writes about presidential power. He maintained an up-to-date tally of the signing statements and provisions of laws challenged by Bush II, at http://www.users.muohio.edu/kelleycs/. See also Charlie Savage, "Obama Looks to Limit Impact of Tactic Bush Used to Sidestep New Laws, *New York Times*, March 10, 2009, http://www.nytimes.com/2009/03/10/us/politics/10signing.html (accessed 3/13/2009).

With regard to Bush II's use of signing statements, as Pfiffner puts it, Bush II has employed signing statements "to assert the unilateral and unreviewable right of the executive to choose which laws to enforce and which to ignore." In issuing signing statements, Bush signaled his lack of obligation to adhere to certain aspects of laws that are of great consequence to the nation. Bush used signing statements both to effectively veto provisions of laws by simply not enforcing them and to decline to provide information to Congress despite laws mandating that the executive branch do so (Pfiffner, *The Modern Presidency*, p. 160). Bush, among other things, threatened to ignore laws that protect whistle-blowers, put restrictions on the congressionally mandated inspectors general who oversee government work, and—most controversially—altered the McCain amendment of 2005 intended to curb the exercise of torture. See, for example, Elizabeth Drew, "Power Grab," *The New York Review of Books* 53, no. 11 (June 22, 2006), http://www.nybooks.com/articles/19092. Bush also issued signing statements that allowed him to sidestep providing information to Congress. For example, in December 2004, Bush signed a law saying that, when requested, scientific information from government researchers and scientists should be given to Congress "uncensored and without delay." However, Bush later wrote in a signing statement that he could order researchers to withhold any information that he deemed might impair U.S. foreign relations or national security. See Charlie Savage, *Takeover: The Return of the Imperial Presidency and the Subversion of American Democracy* (New York: Little, Brown and Company, 2007) p. 238–239. With regard to 9/11 as justification, see Pfiffner, *The Modern Presidency*, p. 159–160. In *Takeover*, Charlie Savage writes that President George W. Bush's legal team has used signing statements "as something better than a veto—something close to a line-item veto." In 1998 the Supreme Court ruled that line-item vetoes, even when approved by Congress, are unconstitutional. See Savage, *Takeover*, p. 231.

77. The American Bar Association panel made specific recommendations to both the president and the Congress. As ABA president Karen Mathis stated in her testimony before the House Judiciary Committee, "James Madison said it best: 'The preservation of liberty requires the three great departments of power should be separate and distinct.'" Statement of Karen J. Mathis, President of the American Bar Association before the Committee on the Judiciary of the U.S. House of Representatives concerning Presidential Signing Statements, January 31, 2007, p. 6, http://www.abanet.org/poladv/letters/antiterror/2007jan31_signingstmts_t.pdf.

78. The Bush administration proposed new pay and personnel rules pertaining to how employees are compensated, hired, promoted, and disciplined for the 850,000 civil servants in the departments of Defense and Homeland Security, which account for almost half of the federal workforce (Stephen Barr, "It Could Be Auld Lang Syne For Annual Pay Raises," *Washington Post*, January 1, 2006, p. C02,

http://www.washingtonpost.com/wp-dyn/content/article/2005/12/31/AR2005123100867_pf.html). Unions in both departments contested aspects of the new rules (see, for example, Stephen Barr and Christopher Lee, "Director of Civil Service Resigns: James Oversaw Key Rule Changes," *Washington Post*, January 11, 2005, p. A13, http://www.washingtonpost.com/wp-dyn/articles/A63283-2005 Jan10.html). In the end, these rules were put into effect on a limited basis only: for a fraction of the DOD workforce and for a short time for the DHS workforce (author's conversation with John Threlkeld, AFGE Legislative Representative, American Federation of Government Employees, March 19, 2008). The Bush Administration proposed to extend the Defense and Homeland Security pay-for-performance systems to a much larger portion of federal employees through the "Working for America Act," which was to do away with the General Schedule by 2010 (Stephen Barr, "Labor Keeps Its Guard Up Against Efforts to Change Workplace Rules," *Washington Post*, November 8, 2005, p. B02, http://www.washington post.com/wp-dyn/content/article/2005/11/07/AR2005110701401.html, and Karen Rutzkik, "Administration Continues Quest to Tie Pay to Performance Across Government," *Government Executive*, July 19, 2005, http://www.govexec.com/dailyfed/0705/071905r1.htm). In 2006 the General Schedule applied to some 1.8 million federal employees (Barr, "It Could Be Auld Lang Syne"). However, some of the pay-for-performance standards for Defense and Homeland Security were struck down in U.S. District Court. (See, for example: http://www.govexec.com/dailyfed/0805/081705r1.htm.)

Light is quoted in Stephen Barr, "Appointees Everywhere, But Try to Count Them," *Washington Post*, Sunday, October 17, 2004, p. C2, http://www.washingtonpost.com/wp-dyn/articles/A38874-2004Oct16.html.

79. For analysis of Obama's use of signing statements, see Charlie Savage, "Obama's Embrace of a Bush Tactic Riles Congress," *New York Times*, August 8, 2009, http://www.nytimes.com/2009/08/09/us/politics/09signing.html?hpw.

Notes to Chapter 5

1. U.S. economic aid to Russia via the Chubais-Harvard players is also a case of what I have called "transactorship," a form of collusion between the representatives of parties on opposite sides. Transactorship is a mode of organizing relations between parties (subnational groups, nations, and/or international organizations) that have been separated, culturally, societally, and perhaps geographically. In transactorship, the separated parties have representatives called transactors, whose job is to build bridges between parties. Although transactors may genuinely share the stated goals of the parties they represent (and they uphold at least the appearance of that representation in public), they develop their own additional goals and ways of operating for their own benefit. The additional goals of transactors, advertently or inadvertently, may diverge from those of their parties in such a way that they undermine the key aims of the parties for whom they came together to begin with and on whose behalf they ostensibly act. See Janine R. Wedel, "Le Developpement Pris en Otage: Comment L'Aide Americaine a la Russie a Ete Detournee Par Les 'Transacteurs'" (Hijacking Development: How Transactors Undermined U.S. Aid to Russia), Laetitia Atlani-Duault, ed., *Revue Tiers Monde* 193 (January-March 2008), pp. 13–36; "Courtage International et Institutions Floues," with Siddarth Chandra, *ACTES de la Recherche en Sciences Sociales*, no. 151–152 (March 2004), pp. 114–125; "Rigging the U.S.-Russia Relationship: Harvard, Chubais, and the Transidentity Game," *Demokratizatsiya: The Journal of Post-Soviet Democratization* 7, no. 4 (Fall 1999), pp. 469–500; "Clique-Run Organizations and U.S. Economic Aid: An Institutional Analysis," *Demokratizatsiya: The Journal of Post-Soviet Democratization* 4, no. 4 (Fall 1996), pp. 571–602.

2. With regard to Hay, see project documents submitted by Jeffrey D. Sachs and Associates Inc. to the Finnish government, one of the firm's funders, which state: "Jonathan Hay, a Harvard law student and Rhodes Scholar, traveled to Moscow to conduct a study of the prospects for mass privatization in Russia. He quickly became a trusted advisor to Deputy Prime Minister Anatoly Chubais, and has provided important economic, legal, and logistical analysis to the staff of the State Committee on Privatization [here called the State Property Committee]. In March, Mr. Hay also joined the team sponsored by the Ford Foundation and will continue his work in Russia over the coming year." ("World Institute for

Development Economic Research Project on the Transformation of Centrally Planned Economics: Report on Activities, First Half of 1992," p. 9.) With regard to Shleifer, see pp. 4 and 7 of the same documents. I obtained these documents from the Finnish government and have put them on my Web site at: http://janinewedel.info/harvardinvestigative.html#3 and http://janinewedel.info/WIDER_Project.pdf.

3. With regard to Shleifer's and Boycko's roles as advisers to the State Property Committee (1991 to 1993), see Maxim Boycko, Andrei Shleifer, and Robert W. Vishny, "Voucher Privatization," *Journal of Financial Economics* 35 (1994), p. 1, http://www.economics.harvard.edu/faculty/shleifer/files/voucher _privatization.pdf.

With regard to Shleifer advising the Federal Securities Commission, it is "one of the many agencies which USAID paid Shleifer to advise" (David Warsh, "In Which, At Last, We Meet, Perhaps, Andrei Shleifer's Evil Twin," *Economic Principals*, April 16, 2006, available at: http://www.economicprin cipals.com/issues/2006.04.16/195.html). With regard to Hay's workplace, the *Boston Globe* refers to an interview conducted in Hay's office "in a high-rise rented by Russia's Federal Securities Commission." David Filipov and David L. Marcus, "Probe of Russian Work Shocks Harvard Adviser," *Boston Globe*, May 25, 1997, p. A1, available at: http://janinewedel.info/media_bostonglobe3.pdf.

4. Quotes are from Olga Kryshtanovskaya, "The Real Masters of Russia," *Argumenty i Fakty*, no. 21 (May 1997), reprinted in *Johnson's Russia List*, by David Johnson, Washington, DC, an authoritative newsletter published via e-mail. For analysis of Russian clans, see also the work of economic sociologist Leonid Kosals, "Interim Outcome of the Russian Transition: Clan Capitalism," *Discussion Paper No. 610* (Kyoto, Japan: Kyoto Institute of Economic Research, January 2006); and "Essay on Clan Capitalism in Russia," *Acta Oeconomica* 57, no. 1 (7), pp. 67–85. For details and documentation regarding the social and political background of the Chubais Clan, see Janine R. Wedel, *Collision and Collusion: The Strange Case of Western Aid to Eastern Europe*, 2nd ed. (New York: Palgrave, 2001), pp. 133–135.

5. On Sachs's projects, see, for example, project documents submitted by Jeffrey D. Sachs and Associates Inc. to the Finnish government: "World Institute for Development Economic Research Project on the Transformation of Centrally Planned Economies: Report on Activities, First Half of 1992." I obtained these documents from the Finnish government and have put them on my Web site at: http:// janinewedel.info/harvardinvestigative.html#3 and http://janinewedel.info/WIDER_Project.pdf.

On Shleifer and Chubais becoming acquainted through Sachs, see Maxim Boycko, Andrei Shleifer, and Robert Vishny, *Privatizing Russia* (Cambridge, MA: MIT Press, 1995), p. viii. Information from Andrei Shleifer is from my interview with him on September 5, 1996.

6. The administration insider cited is Mark C. Medish, then deputy assistant secretary for Eurasia and the Middle East, U.S. Department of Treasury, author's interview, November 26, 1997.

7. Lawrence Summers's biography, as supplied by the U.S. Treasury Department, 1990s.

8. On Summers inspiring Shleifer, see Karen Pennar and Peter Galuszka, "Privatization Expert and Cheerleader," *Business Week*, July 19, 1993. Summers and Shleifer received at least one foundation grant together (vita of Andrei Shleifer on file at HIID, Harvard University, 1990s).

While presenting himself as a Harvard professor offering his advice pro bono, Sachs's little-known consulting firm, Jeffrey D. Sachs and Associates Inc., sometimes solicited fees from clients and would-be clients.

Summers's quote is from David McClintick, "How Harvard Lost Russia," *Institutional Investor Magazine Online*, January 13, 2006, p. 18, http://jboy.chaosnet.org/misc/docs/articles/shleifer.pdf.

9. Facts about Hay's employment are from vita of Jonathan Hay on file at HIID, Harvard University, 1990s.

10. The Harvard Institute's first award from USAID for work in Russia came in 1992, during the Bush I administration. Between 1992 and 1997, the Institute received $40.4 million in competitive grants for work in Russia. It was slated to receive another $17.4 million, but USAID suspended its funding in May 1997, citing allegations of misuse of funds. According to USAID's Deirdre Clifford, since 1992 the Harvard Institute received $40,373,994 in noncompetitive grants under the First Cooperative Agreement (author's interview, 1996). Another $17,423,090 was designated for Harvard under the Second Cooperative Agreement (a three-year agreement that began on September 30, 1995), of which $4.5 million was obligated (USAID documents and author's interview, June 11, 1996).

Approving such a large sum of money as a noncompetitive amendment to a much smaller award (the Harvard Institute's original 1992 award was $2.1 million) was highly unusual, according to U.S. officials. U.S. government procurement officers and GAO officials, including Louis H. Zanardi, who spearheaded GAO's investigation of Harvard activities in Russia and Ukraine, offered this pronouncement. The waiver was endorsed by five U.S. government agencies, including the Department of the Treasury and the National Security Council (NSC), two of the leading bodies making U.S. aid and economic policy toward Russia (and Ukraine). From Treasury, the Harvard-connected Lawrence Summers and David Lipton supported the Harvard Institute projects. In his capacity as USAID's deputy assistant administrator of the Bureau for Europe and the New Independent States, Carlos Pascual signed the waiver on behalf of USAID. Pascual's support for Harvard projects continued, and he was later promoted to the NSC, where he served as director of Russian, Ukrainian, and Eurasian Affairs from 1995 to 1999. (Biography and information supplied by Pascual's office.) Pascual later served as U.S. Ambassador to Ukraine from 2000 to 2003.

11. With regard to the $300 million reform portfolio that the Harvard Institute helped steer and coordinate, see U.S. General Accounting Office, *Foreign Assistance: Harvard Institute for International Development's Work in Russia and Ukraine*, Washington, DC: GAO, SMD-97–27, 1996, p. 18. On Harvard's oversight role and on USAID's laxity, see p. 17 of the same report.

12. U.S. General Accounting Office, *Foreign Assistance: Harvard Institute for International Development's Work in Russia and Ukraine*, Washington, DC: GAO, SMD-97-27, 1996, p. 17.

13. Lawrence Summers's speech printed in *Russia Business Watch* 5, no. 2 (Spring 1997), p. 19. Summers and Chubais were on a first-name basis. For example, a letter Summers wrote to Chubais in April 1997 (obtained and published by a Russian newspaper) which he wrote as deputy Treasury secretary and addressed to "Dear Anatoly," instructed his Russian colleague on the conduct of Russian foreign and domestic economic policy. Summers's dictates included the Russian tax code, oil industry prospects, and how Russia should prepare itself to join the World Trade Organization and deal with U.S. trade laws.

14. The book by Shleifer, Boycko, and a coauthor here quoted is Boycko, Shleifer, and Vishny, *Privatizing Russia*, pp. 142, 128, respectively.

Dine's views are from author's interview with Thomas A. Dine, August 16, 1996. The quote from Morningstar is from author's interview with Richard L. Morningstar, U.S. aid coordinator to the former Soviet Union, February 11, 1997.

For details of unequivocal U.S. support of Boris Yeltsin and the "Reformers," see *Frontline* "Return of the Czar," interviews with former officials at the U.S. Embassy in Moscow, including Thomas Graham, E. Wayne Merry, and Donald Jensen, PBS, http://www.pbs.org/wgbh/pages/frontline/shows/yeltsin/interviews/.

15. The Kryshtanovskaya quote is from Kryshtanovskaya, "The Real Masters of Russia." Hay's view of his role is from author's interview with Jonathan Hay, June 17, 1994.

16. The SEC quote is from "U.S.-Russian Joint Commission on Economic and Technological Cooperation," *SEC News Digest*, Issue 96–134, July 17, 1996. Summers's quote is from Lawrence H. Summers, "Russia's Stake in Global Capital Market Development," speech at the Kennedy School of Government, Harvard University, *Treasury News*, Washington DC, Department of the Treasury, Office of Public Affairs, January 9, 1997, p. 30. The Forum's four working groups were Investor Protection; Capital Markets Infrastructure; Collective Investment Vehicles; and Taxation, Accounting, and Auditing.

When a U.S. Treasury spokesman was asked who named Shleifer and Hebert to the Forum, the answer was that they were appointed by the Chubais group—specifically, according to other sources, by Vasiliev (interview with U.S. Treasury spokesman by Bill Mesler of *The Nation*, summer 1997).

In 1997, Congress asked the GAO to look into Shleifer's role on the Commission. The U.S. Department of Justice, with concurrence from the House International Relations Committee, subsequently requested that the GAO suspend its probe, pending the outcome of Justice's investigation.

17. As a U.S. investigator explained it to me: "Norris would call Jonathan [Hay] who would set up meetings for him [Norris] with Russian officials." Author's interview with Phil Rodokanakis, former senior agent in USAID's Office of the Inspector General, January 25, 2001.

18. With regard to the laws passed by the Russian Supreme Soviet laying the groundwork for privatization: One law established the basic structure and principles of privatization; the other specified

personal privatization accounts as the method of privatization. See Lynn D. Nelson and Irina Y. Kuzes, *Radical Reform in Yeltsin's Russia: Political, Economic, and Social Dimensions* (Armonk, NY: M. E. Sharpe, 1995), pp. 48–51. The laws were passed two months before the August 1991 coup attempt. In the confused political environment that followed it, several schemes to realize privatization were floated before the Supreme Soviet (for details, see Lynn D. Nelson and Irina Y. Kuzes, *Property to the People: The Struggle for Radical Economic Reform in Russia* [Armonk, NY: M. E. Sharpe, 1994], pp. 26–56). At the time "nomenclatura privatization" was well under way, with bureaucrats and managers of state-owned enterprises appropriating property and resources for their own economic benefit.

For an authoritative account of the privatization reforms, see Nelson and Kuzes, *Radical Reform in Yeltsin's Russia*, pp. 48–51. The authors detail how Chubais essentially fooled the Supreme Soviet by pushing through a new voucher idea via Yeltsin's decree (of August 14, 1992) while no one was looking. As Vladimir Mazaev, chairman of the Commission on Economic Reform of the Supreme Soviet, told the authors in 1993, "The parliament was deceived. We approved one privatization program, and Chubais with his foreign advisers created voucher privatization using Yeltsin's emergency powers [to issue decrees]" (p. 50). In September after having analyzed the new approach, the Commission concluded that legally it contradicted the law "On Registered Privatization" accounts that they had passed a year earlier and "promised to offer fertile ground for criminal activity" (p. 51).

The Sachs project documents here cited are: Project documents submitted by Jeffrey D. Sachs and Associates Inc. to the Finnish government (one of many sources of Sachs's funding), World Institute for Development Economic Research Project on the Transformation of Centrally Planned Economies: Report on Activities, First Half of 1992, pp. 4 and 7. (I obtained these documents from the Finnish government and have put them on my Web site at: http://janinewedel.info/harvardinvestigative.html#3 and http://janinewedel.info/WIDER_Project.pdf.

19. For Shleifer-Boycko quote, see *Privatizing Russia*, a book coauthored by Boycko, Shleifer, and Robert Vishny (Shleifer's colleague and business partner and a professor of economics at the University of Chicago who worked with the Chubais-Harvard team). The authors state that the book "looks at the Russian privatization from our perspective *as members of the team that put it together*" [emphasis added] (p. vii). Information about USAID's $58 million privatization effort was supplied by Walter Coles (interview of June 5, 1996), with figure verified at Cole's request by Deirdre Clifford, July 24, 1996.

20. For Yeltsin's quote see, for instance, *Komsomol'skaya Pravda*, August 22, 1992, p. 2, cited in Hilary Appel, "Voucher Privatisation in Russia: Structural Consequences and Mass Response in the Second Period of Reform," *Europe-Asia Studies* 49, no. 8, December 1997, http://findarticles.com/p/articles/mi_m3955/is_n8_v49/ai_20545806/pg_1.

The economist quoted is James R. Millar, "From Utopian Socialism to Utopian Capitalism: The Failure of Revolution and Reform in Post-Soviet Russia," Washington, DC: George Washington University 175th Anniversary Papers, paper 2, 1996, p. 8.

With regard to Chubais's scheme offering "fertile ground for criminal activity," see Nelson and Kuzes, *Radical Reform in Yeltsin's Russia*, p. 51.

With respect to loans for shares: Loans for shares also helped bankrupt the state, leaving it unable to fund many social services, which, of course, alienated the population. Boris Fyodorov, a former finance minister, characterized loans for shares as "a disgusting exercise of a crony capitalism, where normal investors were not invited, where even among Russian so-called investors, only those who were friends of certain people in the government were invited. And there's a big suspicion that no real cash came to the government. . . . These loans for shares unleashed a wave of corruption like never before." *Frontline*, "Return of the Czar," interview with Boris Fyodorov, PBS, http://www.pbs.org/wgbh/pages/frontline/shows/yeltsin/interviews/fyodorov.html.

21. The Merry quote is from interview with E. Wayne Merry, "Return of the Czar," *Frontline*.

22. For analysis of the voucher privatization program and its impact, see Hilary Appel, "Voucher Privatisation in Russia," and Nelson and Kuzes, *Property to the People*, pp. 25–56.

23. With regard to privatization and the popularity of politicians, see Janet Gultsman, "Yeltsin Says Still Pro-Reform, Scathing on Chubais," *Reuters Financial Service*, January 19, 1996. Hilary Appel adds that Yeltsin provided details such as the following: He said that, while the mayor of Moscow managed to create 6,000 billion rubles in revenue in the Russian capital, Chubais managed to create only 8,000 bil-

lion rubles from throughout the country (ITAR-TASS World Service, February 16, 1996, cited in "Russia: Yeltsin Notes Main Tasks of Privatization," *FBIS-SOV-96.33*, February 16, 1996). See Appel, "Voucher Privatisation in Russia."

24. *The Economist* article is "A Survey of Russia's Emerging Market: A Silent Revolution," April 8, 1995.

25. With regard to Harvard players obstructing reform efforts that originated from outside their approved circle: When Stanford University was awarded a contract to work with the Chubais Clan-run Federal Securities Commission, Vasiliev turned down Stanford's help. When I asked Shleifer for an explanation, he said that Vasiliev "had a group of people he was working with," meaning, of course, the Harvard players (author's interview with Andrei Shleifer, September 5, 1996). Later, the clan secured additional funds out of USAID for the same project that Stanford was to have worked on, now with Harvard as a partner. (In September 1995, the Russian Federal Commission and the Harvard Institute received $1.7 million as an amendment to the 1992 cooperative agreement.) GAO sources confirmed that the Harvard-Chubais players obstructed reform efforts that originated from outside their approved circle (conversations of October 28, 1997, and April 23, 1998, with Louis H. Zanardi, who spearheaded the GAO's investigation of the Harvard Institute's activities in Russia and Ukraine). One example of this involves interference by the Russian Privatization Center with efforts by the U.S.-funded Senior Executive Service Corps. With respect to Harvard players blocking legal reform efforts, information was gleaned through interviews with USAID-paid contractors and U.S. government sources. A member of the GAO audit team confirmed this observation (conversations of October 28, 1997, and April 23, 1998 with Louis H. Zanardi). Quote of GAO lead investigator is from author's interview with Louis Zanardi, January 25, 2001.

26. See U.S. General Accounting Office, *Foreign Assistance: Harvard Institute for International Development's Work in Russia and Ukraine* (Washington, DC: GAO, November 1996), p. 8. USAID contracts to design and implement CSOs totaled $13.9 million. For additional details, see also Janine R. Wedel, "Clique-Run Organizations and U.S. Economic Aid: An Institutional Analysis," *Demokratizatsiya: The Journal of Post-Soviet Democratization*, no. 4 (Fall 1996), pp. 592–593.

27. The players do not deny making these investments. For details, see United States District Court, District of Massachusetts, *United States of America, Plaintiff, v. The President and Fellows of Harvard College, Andrei Shleifer, Jonathan Hay, Nancy Zimmerman, and Elizabeth Hebert, Defendants*, Civil Action No. 00CV11977DPW, September 26, 2000, p. 30; and, for example, Thanassis Cambanis, "US Seeking $102M from Harvard, Pair," *Boston Globe*, June 27, 2002. Lawyers for Harvard, Shleifer, and Hay argued that the investments of project staff (Shleifer and Hay) neither affected Harvard's work in Russia (see, for example, Thanassis Cambanis, "Prosecutors Argue Harvard Owes US at Least $34M in Russia Case," *Boston Globe*, December 18, 2002) nor violated the university's agreements with the U.S. government (see, for example, Thanassis Cambanis, "US Seeking $102M From Harvard, Pair").

28. United States District Court, District of Massachusetts, *United States of America, Plaintiff, v. The President and Fellows of Harvard College, Andrei Shleifer, Jonathan Hay, Nancy Zimmerman, and Elizabeth Hebert, Defendants*.

29. The suit, registered by Forum Financial Group of Portland, Maine, states that Hay and Shleifer used their pull with Russian officials to acquire for the company the rights to the country's first mutual fund. They then compelled its owner to sell his interest in the fund. For information about the settlement of the case, see, for example, David H. Gellis, "Harvard in Settlement Talks with Forum," *The Harvard Crimson*, 30 October 2002; and "Harvard Settles With Mutual Funds Company Over Fraud Allegations," Associated Press, November 8, 2002.

30. The Cohen quote is from Stephen F. Cohen, *Failed Crusade: America and the Tragedy of Post-Communist Russia* (New York: W. W. Norton & Company, Inc., 2001), p. 13. Also see Cohen (*Failed Crusade)* for analysis of American media coverage of Russian "reforms."

With regard to Shleifer and Vishny as business partners: In 1994, Shleifer, Vishny, and Josef Lakonishok, all experts in behavioral finance, started LSV Asset Management, a money management company based in Chicago (David McClintick, "How Harvard Lost Russia," *Institutional Investor Magazine Online*, January 13, 2006, p. 30, http://jboy.chaosnet.org/misc/docs/articles/shleifer.pdf). For Vishny's work with the Chubais-Harvard team, see, for instance, Boycko, Shleifer, and Vishny, *Privatizing Russia*, p. vii.

The Harvard Institute supported the writing of Boycko, Shleifer, and Vishny's *Privatizing Russia*, according to the authors. *The New Republic* reports that this support was provided by USAID through the Harvard Institute (Stephen Kotkin, "Stealing the State," April 13, 1998, p. 30). However, I was unable to confirm direct USAID support for the project. The claim that a "large class of owners" was created is found in Boycko, Shleifer, and Vishny, *Privatizing Russia*, p. vii.

31. The Donald Pressley quote is from an interview with him aired on Monitor Radio, May 22, 1997. The U.S. investigator cited here is Phil Rodokanakis, former senior agent in USAID's Office of the Inspector General (author's interview of January 25, 2001).

32. Sources on Åslund's role in Swedish policy and aid include Dan Josefsson, "The Art of Ruining a Country with Some Professional Help from Sweden," *ETC*, English Edition 1, 1999. U.S. officials in the Departments of Treasury and State supplied information (via interviews) about Åslund's participation in meetings in these agencies. On Åslund's business activities, he was, for example, linked to Brunswick, which began as a Moscow-based brokerage firm and evolved into an investment bank, the Brunswick Group (Anne Williamson, *Contagion*, Chapter 13, unpublished manuscript; Williamson writes on economics and Soviet and Russian affairs). Two of Åslund's Swedish associates worked for Chubais at the State Property Committee, where they helped to design and implement voucher privatization (Williamson's interview with Martin Andersson, February 1995). Later, "with still good relations to Chubais," they started Brunswick Brokerage to participate in voucher privatization and to help sell these and other assets to Western investors. (Sven-Ivan Sundqvist, "Svenska Rad Biter Pa Ryssen: Svenska Finansman i Ledningen for Brunswick Group, Foretaget Som Ska Hjalpa Ryska Staten Att Privatisera Industrin," *Dagens Nybeter*, June 15, 1997.) While Åslund claims that he only gives "lectures and briefings" ("Tainted Transactions: An Exchange," *The National Interest*, no. 60 [Summer 2000], p. 101), he attended an April 1997 banking conference in New York sponsored by Brunswick Securities Ltd. *as a representative of Brunswick*. He promoted the Russian stock market to institutional investors and money managers, according to Michael Hudson, who also participated in the conference. (Anne Williamson communication with Michael Hudson of May 16, 1999; and Wedel interview with Hudson, September 8, 1999.) Hudson adds (April 3, 2000) that the minimum acceptable investment was between $400,000 and $500,000. Åslund's current wife, Anna Viktorovna Åslund, Gaidar's former press secretary, has listed an affiliation with Brunswick-Warburg. (Brunswick entered into an association with Warburg, effective November 1997.)

Sources for Åslund's business activities in Russia and Ukraine also include a number of additional reports and sources in Russia, Ukraine, Sweden and Washington. For details of Åslund's Ukraine activities, see Wedel, *Collision and Collusion*, pp. 168–170. Information from the Russian Interior Ministry's Department of Organized Crime on Aslund's investments is from interview with Vyacheslav Razinkin by author Anne Williamson, February 23, 1995.

For Åslund in the press, see, for instance, Anders Åslund, "Russia's Success Story," *Foreign Affairs* vol. 73, no. 5, September-October 1994, pp. 58–71. For Åslund as an oft-cited analyst in the Western press, see Cohen, *Failed Crusade*, p. 287, n40.

33. I have called this practice "transidentity capability," the ability of an individual player, based on official (or apparently official) authorization from two or more parties, to change whom he represents, regardless of which party originally designated him as its representative. See Janine R. Wedel ("Tainted Transactions: Harvard, the Chubais Clan and Russia's Ruin," *The National Interest*, no. 59 [Spring 2000], pp. 23–34; and "Courtage International et Institution Floues" with Siddarth Chandra, *ACTES de la Recherche en Sciences Sociales*, no. 151–152 [March 2004], pp. 114–125). The concept of transidentities draws on anthropologist Fredrik Barth's notion that individuals possess repertoires of identities. Fredrik Barth, *Ethnic Groups and Boundaries: The Social Organization of Culture Difference* (Boston, MA: Little, Brown & Co., 1969).

With regard to players representing more than one nation, notable cases of players doing so simultaneously or interchangeably can be found in the annals of international socialists of the early twentieth century. For instance, Angelica Balabanoff, the Jewish Ukrainian communist and social democratic activist, represented both Italian and Russian parties at various times. See Angelica Balabanoff, *My Life as a Rebel* (Bloomington, IN: Indiana University Press, 1938).

34. Information about Hay's signature authority was obtained from author's interview with and documents provided by Chamber of Accounts auditor Veniamin Sokolov, May 31, 1998. See State Property Committee order no. 188 (which gave Jonathan Hay veto power over the Committee's projects), October 5, 1992.

35. Information about Hay's decisions "as a Russian" were gleaned from author's conversations with Louis H. Zanardi, who spearheaded GAO's investigation of the Harvard Institute's activities in Russia and Ukraine.

36. In one scheme alone, some 10 million investors lost their savings. See Kirill Bessonov, "Pyramid Scheme Bilks Thousands," *Moscow News*, no. 9, June 3, 2008, http://mnweekly.ru/trend/mn09_2008/. See also, for example, Barbara Rudolph and Sally B. Donnelly, "Poof Go the Profits," *Time Magazine*, August 8, 1994, http://www.time.com/time/magazine/article/0,9171,981229,00.html, and Vladimir Kovalev "Pharaoh of Russian Pyramid Scheme Finally Arrested," *Transitions Online*, February 10, 2003, http://www.cdi.org/russia/johnson/7056.cfm##13. Support for the Russian government fund was provided through the World Bank's Investment Protection Fund. With regard to consequences for the fraud victims, Russia's Chamber of Accounts reported that not a single kopeck had been paid to a defrauded investor in the first year and a half of the fund's existence, although the fund's Western consultants had been receiving their salaries. Matt Taibbi, "Picked Clean: How a Small Clique of Americans Scavenged the Remains of Defrauded Russians," *Exile*, January 15, 1998, reprinted in *Johnson's Russia List*, no. 2021, January 16, 1998.

37. For United States's denial of entry to Kokh, see *Radio Free Europe/Radio Liberty Newsletter*, January 4, 1999, http://www.rferl.org/content/article/1141813.html.

38. See, for instance, "Chubays's Business 'Empire' Exposed," *Moskovskiy Komsomolets*, December 10, 1997. Report by Kirill Viktorov, "Shadow Empire: 'Anatoliy Chubays and Co.' Individual Private Enterprise is Successfully Operating in the Country," reprinted in *Johnson's Russia List*, December 19, 1997, no. 1442, http://www.cdi.org/russia/johnson/1442.html.

39. While in fact acting in the interests of the Chubais-Harvard partners, Vasiliev, for instance, could claim that he had made decisions on behalf of "The Russians," not just his own group, thereby lending legitimacy to the decisions. That is how the partners edged their competitors out of contracts that the group itself wanted (as in the Chubais-Harvard partners' rejection of Stanford), secured roles for their members on the Gore-Chernomyrdin Commission, and diluted the accountability of a banking-support institution. With regard to the latter point, an associate of Hay's, Julia Zagachin, an American citizen married to a Russian, was chosen by Federal Securities Commission chairman Vasiliev to assume a position designated for a Russian citizen. Zagachin was to run the First Russian Specialized Depository, which maintains the records of mutual fund investors' holdings and was funded by a 1996 World Bank loan. As journalist Anne Williamson has reported, the World Bank had established that the head of the Depository was to be a Russian citizen. But Vasiliev and other members of the clan apparently had determined that if their associate Zagachin headed the Depository, they would retain greater control over its assets and functions, so as to evade accountability if necessary.

40. For analysis of flex organizations, see Janine R. Wedel, "Blurring the State-Private Divide: Flex Organisations and the Decline of Accountability," *Globalisation, Poverty and Conflict: A Critical Development Reader*, Max Spoor, ed. (Dordrecht, Netherlands and Boston: Kluwer Academic Publishers, 2004), pp. 222–231; and Wedel, *Collision and Collusion*, pp. 145–153.

41. The Russian Privatization Center received some $45 million from USAID (U.S. General Accounting Office, *Foreign Assistance: Harvard Institute for International Development's Work in Russia and Ukraine* [Washington, DC: GAO, November 1996, p. 56]) and millions of dollars more in grants from the EU and Western Governments. As of June 1996, Japan was the largest contributor among the G-7, according to Ralf-Dieter Montag-Girmes, director of postprivatizion support with the Russian Privatization Center (author's interview of June 12, 1996) with Germany, the British Know How Fund, and "many other governmental and non-governmental organizations" contributing, according to the Center's annual report (Russian Privatization Center, *1994 Annual Report*, pp. 5, 24).

42. For the governing role of Harvard in the Center, see, for instance, U.S. General Accounting Office, *Foreign Assistance: Harvard Institute for International Development's Work in Russia and Ukraine* (Washington, DC: General Accounting Office, November 1996), p. 60.

In one example of U.S. government officials treating the Center as a governmental entity, U.S. assistance authorities asked the Center to nominate one person to serve on a technical evaluation panel to select a contractor. U.S. General Accounting Office, *Foreign Assistance: Harvard Institute for International Development's Work in Russia and Ukraine* (Washington, DC: GAO, November 1996), pp. 26, 27, 50. According to USAID contracts officer Stanley R. Nevin, USAID normally chooses this representative from a recipient government ministry, not from private bodies (author's conversation with Stanley R. Nevin, September 24, 1996). Dine quote is from author's interview with Thomas A. Dine, August 16, 1996.

With respect to loans from the international financial institutions to the Russian Privatization Center, the World Bank figure was provided by Ira Lieberman, senior manager in the Private Sector Development Department (author's interview of July 23, 1996), while the EBRD figure was supplied by Renae Ng (author's conversation of September 24, 1996). The World Bank official quoted here is Ira Lieberman, who helped design the Center (author's conversation of August 27, 1996).

With regard to the nongovernmental Center, repayment was to be made by the Ministry of Finance, the official borrower of the Russian government, while the Center served as the implementing agency (author's conversations with Ira Lieberman).

43. With regard to Clan members appointing one another: For example, while the supervisory board nominated Maxim Boycko, a member of the Chubais Clan, to run the Center, Boycko chose its directors, of which Vasiliev is one (based on information provided to author by Ralf-Dieter Montag-Girmes of the Russian Privatization Center, July 26, 1995). Boycko served as managing director until July 1, 1996; Eduard Boure, another Chubais Clan member, as managing director after July 1, 1996; and Vasilev, who also served as a vice chair of the State Property Committee, deputy chairman of the board. Chubais, for his part, continued to serve on the Center's board even after Yeltsin dismissed him as first deputy prime minister in January 1996. (Later that year, however, Yeltsin made Chubais head of his successful reelection campaign and then named him chief of staff.) In addition, soon after his dismissal, Chubais was placed on the Harvard Institute payroll, a demonstration of solidarity for which senior U.S. officials openly declared their support (author's interviews with William B. Taylor, then deputy coordinator—later coordinator—of NIS assistance August 9, 1996; and Thomas A. Dine, August 16, 1996). When I asked Dine why this favor was extended to Chubais, he replied that "the Harvard people said they could use him as a consultant to them" (author's interview with Thomas A. Dine, August 16, 1996).

44. Hay, together with Dart Management, Inc., was the subject of a civil suit (under U.S. racketeering laws) filed in the U.S. District Court of New Jersey brought by Avisma Titano-Magnesium Kombinat over an alleged fraud and money laundering scheme. Avisma sought $150 million in damages. (In the United States District Court for the District of New Jersey, Civil Action no. 99-CV-3979 [JWB], filed on December 13, 1999.) The suit alleged that a group of American investors who took over the company from the Russian bank Menatep skimmed at least $50 million from profits over a period of two years. The suit also alleged that Hay arranged the purchase from Menatep through the Institute for Law-Based Economy. According to documents presented by Avisma, Hay "assisted in structuring the transfer of the illegal scheme from Menatep to the investors." "Avisma Court Case Filing Targets More Banks," *Metals Week* 71, no. 1 (January 3, 2000), p. 2.

The suit also alleged that Natasha Garfinkel Kagalovsky, wife of Menatep executive Konstantin Kagalovsky and Bank of New York employee, arranged accounts at the bank to help channel funds that Menatep had diverted. According to *Metals Week*, "the deal . . . included back-door payoffs to the investors through the same network of bank accounts and offshore entities as Menatep had used." (For further details, see "Avisma Court Case Filing Targets More Banks," p. 2; John Helmer, "Deliberate Blindness to Fraud," *The Moscow Tribune*, December 17, 1999, p. 3; and Padraic Cassidy, "From Russia with Suit: Russian Factory Files RICO Suit Against U.S. Investor and Company," *New Jersey Law Journal*, August 30, 1999.) Little information about the resolution of the suit is publicly available, except that it resulted in a "favorable" outcome for the plaintiff (Avisma). See the SEC database (at sec.edgar-online.com/2000/01/14/10/0000006383-00-000004/Section8.asp) and a statement by the plaintiff's law firm concerning the settlement (http://www.marks-sokolov.com/about_the_firm.htm).

45. Information about the political agendas of the Chubais associates in local offices was offered by a representative of Price Waterhouse (author's interview of July 18, 1996), Dennis Mitchem of Arthur Andersen (author's interview of August 18 and 19, 1996), and Robert Otto of Carana (author's interview of August 27, 1996). Cecilia Ciepiela, the USAID official in Moscow handling the local offices, told me that Maxim Boycko chose the local directors (author's interview of August 5, 1996). The quote is from Dennis Mitchem of Arthur Andersen (author's interview of August 19, 1996).

46. On the government's and parliament's lack of decision-making authority or control over the Center's spending, see report by Russia's Chamber of Accounts: "Report on the Results of the Audit of the Russian Privatization Center on its Legality and Efficiency of Using Loans Granted by International Financial Organizations for Assistance in Performing Privatization and Support of Enterprises," *Accounting Chamber Bulletin*, no. 2, 2000, http://www.ach.gov.ru/bulletins/2000/arch2/3.doc, accessed January 16, 2009.

47. Information on the influence of the Center was provided by Chamber of Accounts auditor Veniamin Sokolov (author's interview with and documents supplied by Sokolov, May 31, 1998).

48. Author's interview with consultant Bill McCulloch, May 30, 2001.

49. The GAO's investigation into the Harvard Institute's activities in Russia found that "None of the USAID or Department of State documents authorizing the program discuss accomplishing legal reform through the issuance of decrees, only the passage of legislation." U.S. General Accounting Office, *Foreign Assistance: Harvard Institute for International Developments Work in Russia and Ukraine*, Washington, DC: GAO, SMD-97-27, 1996, p. 50. With regard to the Office of Democracy Assistance specifically, see the same GAO report, p. 50.

50. See the work of economic sociologist Leonid Kosals for a discussion of the different types of clans, as well as descriptions of specific clans. Leonid Kosals, "Interim Outcome of the Russian Transition: Clan Capitalism," *Discussion Paper No. 610* (Kyoto, Japan: Kyoto Institute of Economic Research, January 2006); and "Essay on Clan Capitalism in Russia," *Acta Oeconomica* 57, no. 1 (2007), pp. 67–85.

My notion of the "clan-state" also builds on political scientist Thomas Graham's observation of clans in the 1990s. See Thomas E. Graham, "The New Russian Regime," *Nezavisimaya Gazeta*, November 23, 1995; and "Russia's New Non-Democrats," *Harper's Magazine* 292, no. 1751 (1996), pp. 26–28. See Janine R. Wedel, "Flex Organizing and the Clan-State: Perspectives on Crime and Corruption in the New Russia," *Ruling Russia: Crime, Law, and Justice in a Changing Society*, William Pridemore, ed. (New York: Rowman and Littlefield Publishers, Inc., 2005), pp. 101–116; "Dirty Togetherness: Institutional Nomads, Networks, and the State-Private Interface in Central and Eastern Europe and the Former Soviet Union," *Polish Sociological Review* 2, no. 142 (2003), pp. 139–159; and "Clans, Cliques and Captured States: Rethinking 'Transition' in Central and Eastern Europe and the Former Soviet Union," *Journal of International Development* 15 (2003), pp. 425–440.

51. For mainstream media coverage that attracted considerable attention, see Carla Anne Robbins and Steve Liesman, "How an Aid Program Vital to New Economy of Russia Collapsed," *The Wall Street Journal*, August 13, 1997.

52. For information about Zimmerman working for Goldman Sachs and Robert Rubin, see, for instance: "Steyer Power," *Institutional Investor Magazine*, February 23, 2005, http://www.emii.com/article.aspx?ArticleID=1024622; and David Warsh, "The Tick-Tock," *Economic Principals*, January 22, 2006, http://www.economicprincipals.com/issues/06.01.22.html.

53. On Zimmerman and the Yale endowment, see "Yale Connection to Harvard Russian Fraud Case," *Yale Insider*, October 1, 2002, http:/www.yaleinsider.org/article.jsp?id=16, accessed October 1, 2002. On Shleifer's advisory role with regard to GKOs, see United States District Court District of Massachusetts, *US Complaint and Jury Trial Demand, USA, Plaintiff, vs. The President and Fellows of Harvard College, Andrei Shleifer, Jonathan Hay, Nancy Zimmerman, and Elizabeth Hebert*, pp. 25, 27; and Bruce Rubenstein, "Harvard Accused of Ignoring Russian Aid Scam: Academics Rigged Russian Market," *Corporate Legal Times*, January 2001.

On Harvard Management Company's deals, see Wedel, *Collision and Collusion*, pp. 160–165. Aside from these deals, the Harvard Management Company also may have benefited from information provided by this nexus of players. Andrei Shleifer acknowledges in his deposition that he had numerous conversations with a Harvard Management Company representative. He said that that representative also met with Jonathan Hay and Maxim Boycko in Russia. See *United States District Court for the District of Massachusetts, United States of America, Plaintiff, v. The President and Fellows of Harvard College, Andrei Shleifer, Jonathan Hay, Nancy Zimmerman, and Elizabeth Hebert, Defendants*, Civil Action No. OOCV11977DPW, Deposition of Andrei Shleifer, October 16, 2001, pp. 838-842. It remains for financial investigators to discover just how much of the mushrooming Harvard endowment (from $4.683 billion in 1990 to $19.200 billion in 2000, with this 310 percent increase [http://www.ilr.cornell.edu/cheri/wp/cheri_wp16.pdf] largely attributed to "emerging markets") is due to investments in Russia. That some people made themselves instant millionaires—even billionaires—during the period is a fact.

54. See Deposition of Lawrence Summers in: *United States District Court for the District of Massachusetts, United States of America, Plaintiff, v. The President and Fellows of Harvard College, Andrei Shleifer, Jonathan Hay, Nancy Zimmerman, and Elizabeth Hebert, Defendants*, Civil Action No. OOCV11977DPW, Deposition of Lawrence Summers, March 13, 2002, pp. 109-114, especially p. 112.

55. With regard to Chubais receiving money for privatization favors, the money came from Potanin's Oneximbank through a Swiss subsidiary as a front. See, for example, Dimitri K. Simes, "Moscow on the Potomac–Russian Foreign Policy," *National Review*, January 26, 1998, http://findarticles.com/p/articles/mi_m1282/is_n1_v50/ai_20221441/print (accessed 4/9/2008). See also http://www.pbs.org/wgbh/pages/frontline/shows/crash/etc/russia.html and *Global Integrity Report*, which reported in November 1997: "President Yeltsin removes Anatoly Chubais from his post as Finance minister after it is revealed that Chubais and three other top officials received a US$90,000 book advance in an alleged 'sweetheart' deal" (http://report.globalintegrity.org/Russia/2008/timeline).

56. For Russian corruption in the headlines, see, for instance, Eric Schmitt, "State Dept. Expert Upbeat About Russian Fund Case," *New York Times*, September 24, 1999, http://query.nytimes.com/gst/fullpage.html?res=9400E4DB123FF937A1575AC0A96F958260.

For Chubais's statement with regard to IMF funds, see *Kommersant Daily*, September 8, 1998, and *Los Angeles Times*, September 9, 1998.

For the meeting in Summers's home, see Michael R. Gordon and David E. Sanger, "Rescuing Russia: A Special Report; The Bailout of the Kremlin: How U.S. Pressed the IMF," *New York Times*, July 17, 1998, p. A1.

For Summers's congressional testimony: Summers, "The United States and Russia, Part II: Russia in Crisis," U.S. House of Representatives, Committee on International Relations, Washington, DC: U.S. House of Representatives, September 17, 1998, Hearing Transcript, pp. 29–30.

With respect to the Bank of New York, in August and September 1999, newspapers reported that billions of dollars had been laundered through it. See Raymond Bonner with Timothy L. O'Brien, "Activity at Bank Raises Suspicions of Russia Mob Tie: Billions Thought to Be Laundered Through Bank of New York," *New York Times*, August 19, 1999, p. A1.

For details regarding the alleged involvement of Chubais and Kokh, see, for instance, Oleg Lurye, "Alfred i ego barbadoss," *Novaya Gazeta*, July 16, 2001, http://www.novayagazeta.ru/data/2001/49/02.html, and a summary of the article in *Jamestown Foundation Monitor*, "Did Chubais Launder Money Through The Bank of New York?" July 18, 2001, http://www.jamestown.org/publications_details.php?volume_id=24&issue_id=2066&article_id=18551.

For details about the Bank of New York case, see Alan A. Block and Constance A. Weaver, *All Is Clouded by Desire: Global Banking, Money Laundering, and International Organized Crime* (Westport, CT: Praeger, 2004).

57. The name of Moscow's energy conglomerate is Mosenergo.

For information on Chubais's current positions, see: http://document.kremlin.ru/doc.asp?ID=47868 and http://www.marketwatch.com/story/jp-morgan-appoints-anatoly-chubais-to-advisory-council. For information on Vasiliev's positions, see: http://corp-gov.ru/bd/db.php3?db_id=3623&base_id=3.

58. The Donnelly quote is found in John Donnelly, "The New Crusade: Jeffrey Sachs's Mission to Reform the Russian Economy Was a Bust. The Harvard Economist's Campaign for Global Health Is Faring Better—So Far," *Boston Globe Magazine*, June 3, 2001, p. 14.

Sachs honed his skills as a flexian in the late 1980s and early 1990s—most famously in central and eastern Europe and the former Soviet Union. For instance, while in the United States Sachs presented himself as a pro bono consultant in eastern Europe (when in fact he often worked under the umbrella of his consulting firm, Jeffrey D. Sachs and Associates Inc.). He and his colleagues also appeared as advisers to the Russian side during negotiations in 1992 between the IMF and the Russian government. At the same time, according to journalist John Helmer, they were writing secret memoranda advising the IMF negotiators. (See John Helmer, "Russia and the IMF: Who Pays the Piper Calls the Tune." *Johnson's Russia List*, no. 3057, February 17, 1999.) And when the future of Yegor Gaidar, the first "architect" of economic reform, with whom Sachs had been working, was precarious and he came under attack in the Russian parliament, Sachs switched loyalties and offered his services to Gaidar's opposition. (Memorandum from Jeffrey Sachs to Ruslan Khasbulatov of November 19, 1992, in author's possession; author's interviews with Stanford University economist Michael Bernstam of August 21, 1997 and October 17, 1997.)

With regard to activities in the 2000s, in 2002, Sachs, by then head of Columbia University's Earth Institute, obtained an appointment as a special adviser to Secretary General Kofi Annan on the Millennium Development Goals (MDGs). He also became director of the Millennium Project, commissioned as an independent advisory body underwritten by a special Millennium Trust Fund administered by the United Nations Development Program (UNDP), the UN's global poverty-fighting network and its biggest provider of development grants. Through this arrangement, Sachs set up a UNDP-funded parallel informal structure. At the same time he became identified with other initiatives that blurred into what John McArthur, his right-hand man, described as a "hodgepodge" of all things Millennium—among them the Millennium Villages Project, model development experiments to mitigate poverty in selected African villages, and Millennium Promise, the project's financing arm (author's conversation with John McArthur, October 2, 2007). (For a blog that shows the interconnectedness of these projects, see http://blogs.ei.columbia.edu/blog/author/jsachs/. For a Web site describing Millennium Promise and Millennium Villages Project, see http://www.millenniumpromise.org/site/PageServer?pagename =about.) While of these initiatives the UNDP housed only the Millennium Project, no one in Sachs's parallel hodgepodge formally reported to the UNDP management, according to UNDP sources here cited. This meant that Sachs et al. were able to circumvent many of the UNDP's institutional standards, regulations, procedures, and training requirements, while appearing to be sanctioned by the secretary general (or someone at the top), as well as the administrator of UNDP, a strong supporter and longtime associate of Sachs. McArthur's characterization of the Millennium Project as a "special status project" that was "*for* the UN, but not *of* the UN" is telling. The ten or so full-time equivalent staff (at any given time) on the project (author's conversation with John McArthur, October 2, 2007) were granted UN passports and UNDP identification and they enjoyed the same salaries, benefits, and privileges of UNDP employees. Yet these staff were not recruited, vetted, or trained by the UNDP, though their contracts and paychecks were issued by the UNDP. They did not report to the UNDP, but to Sachs. UNDP staff did not evaluate the Millennium Project or approve the publications it issued. Yet all these actions were sanctified under the mantle of Annan's authority, if not undertaken with his knowledge or direction. (Information and documents provided to author by UNDP sources, including Dorothy Rosenberg, former senior adviser for MDGs and civil society, UNDP; author's interview of March 13, 2007 and e-mail messages of February 20, 2007, and March 12, 2007.) Rosenberg recalls: "They continually made clear that their mandate came from the Secretary General and they were not subordinate to anyone in UNDP." (E-mail of October 16, 2007 to Janine Wedel from Dorothy Rosenberg.) Eventually, in 2006, under criticism from numerous quarters, the UN set out to wrest control of the project. Yet the distinctions and lines of authority remained messy as of 2008, with people who converted to regular UNDP staff still taking orders and doing work for Sachs et al.

59. See http://janinewedel.info/harvard.html. See also: Matt Taibbi, "Chubais: Our Media Darling," *The eXile* 22, November 20, 1997, and http://janinewedel.info/harvardinvestigative_exile2.html; and Anne Williamson, *Contagion*.

60. This draft of the GAO report, dated August 23, 1996, was given to me by GAO staff on January 5, 1998.

61. In 2000 the U.S. Department of Justice alleged that Shleifer and Hay had been "using their positions, inside information and influence, as well as USAID-funded resources, to advance their own personal business interests and investments and those of their wives and friends" (United States Attorney, District of Massachusetts, "United States Sues Harvard and Others for False Claims Relating to USAID

Programs in Russia," Press Release, U.S. Department of Justice, September 26, 2000). Harvard was cleared of fraud charges but had to pay damages for breaching its contract with USAID. Harvard was prohibited from paying on behalf of either Shleifer or Hay. The exact amount of Hay's fine was made contingent upon his earnings over the next decade. Marcella Bombardieri, "Harvard, teacher, and lawyer to pay US $30 m," *Boston Globe*, 4 August 2005.

Investigations that have been initiated, then suspended, include the separate GAO investigation looking into Shleifer's role on the Gore-Chernomyrdin Commission.

62. The *Foreign Affairs* article referred to here is Andrei Shleifer and Daniel Treisman, "A Normal Country," *Foreign Affairs*, March/April 2004, www.foreignaffairs.org/20040301faessay83204/andrei-shleifer-daniel-treisman/a-normal-country.html.

For the settlement paid by Harvard being a record one, see David McClintick, "How Harvard Lost Russia," *Institutional Investor Magazine Online*, January 13, 2006, p. 3, http://jboy.chaosnet.org/misc/docs/articles/shleifer.pdf.

63. For Summers's side jobs in finance while president of Harvard, see Frank Rich, "Awake and Sing!," *New York Times*, April 11, 2009, http://www.nytimes.com/2009/04/12/opinion/12rich.html?pagewanted=all. For more on his work at D. E. Shaw & Co, see: Louise Story, "A Rich Education for Summers (After Harvard)," *New York Times*, April 5, 2009, http://www.nytimes.com/2009/04/06/business/06summers.html?_r=1&partner=rss&emc=rss.

For Summers's financial and Wall Street associations and its bearing on his policymaking in the Obama administration, see, for instance, Frank Rich, "Obama's Make-or-Break Summer," *New York Times*, June 21, 2009, http://www.nytimes.com/2009/06/21/opinion/21rich.html; Story, "A Rich Education for Summers"; Matt Taibbi, "Inside The Great American Bubble Machine," *Rolling Stone*, July 2, 2009, http://www.rollingstone.com/politics/story/28816321/the_great_american_bubble_machine/3; and Matt Taibbi's blog, at http://smirkingchimp.com/thread/22127.

64. According to the Web site of Delin Development, Hay has worked for the company since 2005. The company describes itself as "a real estate development company with contracts in the Ukraine, Russia, and other Eastern European countries. The company specializes in office, residential and retail buildings; over $1 billion has been invested in upcoming projects." With regard to Hay, the Web site states that "Jonathan has been involved in real estate investment and development in Russia and Ukraine for more than 10 years. Since 2005 Jonathan has had operational responsibility for Delin's real estate development activities in Ukraine." See http://www.delin-d.com.

65. "Excellence without a Soul: Higher Education and the Shaping of Moral Character," *Leaders on Ethics: Real-World Perspectives on Today's Business Challenges*, John C. Knapp, ed. (Santa Barbara, CA: Greenwood Publishing Group, Inc., 2007), p. 69.

Notes to Chapter 6

1. Interview with Stephen Green, August 30, 2004; see also Stephen Green, "Damage Caused by 'Friendly' Spies," *Christian Science Monitor*, May 22, 1989, pp. 18–19. On the 1978 investigation of Wolfowitz, see also: Philip Giraldi, "Saving Feith," *The American Conservative*, March 12, 2007, http://www.amconmag.com/article/2007/mar/12/00024/.

2. The first instance referenced here was reported by Sidney Blumenthal in "Richard Perle, Disarmed but Undeterred," *Washington Post*, November 23, 1987, p. B1. The second instance was reported by investigative journalist Seymour Hersh in "Kissinger and Nixon in the White House," *Atlantic Monthly*, May 1982, http://www.theatlantic.com/issues/82may/hershwh2.htm.

3. For Perle enlisting Feith as an intern, see Douglas J. Feith, *War and Decision: Inside the Pentagon at the Dawn of the War on Terrorism* (New York: HarperCollins Publishers, 2008), pp. 26–27; http://www.lib.washington.edu/specialcoll/portals/pnw/Jackson/2-Reference/5-Staff/Staff.html. See also Stephen Green, "Damage Caused by 'Friendly' Spies," *Christian Science Monitor*, May 22, 1989, pp. 18–19. On the 1982 investigation of Feith, see also Philip Giraldi, "Saving Feith," *The American Conservative*, March 12, 2007, http://www.amconmag.com/article/2007/mar/12/00024/.

4. See, for example, David S. Hilzenrath, "The Ultimate Insider: Richard N. Perle's Many Business Ventures Followed His Years as a Defense Official," *Washington Post*, May 24, 2004, p. E01, http://www.washingtonpost.com/ac2/wp-dyn/A50388–2004May23?language=printer; and Jack Shafer, "Richard Perle Libel Watch, Week 4: He's Just Too Busy Resigning to Sue This Week!" Slate.com, April 2, 2003, http://slate.msn.com/id/2081053/.

5. In his book Feith says that Fred Iklé was the first to approach him about this position and helped talk him into considering the job (Feith, *War and Decision*, p. 42). For an astute analysis of Feith's book, see Robert Jervis, "War, Intelligence, and Honesty: A Review Essay," *Political Science Quarterly* 123, no. 4 (Winter 2008–2009), pp. 645–675.

The same pattern—of getting into hot water with government authorities, then getting each other off and even promoting one another afterward—also played out with Perle's friend Stephen J. Bryen. In 1979, Bryen, a staff member on the Senate Foreign Relations Committee, was investigated by the Justice Department and the FBI for "unauthorized disclosure" of classified information. He resigned under pressure, and the charges were quietly dropped. See Michael P. Saba and Evan Hendricks, *The Armageddon Network* (Brattleboro, VT: Amana Books, 1984), especially chapter 6. A few years later, Perle, after being named assistant secretary of defense for international security policy, not only lobbied hard enough to bring Bryen back into government as his deputy but saw to it that he received top security clearances. Alan Weisman, *Prince of Darkness: Richard Perle: The Kingdom, the Power & the End of Empire in America* (New York: Union Square Press, 2007), pp. 68–69.

6. Author's interview with Stephen Green, August 30, 2004.

7. Narratives by former insiders and investigative reports of congressional committees, inspectors general, investigative journalists (see especially the work of Jim Lobe, Seymour Hersh, Jane Mayer, and Laura Rozen) and reputable bloggers (Steve Clemons's *The Washington Note*, http://www.thewashingtonnote.com/) have established at least some of the pivotal parts played by members of the group (as well as other players). See also Right Web: http://rightweb.irc-online.org/. Conversations with people who are or have been close to the inner core, including "defectors" from it, as well as functions I have attended organized by Neocon organizations, have helped fill in some of the gaps.

8. I look into the Neocon core members' activities, roles, relationships, sponsors, and organizations they empower, and how they shift and pool them—both inside and outside government—to achieve mutual goals. (I do not attempt to summarize the reams of material on record, or detail all, or even most of, the players' interconnections. Instead, I provide representative examples based on well-confirmed accounts.)

9. As Gary Dorrien writes, "Kristol broke from liberalism in the 1950s; Podhoretz turned Right at the end of the 1960s; the right-wing social democrats became neoconservatives in the early 1970s." Gary Dorrien, *The Neoconservative Mind: Politics, Culture and the War of Ideology* (Philadelphia, PA: Temple University Press, 1993), p. 15. See also Irving Kristol, *Neoconservatism: The Autobiography of an Idea*, New York: Free Press, 1995. For neoconservatism as a force on the political scene, see, for instance, ibid., pp. 8–18. See also Jim Lobe, "What Is a Neoconservative Anyway?" *Asia Times*, August 3, 2003, http://ipsnews.net/news.asp?idnews=19618.

10. The Heilbrunn book is Jacob Heilbrunn, *They Knew They Were Right: The Rise of the Neocons* (New York: Doubleday, 2008), p. 68.

11. RAND was one of the government's first major forays into contracting out expertise. It was set up in the late 1940s to conduct research for the U.S. armed forces and has been a powerful contributor to military and intelligence analysis ever since.

On Wohlstetter as inspiration for Perle and Wolfowitz, see, for example, ibid., pp. 98–99. According to Heilbrunn, Wohlstetter "even believed that protracted wars, rather than short ones, could be a good thing. Why? Because the West had superior economic resources and could outlast its foes . . . Wohlstetter focused on devising and promoting new weapons systems, ranging from missile defense to more accurate weaponry that would lower civilian casualties, in order to wage and win more wars. Some of his ideas came to grief in both Vietnam and Iraq. All of these themes, however, would be pounded home by the neoconservatives, culminating in the Bush Doctrine" (p. 106).

Andrew Marshall, an octogenarian and still director of the Pentagon's Office of Net Assessments, has also long provided substantial intellectual justification for rethinking military affairs along neoconservative lines.

12. PBS, "Richard Perle: The Making of a Neoconservative," *Think Tank with Ben Wattenberg*, 2003, http://www.pbs.org/thinktank/transcript1017.html.

13. For Wohlstetter's influence on Jackson, see, for example, Heilbrunn, *They Knew They Were Right*, p. 106. For Jackson's, strong-on-defense stance, see, for example, Elizabeth Drew, "The Neocons in Power," *New York Review of Books* 50, no. 10 (June 12, 2003). With regard to Gaffney's working for Jackson, see Frank Gaffney's biography, Center for Security Policy, http://www.centerforsecurity policy.org/Home.aspx?Search=gaffney. For "Senator from Boeing" reference, see, for instance, Roger Morris, "P-I Focus: The Road the U.S. Traveled to Baghdad Was Paved by 'Scoop' Jackson," *Seattle PI*, April 6, 2003, http://www.seattlepi.com/opinion/115505_focus06.shtml.

14. Jacob Heilbrunn calls Jackson "effectively the first prominent neoconservative politician" (Heilbrunn, *They Knew They Were Right*, p. 115). Neoconservatives, with Podhoretz a key player, conceived of the Coalition for Democratic Majority, which they announced in 1972 (ibid., p. 114). The neoconservatives supported Jackson's presidential campaign and Jackson, leader of this coalition and the conservative faction of the Democratic Party, endorsed a strong military and pushed the idea of "peace through strength."

15. Feith was appointed special counsel by Perle in 1982 and served until 1986 (Feith, *War and Decision*, pp. 36–37).

Frank Gaffney's biography, Center for Security Policy, http://www.centerforsecuritypolicy.org/ Home.aspx?Search=gaffney. For "Senator from Boeing" reference, see, for instance, Roger Morris, "P-I Focus: The Road the U.S. traveled to Baghdad was paved by 'Scoop' Jackson," *Seattle PI*, April 6, 2003, http://www.seattlepi.com/opinion/115505_focus06.shtml.

Joining Perle, Feith, and Gaffney in the Department of Defense was Stephen Bryen. Bryen first served as deputy assistant secretary of defense for trade policy and later became the first director of the Defense Technology Security Administration (which was later absorbed into the Defense Threat Reduction Agency). He was in charge of regulating the transfer of U.S. military technology to foreign countries. Perle and Bryen met in the early 1970s when Perle worked for Senator Jackson and Bryen for Senator Clifford Case (R-NJ). Bryen, who began working for Case in 1971, became Case's personal staff member responsible for foreign policy issues in 1973, and, beginning in 1975, a staff member on the Senate Foreign Relations Committee. See Michael P. Saba and Evan Hendricks, *The Armageddon Network*, pp. 67–68.

16. With regard to Perle and his age cohorts as part of the "second" or "younger" generation, see Sidney Blumenthal, *The Rise of the Counter-Establishment: From Conservative Ideology to Political Power* (New York: Times Books, 1986), pp. 160–165; and Heilbrunn, *They Knew They Were Right*, pp. 106–113.

The Meyrav Wurmser quote is from Comments of Meyrav Wurmser, "The War Party," *BBC Panorama*, May 18, 2003, http://news.bbc.co.uk/nol/shared/spl/hi/programmes/panorama/transcripts/ thewarparty.txt.

An additional example is Neocon core ally Dov Zakheim, a member of the Advisory Council of Frank Gaffney's Center for Security Policy (and undersecretary of defense and comptroller). He said in September 2002 about the Center and their efforts: "Basically this is family. We have been in the trenches together now well before Frank set up the Center for Security Policy. It's an honor to be back with people that we know—in the Pentagon—are always with us." Dov Zakheim, quoted in Center for Security Policy, *Precision-Guided Ideas*, 2002 Annual Report, Center for Security Policy, http://www.centerforsecuritypolicy.org/modules/newsmanager/inside%20the%20ctr%20images%20pdfs/annualreport2002.pdf (accessed 7/21/2008), p. 7.

17. Sources for Israeli embassy officials referring to the "Perle group" include W. Patrick Lang, author's interview of June 12, 2009. Lang, a Defense Intelligence Officer for the Middle East, South Asia and Counter-Terrorism from 1985 to 1992 and Director of Defense HUMINT from 1992-1994, was awarded the Presidential Rank of Distinguished Executive.

With regard to Perle serving as a mentor, see, for example, Weisman, *Prince of Darkness: Richard Perle*, pp. 66–68.

The Feith quote is from ibid., p. 67.

18. A key question for an analyst trying to make sense of the parameters of the network is the extent to which individuals are intertwined with other individuals with whom they work to shape the habitat.

19. Some analysts characterize this as a "mindset" or a "worldview," assessing it as not coherent enough to warrant the label ideology. See, for example, Heilbrunn, *They Knew They Were Right*, pp. 106–113.

20. Hannah Arendt, *Origins of Totalitarianism* (New York: Harcourt Brace & Company, 1951), p. 423. Arendt posits that absolute enemies were at the core of the world views of both Stalin and Hitler—for Stalin they were the West, for Hitler, the Jews.

21. Comments of Richard Perle, "The War Party," *BBC Panorama*, May 18, 2003, http://news.bbc.co.uk/nol/shared/spl/hi/programmes/panorama/transcripts/thewarparty.txt. Wolfowitz and Feith are among those members of the Neocon core whose parents (their fathers were Polish Jews) lost many family members in the Holocaust.

22. For history of the neoconservative movement and thought, see Alan M. Wald, *The New York Intellectuals: The Rise and Decline of the Anti-Stalinist Left From the 1930s to the 1980s* (Chapel Hill, NC: University of North Carolina Press, 1987); Gary Dorrien, *The Neoconservative Mind: Politics, Culture and the War of Ideology* (Philadelphia, PA: Temple University Press, 1993); Blumenthal, *The Rise of the Counter-establishment*, especially pp. 122–165; and James Mann, *Rise of the Vulcans: The History of Bush's War Cabinet* (New York: Viking, 2004), especially pp. 21–36 and pp. 90–94. The quote from Jim Lobe is from "From Holocaust to Hyperpower," Inter Press Service News Agency, January 26, 2005, http://ipsnews.net/print.asp?idnews=27188.

23. Wolfowitz may be an exception in this regard. Jim Lobe points out that, in contrast to most of "his ideological fellow-travelers," Wolfowitz has long expressed sensitivity to the plight of Palestinians, support for their national aspirations, and opposition to the Jewish settler movement. Jim Lobe, "Wolfowitz Pick for World Bank Prompts Head-Scratching," Inter-Press Service, March 17, 2005, http://www.commondreams.org/cgi-bin/print.cgi?file=/headlines05/03.

24. Author interview of June 12, 2009, with W. Patrick Lang, an American who served as a liaison to the Israeli embassy.

25. Wolfowitz is quoted in Jim Lobe, "From Holocaust to Hyperpower."

The senior fellow here cited is Caroline B. Glick. She published her sentiments in "Shackled Warrior: An NRO Q&A," *National Review Online*, June 17, 2008, http://article.nationalreview.com/?q=ZTVkMWYzYjRkOWViM2NmYzYyOTU3NTg5NTlhMTNlYTc=.

Perle's coauthored book is David Frum and Richard Perle, *An End to Evil: How to Win the War on Terror* (New York: Random House, 2003). Quote is from pp. 6–7.

26. Frum and Perle, *An End to Evil*, quote is from p. 193; list of institutions from p. 196.

27. Ibid., pp. 227, 226, and 227.

28. Feith's thoughts are from author's interview with Douglas Feith, October 16, 2008; see also Feith, *War and Decision*.

29. Feith's thoughts are from author's interview with Douglas Feith, October 16, 2008; see also Douglas J. Feith, *War and Decision: Inside the Pentagon at the Dawn of the War of Terrorism* (New York: HarperCollins Publishers, 2008).

30. Frum and Perle, *An End to Evil: How to Win the War on Terror*, pp. 224, 228–229.

31. Moynihan is quoted in Jim Lobe, "From Holocaust to Hyperpower," Inter Press Service News Agency, January 26, 2005, http://ipsnews.net/print.asp?idnews=27188. See also Daniel Patrick Moynihan, *Pandaemonium, Ethnicity in International Politics* (New York: Oxford University Press, 1994).

32. On alliances with the Christian Right, see, for example, Donald E. Wagner, "Marching to Zion: The Evangelical-Jewish Alliance," *Christian Century*, June 28, 2003, http://findarticles.com/p/articles/mi_m1058/is_13_120/ai_104681907/; and Heilbrunn, *They Knew They Were Right*, p. 20.

33. See, for example, Anne Hessing Cahn, *Killing Détente* (University Park, PA: The Pennsylvania State Press, 1998), pp. 138–139, 136.

34. The first article was Albert Wohlstetter, "Is There a Strategic Arms Race?" *Foreign Policy*, no. 15 (Summer 1974), pp. 3–20. The second article, Albert Wohlstetter, "Optimal Ways to Confuse Ourselves," *Foreign Policy*, no. 20 (Autumn 1975), pp. 170–198, was published a year after the first and responded

to critics of the earlier piece. With regard to the United States risking being outdone militarily, see Wohlstetter, "Optimal Ways to Confuse Ourselves," especially pp. 179 and 181.

35. With regard to unprecedented entrée, see Frances Fitzgerald, *Way Out There in the Blue: Reagan, Star Wars and the End of the Cold War* (New York: Touchstone, 2000), p. 83.

See also Cahn, *Killing Détente*, p. 113 and p. 153.

36. Perle quotes are from author's interview with Richard Perle, July 17, 2009.

37. Pipes quotes are from author's interview with Richard Pipes, May 12, 2009. Pipes similarly told former defense official and political scientist Anne Hessing Cahn, who has written a book on Team B, that the reason he selected Wolfowitz was "because Richard Perle recommended him so highly." Cahn, *Killing Détente*, p. 150.

38. With regard to Perle being in the know, he likewise told Weisman: "I knew everybody on the team so I was aware of their findings." See Weisman, *Prince of Darkness: Richard Perle*, p. 49.

39. Paul C. Warnke, "Killing Détente: The Right Attacks the CIA (Review)," *Bulletin of the Atomic Scientists* 55, no. 1 (January 1999), pp. 70–71.

40. The Pipes quote is from Weisman, *Prince of Darkness: Richard Perle*, p. 49.

41. With regard to Team B findings used as ammunition by cold warriors, see, for example, Michael Krepon and Dan Caldwell, *The Politics of Arms Control Treaty Ratification* (New York: Palgrave Macmillan Publishing, 1991), pp. 459–460.

With regard to the resurrection of the Committee on the Present Danger, see Fitzgerald, *Way Out There in the Blue*, p. 83; and Cahn, *Killing Détente*, p. 184. The Pipes's quote is from author's interview with Richard Pipes, May 12, 2009. See also Richard Pipes's remarks on Team B in "Why the Soviet Union Thinks It Could Fight & Win a Nuclear War," *Commentary*, July 1977; Richard Pipes, "Team B: The Reality Behind the Myth," *Commentary*, October 1986; and his memoirs, Richard Pipes, *Vixi: Memoirs of a Non-Belonger* (New Haven: Yale University Press, 2005).

With regard to the conclusions of Team B, more than two decades after the Team B exercise, we now know, especially with benefit of Soviet archival data, that even the CIA's more modest assessments at the time overpredicted Soviet defense spending and some of its weapons production. According to some analysts, even at the time plenty of information was available to demonstrate that Team B's conclusions were off the mark. "Team B definitely did overestimate Soviet military prowess," according to Nicholas Thompson, who has written a book that examines the subject (*The Hawk and the Dove: Paul Nitze, George Kennan and the History of the Cold War* [New York: Henry Holt, 2009]). Richard Pipes, of course, counters: "We were right that the Russians believed that nuclear weapons can fight and win a war, which is why having nuclear superiority in terms of numbers of weapons, explosive power and defense against weapons made sense. The Russians did all these things [while] we did not" (author's interview with Richard Pipes of May 12, 2009).

42. Report of Team "B," *Soviet Strategic Objectives: An Alternative View: Report of Team B, Intelligence Community Experiment in Competitive Analysis*, Reproduced at the National Archives, http://www.gwu.edu/~nsarchiv/NSAEBB/NSAEBB139/nitze10.pdf, Summary and Introductory Remarks. With regard to motivations rather than actual capacities, see also Anne Hessing Cahn, *Killing Détente* (University Park, PA: The Pennsylvania State Press, 1998), p. 163, for example.

43. Wolfowitz quote is from Jack Davis, "The Challenge of Managing Uncertainty: Paul Wolfowitz on the Intelligence Policy-Relations," *Studies in Intelligence* 39, no. 5, 1996, http://www.cia.gov/csi/studies/96unclass/davis.htm.

44. Mann, *Rise of the Vulcans*, p. 74.

45. When National Security Advisor John Poindexter was questioned during the famous 1987 joint congressional hearings (before the House Select Committee to Investigate Covert Arms Transactions with Iran and the Senate Select Committee on Secret Military Assistance to Iran and the Nicaraguan Opposition) about what the president knew of the meetings about illegal weapons sales to Iran, Poindexter acknowledged having discussed with him the results of a "nine-point plan" agreed upon by Albert Hakim and an Iranian representative in October 1986 in Frankfurt. He reported that the president approved of these negotiations—which were adapted from an earlier version of an Oliver North plan—with only small exceptions. Theodore Draper, "Out of Control," *A Very Thin Line* (New York: Hill and Wang,

1991), pp. 434–435. The Contra side of the affair, too, carried the presidential seal of approval: Reagan had vowed to keep the anticommunist Contras alive "body and soul."

46. This term was used by Independent Counsel Lawrence Walsh (United States Court of Appeals District of Columbia Circuit, *Final Report of the Independent Counsel for Iran-Contra Matters: Volume 1: Investigations and Prosecutions*, Washington, DC, August 4, 1993). See Part 5, "The Flow of Funds and the Private Operatives," http://www.fas.org/irp/offdocs/walsh/part_v.htm.

47. For information on Reagan's approval of the sale of missiles to Iran, see Arthur L. Liman, "Hostile Witnesses," *Washington Post* magazine, August 16, 1998, http://www.washingtonpost.com/wp-srv/national/longterm/irancontra/contra1.htm.

48. These U.S. laws and policies include Reagan's professed hardliner approach "Operation Staunch," which placed economic and political sanctions on Iran (1983); the Boland Amendment I and II (1983 and 1984), passed by Congress and signed into law by President Reagan, which placed limits on U.S. assistance to Central America in the form of weapons; and the Arms Export Control Act of 1976 and rules governing the mandatory reporting to Congress of Department of Defense weapon sales to the CIA, both of which would have severely restricted the Enterprise's activities (Theodore Draper, "Finding No. 3," *A Very Thin Line*, pp. 120–121, 18, 24, and 247–248).

49. North occupied a position—deputy director for political-military affairs—that had been created for him at the NSC in 1984 while he was on temporary detail there. According to North, it was Casey's idea to set up "outside entities" to aid the Contras, "ostensibly to 'comply' with the Boland Amendment by going around it," as the historian Theodore Draper writes, and it was Casey who suggested bringing Secord on board. Theodore Draper, "Body and Soul," *A Very Thin Line*, p. 37. McFarlane, like North, was a Naval Academy graduate and U.S. Marine Corp officer (p. 40). Even before Poindexter took over as NSC Advisor, all NSC staff, except North, were required to send correspondence through an executive secretary. North signed correspondence to Poindexter with the code name "Blank Check" (p. 220).

50. Secord and Hakim met while Secord was stationed on an Air Force mission in Iran, where Hakim made a business selling U.S. electronic equipment to the Iranian Air Force (Draper, "Out of Control," *A Very Thin Line*, p. 37).

With regard to Hakim's meetings with Iranians: Frankfurt, Germany was the scene of two such meetings in February and October of 1986; another meeting took place in Tehran in May 1986 (p. 420).

With regard to Hakim's reimbursement, the Walsh report states that in 1985 and 1986 Hakim received $2.06 million from the Enterprise (*Final Report of the Independent Counsel for Iran/Contra Matters, Volume I: Investigations and Prosecutions*, Lawrence E. Walsh, Independent Counsel, August 4, 1993, Washington, D.C., United States Court of Appeals for the District of Columbia Circuit, Division for the Purpose of Appointing Independent Counsel, Division No. 86–6, Chapter 10, http://www.fas.org/irp/offdocs/walsh/). *New York Times*, "Iran-Contra Affair: Accounts of Guns, Money and Promises," June 14, 1987, http://www.nytimes.com/1987/06/14/weekinreview/iran-contra-affair-accounts-of-guns-money-and-promises.html.

51. Leaders of crucial CIA operations included the head of the CIA's Central American Task Force, a CIA station chief in Costa Rica, and others. Abrams also convinced the Costa Rican government to build an airstrip that would facilitate Contra resupply operations. Former CIA operatives collected generous profits carrying out Contra resupply missions for front companies with names like Southern Air Transport and Corporate Air Services for the CIA (Draper, "Body and Soul," *A Very Thin Line*, p. 39).

Representatives of the CIA, the NSC, the departments of Defense and State, and the Joint Chiefs of Staff participated in the high-level interagency working group known as the Restricted Inter-Agency Group (RIG). For information about Abrams's role in raising private funds for the Contras, see Scott Armstrong, "Cast of Characters," in Malcolm Byrne, ed., *The Chronology: The Documented Day-to-Day Account of the Secret Military Assistance to Iran and the Contras* (New York: Warner Books, 1987), p. xi.

With regard to Abram's private fund raising, see Draper, "Big Money," *A Very Thin Line*, p. 62.

52. Ledeen served as a special adviser to Secretary of State Alexander M. Haig Jr. (from 1981 to 1982) and a consultant to the Pentagon in 1983.

With regard to Ledeen's briefing of McFarlane, see Charles R. Babcock, "Key Iran-Contra Figure Ledeen Might Not Testify; Scheduled Hill Appearance by Former NSC Consultant on Terrorism Postponed," *Washington Post*, July 5, 1987.

With respect to Ledeen's working with North on counterterrorism, see Scott Armstrong, *Secret Military Assistance to Iran and the Contras: A Chronology of Events and Individuals*, Scott Armstrong, Malcolm Byrne, and Tom Blanton, authors, The National Security Archive, 1987, p. xviii.

With regard to Ledeen's relations with foreign nations, see, for instance: http://www.nytimes.com/ 1987/02/01/world/adding-peices-to-the-puzzle-a-new-chronology-of-the-iran-contra-affair.html.

With regard to the Walsh quotes: The first one is found in Lawrence E. Walsh, "Opening View," *Firewall: The Iran-Contra Conspiracy and Cover-Up* (New York: W. W. Norton & Company, 1997), p. 37. Discussion between Ledeen and Peres is reported in Draper, "Big Money," *A Very Thin Line*, p. 139. The second Walsh quote is found in Walsh Report, Chapter 1.

Khashoggi, who had handled billions of dollars worth of sales in arms and aircraft for the Saudi royal family in the 1970s, has been called the "Modern Multinational Man—placeless and rootless" (Draper, "Middlemen," *A Very Thin Line*, p. 123). In Iran-Contra Khashoggi served as a bridge financier, putting down funds on behalf of the Iranian side contingent on repayment by arms dealers upon completion of sale. Despite being considered highly unreliable by the American intelligence community (p. 127), Ghorbanifar served as the U.S. link to moderate Iranian government insiders (by continually convincing Ledeen and North that he would bring relevant Iranians to the table; whether the people he brought were legitimately moderate and/or influential has not been established).

Walsh's commentary on Ledeen's secrecy vis-à-vis North is reported in Draper, "Catalysts," *A Very Thin Line*, p. 137. With regard to Ledeen's potential making of money from weapons sales, see, for instance, Oliver North's note to John Poindexter; Iran-Contra Affair, Item IC02202; Digital National Security Archives; January 24, 1986. In this note, "Oliver L. North informs John M. Poindexter of his suspicion that Michael A. Ledeen may be making profits with [Adolph ("Al") Schwimmer; Manucher Ghorbanifar] on current operations." Walsh quote is from Walsh, "Opening View," *Firewall*, pp. 42–43.

53. Keith Schneider, "Washington Talk: Contra Drug Inquiry Stirs Growing Interest," February 24, 1987, in the *New York Times*, and author's interview with Jack Blum, November 2, 2004.

54. In addition to a congressional investigation, separate trials for some of the protagonists of the tale ensued. Before being pardoned, North was convicted on three felony counts; Abrams pled guilty to two misdemeanor charges of withholding information from Congress; and Ledeen was not charged. See, for example, Federation of American Scientists, "Walsh Iran / Contra Report – Summary of Prosecutions," http://www.fas.org/irp/offdocs/walsh/summpros.htm. With regard to the pardons, see: "Bush Pardons 6 in Iran Affair, Aborting a Weinberger Trial; Prosecutor Assails 'Cover-Up'" *New York Times*, December 25, 1992, http://www.nytimes.com/books/97/06/29/reviews/iran-pardon.html.

55. The first two post–Cold War commanders-in-chief, presidents Bush (the elder) and Clinton, were unenthusiastic about missile defense. (Clinton's defense secretary, Les Aspin, even proposed cutting the ground-based portion of it.) See, for instance, *New York Times*, "Reagan's Missile Shield in Space, 'Star Wars,' Is Pronounced Dead," May 14, 1993.

56. With regard to scientists challenging the viability of missile defense, see, for example, *Briefing Book on Ballistic Missile Defense* (May 18, 2004) published by the Center for Arms Control and Non-Proliferation, in cooperation with the Center for Defense Information and the Union of Concerned Scientists.

Regarding both capability and cost of the current program, see GAO, *Missile Defense: Actions Are Needed to Enhance Testing and Accountability*, GAO-04–409, Washington, DC, April 2004. While Clinton's missile defense plan carried a $60 billion price tag, William Hartung estimates that the cost of system proposed by Bush II would be as high as $240 billion over the coming two decades. William Hartung, "Ballistic Missile Defense in the Bush Defense Review: Problems and Prospects," *Foreign Policy in Focus*, June 2, 2003, http://www.fpif.org/presentations/0105briefingbook/hartung01.html. On the cost of the SDI program, see Fitzgerald, *Way Out There in the Blue*, p. 481.

57. Non-Neocon core members also active in Star Wars include William R. Van Cleave and Daniel O. Graham.

58. For Dov Zakheim at Booz Allen, see http://www.boozallen.com/publications/article/658016?lpid=827904.

59. With regard to Star Wars advocates as civilians, see, for example, Fitzgerald, *Way Out There in the Blue*, p. 188.

60. Hartung's views are from author's interview with William D. Hartung, July 31, 2007. Douglas Feith, Richard Perle, and Dov Zakheim serve on the Advisory Council of the Center for Security Policy. With regard to the coordinating role played by the Center: author's interview with William D. Hartung, July 31, 2007. The Center was funded in part by conservative foundations and military contractors (including three of the four big missile defense contractors—Boeing, Lockheed Martin, and TRW). Since it was created in 1988, the Center for Security Policy has received upwards of $2 million in corporate donations (http://www.fpif.org/papers/micr/star_warriors_body.html). The fourth contractor is Raytheon. William D. Hartung, with Jonathan Reingold, *About Face: The Role of the Arms Lobby in the Bush Administration's Radical Reversal of Two Decades of U.S. Nuclear Policy, A World Policy Institute Special Report* (New York: Arms Trade Resource Center, May 2002), http://www.worldpolicy.org/projects/arms/reports/reportaboutface.html.

With regard to organizations advocating missile defense: For instance, eight organizations known for missile defense advocacy sponsored a working group that issued a major 2007 report. The Claremont Institute's MissileThreat.com project (which has Frank Gaffney as a member of its advisory board), one of the cosponsors of the report, summarized the work as "outlining the need for more ambitious efforts in ballistic missile defense policy" (http://www.claremont.org). Another report cosponsor, the Department of Defense and Strategic Studies, features some of the leading lights in missile defense advocacy on its roster (see http://www.missouristate.edu/dss/). The Department of Defense and Strategic Studies was established at the University of Southern California in 1971 and moved to Southwest Missouri State University, (now Missouri State University) in 1987. Since 2005 it has been based, still as a department of Missouri State University, in Fairfax, Virginia, not far from Washington, D.C.

61. The Hartung quote is from author's interview with William D. Hartung, July 31, 2007.

62. Michelle Ciarrocca and William D. Hartung, *Axis of Influence: Behind the Bush Administration's Missile Defense Revival, A World Policy Institute Special Report* (New York: Arms Trade Resource Center, July 2002), http://www.worldpolicy.org/projects/arms/reports/execsumaxis.html.

63. The Commission to Assess the Ballistic Missile Threat to the United States (often called the Rumsfeld Commission or the Rumsfeld Missile Commission) began operations in January 1998 and released its final report in July of that year. Among the Neocon core members who dominated the commission were Paul Wolfowitz, an important member (Mann, *Rise of the Vulcans*, pp. 74–75), and James Woolsey. The commission relied on estimates from Lockheed Martin, the gigantic defense contractor, which had gone into missile defense. See Bradley Graham, *Hit to Kill: The New Battle Over Shielding America from Missile Attack* (New York: Public Affairs, 2001), pp. 43–44. The commission's report was used to promote missile defense and helped change the tone and substance of the debate in Congress. Using the commission's findings as the theme of his remarks, for instance, Rumsfeld conducted a closed-door briefing for 250 House members before their key vote calling for deployment of a missile defense system (ibid., pp. 101–112. See also Fitzgerald, *Way Out There in the Blue*, pp. 494–495).

Cambone was part of an earlier team that issued a January 2001 report sponsored by the National Institute for Public Policy, a missile defense advocacy organization, to urge the incoming administration to adopt a more aggressive nuclear weapons policy. Stephen Hadley was part of that same team.

With regard to the goal of the commissions, see George Lewis, Lisbeth Gronlund, and David Wright, "National Missile Defense: An Indefensible System," *Foreign Policy* (Winter 1999–2000), pp. 120–137. The authors state that the missile defense commission "enhanced the perception of a threat from emerging missile states" (p. 122).

64. For Weldon quote, see Michael Dobbs, "How Politics Helped Redefine Threat," *Washington Post*, January 14, 2002, p. A1.

The second commission (the result of an amendment to the Defense authorization bill of 1999), was convened in 2000. The Commission to Assess United States National Security Space Management and Organization (informally dubbed the Space Commission, the Rumsfeld Space Commission, or the second Rumsfeld Commission) focused on U.S. space-based defense capabilities. Members of that commission included Neocon core ally David Jeremiah, a member of the board of advisers of the Jewish Institute for National Security Affairs (JINSA is a Neocon core–associated think tank that pays special attention to missile defense), as well as two members of Gaffney's Center for Security Policy advisory board. For the effects of the second commission on policy, see, for example, Jeremy Singer, *Space News*, January 23, 2006, http://www.space.com/spacenews/archive06/Space_012306.html.

For updates on Weldon, see Laura Rozen's blog posts, including http://www.warandpiece.com/blogdirs/007525.html, http://www.warandpiece.com/blogdirs/007661.html.

65. On Rumsfeld creating the position, see, for instance: Jim Garamone, "New Office to Help Set DoD Intelligence Priorities," American Forces Press Service, May 20, 2003, http://www.defense link.mil/news/newsarticle.aspx?id=28963. Wolfowitz, Zakheim, and Feith all have served as consultants or on paid advisory boards for Northrop Grumman, the nation's third largest defense contractor. Hartung, with Reingold, *About Face*, http://www.worldpolicy.org/projects/arms/reports/reportabout-face.html. In his book *War and Decision*, Feith writes that, as under secretary of Defense for policy, "my office was . . . supporting the development of ballistic missile defense" (p. 44).

66. Information about the "Freedom to Manage" program is contained in: Hartung, with Reingold, *About Face*, http://www.worldpolicy.org/projects/arms/reports/reportaboutface.html.

For Rumsfeld quote, see Bradley Graham, "Rumsfeld Pares Oversight of Missile Defense Agency," *Washington Post*, February 16, 2002, p. A2. For exemption language, see: "Rumsfeld Pares Oversight of Missile Defense Agency," *Washington Post*, February 16, 2002.

67. The speaker was Admiral Leon Edney, USN (ret). The symposium was held on December 4, 2007.

68. This comparison is also made in Greg Thielmann, "Rumsfeld Reprise? The Missile Defense Report that Foretold the Iraq Intelligence Controversy," *Arms Control Today*, July/August 2003, pp. 3–9.

69. The study group effort was orchestrated by the Jerusalem-based Institute for Advanced Strategic and Political Studies, where David Wurmser served as director of research in the Strategy and Politics Program. He later became director of Middle East studies and Perle's colleague at the American Enterprise Institute and author of the 1999 *Tyranny's Ally: America's Failure to Defeat Saddam*, with a foreword by Perle (Washington, DC: The AEI Press, 1999). Meyrav Wurmser two years later cofounded MEMRI, the Middle East Media Research Institute, an organization that "monitors the Arab press for anti-Semitic opinions," with Yigal Carmon, a former colonel in Israel's military intelligence. MEMRI, according to journalist Jim Lobe, focuses on translating and circulating "particularly virulent anti-U.S. and anti-Israel articles appearing in the Arab press to key U.S. media and policymakers" (*Dawn*, March 9, 2003). She also directs the Center for Middle East Policy at the conservative-allied Hudson Institute.

70. See Study Group on "A New Israeli Strategy Toward 2000," *A Clean Break: A New Strategy for Securing the Realm*, Institute for Advanced Strategic and Political Studies, July 2006. Available at http://www.iasps.org/strat1.htm. For Perle's involvement, see James Bamford, *A Pretext for War* (New York: Doubleday, 2004), p. 265.

71. Rumsfeld, who that year was chairing the first ballistic missile commission, also signed the letter. "Letter to the Honorable William J. Clinton," *Project for the New American Century*, January 26, 1998, http://www.newamericancentury.org/iraqclintonletter.htm.

72. The Lobe quote is from Jim Lobe, "U.S. Right Weaves Tangled but Effective Web," IRC Right Web, January 13, 2004, http://rightweb.irc-online.org/rw/844.html.

73. Organizations of wider or somewhat different circles set up for similar purposes include the Foundation for the Defense of Democracies, the Washington Institute for Near East Policy, the Committee on U.S. Interests in the Middle East, and the Middle East Forum.

74. For Feith as founding member, see http://www.centerforsecuritypolicy.org/Home.aspx?Search =douglas%20feith. See also: http://www.csmonitor.com/specials/neocon/index.html.

75. The sociologist referred to here is Lawrence A. Toenjes, "U.S. Policy Towards Iraq: Unraveling the Web of People, Think Tanks, Etc.," OpEdNews.com, http://www/opednews.com/toenjessum-mary.htm.

76. With regard to civil society, see Janine R. Wedel, *Collision and Collusion: The Strange Case of Western Aid to Eastern Europe* (New York, NY: Palgrave, 2001), Chapter 3.

77. Quoted in George Packer, *The Assassins' Gate: America in Iraq* (Farrar Strauss and Giroux, New York: 2005), p. 41.

78. Quoted in ibid., p. 29.

79. Perle is known for hosting dinners and salons in which Neocon core members, allies, and brokers such as Chalabi participate. See, for instance, Dexter Filkins, "Where Plan A Left Ahmed Chalabi," *New York Times Magazine*, November 5, 2006, p. 51.

With regard to Eleana Benador, see Benador's Web site: http://www.benadorassociates.com/bio.php. Eleana is also sometimes spelled Eliana. For Benador as an adviser to the Middle East Forum, see Holly Yeager, "Of All Things: Power Behind the Throne—Eleana Benador," *Financial Times*, August 9, 2003. In 2007, Benador said she would be devoting her energies to her new firm, Benador Public Relations, which appears to have distanced itself from any particular political persuasion. For Benador clients, see http://www.sourcewatch.org/index.php?title=Benador_Associates. For a profile of Eliana Benador and information about her clients, see Jim Lobe, "The Andean Condor Among the Hawks," *Asia Times*, August 15, 2003, http://www.atimes.com/atimes/Front_Page/FH15Aa01.html.

80. The Neocon core has ties with Chalabi that go back more than two decades. Perle met Chalabi, another protégé of Albert Wohlstetter, through Wohlstetter in 1985. Aram Roston, *The Man Who Pushed America to War: The Extraordinary Life, Adventure, and Obsessions of Ahmad Chalabi* (New York: Nation Books, 2008), p. 134. Perle invited Chalabi to conferences at the American Enterprise Institute, where he met Wolfowitz and others who became key players under Bush II—Dick Cheney and Donald Rumsfeld. Chalabi maintained close ties to Cheney, as well as to members of the Neocon core at Bush II's Pentagon, notably Wolfowitz, Feith, Ledeen, Harold Rhode (a core ally and U.S. Defense Department analyst), and William Luti (a core ally and undersecretary of defense for Near Eastern and South Asian Affairs (ibid., p. 183; pp. 134–135).

The Neocon core and Chalabi needed each other in the service of promoting their own interests—the first stop being the use of American might to overthrow Hussein. They needed his persona as a potential Iraqi leader; he needed the legitimacy, contacts, and funds they would help him secure. Despite his record of conviction for bank fraud and untold frozen assets, in 1992 the CIA put him on their payroll via a front company (pp. 99–100). The Agency aimed to assemble what looked like a solid Iraqi opposition (pp. 87–90). From the very beginning, Chalabi had a plan: As Roston put it: "CIA officers who knew him best, even those who like him," say that "his goal . . . was always simply to rush America to war. . . . One of the former officers who knew Chalabi throughout said there is simply no doubt: 'an invasion is what he always wanted'" (p. 107).

Toward that end, Neocon core members helped Chalabi secure many of the millions of U.S. taxpayer dollars he received beginning in the 1990s and through the first several years of the U.S. occupation of Iraq. With the Neocon core and the neoconservative Project for the New American Century as lobbyists (including core member Woolsey and his law firm, Shea & Gardner [Chris Suellentrop, "Ahmed Chalabi: Why Shouldn't a Politician Be President of Iraq?" Slate.com, April 9, 2003, p. 167]), the Republican-controlled Congress passed and President Clinton signed the 1998 Iraq Liberation Act. This rendered the toppling of Saddam Hussein official U.S. policy and provided $100 million to support democracy promotion, of which the INC was the principal beneficiary (ibid.). In the late 1990s, separate taxpayer dollars were given to a Washington public relations firm, with ties to Bush II, to promote the INC (Roston, *The Man Who Pushed America to War*, p. 169).

After 9/11, Chalabi's activities in the service of the neoconservatives' agenda became even more vital. He made the case to officials and the public alike. Not long after the attacks on the Pentagon and the World Trade Center, he spoke at a secret meeting of the Defense Policy Board (held on September 19 and 20, 2001), at the invitation of Chairman Perle —a nineteen-hour meeting to which Secretary of State Colin Powell was not invited, and of which he was not informed or briefed (Elaine Sciolino and Patrick E. Tyler, "A Nation Challenged: Saddam Hussein; Some Pentagon Officials and Advisors Seek to Oust Iraqi Leader in War's Next Phase," *New York Times*, October 12, 2001, http://query.nytimes.com/gst/fullpage.html?res=950DE2DD153FF931A25753C1A9679C8B63 [accessed 19 August, 2008]). Chalabi told audiences "that it would be easy" to remove "Saddam" and replace him with a government that was friendly to Israel—if the United States would provide minimal support to an armed insurgency organized by the INC. Ultimately, under Bush II, Chalabi and the INC would be granted close to $40 million from the U.S. State Department. Exactly what the United States received in return for these dollars has been questioned by numerous commentators (Jane Mayer, "The Manipulator Ahmad Chalabi Pushed a Tainted Case for War. Can He Survive the Occupation?" *The New Yorker,* June 7, 2004, p. 58). On the latter point, see also Roston, *The Man Who Pushed America to War,* p. 116. For reporting on Chalabi's funding and history of support from members of the Neocon core, see also Bamford, *A Pretext for War.*

81. Author's interview with Lawrence B. Wilkerson, June 12, 2009.

82. Quotations are from the following: Interview with Lawrence B. Wilkerson, June 12, 2009, and interview with Paul Pillar, June 10, 2009. With regard to decision-making process and going to war, Leslie H. Gelb and Richard K. Betts show that, while the foreign policy of intervention in Vietnam failed, the system of decision-making worked (*The Irony of Vietnam: The System Worked* [Washington, DC: Brookings Institution Press, 1979]). For further confirmation of the lack of standard bureaucratic and interagency process in the decision to go to war, see also the memoir of Richard N. Haass, director of policy planning in the State Department for Bush II (*War of Necessity, War of Choice: A Memoir of Two Iraq Wars* [New York: Simon & Schuster, 2009], especially p. 5 and pp. 212–213).

83. For example, David L. Phillips writes: "Cheney's seniority, experience, and bureaucratic abilities gave him vast influence in the White House. . . . Cheney was given unprecedented permission to participate in all meetings of the (principals) committee. The Office of the Vice President (OVP) functioned like an independent body wielding enormous influence. Cheney asserted a major role in national security policy and created his own National Security Council staff" (David L. Phillips, *Losing Iraq: Inside the Postwar Reconstruction Fiasco* [New York: Basic Books, 2005], p. 59). John Prados, a senior fellow with the National Security Archives in Washington has come to the same conclusion (John Prados, "The Pros from Dover," *Bulletin of the Atomic Scientists* 60, no. 01 [January/February 2004], pp. 44–51). Veteran observers of executive branch decision-making processes reinforce this point (for instance, interview with Larry Wilkerson, June 12, 2009; interview with Paul Pillar, June 10, 2009). On this point, see Chapter 4, Enhanced Executive Power.

84. With regard to Libby, he allegedly leaked Plame's identity in an attempt to discredit former ambassador Joseph Wilson, her husband, who had written an op-ed in the *New York Times* challenging intelligence regarding Iraq's attempt to purchase uranium from an African country, thus posing an immediate threat.

David Addington also was a key player in the vice president's office. While long associated with Cheney more than the Neocon core, Addington helped fulfill core missions, both as chief of staff to Libby and after he replaced him when Libby left under a cloud of legal troubles. According to the *New Yorker's* Jane Mayer, Addington is the architect of the NSA's warrantless wiretapping program and a new legal anti-terror strategy that supplants the American constitution. See Jane Mayer, *The Dark Side: The Inside Story of How the War on Terror Turned into a War on American Ideals* (New York: Doubleday, 2008), p. 70.

Continuity was maintained after Libby's forced retirement. John Hannah, who previously had been the liaison between Cheney's office and Chalabi, became the vice president's national security adviser, with David Wurmser, formerly of the Pentagon Counter Terrorism Evaluation Group who joined Cheney's office as Mideast adviser in 2003, still in that post. Jim Lobe and Michael Flynn, "The Rise and Decline of the Neoconservatives," A Right Web Special Report, November 17, 2006, http://rightweb.irc-online.org/rw/3713. Wurmser served as special adviser to the Undersecretary of State for Arms Control and International Security in the State Department from 2001 to 2003 and as Mideast adviser in the office of the vice president from 2003 to 2007. In his Washington Note blog of July 24, 2007, Steven Clemons described Wurmser as "one of the Vice President's most dedicated neoconservative spear-carriers," http://www.thewashingtonnote.com/archives/002240.php.

For Wilkerson quote, see Lawrence B. Wilkerson, "The Whitehouse Cabal," *Los Angeles Times,* October 25, 2005, p. B11. With regard to undercutting the NSC, Wilkerson reported this in National Public Radio (cited in "Former Powell Aide Links Cheney's office to Abuse Directives," *New York Times,* November 3, 2005, http://www.nytimes.com/2005/11/03/world/americas/03iht-cheney.html.) See also James Risen, *State of War: The Secret History of the CIA and the Bush Administration* (New York: Free Press, 2006). Tellingly, the "Cheney team had . . . technological supremacy over the National Security

Council staff" and read their e-mail messages, according to Wilkerson (Cullen Murphy and Todd S. Purdum, "Farewell to All That: An Oral History of the Bush White House," *Vanity Fair*, February 2009, p. 30, http://www.vanityfair.com/politics/features/2009/02/bush-oral-history200902).

Patrick Lang, a Middle East analyst and former director of human intelligence collection for the Defense Intelligence Agency, adds that, under Libby's direction, Undersecretary of Defense (and Neocon core ally) Luti did the bidding of this "shadow National Security Council" (W. Patrick Lang, "Drinking the Kool-Aid," *Middle East Policy Council Journal* XI, no. 2 [Summer 2004], p. 51, http://www.mepc.org/journal_vol11/0406_lang.asp).

85. Leverett quotes are from author's interview with Flynt Leverett, May 8, 2009.

With regard to claims that Libby and the vice president helped assemble: These included the allegation that, in the months leading up to 9/11, lead hijacker Mohamed Atta had met with an Iraqi agent in the Czech Republic (Dana Priest and Glenn Kessler, "Iraq, 9/11 Still Linked to Cheney," *Washington Post*, September 29, 2003).

For further reference, see David Corn and Michael Isikoff, *Hubris: The Inside Story of Spin, Scandal, and the Selling of the Iraq War* (New York: Crown Publishers, 2006).

86. The Perle quote is from Weisman, *Prince of Darkness: Richard Perle*, p. 172.

With regard to think tanks with which the neoconservatives are affiliated: These think tanks included JINSA, the AEI, the Middle East Media Research Institute, and the Washington Institute for Near East Policy. See, for example, Jim Lobe, "Pentagon Office Base for Neoconservative Network Manipulating Iraq Intelligence," September 15, 2003, http://www.fpif.org/commentary/2003/0309feith.html.

The Kwiatkowski quote is from: Karen Kwiatkowski, "Conscientious Objector: A Senior Air Force Officer Watches Civilians Craft the War Plan," *The American Conservative*, December 15, 2003. Kwiatkowski also points out that the civilian head of the Israel, Lebanon, and Syria desk office was replaced by a political appointee from the neoconservative Washington Institute for Near East Policy, although previously such appointees were seldom given positions as country desk officers. Karen Kwiatkowski, "The New Pentagon Papers," Salon.com, March 10, 2004, p. 1, http://dir.salon.com/story/opinion/feature/2004/03/10/osp_moveon/index.html.

87. Lang's encounter with Feith is recounted in Steve Clemons, thewashingtonnote.com, May 26, 2007, http://www.thewashingtonnote.com/archives/2007/05/pat_lang_lawren/. Lang, who served as Defense Intelligence Officer for the Middle East, South Asia and Counter-Terrorism from 1985 to 1992 and Director of Defense HUMINT from 1992-1994, was awarded the Presidential Rank of Distinguished Executive. See also James Risen, "How Pair's Finding on Terror Led to Clash on Shaping Intelligence," *New York Times*, April 28, 2004, p. A2, http://www.nytimes.com/2004/04/28/politics/28INTE.html?ex=1216785600&en=a425abba18379e73&ei=5070 (accessed 7/21/2008), and Lang, "Drinking the Kool-Aid."

88. The Pillar quote is from Paul R. Pillar, "Intelligence, Policy, and the War in Iraq," *Foreign Affairs*, March/April 2006, http://www.foreignaffairs.org/20060301faessay85202/paul-r-pillar/intelligence-policy-and-the-war-in-iraq.html.

Jane Mayer's reporting on this issue can be found in Mayer, "The Manipulator," p. 64.

89. Kwiatkowski is cited in Faiz Shakir, Amanda Terkel, Satyam Khanna, Matt Corley, Ali Frick, Benjamin Armbruster, and Matt Duss, "Iraq: Douglas Feith's Blame Game," *The Progress Report*, March 11, 2008, http://www.americanprogressaction.org/progressreport/2008/03/pr20080311.

90. Kwiatkowski, "The New Pentagon Papers," p. 1. PBS's 2005 *Frontline* special on "The Long Road to War," http://www.pbs.org/wgbh/pages/frontline/shows/longroad/etc/script.html, makes similar points.

91. Seymour Hersh, "Selective Intelligence," *New Yorker*, May 12, 2003, http://www.newyorker.com/archive/2003/05/12/030512fa_fact.

92. For Chalabi and the INC as core suppliers of intelligence, see: Kwiatkowski, "The New Pentagon Papers," p. 3. Chalabi and his INC provided "intelligence" to Undersecretary of Defense (and Neocon core ally) Luti and Libby's deputy (John Hannah), according to information from inside the INC itself. This was revealed in a 2002 letter from the Washington office of the INC to the Senate Appropriations Committee. Reported in Lang, "Drinking the Kool-Aid."

For further confirmation that Ahmad Chalabi had a special relationship with the vice president's office, see also Karen Kwiatkowski, "The New Pentagon Papers," p. 1.

For Chalabi's operation seen as providing questionable intelligence, see, for instance, former CIA officer Robert Baer in Jane Mayer, "The Manipulator," p. 58, http://www.newyorker.com/archive/2004/06/07/040607fa_fact1?currentPage=1.

93. The chummy relationship with Chalabi extended to designs for postwar Iraq, in which Chalabi was a ubiquitous figure. A senior State Department official reported about the Office of Special Plans that, "Every list of Iraqis they wanted to work with for positions in the government of postwar Iraq included Chalabi and all the members of his organization." Mayer, "The Manipulator," p. 58, http://www.newyorker.com/archive/2004/06/07/040607fa_fact1?currentPage=1. For additional information on how the Counter Terrorism group acquired its intelligence, see http://www.pbs.org/wgbh/pages/frontline/darkside/interviews/maloof.html.

94. With regard to Maloof and Wurmser and the CTEG, see Risen, "How Pair's Finding on Terror," p. A1. Maloof also served as a deputy to Stephen Bryen in Reagan's Pentagon (Lang, "Drinking the Kool-Aid").

With regard to the pair's findings, see Kwiatkowski, "The New Pentagon Papers," p. 1; and PBS's 2008 *Frontline* special on "Bush's War" regarding the post-9/11 strategizing that went into planning for Iraq, http://www.pbs.org/wgbh/pages/frontline/bushswar/etc/script.html.

95. With regard to Maloof meeting Perle in his home, see, for instance, http://www.nytimes.com/2004/04/28/us/how-pair-s-finding-on-terror-led-to-clash-on-shaping-intelligence.html?pagewanted=all. For Kwiatkowski quote, see Kwiatkowski, "The New Pentagon Papers," p. 1. Kwiatkowski calls this commandeering of intelligence bodies by executive appointees in the Pentagon a "neoconservative capture of the policy-intelligence nexus" (Kwiatkowski, "The New Pentagon Papers," p. 1).

The leaked report is marked: "NSC/OVP BREIFING (sic)." For the report, see http://www.fas.org/irp/news/2007/04/feithslides.pdf.

For further reference, see David Corn and Michael Isikoff, *Hubris: The Inside Story of Spin, Scandal, and the Selling of the Iraq War* (New York: Crown Publishers, 2006).

96. Jim Lobe, "POLITICS-U.S.: Pentagon Office Home to Neo-Con Network," Inter Press Service, August 7 2003, http://www.ipsnews.net/interna.asp?idnews=19565.

97. For 2007 IG finding on Office of Special Plans: The first quote here is from Deputy Inspector General for Intelligence, *Review of the Pre-Iraqi War Activities of the Office of the Under Secretary of Defense for Policy, Inspector General, United States Department of Defense, Report No. 07-INTEL-04*, February 9, 2007, Review, p. 4. In fall 2005 Senator Pat Roberts (R-KS), then chairman of the Senate Select Committee on Intelligence, requested the report (Walter Pincus and R. Jeffrey Smith, "Official's Key Report on Iraq is Faulted," *Washington Post*, February 9, 2007, p. A1, http://www.washingtonpost.com/wp-dyn/content/article/2007/02/08/AR2007020802387.html).

The second quote is from Deputy Inspector General for Intelligence, *Review of the Pre-Iraqi War Activities of the Office of the Under Secretary of Defense for Policy*, p. 34.

For Senate Select Committee on Intelligence 2004 finding that the unit exaggerated the Iraqi threat, see executive summary from the office of Inspector General referring to this report at: http://www.fas.org/irp/agency/dod/ig020907-decl.pdf. For June 2008 report, see Press Release of Intelligence Committee, "Senate Intelligence Committee Unveils Final Phase II Reports on Prewar Iraq Intelligence—Two Bipartisan Reports Detail Administration Misstatements on Prewar Iraq Intelligence, and Inappropriate Intelligence Activities by Pentagon Policy Office," http://intelligence.senate.gov/press/record.cfm?id=298775.

For quote from Senate Select Committee on Intelligence report: According to a report by the Senate Select Committee on Intelligence, "when the analytical judgments of the intelligence community did not conform to the more conclusive and dire administration views of Iraqi links to al-Qaeda . . . policymakers within the Pentagon denigrated the intelligence community's analysis and sought to trump it by circumventing the CIA and briefing their own analysis directly to the White House." The Senate report also notes that in a communication sent to Wolfowitz and Secretary of State Donald Rumsfeld regarding a CIA report that failed to establish a convincing connection between Iraq and Al Qaeda, Feith's people recommended that the "CIA's interpretation ought to be ignored." Senator Jay Rockefeller, vice chairman of the intelligence committee, said in a news conference that Feith's "private intelligence" operation was "not lawful." (Senate Select Committee on Intelligence, "Report on the U.S. Intelligence Community's Prewar Intelligence Assessments on Iraq," July 7, 2004, p. 457, section containing the "additional views" of Senators John Rockefeller, Carl Levin, and Richard Durbin.)

For conclusions of the inspector general, see Deputy Inspector General for Intelligence, Review of Pre-Iraqi War Activities.

98. For information on the cross agency clique, see Jim Lobe, "U.S.: Ex-Pentagon Aide Hits 'Deceit' and 'Subversion' on Iraq," InterPress Service, August 5, 2003.

Regarding Abrams: In posts that did not require congressional approval, Abrams served as special assistant to the President and senior director for Near East and North African Affairs from 2002 to 2009; deputy assistant to the President and deputy national security advisor for Global Democracy Strategy from 2005 to 2009; and senior director for Democracy, Human Rights, and International Operations from 2001 to 2002.

Kwiatkowski is cited in Jim Lobe, "Insider Fires a Broadside at Rumsfeld's Office," *Asia Times*, 7 August 2003, http://www.atimes.com/atimes/Middle_East/EH07Ak01.html.

99. See, for instance, author's interview with Paul Pillar, June 10, 2009.

100. John Judis, *The Folly of Empire: What George W. Bush Could Learn from Theodore Roosevelt and Woodrow Wilson* (New York: Scribner, 2004), p. 169.

101. Weisman, *Prince of Darkness: Richard Perle*, p. 175.

102. Author's interview with Lawrence B. Wilkerson, June 12, 2009.

103. Holly Yeager, "Of All Things: Power Behind the Throne—Eleana Benador," *Financial Times*, August 9, 2003.

104. See "EB-NEWS 769: Krauthammer, Gaffney, Hanson and Taheri," EB Benador Associates, www.benadorassociates.com, May 2, 2004, https://mserver3.gmu.edu/frame.html?rtfPossible=true.

105. Jim Lobe, "Tenet v Perle," Lobel og.com, 2007, http://www.ips.org/blog/jimlobe/?p=13.

106. Jim Lobe, "Dating Cheney's Nuclear Drumbeat," Tom Dispatch, August 1, 2005, http://www.tomdispatch.com/post/print/9301/Tomgram%253A%252. *The American Conservative* argues that, "far from being a martyr for press freedom, the New York Times reporter [Judith Miller] was Chalabi's mouthpiece" (Justin Raimondo, *The American Conservative*, November 7, 2005, p. 21, http://www.amconmag.com/2005/2005_11_07/feature.html).

107. Charles Lewis and Mark Reading-Smith, "False Pretenses," The Center for Public Integrity, January 23, 2008, http://projects.publicintegrity.org/WarCard/.

108. With regard to the mushroom cloud, on October 8, 2002, President Bush said on CNN: "America must not ignore the threat gathering against us. Facing clear evidence of peril, we cannot wait for the final proof—the smoking gun—that could come in the form of a mushroom cloud" (http://archives.cnn.com/2002/ALLPOLITICS/10/07/bush.transcript/). See, for example, Fred Barnes, "Mohamed Atta Was Here . . . And Met with Saddam Hussein's Man in Prague," *Weekly Standard* 007, issue 46, August 12, 2002.

109. See, for example, Joby Warrick and Walter Pincus, "Bush Inflated Threat from Iraq's Banned Weapons, Report Says," *Washington Post*, June 6, 2008, p. A3.

110. Richard Perle on November 3, 2006, quoted in "Mission Accomplished?" *The American Conservative*, May 5, 2008.

111. Comments of Meyrav Wurmser, "The War Party," *BBC Panorama*, May 18, 2003, http://news.bbc.co.uk/nol/shared/spl/hi/programmes/panorama/transcripts/thewarparty.txt. See also Dov Zakheim quote in note 16.

112. See, for instance, Jacob Heilbrunn, "Where Have All the Neocons Gone?" *The American Conservative*, February 11, 2009, http://www.amconmag.com/article/2009/jan/12/00006//.

113. Damascus has been a serious target for the Neocon core for regime change, as Jim Lobe has established. For example, Elliott Abrams, in his capacity as U.S. deputy national security adviser, intimated to a senior Israeli official during Israel's 2006 incursion into Lebanon that Washington would not object if Israel expanded the war to Syria. Abrams's colleagues David and Meyrav Wurmser and John Hannah are also big supporters of regime change in Syria (Jim Lobe, "Neo-Cons Wanted Israel to Attack Syria,"

Interpress News, December 18, 2006). Members of the Neocon core–powered U.S. Committee for a Free Lebanon (including Perle, Feith, Abrams, Gaffney, Ledeen, and Wurmser) were instrumental in the passage of the 2003 Syria Accountability and Lebanese Sovereignty Restoration Act. That act established the justification for "regime change" invasion in the region. The appointment of Wurmser to Cheney's staff in September 2003 was seen by many as a sign that the United States might soon be taking "the road to Damascus." Tom Barry, "On the Road to Damascus with the Neo-cons," *Asia Times*, March 12, 2004, http://www.atimes.com/atimes/Middle_East/FC12Ak04.html.

114. Norman Podhoretz, "The Case for Bombing Iran," *Commentary*, June 2007, p. 23, commentary magazine.com.

115. See, for example, Ledeen, *The Iranian Time Bomb: The Mullah Zealots' Quest for Destruction* (New York: St. Martin's Press, 2007), as well as countless articles (such as Michael A. Ledeen, "Do the Right Thing: Let's Avoid Making a Catastrophe Out of an Embarrassment," *National Review Online*, January 18, 2006, http://www.aei.org/include/pub_print.asp?pubID=23696). At AEI Ledeen spoke to a mostly supportive audience about "the evil of Islamic fascism," "Iranian support of international terrorism," and the threat to American security. The event, which I attended, took place in AEI's Wohlstetter Conference Center on September 10, 2007.

116. Ledeen's Iraq activities are murky: It has been established that, ostensibly as a private citizen, he had unescorted access to the Pentagon. Karen Kwiatkowski saw an unescorted Ledeen multiple times after 9/11, when procedures were especially strict (author's conversation with Karen Kwiatkowski, July 21, 2009).

Regarding Ledeen as point person on Iran, also noteworthy is that Ledeen regularly offered foreign policy advice to Bush II aide Karl Rove, and, according to the *Washington Post*, "more than once, Ledeen has seen his ideas, faxed to Rove, become official policy or rhetoric." Thomas B. Edsall and Dana Milbank, "White House's Roving Eye for Politics; President's Most Powerful Adviser May Also Be the Most Connected," *Washington Post*, March 10, 2003, p. A1. See also Jim Lobe, "U.S.: Shadowy Neo-Con Adviser Moves on Iran," Inter Press Service, June 24, 2003.

With regard to Shulsky, he also roomed with Wolfowitz at Cornell; Packer, *The Assassins' Gate*, p. 150.

With regard to OSP veterans being tapped to head the new office, see Laura Rozen, "U.S. Moves to Weaken Iran," *Los Angeles Times*, May 19, 2006, p. A29, http://articles.latimes.com/2006/may/19/world/fg-usiran19; and Mary Louise Kelly, "Pentagon Iran Office Mimics Former Iraq Office," National Public Radio, Morning Edition, September 20, 2006, http://www.npr.org/templates/player/mediaPlayer.html?action=1&t=1&islist=false&id=6108983&m=6108984. See also Craig Unger, "From the Wonderful Folks Who Brought You Iraq," *Vanity Fair*, March 2007.

Ghorbanifar resurfaced in 2003, this time as an informant to Undersecretary of Defense Douglas Feith, after the U.S. invasion of Iraq. Specifically, he met with a Defense Department official, Neocon core collaborator Harold Rhode, in 2001 in Rome, to put U.S. officials in touch with Iranian dissidents, according to Michael Ledeen, who helped broker the meeting (Warren P. Strobel, "Alleged Pentagon Leaks May Be Connected to Battle Over Iran Policy," Knight Ridder Newspapers, September 3, 2004, www.highbeam.com/DocPrint.aspx?DocId=1G1:121554067). These meetings took place in Rome in December 2001 and Paris in June 2003 (see Joshua Micah Marshall, Laura Rozen, and Paul Glastris, "Iran-Contra II?" *Washington Monthly*, September 2004, http://www.washingtonmonthly.com/features/2004/0410.marshallrozen.html). In addition to the meetings in Rome, Ghorbanifar helped finance business deals and broker relationships for Richard Perle, as Seymour Hersh has reported. So has the equally enigmatic Saudi financier Adnan Khashoggi. Khashoggi resurfaced in the 1990s with his arrest and extradition to the United States for his borrowing of funds from the Bank of Credit and Commerce International (BCCI), which collapsed in 1991. He was acquitted. He reemerged again in the 2000s, this time in connection with Richard Perle. In a 2003 article by Seymour M. Hersh, "Lunch with the Chairman: Why Was Richard Perle Meeting with Adnan Khashoggi?" Hersh offers the viable theory that Khashoggi hoped to flaunt his and fellow Saudi Harb Zuhair's interest in investing in Perle's company Trireme Partners L.P. for the chance for Zuhair to discuss peaceful alternatives to a U.S. invasion of Iraq (*The New Yorker*, March 17, 2003, www.newyorker.com/archive/2003/03/17/030317fa_fact?currentPage=5).

With regard to Franklin's conviction, see, for example, Jerry Markon, "Pentagon Analyst Given 12½ Years in Secrets Case," *Washington Post*, January 21, 2006, p. A1. Franklin's sentence was reduced to house arrest. See http://www.washingtonpost.com/wp-dyn/content/article/2009/06/11/AR2009061104280.html.

The Rozen quote is from Laura Rozen, "Does Investigation of the Pentagon's Channel to an Iran Contra Arms Dealer Continue?" *Mother Jones*, June 20, 2008. See also Senate Select Committee on Intelligence, Report on Intelligence Activities Relating to Iraq Conducted by the Policy Counterterrorism Evaluation Group and the Office of Special Plans Within the Office of the Under Secretary of Defense for Policy, June 2008, http://intelligence.senate.gov/080605/phase2b.pdf.

117. See chapter 1 for discussion of how flex nets differ from the issue networks defined by Heclo.

118. Bradley Graham, "Levin Assails Officials' Post-Resignation Roles," *Washington Post*, April 20, 2005, p. A22. For Feith resigning for personal reasons, see Department of Defense, "DoD Announces Departure of Undersecretary Douglas Feith," January 26, 2005, http://www.defensclink.mil/releases/release.aspx?releaseid=8160.

119. Libby was convicted of "four felony counts: obstruction of justice, giving false statements to the Federal Bureau of Investigation and committing perjury twice before the grand jury" (Neil A. Lewis, "Libby Guilty of Lying in CIA Leak Case," *New York Times*, March 6, 2007). In July 2007 President Bush commuted his two-and-a-half-year prison sentence. In March 2008 Libby was barred from practicing law in Washington, D.C. (See, for example, Carol D. Leonnig, "Court Disbars Cheney Ex-Aide," *Washington Post*, March 21, 2008.)

120. For a description of the letters sent on Libby's behalf in hopes of securing him a reduction in prison time (from a Who's Who of neoconservatives, as well as Cheney and Rumsfeld), see Sidney Blumenthal, "The Libby Lobby's Pardon Campaign," Salon.com, June 7, 2007, http://www.salon.com/opinion/blumenthal/2007/06/07/scooter_libby/print.html.

121. Petraeus is cited in Nancy A. Youssef, "Chalabi Back in Action in Iraq," McClatchy Newspapers, October 28, 2007. See also: http://www.guardian.co.uk/world/2004/may/26/usa.iraq3.

122. With regard to severing ties, see Nancy A. Youssef, "U.S. Once Again Cuts Off Ties to Chalabi, This Time Over Rivalry with Malaki," McClatchy Newspapers, May 15, 2008.

123. See, for example, Richard Perle, "We Made Mistakes in Iraq, but I Still Believe the War Was Just," *Sunday Telegraph* (London), March 16, 2008, posted on AEI Web site on March 17, 2008, http://www.aei.org/include/pub_print.asp?pubID=27655.

Notes to Chapter 7

1. Susan Strange, *The Retreat of the State* (Cambridge, UK: Cambridge University Press, 1996), p. 199.

2. With regard to flexlike structures at Enron: Andrew S. Fastow, for example, played dual roles as chief financial officer of Enron and as manager of the LJM partnerships that he had created. Using Enron stock as collateral, Fastow signed off on deals for both and hid Enron losses by putting them under the partnerships. According to a report issued by Enron's board after the misdeeds were brought to light, the transactions were illusory since Enron was essentially on both sides of each deal (Kurt Eichenwald, "Talk of Crime Gets Big Push," *New York Times*, February 4, 2002, p. A19). William C. Powers Jr., an Enron director who chaired the committee that wrote the report, said that Fastow was plagued by dual loyalties. "Fastow couldn't mind the store," Powers said, "because he was involved in the transactions" (Kurt Eichenwald, "Enron's Many Strands: The Ex-Chairman; Questions Were Answered at Board's Investigation," *New York Times*, February 13, 2002, p. C9). Jordan Mintz, a lawyer with Fastow's finance division, was troubled by this state of affairs: "Mr. Fastow was negotiating deals on behalf of the partnerships across the table from his own subordinates, who were representing Enron. Approval sheets for those deals had not been signed off by Mr. Skilling, the chief operating officer, even though they all had a line for his signature" (Kurt Eichenwald and Diana B. Henriques, "Web of Details Did Enron In as Warnings Went Unheeded," *New York Times*, February 10, 2002, p. A27). Fastow's dual roles (as CFO of

Enron and manager of the partnerships), and the ambiguity as to which role he was playing during cru-cial transactions, facilitated his ability to hide the partnerships and his success in money making.

For details about the relationship between Enron and Arthur Andersen, see, for instance, Jane Mayer, "The Accountants' War," *The New Yorker*, April 22, 2002. The quote from Jack Blum is from my inter-view with Jack Blum, August 12, 2004.

Quote by John Cassidy is from John Cassidy, "The Greed Cycle," *The New Yorker*, September 23, 2002, http://www.newyorker.com/archive/2002/09/23/020923fa_fact_cassidy. John Cassidy is from John Cassidy, "The Greed Cycle," The New Yorker, September 23, 2002, http://www.newyorker.com/archive/2002/09/23/020923fa_fact_cassidy.

3. Lloyd J. Dumas has analyzed the behavior of Enron executives in light of a broader definition of corruption (see Lloyd J. Dumas, Janine R. Wedel, and Greg Callman, *Confronting Corruption, Building Accountability: Lessons from the World of International Development Advising* [New York: Palgrave, forthcoming, 2010]).

Sources on Enron include Andrew Hill and Stephen Fidler, "Enron Ties Itself Up In Knots, Then Falls Over," *Financial Times*, January 29 2002, http://specials.ft.com/enron/FT3A5RP52XC.html; Sheila McNulty, "Enron: Big Bucks from a Company," *Financial Times*, February 8, 2002, http://specials.ft.com/enron/FT3HR1OBGXC.html; Daniel Kadlec, "Enron: Who's Accountable?" *Time Magazine*, January 13, 2002, http://www.time.com/time/business/article/0,8599,193520,00.html; Eichenwald, "Talk of Crime Gets Big Push," p. A19; Eichenwald and Henriques, "Web of Details Did Enron In as Warnings Went Un-heeded," p. A27; and Eichenwald, "Enron's Many Strands," p. C9.

The quote from Dipak Gyawali is cited in Dumas, Wedel, and Callman, *Confronting Corruption, Building Accountability*.

4. For Power work, see Michael Power, *The Audit Explosion* (London: Demos, 1994) and *The Audit Society: Rituals of Verification* (New York: Oxford University Press, 1999).

In the UK, the migration of the audit from finance to other areas of life followed this course: After the election of Margaret Thatcher as prime minister in 1979, the government of Britain sought to revamp the public sector by introducing operating methods from the supposedly more efficient and dynamic pri-vate sector (Cris Shore, Susan Wright, and Martin Mills, "Audit Culture and Anthropology: Neo-liber-alism in British Higher Education," *The Journal of the Royal Anthropological Institute* 5, no. 4 [December 1999], p. 561).

The quote from the UK's Audit Commission on audit functions is from the "Audit Commission for England and Wales: Report of Accounts for Year Ended 31 March 1984," London HMSO, p. 3, quoted in Shore, Wright and Mills, "Audit Culture and Anthropology," p. 562. Additional quotations in this paragraph appear on p. 562.

With respect to the introduction of cost-benefit analysis at the Department of Defense, see Tevfik F. Nas, *Cost-Benefit Analysis: Theory and Application* (Thousand Oaks, CA: Sage Publications, 1996). With regard to the introduction of audit in the United States in the 1980s, see Marilyn Strathern, *Audit Cultures: Anthropological Studies in Accountability, Ethics, and the Academy* (Oxford and New York: Routledge, 2000), especially, p. 60.

5. The Power quote is from Michael Power, *The Audit Explosion*, p. 19.

6. For information on Perle's early role in the administration of George W. Bush, see Seymour M. Hersh, "Lunch with the Chairman," *The New Yorker*, March 17, 2003, http://www.newyorker.com. For sources on Perle's role in pushing information manufactured by Chalabi, see chapter 6. The Goldman Sachs information is from Ken Silverstein and Chuck Neubauer, "Consulting and Policy Overlap," *Los Angeles Times*, May 7, 2003. Sources on Perle's work with the American satellite manufacturer (Loral Space & Communications) and telecommunications company (Global Crossing Ltd.) here referenced are Stephen Labaton, "Pentagon Adviser Is Also Advising Global Crossing," *New York Times*, March 21, 2003, www.nytimes.com/2003/03/21/business/21GLOB.html-44k; and Stephen Labaton, "Pentagon Ad-viser Is Stepping Down," *New York Times*, March 28, 2003, http://www.nytimes.com/2003/03/28/business/28GLOB.html; and Jack Shafer, "Richard Perle Libel Watch, Week 4: He's Just Too Busy Re-signing to Sue This Week!" Slate.com, April 2, 2003, http://slate.msn.com/id/2081053/.

7. Department of Defense, Inspector General, "Alleged Conflict of Interest and Misuse of Public Of-fice: Mr. Richard N. Perle, Former Chairman Defense Policy Board Advisory Committee," November

10, 2003, http://www.dodig.mil/fo/Foia/RichardPerleReport.pdf. For further information about the re-port issued by the Pentagon's inspector general, see Stephen Labaton, "Report Finds No Violations at Pentagon by Adviser," *New York Times*, November 15, 2004, http://www.nytimes.com/2003/11/15/business/15global.html?th.

8. Melvin J. Dubnick, "Seeking Salvation for Accountability," prepared for delivery at the 2002 An-nual Meeting of the American Political Science Association, Boston, August 29–September 1, 2002, pp. 6–7, http://pubpages.unh.edu/dubnick/papers/2002/salv2002.pdf. This scholar further notes that today's practice of accountability, by contrast, "holds the promise of bringing someone to justice, of generating desired performance through control and oversight, of promoting democracy through institutional forms" (p. 2).

9. The Power quote is found in Power, *The Audit Explosion*, p. 21.

10. With regard to nonstate actors playing off the rules of any particular country in which they op-erate against the rules of others: Multinational corporations have been doing just this for years. For ex-ample, as Lloyd J. Dumas has written, "suppose one nation in which they [a multinational corporation] have a subsidiary increases a tax on the profits of companies operating in their country. The multina-tional can lower the price at which its subsidiary in that country 'sells' its output to another division of the same multinational located in a country without a profits tax. (This is called 'transfer pricing.') That will reduce the profits of the subsidiary in the country that raised taxes and increase the profits of the division operating where there is no tax. The result: the multinational completely avoids the tax increase without violating any country's laws." Dumas, Wedel, and Callman, *Confronting Corruption, Building Accountability*.

11. Author's interview with Gaston L. Gianni, June 16, 2009. Author's interview with Monique Helfrich, September 1, 2008.

12. International development specialist Dipak Gyawali outlines the concept of "social audit," a ho-listic notion that captures "the larger processes of social critique that are not limited to procedural mis-takes only. . . . It is not enough for procedures to have been followed: it is important that the entire enterprise itself be right" (Dumas, Wedel, and Callman, *Confronting Corruption, Building Accountability*). The quotations from Monique Helfrich are from my interview of September 1, 2008.

13. Book by Moisés Naím, *Illicit: How Smugglers, Traffickers and Counterfeiters are Hijacking the Global Economy* (New York: Random House, Inc., 2006); Moisés Naím, talk at New America Founda-tion, April 29, 2009.

INDEX